FURTHER WITH KNOWLEDGE GRAPHS

.

Studies on the Semantic Web

Semantic Web has grown into a mature field of research. Its methods find innovative applications on and off the World Wide Web. Its underlying technologies have significant impact on adjacent fields of research and on industrial applications. This book series reports on the state of the art in foundations, methods, and applications of Semantic Web and its underlying technologies. It is a central forum for the communication of recent developments and comprises research monographs, textbooks and edited volumes on all topics related to the Semantic Web.

Volume 53

ISSN 1868-1158 (print)
ISSN 2215-0870 (online)

Further with Knowledge Graphs

Proceedings of the 17th International Conference on Semantic
Systems, 6–9 September 2021, Amsterdam, The Netherlands

Edited by

Mehwish Alam
FIZ Karlsruhe, Leibniz Institute for Information Infrastructure, Germany

Paul Groth
University of Amsterdam, The Netherlands

Victor de Boer
Vrije Universiteit Amsterdam, The Netherlands

Tassilo Pellegrini
University of Applied Sciences St. Poelten, Austria

Harshvardhan J. Pandit
ADAPT Centre – Trinity College Dublin, Ireland

Elena Montiel
Universidad Politécnica de Madrid, Spain

Víctor Rodríguez Doncel
Universidad Politécnica de Madrid, Spain

Barbara McGillivray
University of Cambridge and The Alan Turing Institute, UK

and

Albert Meroño-Peñuela
King's College, London, UK

IOS Press

ISBN 978-3-89838-765-1 (AKA, print)
ISBN 978-1-64368-200-6 (IOS Press, print)
ISBN 978-1-64368-201-3 (IOS Press, online)
doi: 10.3233/SSW53

Bibliographic information available from the Katalog der Deutschen Nationalbibliothek (German National Library Catalogue) at https://www.dnb.de

Publisher
Akademische Verlagsgesellschaft AKA GmbH, Berlin

Represented by Co-Publisher IOS Press
IOS Press BV
Nieuwe Hemweg 6B
1013 BG Amsterdam
The Netherlands
Tel: +31 20 688 3355
Fax: +31 20 687 0019
email: order@iospress.nl

LEGAL NOTICE
The publisher is not responsible for the use which might be made of the following information.

Preface

This volume contains the proceedings of the 17th International Conference on Semantic Systems, SEMANTiCS 2021. SEMANTiCS is the annual meeting place for professionals and researchers who make semantic computing work, who understand its benefits and encounter its limitations. Every year, SEMANTiCS attracts information managers, IT-architects, software engineers, and researchers from organisations ranging from research facilities, NPOs, through public administrations to the largest companies in the world.

SEMANTiCS offers a forum for the exchange of the latest scientific results in semantic systems and complements these topics with new research challenges in areas like data science, machine learning, logic programming, content engineering, social computing, and the Semantic Web. The conference is in its 17th year and has developed into an internationally visible and professional event at the intersection of academia and industry.

Contributors to and participants of the conference learn from top researchers and industry experts about emerging trends and topics in the wide area of semantic computing. The SEMANTiCS community is highly diverse; attendees have responsibilities in interlinking areas such as artificial intelligence, data science, knowledge discovery and management, big data analytics, e-commerce, enterprise search, technical documentation, document management, business intelligence, and enterprise vocabulary management.

The conference's subtitle in 2021 was "In the Era of Knowledge Graphs", and especially welcomed submissions on the following topics:

- Web Semantics & Linked (Open) Data
- Enterprise Knowledge Graphs, Graph Data Management, and Deep Semantics
- Machine Learning & Deep Learning Techniques
- Semantic Information Management & Knowledge Integration
- Terminology, Thesaurus & Ontology Management
- Data Mining and Knowledge Discovery
- Reasoning, Rules, and Policies
- Natural Language Processing
- Data Quality Management and Assurance
- Explainable Artificial Intelligence
- Semantics in Data Science
- Semantics in Blockchain environments
- Trust, Data Privacy, and Security with Semantic Technologies
- Economics of Data, Data Services, and Data Ecosystems

We additionally issued calls for three special sub-topics:

- Digital Humanities and Cultural Heritage
- LegalTech
- Distributed and Decentralized Knowledge Graphs

Due to the health crisis caused by the Corona-Virus pandemic, 2021's SEMANTiCS took place in a hybrid form in Amsterdam. A call for papers was distributed publicly and we received 66 submissions to the Research and Innovation track.

In order to properly provide high-quality reviews, a program committee comprising 99 members supported us in selecting the papers with the highest impact and scientific merit. For each submission, at least 3 reviews were written independently from the assigned reviewers in a single–blind review process (author names are visible to reviewers, reviewers stay anonymous). After all reviews were submitted the PC chairs compared the reviews and discussed discrepancies and different opinions with the reviewers to facilitate a meta-review and suggest a recommendation to accept or reject the paper. Overall, we accepted 19 papers which resulted in an acceptance rate of 29%.

In addition to the peer-reviewed work, the conference had four renowned keynote speakers: Joe Pairman (Senior Product Manager, Tridion Docs; Prof. Enrico Motta (Professor of Knowledge Technologies at the Knowledge Media Institute – The Open University); Prof. Maria-Esther Vidal (Head of Scientific Data Management Research Group TIB – Leibniz Information Centre for Science and Technology and University Library); and Dr. Vanessa Lopez (Research Scientist and Manager – AI for Health and Social Care – IBM).

Additionally, the program had posters and demos, a comprehensive set of workshops, as well as talks from industry leaders.

We thank all authors who submitted papers. We particularly thank the program committee which provided careful reviews in a quick turnaround time. Their service is essential for the quality of the conference.

Sincerely yours,

The Editors

Amsterdam, September 2021

Contents

Further with Knowledge Graphs. M. Alam et al. (Eds.)
AKA Verlag and IOS Press, 2021
© 2021 Akademische Verlagsgesellschaft AKA GmbH, Berlin
This article is published online with Open Access by IOS Press and distributed under the terms
of the Creative Commons Attribution License 4.0 (CC BY 4.0).
doi:10.3233/SSW210031

TODO: A Core Ontology for Task-Oriented Dialogue Systems in Industry 4.0

Cristina ACETA [a,1], Izaskun FERNÁNDEZ [a] and Aitor SOROA [b]

[a] *TEKNIKER, Basque Research and Technology Alliance (BRTA), Spain*
[b] *CCIA Group, University of the Basque Country, Spain*

Abstract. Nowadays, the demand in industry of dialogue systems to be able to naturally communicate with industrial systems is increasing, as they allow to enhance productivity and security in these scenarios. However, adapting these systems to different use cases is a costly process, due to the complexity of the scenarios and the lack of available data. This work presents the Task-Oriented Dialogue management Ontology (TODO), which aims to provide a core and complete base for semantic-based task-oriented dialogue systems in the context of industrial scenarios in terms of, on the one hand, domain and dialogue modelling and, on the other hand, dialogue management and tracing support. Furthermore, its modular structure, besides grouping specific knowledge in independent components, allows to easily extend each of the modules, attending the necessities of the different use cases. These characteristics allow an easy adaptation of the ontology to different use cases, with a considerable reduction of time and costs. So as to demonstrate the capabilities of the the ontology by integrating it in a task-oriented dialogue system, TODO has been validated in real-world use cases. Finally, an evaluation is also presented, covering different relevant aspects of the ontology.

Keywords. Semantic Web, Dialogue Systems, Natural Language Processing, Industry 4.0.

1. Introduction

Factory workers are a core factor in production environments. These environments are becoming more automatized over time, and workers require of intuitive and powerful interaction techniques so as to successfully perform their assigned tasks in collaboration with automatisms [1]. To cover this necessity, Human-Machine Interfaces (HMI) have increasingly evolved in last years with the development of new mobile techniques and new gadgets such as smartphones, tablets or Augmented Reality (AR) glasses. In this context, a big number of systems have been developed, especially in collaborative robotics, with human-machine interaction capabilities in different degrees [2,3].

In this sense, task-oriented dialogue systems are a very useful tool that allow workers to work on multiple tasks at once without reducing the quality of their work, by perform-

---

[1]Corresponding Author: Cristina Aceta, Tekniker, C/Iñaki Goenaga 5, 20600 Eibar, Spain; E-mail: cristina.aceta@tekniker.es.

ing secondary tasks simply by communicating with the target system. It is also worth noting that the capacity of dialogue systems of communicating in natural language has a positive impact in acceptation from humans [4]. However, the capacity of the system to interpret human commands in most current frameworks in industrial environments is basically based on a predefined vocabulary that allows the worker to interact with the target system, making use of templates [5,6]. These templates are based on human-readable models, but all of them depend on expert manual work, which in most cases supposes high costs, and they cannot be directly reused in other scenarios. Furthermore, these approaches negatively affect the naturality of the interaction and, thus, human acceptation [7]. Also, the capacity of current interfaces to semantically understand natural human commands is still limited and the required effort to do so is usually high.

This evidence motivates the development of the ontology presented in this work: the Task-Oriented Dialogue management Ontology (TODO). TODO is a core, modular ontology that provides task-oriented dialogue systems with the necessary means to be capable of naturally interacting with workers (both at understanding and at communication level) and that can be easily adapted to different industrial scenarios, reducing adaptation time and costs. Moreover, it allows to store and reproduce the dialogue process to be able to learn from new interactions. To the best of the authors' knowledge at the time of presenting this work, there are not core ontologies in the literature that deal with natural interaction in industrial scenarios at this level, which gives special relevance to TODO.

This paper is organized as follows: Section 2 provides related work that is relevant to this paper. Section 3 presents TODO, following the methodology used to develop it; Section 4 makes some remarks on the instantiation process of TODO and its use in several industry-related use cases. Finally, Section 5 includes a set of final considerations for this work.

2. Related Work

According to [8], the basic architecture of a task-oriented dialogue system consists of a **natural language understanding** component, a **dialogue state tracker**, a **dialogue policy** and a **natural language generation** module. The first aims to extract an interpretation from the command, the second and the third ones deal with the dialogue process and management, and the latter generates the response directed to the user.

In general, for the natural language understanding component, most modern task-oriented dialogue systems are somewhat based in frames, which consist of a representation on the information to be provided as slots, to be filled with the information provided by the user [8] and supported by a knowledge base [9]. To assure the correct interpretation for a given command in this kind of dialogue systems, natural language technologies are used in several solutions in the literature [10,11]. Classical architectures made use of rules to detect the intent of the user and to perform slot filling, mainly semantic grammars, as it can be seen in [9], or templates [12]. However, modern approaches generally do not make use of rules and rely on machine-learning-based (both classic machine learning and deep learning) techniques [8]. Nevertheless, and as pointed out by [8], industrial approaches often make use of rules and templates for slot-filling techniques, as the domain is limited enough for this approach to work.

As for dialogue management, rules have also been traditionally used in task-oriented dialogue systems [13]. However, and as in the previous case, these techniques are being replaced by machine-learning-based methods such as conditional random fields [14,15], maximum entropy models [16] and, more recently, deep learning models [17,18] [19].

Although they are proven to be widely used, machine-learning-based methods require of great amounts of data to train the systems, which is not easy to obtain for industrial task-oriented dialogue systems, and rules are often generated for both natural language understanding and dialogue management. However, constructing rules is time and cost consuming and may be prone to errors, and supervised machine learning techniques are being added to the paradigm by combining them with these rules to optimize results [20,21].

In current approaches, ontologies have also been considered both for the natural language understanding and the dialogue management components of task-oriented dialogue systems, as they are a powerful tool that allows to define in detail the domain and reduce ambiguity between agents [10]. However, most dialogue systems that use ontologies found in the literature are limited to highly specific use cases and mainly to model the domain. In [22], for the banking and finance domain, domain information, such as products and services, is modelled in the ontology, as well as certain state-related dialogue information (e.g., which is the current product that is discussed in the conversation). In industrial scenarios, the work in [11] makes use of an ontology to model the domain in terms of possible actions to be performed by the robot and a description of the scenario.

As far as the authors of this paper are concerned, OntoVPA [23] is currently the only intent to achieve a generic approach to semantic-based task-oriented dialogue systems both at domain and dialogue management level. This commercial tool, aims to provide a general approach to manage dialogue through ontologies and, more precisely, by making a distinction between a domain and a dialogue management ontology. The domain ontology and its instantiation store the knowledge related to the domain and the slots to be filled for any of the modelled actions. The dialogue ontology, which is inspired by the Speech Act Theory [24], has the capability of managing the dialogue process, perform state tracking and can also manage responses and answers. However,the documentation for this tool is limited and the ontologies developed are not publicly available, what makes its reuse impossible.

The advances in last decades regarding ontologies have allowed to associate their building process to an engineering task through the creation of methodologies for that matter to obtain quality ontologies [25]. However, as pointed by [25], traditional methodologies such as METHONTOLOGY [26] or NeOn [27] propose actions that are time and resource consuming. Modern methodologies –such as eXtreme Method [28] or Rapid-OWL [29]–, on the other hand, tend to include guidelines that are more consumption friendly, but do not consider basic characteristics of Linked Data such as reuse of ontologies or ontology maintenance and updating [25]. For that purpose, [30] have defined Linked Open Terms (LOT), a light methodology that also complies with reuse and maintenance aspects. Moreover, this methodology has an industrial version, especially optimised for ontology building for industrial scenarios.

The remarks above illustrate that the use of ontologies is a current trend in the literature referring to task-oriented dialogue systems, especially for *ad-hoc* domain modelling, with great capabilites, but still in an early stage for dialogue management and generic implementations. Indeed, since the only approach for this last issue is not available to reuse, a new ontology development is motivated.

3. The Task-Oriented Dialogue management Ontology (TODO)

With the aim of enhancing natural communication between workers in industrial environments and the systems to be used by them, TODO (Task-Oriented Dialogue management Ontology) has been developed to be the core of task-oriented dialogue systems. This section describes TODO in detail, following the methodology used for that purpose.

3.1. Ontology Development Methodology

In ontology development, two main considerations arise: on the one hand, ontologies have to be "carefully designed and implemented" [31], so as to properly model all the necessary information for their final use. On the other hand, ontology development is becoming more and more centered in reuse [32]. Considering the above, it is important to follow a well-defined design methodology to develop ontologies that are optimal both for their intended function and to be reused by others. In the development process of TODO, the methodology followed is LOT (Linked Open Terms), in its industrial version [30], as it focuses on design of ontologies oriented to industrial scenarios. This methodology sets four main steps of development:

- **Requirements specification**. It defines the motivation and the requirements to be fulfilled by the ontology, through the Ontology Requirement Specification Document (OSRD) [33]. The ORSD defines the purpose, scope, intended uses and requirements –defined as Competency Questions (CQ)– of the ontology.
- **Implementation**. By considering the requirements set in the previous step, the ontology is constructed and evaluated.
- **Publication**. Once the ontology has been created and properly annotated, its documentation is generated, and both ontology and documentation are published and made accessible online.
- **Maintenance**. This step includes periodical revisions with the aim to solve issues, add improvements, etc.

The following sections will document TODO ontology design process in terms of the first three steps defined in LOT, as the last one is understood as further periodic maintenance work after an initial version of TODO has been released.

3.2. Requirements Specification Step

Besides the motivation of the ontology, which has been previously documented in the introduction, the ORSD leads to determine the specifications for the functional requirements of the ontology; that is, the knowledge that the ontology must cover. In this sense, it is important to bear in mind that the main objective of the dialogue is to obtain a command that is understandable for the target system from a natural language request.

To determine the required knowledge, three experts in collaborative industrial work and dialogue systems were interviewed to gather information about their necessities and the characteristics they considered to be covered by a task-oriented dialogue system and which type of interactions were expected. By using the information obtained, a series of requirements that had to be covered by the ontology were identified and codified as CQs. For TODO, a total of 93 CQs were obtained, which can be grouped into the following 10 basic CQs:

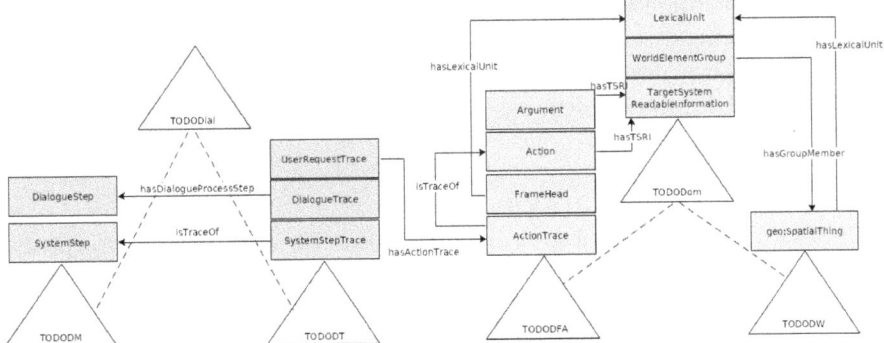

Figure 1. Overview of TODO. Triangles represent ontology modules, whereas rectangles correspond to classes.

- **CQ01**. What are the elements that are present in the scenario?
- **CQ02**. Which is the action to be performed by the target system given a series of key elements obtained from a user request?
- **CQ03**. Which are the arguments of a specific action?
- **CQ04**. Given a set of arguments from a specific action, to what argument can a key element from the user request be associated to?
- **CQ05**. Which is the format of the information that has to be provided to the target system?
- **CQ06**. Which is the first/next step of the dialogue?
- **CQ07**. What should be told to the user given a specific situation?
- **CQ08**. Given some output to the user, it is some input from the user required or not?
- **CQ09**. Which step is currently being performed in the dialogue?
- **CQ10**. Which is the trace –and the information that includes– for an element?

These CQs have helped to define the scope of the ontology and to delimit its different areas of knowledge, along with the classes and relations to be modelled. These CQs have also helped to define the criteria to search for relevant ontological resources for reuse, which will be specified in the implementation section.

3.3. Implementation Step

Ontology Implementation

TODO has been implemented as a modular ontology, inspired in the modules in [23], which distinguish between domain-related and dialogue-related information. This modular approach provides many beneficial aspects to ontologies in terms of maintenance, reasoning-processing[2], validation, comprehension, collaborative effort and reuse [34].

Considering the CQs, the domain and dialogue modules have been divided in submodules in TODO, so as to cover more specific areas of knowledge that have certain independence. The definition of the CQs also contributes to the identification of reusable concepts from other ontologies, a task that is considered as good practice in ontology

---

[2]Reasoners and processing tools may take more time to work over big ontologies.

development [35]. More details on the reused concepts for each module are specified in the following sections.

The general overview of TODO and its modules can be seen in Figure 1. The following lines will describe the dialogue- and domain-related modules, along with each of their submodules.

Dialogue Ontology Module - TODODial

The TODODial module, which covers basic CQs 06 to 10, deals with the concepts used for dialogue modelling, both for dialogue management and dialogue tracing. The knowledge covering the former is intended to be implemented as static, and the latter as dynamic, as it will be instantiated during the dialogue process. Considering this, the module consists of two submodules: **Dialogue Management** (TODODM) and **Dialogue Tracing** (TODODT).

TODODM, which covers basic CQs 06 to 08, models the concepts that allow to manage the dialogue process. In this sense, the dialogue process consists of two main types of steps: **Dialogue steps** and **Process steps**. The former require of some interaction with the user by the system (SystemStep) and, depending on the modelling of the dialogue step, it may prompt the user to obtain information (SystemRequest) or it may output some information (SystemResponse). The output to be presented to the user is defined in a data property (outputSentence).

A system response will typically imply a system request, although it may also imply a predefined action in dialogue control (DialogueControlMarkers), which might establish that the dialogue process needs to **continue, finish** or to **restart**.

On the other hand, process steps do not require from interaction with the user. Both **dialogue** and **process steps** have a **step function** associated. **Step functions** are a very important concept in the dialogue process, since they are directly linked to specific functions in the dialogue system component that manages the dialogue process (usually known as dialogue manager). Furthermore, **step functions** have a set of implications (through the object property implies and its subproperties) that determine the next step of the dialogue process, considering the output of the **step function**s when executed in the dialogue manager.

The **TODODT** module deals with basic CQs 09 to 10, and aims to model the necessary concepts to allow dialogue recreability; that is, to gather the necessary information to be able to reproduce the dialogue process, so as to detect possible errors or check the flow of a specific piece of dialogue. Furthermore, this information can be exploited to learn from finished interactions.

In this module, three main dialogue elements are subject to tracing: **dialogues, user steps** and **system steps**. For dialogues, two types are distinguished: **Dialogues** and **Secondary dialogues**. **Dialogues** are the main concept of the dialogue, whereas **Secondary dialogues** are the subdialogues that emerge in the context of a **Dialogue**. For example, given the user request "I want information": a dialogue trace would be created, and that dialogue trace would have an associated user request trace. However, the user has not specified the element they want information about, and the system generates a secondary dialogue, with a trace of the request that asks for the missing information –which will

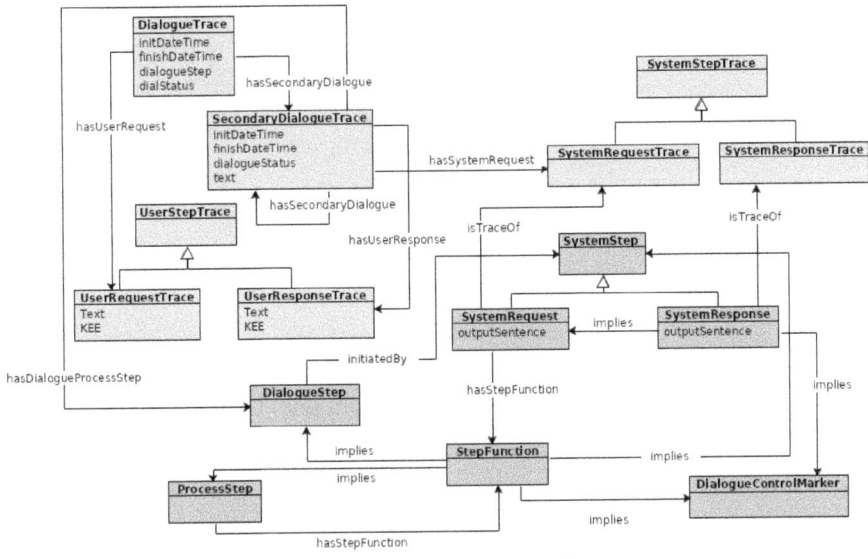

Figure 2. Simple overview of TODODial.

recreate the output sentence(s) that the user has received as output. If the system output is a request, a trace for the user response will also be created.

Figure 2 shows a simple overview of the main relations in TODODial, showing the Tracing module in purple and the Management module in magenta. As it can be seen, both modules are joined in terms of traces.

Domain Ontology Module - TODODom

The TODODom module, which covers basic CQs 01 to 05, deals with the concepts used for domain modelling, in terms of the actions that the target system can perform and the elements that are present in the scenario. Most importantly, this module is in charge of obtaining a target-system-readable command from a natural interaction.

Taking into account these considerations, this module includes two submodules: **Frame-Action** (TODODFA), which deals with the former, and **World** (TODODW), which deals with the latter.

TODODFA, which covers basic CQs 02 to 05, models the actions that can be performed by the target system and the arguments required by said action to be executed. It also establishes the concepts that help identify the action from a natural command.

This module, which is inspired by the GUS architecture [36], considers the **skills** of the target system[3], and associates each **skill** to an **intent**, which is the user objective when directing a request to the dialogue system (e.g. *pick something*). This **intent** is both associated to a **frame** (inspired by Frame Semantics [37]) and to the **action** to perform by the target system.

In this approximation, **frames** are the means by which an **intent** –and, thus, an **action**– can be identified from an user request. In a nutshell, **frames** model situations that can be elicited by specific words (FrameHeads). These specific words are extracted

---

[3]e.g. a robot that can *give directions* and that can *pick objects* can perform two skills.

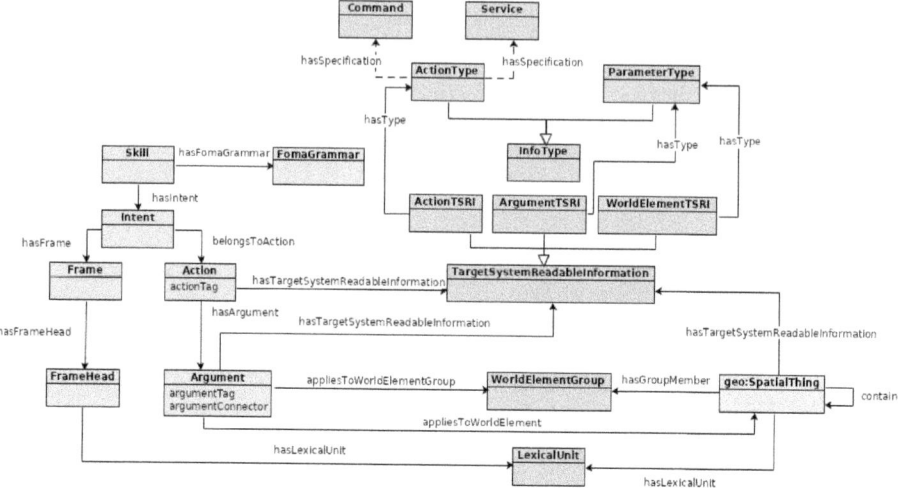

Figure 3. Simple overview of TODODom.

from the user request and, in a dialogue process, the ontology will be in charge of associating them to a **frame** and to their corresponding **intent**. After obtaining the **intent**, it is possible to obtain the **action** to be directed to the target system and its corresponding **arguments** to be fulfilled. The object properties in Frame-Action, besides modelling the relations between classes that have been described above, also allow to define which arguments are compulsory (hasCoreArgument) and which are optional (hasOptionalArgument) for a specific action. Finally, **actions** and **arguments** have a set of tags associated as data properties, in order to fill the corresponding parametric values in a sentence directed to the user (outputSentence).

Frame-Action also includes **Traces** for **skills**, **intents**, **frames**, **actions**, and **arguments**. The **action trace** is the link between TODODom and TODODial, since each user request **trace** is related to the **trace** of the **action** obtained through the user command they represent.

The complete set of classes and object and data properties can be found in the documentation, accessible through the ontology URI in Section 3.4.

TODODW, which covers basic CQ 01, models the set of elements that are available in the scenario. Examples of these elements are spaces, objects or people, depending on the use case. For this, the WGS84 Geo Positioning ontology[4] was considered to reuse. Taking into account the strong dependence of this module on the scenario, this module is practically empty, with an only class, geo:SpatialThing, and the relations dcterms:hasPart and its inverse dcterms:hasPartOf[5], that aim to model the world elements contained by others. This is a module, thus, that must be customized according to the use case. To do so, LOT methodology should be applied, as described in Section 4.

---

[4]http://www.w3.org/2003/01/geo/wgs84_pos
[5]http://purl.org/dc/terms/

Back to **TODODom**, the role of this upper module is to join its two submodules – described above– through intermediate classes and relations to obtain a complete modelling of the domain of the use case as shown in Figure 3. This TODODom modelling approach allows the dialogue system to associate instructions in natural language to their corresponding commands in the appropriate format for the target system.

These intermediate classes are the **target system readable information** (TSRI), **world element groups** and **lexical units**. The first one models information in a format that is understandable to the target system, which is common to the concepts that have to be provided to the target system. Depending on the **TSRI**, an **information type** (InfoType) is associated, which will determine, on the one hand, the implementation of the **action** in regard to the target system (in this case, whether the target system is reachable through a Service[6] or simply receives (robot) commands (Command)) and, on the other hand, the format of the argument information to be provided to the target system. The second may group similar world elements to relate them to specific arguments, modelling the possible values that an **argument** may have in the context of a specific action. Finally, the third one is common to the concepts that are provided by the user (that is, world elements and actions through **frame heads**). **Lexical units** basically represent the different variants to refer to a **frame head** or a world element.

So as to define the implementation of Services, the OWL-S [7] and RESTful Grounding[8] ontologies were reused and reengineered, since they define a semantic markup for web services, including RESTful services.

Ontology Evaluation

According to [38], there are several metrics in the literature to perform ontology evaluation and validation. However, most of these metrics evaluate ontologies from a structural point of view (e.g. whether there are inconsistencies or ill-formed data) or subject-related data (e.g. whether the information in the ontology is correct or whether the domain is fully covered). In the first case, although relevant, these metrics may not be descriptive enough to properly assess the quality of an ontology, whereas in the second case, the metrics must rely on other sources (e.g. gold standards) in order to perform evaluation [39], which in some cases is not viable due to the nature of the ontology to evaluate.

Following the considerations above and the approach and tools described in [31], the following sections present the ontology evaluations from three points of view (**structural metrics**, **design correctness** and **modularity quality**), that aim to provide a non-biased ontology evaluation. Some discussion is also provided on the possibility of customizing the ontology through module modification, so as to obtain descriptive, comprehensive and objective information regarding the quality of the ontologies[9].

Structural Metrics
This evaluation approach aims to provide some figures describing the data modelled in the ontology, more than assessing its quality [31]. The source of such information is

---

[6]http://www.daml.org/services/owl-s/1.1/Service.owl
[7]See previous Note.
[8]https://sites.google.com/site/owlsrestful/RESTfulGrounding.owl
[9]The evaluations have been performed in the 2.0 release of TODO: https://github.com/cristinacm/todo/releases/tag/2.0

Table 1. Structural metrics obtained through Protégé's Ontology Metrics tab. Values in parentheses do not consider imported modules.

Ontology	Axioms	Class	OP	DP	Annotation	DL Expressivity
TODODial	560 (29)	66 (0)	22 (3)	13 (0)	17	SHIQ(D)
TODODM	398	52	15	4	17	ALCHI(D)
TODODT	133	14	4	9	17	SHQ(D)
TODODom	442 (376)	35 (26)	40 (20)	16 (13)	17	ALCHIQ(D)
TODODFA	149	8	18	3	17	ALCHIQ(D)
TODODW	17	1	2	0	15	ALI

Table 2. Results of the evaluation on design correctness performed by OOPS!

Ontology	M	I	C	Notes
TODODial	2	1	0	P11, P13, P22
TODODM	2	1	0	P11, P13, P22
TODODT	1	2	0	P04, P11, P13
TODODom	4	1	0	P04, P08, P11, P13, P22
TODODFA	0	1	0	P13
TODODW	2	1	0	P04, P08, P11

Protégé, which includes this specific information in its Ontology Metrics tab. Table 1 provides with the most relevant information in said tab.

Apart from offering statistical measures (e.g., number of axioms, classes and properties), Table 1 also provides information about the expressivity of the ontology at hand. In this sense, due to the nature of the ontologies involved, which aim to model complex relationships between concepts, the presented ontologies show a considerably rich expressivity. However, TODODW is not as rich as the others, which makes sense taking into consideration its out-of-the-box simplicity.

Design Correctness Metrics

So as to assess the design of the ontologies presented in this work, the tool OOPS! [40] is used. This tool checks the ontology to evaluate against a set of 41 pitfalls, classified according to three levels of importance, which are considered to be the most common pitfalls in ontology design.

Table 2 shows the results obtained by OOPS! for each of the modules of the ontology in terms of number of minor (M), important (I) and critical (C) pitfalls. Note that some of the pitfalls detected for TODODial and TODODom are inherited from their submodules.

For the minor pitfalls, the most repeated are **P8**, **P13** and **P22**. **P8** arises when any *class/property lacks some annotation* (e.g. description, label). In these ontologies, this pitfall refers to imported classes and properties. On the other hand, **P13** points out the *lack of inverse object properties*. Due to the purpose of the ontology they are modelled in, the object properties detected do not require an inverse relationship. Finally, **P22** states that *name conventions are not correctly followed*. Since this pitfall does not indicate the specific elements to be reviewed, all the affected modules have been manually reviewed and all classes and properties follow the same naming conventions.

For the important pitfalls, as it can be seen in the table, the one that all modules share is **P11**, which states that *properties lack the modelling of domain and range*. In

Table 3. Results of the evaluation on modularity quality

	TODODom		TODODial		TODO		
Metrics	DFA	DW	DM	DT	Dial	Dom	T2
Cohesion	0.01	0.0	0.07	0.03	0.04	0.004	*0-0.25*
Encapsulation	0.96	0.62	0.98	0.95	0.99	0.98	*0.75-1*
Coupling	0.0	0.0	0.0	0.0	0.0	0.0	*0-0.25*
Redundancy	0.08	0.08	0.03	0.03	0.01	0.01	*0-0.25*
Size	29	3	71	27	101	91	*10-1103*
Number of axioms	149	17	398	133	532	414	*46-3954*
Appropriateness	0.65	0.01	0.36	0.55	-1.0	0.26	*0.51-0.75*
Atomic size	3.97	1.67	4.18	3.22	4.0	5.18	*3.42-7.66*
Intramodule distance	8.0	0.0	3104.0	74.0	3178.0	62.0	*0-340833*
Attribute richness	3.75	0.0	1.21	1.0	1.32	4.14	*0-3.44*
Inheritance richness	NaN	NaN	5.88	2.2	4.46	2.0	*1-6.44*

the scope of this work, this modelling would be problematic and would not be useful for the purpose of the ontologies, so the correction of this pitfall has been discarded by now.

Finally, it is worth noting that no critical pitalls have been observed in any of the modules of TODO. This fact, in combination with the previous considerations for the rest of pitfalls detected, proves that the modules in TODO are correctly designed.

Modularity Quality
Finally, and considering that TODO is a modular ontology, it is of special relevance to evaluate the quality of each of the ontology modules. For this, the approach in [41] is considered to provide a set of comprehensive measures to be able to determine the quality of an ontology module. The work proposes a set of 14 different module types to be used depending on the final usage of the evaluated ontology module, along with some reference metrics and values in order to be able to evaluate if the ontology module is of high quality. In regard to TODO, all modules belong to the T2 type –*Subject domain modules*, which correspond to subdomains inside a large domain [41].

Considering the complexity of the modular hierarchy in TODO, three evaluations have been performed: the quality of TODODFA and TODODW in relation to TODODom, the quality of TODODM and TODODT in relation to TODODial, and the quality of TODODial (including TODODT and TODODM) and TODODom (including TODODFA and TODODW) in relation to TODO, using the TOMM evaluation tool [41]. The results are included in Table 3, which include the relevant metrics to the T2 module types and their reference values. Some of these reference values for the metrics are small cohesion (i.e. "the extent to which entities in a module are related to each other" [41]), coupling (i.e. the degree in which the concepts in a module are related to concepts in other modules) and redundancy (i.e. "the duplication of axioms within a set of ontology modules" [41]) and large encapsulation (i.e. whether a module can be easily replaced by another or modified without side effects), among others.

In Table 3, for TODODom-related metrics, it can be observed that TODODFA achieves the reference values in general, so it can be stated that it is a module of high quality. In the case of TODODW, size-related metrics (size, number of actions, appropriateness and atomic size) do not fit the defined reference values. This is due to the fact that this ontology is intended to be expanded according to the use case and, thus, it has a reduced size. In the case of TODODial- and TODO- related metrics, the results show that in both cases the implicated modules widely satisfy the established criteria and, thus, are of high quality.

Ontology Customization by Module Modification

One of the advantages of the modularity of TODO is that it is possible to easily modify the ontology by means of specific parts of each module, according to the requirements of the use case. In general, these modifications may be performed in TODODom, since it is the module that is inherently linked to the use case. The clearest example of this customization is TODODW, which, as noted in Section 3.3, must be extended taking into account the scenario the dialogue system will be implemented in, which will define the classes and further relations between them. However, any module from TODO can be easily modified, as shown in the use cases in Section 4.

3.4. Publication Step

Once the ontology has been implemented, it has been made accessible online, both at human- and machine- readable level.

Each of the modules in TODO include all the recommended metadata following Garijo and Poveda-Villalón guidelines [42]. To generate the documentation, WIDOCO (a WIzard for DOCumenting Ontologies) [43], which creates enriched documentation for ontologies, has been used. Furthermore, it is fully compatible with the metadata from the selected guidelines.

The URI for TODO is the following: https://w3id.org/todo. Through this address, the URIs for the rest of the modules can be accessed. This information is also available in TODO's GitHub repository[10].

4. TODO in Use

To assess TODO's usability as core of a task-oriented dialogue system –which is its main motivation–, a validation process has been performed through three industrial use cases for interaction in Spanish: a guide robot, a computerized maintenance management system (CMMS) and a pick-place robot. This validation consists on the definition of TODODW and the instantiation of TODO as a whole, assuring that all the required classes and relations are present. In this process, the suitability of the modularity of the ontology is also reinforced, since each of these solutions have used different configurations of the ontology depending on the necessities of each application[11].

For the modelling of TODODW for each use case, the LOT methodology has been applied: for each use case, two experts in the application field have been interviewed to define the necessities of the use case and recorded as CQs. Based on these CQs, the relevant classes and relations for the Guide and Pick-Place use cases[12] have been defined in the TODODW module[13] (see Table 4 for details).

---

[10]https://github.com/cristinacm/todo

[11]**Guide robot:** TODO; **CMMS:** TODODom and TODODM; **Pick-place robot:** TODODom.

[12]Due to the characteristics of the CMMS use case, TODODW modelling was not necessary.

[13]Specific TODODW files can be found at Github in the following link: https://git.io/Jnly4.

Table 4. Created classes and relations for TODODW modelling for each use case.

	Guide	Pick-Place
Classes	8	5
Relations	4	-

Table 5. Number of instances for each use case and ontology module.

Use case	Total instances	TODODial instances	TODODom instances	
			Through strategy in [44]	Rest
Guide	589	58	47	484
CMMS	208	58	51	99
Pick-Place	242	N/A	184	58

For the ontology instantiation task, the TODODial population has been performed only once, since it is common for all use cases, and only a specific domain instantiation has been required for each of them. To reduce the manual effort for each of these instantiations, and considering the number of different words that can be used in a natural-language-based interaction to describe the same circumstances, a strategy to semi-automatically obtain this information has been explored [44] and applied to instantiate TODODFA frames, frame heads and lexical units. The rest of the instances are included by mapping the ontology with existing target system data (e.g. personnel databases) and, when necessary, manually. Table 5 shows the main figures.

This validation evidences that the classes and relations in the ontology, identified through expert knowledge, allow to comprehensively model the domain at play and the dialogue-relevant information to successfully enable a natural interaction between workers and industrial systems.

5. Conclusions

This work has presented TODO, a core ontology that is aimed to provide easily-adaptable dialogue systems that allow natural communication between workers and industrial systems in the context of Industry 4.0.

TODO has been developed following a well-defined methodology, which has been specially designed for industrial contexts. First, the requirements of the ontology have been established by describing its motivation and setting them as 10 basic CQs. Considering the requirements, TODO has been implemented using a modular structure, which allows to gather related knowledge in specific modules and to facilitate the extension or modification of said areas of knowledge without affecting the rest of the ontology.

So as to provide information about the quality of TODO and its modules, a set of evaluations have been carried out, which have proven that the modules are expressively rich –which is of special relevance to the area of application–, well designed and of high quality –according to the relevant characteristics of their module type. To reinforce the information provided in the evaluation step, a set of use cases in which TODO has been instantiated and extended where necessary –so as to be used in a dialogue system– have been presented. All in all, the implementation of TODO in these use cases has provided satisfactory results, as common instances for all use cases have been identified and part of the instantiation process can be performed automatically.

Further work includes fine-tuning the dialogue manager to obtain a stable, robust dialogue system using TODO as its core and the definition of a user study to test the whole dialogue system implementation in real industrial settings.

Acknowledgements

This work was partially supported by the Basque Government's Elkartek research and innovation program, projects EKIN (KK-2020/00055) and DeepText (KK-2020/00088).

References

[1]   Oborski P. Man-Machine Interactions in Advanced Manufacturing Systems. The International Journal of Advanced Manufacturing Technology. 2004;23(3-4):227–232.

[2]   Messner L, Gattringer H, Bremer H. Efficient Online Computation of Smooth Trajectories along Geometric Paths for Robotic Manipulators. In: Multibody System Dynamics, Robotics and Control. Springer; 2013. p. 17–30.

[3]   Müller R, Vette M, Scholer M. Inspector Robot–A New Collaborative Testing System Designed for the Automotive Final Assembly Line. Assembly Automation. 2014.

[4]   Kildal J, Fernández I, Lluvia I, Lázaro I, Aceta C, Vidal N, et al. Evaluating the UX Obtained from a Service Robot that Provides Ancillary Way-Finding Support in an Industrial Environment. In: Advances in Manufacturing Technology XXXIII: Proceedings of the 17th International Conference on Manufacturing Research, 10-12 Sep 2019, Belfast. vol. 9. IOS Press; 2019. p. 61.

[5]   Bugmann G, Pires JN. Robot-by-voice: Experiments on Commanding an Industrial Robot Using the Human Voice. Industrial Robot: An International Journal. 2005.

[6]   Veiga G, Pires J, Nilsson K. Experiments with Service-Oriented Architectures for Industrial Robotic Cells Programming. Robotics and Computer-Integrated Manufacturing. 2009;25(4-5):746–755.

[7]   Villani V, Pini F, Leali F, Secchi C. Survey on Human–Robot Collaboration in Industrial Settings: Safety, intuitive interfaces and applications. Mechatronics. 2018;55:248 – 266.

[8]   Jurafsky D, Martin JH. Speech and Language Processing (Draft). Hentet; 2020.

[9]   Ward W, Issar S. Recent Improvements in the CMU Spoken Language Understanding System. Carnegie-Mellon University Pittsburgh, PA School of Computer Science; 1994.

[10] Antonelli D, Bruno G. Human-Robot Collaboration using Industrial Robots. In: 2nd International Conference on Electrical, Automation and Mechanical Engineering. Atlantis Press; 2017. p. 99–102.

[11] Maurtua I, Fernández I, Tellaeche A, Kildal J, Susperregi L, Ibarguren A, et al. Natural Multimodal Communication for Human Robot Collaboration. International Journal of Advanced Robotic Systems. 2017;14(4):1–12.

[12] Wei Z, Liu Q, Peng B, Tou H, Chen T, Huang XJ, et al. Task-Oriented Dialogue System for Automatic Diagnosis. In: Proceedings of the 56th Annual Meeting of the Association for Computational Linguistics (Volume 2: Short Papers); 2018. p. 201–207.

[13] Goddeau D, Meng H, Polifroni J, Seneff S, Busayapongchai S. A Form-Based Dialogue Manager for Spoken Language Applications. Proceedings of Fourth International Conference on Spoken Language Processing ICSLP '96. 1996;2:701–704 vol.2.

[14] Lee S, Eskenazi M. Recipe For Building Robust Spoken Dialog State Trackers: Dialog State Tracking Challenge System Description. In: Proceedings of the SIGDIAL 2013 Conference. Metz, France: Association for Computational Linguistics; 2013. p. 414–422.

[15] Lee S. Structured Discriminative Model for Dialog State Tracking. In: Proceedings of the SIGDIAL 2013 Conference; 2013. p. 442–451.

[16] Williams JD. Multi-Domain Learning and Generalization in Dialog State Tracking. In: Proceedings of the SIGDIAL 2013 Conference; 2013. p. 433–441.

[17] Mrkšić N, Séaghdha DO, Thomson B, Gašić M, Su PH, Vandyke D, et al. Multi-Domain Dialog State Tracking Using Recurrent Neural Networks. arXiv preprint arXiv:150607190. 2015.

[18] Henderson M, Thomson B, Young S. Deep Neural Network Approach for the Dialog State Tracking Challenge. In: Proceedings of the SIGDIAL 2013 Conference; 2013. p. 467–471.

[19] Chen, Hongshen and Liu, Xiaorui and Yin, Dawei and Tang, Jiliang. A Survey on Dialogue Systems: Recent Advances and New Frontiers. SIGKDD Explor Newsl. 2017 Nov;19(2):25–35.

[20] Aceta C, Kildal J, Fernández I, Soroa A. Towards an Optimal Design of Natural Human Interaction Mechanisms for a Service Robot with Ancillary Way-Finding Capabilities in Industrial Environments. Production & Manufacturing Research. 2021;9(1):1–32.

[21] Suendermann D, Evanini K, Liscombe J, Hunter P, Dayanidhi K, Pieraccini R. From Rule-Based to Statistical Grammars: Continuous Improvement of Large-Scale Spoken Dialog Systems. In: 2009 IEEE International Conference on Acoustics, Speech and Signal Processing. IEEE; 2009. p. 4713–4716.

[22] Altinok D. An Ontology-Based Dialogue Management System for Banking and Finance Dialogue Systems. arXiv preprint arXiv:180404838. 2018.

[23] Wessel M, Acharya G, Carpenter J, Yin M. OntoVPA-an Ontology-Based Dialogue Management System for Virtual Personal Assistants. In: Advanced Social Interaction with Agents. Springer; 2019. p. 219–233.

[24] Searle JR, Kiefer F, Bierwisch M, et al. Speech Act Theory and Pragmatics. vol. 10. Springer; 1980.

[25] Poveda-Villalón M. A Reuse-Based Lightweight Method for Developing Linked Data Ontologies and Vocabularies. In: Extended Semantic Web Conference. Springer; 2012. p. 833–837.

[26] Fernández-López M, Gómez-Pérez A, Juristo N. Methontology: from Ontological Art towards Ontological Engineering. 1997.

[27] Suárez-Figueroa MC. NeOn Methodology for Building Ontology Networks: Specification, Scheduling and Reuse. Informática; 2010.

[28] Hristozova M, Sterling L. An eXtreme Method for Developing Lightweight Ontologies. In: In Workshop on Ontologies in Agent Systems, 1st International Joint Conference on Autonomous Agents and Multi-Agent Systems. Citeseer; 2002. .

[29] Auer S, Herre H. RapidOWL—An Agile Knowledge Engineering methodology. In: International Andrei Ershov Memorial Conference on Perspectives of System Informatics. Springer; 2006. p. 424–430.

[30] Poveda-Villalón M, Fernández-Izquierdo A, García-Castro R. Linked Open Terms (LOT) Methodology. Zenodo; 2019. Available from: https://doi.org/10.5281/zenodo.2539305.

[31] Esnaola-González I, Bermúdez J, Fernández I, Arnaiz A. EEPSA as a Core Ontology for Energy Efficiency and Thermal Comfort in Buildings. Semantic Web. 2021;Pre-press.

[32] Suárez-Figueroa MC, Gómez-Pérez A, Fernández-López M. The NeOn Methodology for Ontology Engineering. In: Ontology Engineering in a Networked World. Springer; 2012. p. 9–34.

[33] Suárez-Figueroa MC, Gómez-Pérez A, Villazón-Terrazas B. How to Write and Use the Ontology Requirements Specification Document. In: OTM Confederated International Conferences "On the Move to Meaningful Internet Systems". Springer; 2009. p. 966–982.

[34] Keet M. An Introduction to Ontology Engineering. vol. 1; 2018.

[35] Rudnicki R, Smith B, Malyuta T, Mandrick W. Best Practices of Ontology Development. CUBRC; 2016.

[36] Bobrow DG, Kaplan RM, Kay M, Norman DA, Thompson H, Winograd T. GUS, a Frame-Driven Dialog System. Artificial Intelligence. 1977;8(2):155–173.

[37] Fillmore CJ, et al. Frame Semantics and the Nature of Language. In: Annals of the New York Academy of Sciences: Conference on the Origin and Development of Language and Speech. vol. 280; 1976. p. 20–32.

[38] Villalón MP. Ontology Evaluation: a Pitfall-Based Approach to Ontology Diagnosis; 2016.

[39] Raad J, Cruz C. A Survey on Ontology Evaluation Methods; 2015. .

[40] Poveda-Villalón M, Gómez-Pérez A, Suárez-Figueroa MC. OOPS! (OntOlogy Pitfall Scanner!): An On-line Tool for Ontology Evaluation. International Journal on Semantic Web and Information Systems (IJSWIS). 2014;10(2):7–34.

[41] Khan ZC, Keet CM. Dependencies Between Modularity Metrics Towards Improved Modules. In: Blomqvist E, Ciancarini P, Poggi F, Vitali F, editors. Knowledge Engineering and Knowledge Management. Cham: Springer International Publishing; 2016. p. 400–415.

[42] Daniel Garijo and María Poveda-Villalón. A Checklist for Complete Vocabulary Metadata;. https://w3id.org/widoco/bestPractices.

[43] Garijo D. WIDOCO: a Wizard for Documenting Ontologies. In: International Semantic Web Conference. Springer, Cham; 2017. p. 94–102.

[44] Aceta C, Fernández I, Soroa A. Ontology Population Reusing Resources for Dialogue Intent Detection:Generic and Multilingual Approach. Acceptation pending.

Further with Knowledge Graphs. M. Alam et al. (Eds.)
AKA Verlag and IOS Press, 2021
© 2021 Akademische Verlagsgesellschaft AKA GmbH, Berlin
This article is published online with Open Access by IOS Press and distributed under the terms
of the Creative Commons Attribution License 4.0 (CC BY 4.0).
doi:10.3233/SSW210032

Interlinking Valency Frames and WordNet Synsets in the LiLa Knowledge Base of Linguistic Resources for Latin

Francesco MAMBRINI [a,1], Marco PASSAROTTI [a] Eleonora LITTA [a]
Giovanni MORETTI [a]

[a] *Università Cattolica del Sacro Cuore, Milan (Italy)*

Abstract. This paper describes the steps taken to model a valency lexicon for Latin (Latin Vallex) according to the principles of the Linked Data paradigm, and to interlink its valency frames with the lexical senses recorded in a manually checked subset of the Latin WordNet. The valency lexicon and the WordNet share lexical entries and are part of the LiLa Knowledge Base, which interlinks multiple linguistic resources for Latin. After describing the overall architecture of LiLa, as well as the structure of the lexical entries of Latin Vallex and Latin WordNet, the paper focuses on how valency frames have been modeled in LiLa, in line with a submodule of the Predicate Model for Ontologies (PreMOn) specifically created for the representation of grammatical valency. A mapping of the valency frames and the WordNet synsets assigned to the lexical entries shared by the two resources is detailed, as well as a number of queries that can be run across the interoperable resources for Latin currently included in LiLa.

Keywords. Linguistic valency, Linguistic Linked Open Data, Latin, WordNet.

1. Introduction

In lexicography, a widespread approach to the representation of lexical meaning is based on the fundamental assumption of frame semantics by C. Fillmore [1], namely that the meaning of some words can be fully understood only by knowing the frame elements that those lexical items evoke. Such an approach is related to the concept of linguistic valency [2] [3]. The latter concept is used to denote the number of obligatory complements (called 'arguments', but also 'actants' [3] or 'inner participants' [4]) controlled by a word, usually a content verb. The different types of argument are generally represented in valency frames through labels for semantic roles, such as Agent, Patient and Beneficiary.

Several lexical resources are built around the concept of valency and argument frames that describe the argument structure of words with the help of various sets of labels for semantic roles. For instance, the criteria for distinguishing obligatory and non-obligatory complements and the degree of granularity of the set of semantic roles are

---

[1]Corresponding Author: Francesco Mambrini, CIRCSE, Università Cattolica del Sacro Cuore, Largo Gemelli 1, 20123 Milano, Italia; E-mail: francesco.mambrini@unicatt.it.

what mostly distinguishes valency-based resources like PropBank [5] (and NomBank [6]), VerbNet [7] and FrameNet [8] one from the other.

Another kind of lexical resource largely used in both theoretical and computational linguistics is WordNet (WN) [9], which is built around the idea of synonymy in the broad sense. In WordNet, words are included in synsets, which are sets of lexical items that share the same sense, so "that [they] are interchangeable in some context without changing the truth value of the proposition in which they are embedded".[2]

Despite their differences, not only are the valency-based and the WN approaches to lexical meaning not incompatible, but they are strictly related, because valency frames tend to correspond to lexical senses. This is precisely the case in the PDT-VALLEX valency lexicon for Czech [10], where one valency lexicon entry (i.e., valency frame) is created for each sense of a word. Given that in WN the different senses of a polysemic word are represented through assignments to different synsets, mapping the frame entries of a valency lexicon with the synsets of a WN promises to be an effective way to provide a comprehensive representation of lexical meaning that joins the valency-based and the synset-based approaches.

In order to perform such mapping, two conditions must hold. Firstly, both a WN and a valency lexicon must be available for a specific language, with a substantial number of lexical entries in common. Secondly, the mapping process entails the design of a specific technique for interlinking these two kinds of lexical resources in the most standard fashion as possible, so as to make the process applicable to data in any language.

For Latin, the former condition is satisfied by the existence of both a Latin WN and a Latin valency lexicon. In this paper, we will address the challenges in the second condition with the help of a set of models and ontologies developed by the community working in the area of the Linguistic Linked Open Data (LLOD), whose objective is to make (meta)data of distributed linguistic resources interoperable on the web. We describe the process to represent a valency lexicon for Latin according to the principles of LLOD and to interlink its valency frames with the lexical senses recorded in a manually checked subset of the Latin WN. The valency lexicon and the WN are included together (with shared lexical entries) in the LiLa Knowledge Base, which makes distributed linguistic resources for Latin interoperable by applying LLOD principles. The outcome of the work is a new sub-module of the *PreMOn* ontology (see Section 5.1) dedicated to valency frames and the two linked datasets of the Latin WordNet,[3] and Latin Vallex.[4]

The paper is organized as follows. Section 2 provides an overview of the related work about (inter)linking valency-based lexical resources between them and with WNs. Section 3 presents the fundamental architecture of the LiLa Knowledge Base. Section 4 describes the Latin WN and the Latin Vallex resources. Section 5 details how we modelled valency in LiLa and the mapping between the valency frames of Latin Vallex and the synsets of WN. Finally, Section 6 concludes the paper.

---

[2]Quoted from the glossary of WordNet: http://wordnet.princeton.edu.
[3]http://lila-erc.eu/lodview/data/lexicalResources/LatinWordNet/Lexicon.
[4]http://lila-erc.eu/lodview/data/lexicalResources/LatinVallex/Lexicon.

2. Related Work

Over the last decade, several attempts at (inter)linking different lexical resources together have been performed. One of the best known projects is Semlink, which makes use of a set of mappings to link PropBank, VerbNet, FrameNet and WN [11]. Pazienza et alii [12] study the semantics of verb relations by mixing WN, VerbNet and PropBank. Shi and Mihalcea [13] integrate FrameNet, VerbNet and WN into one knowledge-base for semantic parsing purposes.

In the LLOD context, the *PreMOn* (*pre*dicate *m*odel for *on*tologies) resource [14] exposes predicate models for PropBank, NomBank, VerbNet, and FrameNet and mappings between them. More information on *PreMOn* will be provided in Section 5.1.

Regarding the relations between valency lexica and WNs, Hlaváčková [15] describes the merging of the Czech WordNet (CWN) with the database of verb valency frames for Czech VerbaLex, whose lexical entries are related to each other according to the CWN synsets. Hajič et alii [16] use CWN while performing the lexico-semantic annotation of the Prague Dependency Treebank for Czech (PDT), which is in turn exploited to improve the quality and the coverage of CWN. To pick out the semantic constraints of the verbal arguments in the Polish WordNet (PolNet), the valency structure of verbs is used as a property of verbal synsets, because it is "one of the formal indices of the meaning (it is so that all members of a given synset share the valency structure)" (page 402 of [17]). Finally, Passarotti et alii [18] compare the different views on lexical meaning conveyed by the Latin WN and by a valency lexicon for Latin, evaluating the degree of overlapping between a number of homogeneous lexical subsets extracted from the two resources.

3. The LiLa Knowledge Base

The *LiLa: Linking Latin* project (2018-2023)[5] was awarded funding from the European Research Council (ERC) to build a Knowledge Base (KB) of linguistic resources for Latin based on the Linked Data paradigm. Our aim is to build a collection of multifarious, interlinked data sets of Latin resources represented with the same vocabulary of knowledge description (by using common data categories and ontologies) [19].

According to the Linked Data paradigm, data in the Semantic Web [20] are interlinked through connections that can be semantically queried, so as to make the structure of web data better serve the needs of users. In order to achieve interoperability between distributed resources for Latin, LiLa makes use of a set of Semantic Web and Linked Data standards and practices. These include ontologies to describe linguistic annotation (OLiA: [21]), corpus annotation (CoNLL-RDF: [22]) and lexical resources (Ontolex-Lemon: [23]).

Following Bird and Liberman [24], the Resource Description Framework (RDF) [25] is used to encode graph-based data structures to represent linguistic annotations in terms of triples: (i) a predicate-property (a relation; in graph terms: a labeled edge) that connects (ii) a subject (a resource; in graph terms: a labeled node) with (iii) its object (another resource/node, or a literal, e.g. a string).

Given the presence and role played by lemmatization in various linguistic resources, and the good accuracy rates achieved by the best performing lemmatizers for Latin (up

---

[5]https://lila-erc.eu.

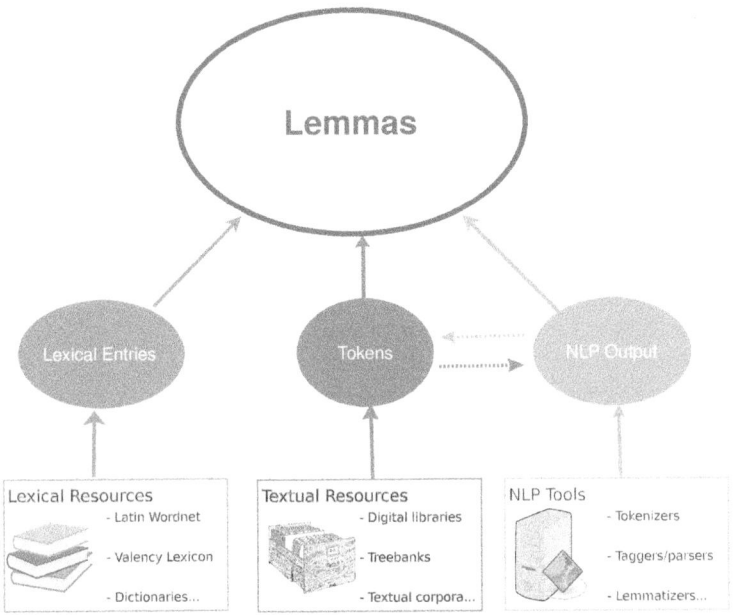

Figure 1. The main components of the LiLa ontology model.

to 0.96, as per the results of the EvaLatin 2020 evaluation campaign [26]), LiLa uses the lemma as the most productive interface between lexical resources, annotated corpora and Natural Language Processing (NLP) tools. Consequently, the ontology model of the LiLa KB is highly lexically based, grounded on a simple, but effective assumption that strikes a good balance between feasibility and granularity: textual resources are made of (occurrences of) words, lexical resources describe properties of words, and NLP tools process words.

Fig. 1 presents the main components of the ontology model of the LiLa KB, showing the key role of interlinking played by lemmas.

Fig. 1 shows that there are three kinds of (meta)data sources in LiLa, namely: (1) lexical resources, which include lexical entries, (2) textual resources, which are made of occurrences of words (tokens), and (3) NLP tools, which produce different outputs according to their task(s) of automatic linguistic analysis.[6] In LiLa, lexical entries, tokens and NLP outputs are interlinked via lemmas.

To make this conceptual architecture work, the core of the LiLa KB consists of a large collection of Latin lemmas: interoperability is achieved by linking all those entries in lexical resources and tokens in corpora that point to the same lemma. The lexical basis of the Latin morphological analyzer Lemlat [27] was used to populate the LiLa collection. Lemlat's database reconciles three reference dictionaries for Classical Latin [28] [29] [30], the entire Onomasticon from Forcellini's *Lexicon Totius Latinitatis* [31]

---

[6]The arrows that double link the nodes for 'Tokens' and 'NLP Output' in Fig. 1 represent that tokens can be both the output of an NLP tool (a tokenizer) and the input of another (e.g., a PoS tagger).

and the Medieval Latin *Glossarium Mediae et Infimae Latinitatis* by du Cange et alii [32], for a total of over 150,000 lemmas.

Beside the collection of Latin lemmas, the linguistic resources linked so far via the LiLa KB are the following:[7]

- the *Index Thomisticus* Treebank, both in its original and in the *Universal Dependencies* version [33];[8]
- the Latin works of Dante Alighieri, taken from the *DanteSearch* corpus [34];[9]
- the text of the Late Antiquity comedy *Querolus sive Aulularia*;[10]
- the *Etymological Dictionary of Latin and the other Italic Languages* by M. De Vaan [35] [36];[11]
- the *LatinAffectus* sentiment lexicon of Latin [37];[12]
- the collection of Ancient Greek loanwords in the Latin language *Index Graecorum vocabulorum in linguam Latinam translatorum quaestiunculis auctus* by G. Saalfeld [38] [39];[13]
- a manually checked set of 1,424 entries of the Latin WordNet [40];[14]
- the valency lexicon *Latin Vallex* [41];[15]
- the derivational lexicon *Word Formation Latin*[42]. [16]

Both the lemma collection and the source (meta)data of the resources linked to LiLa (together with their Turtle files, which provide the RDF triples) are freely available from the GitHub page of the CIRCSE research center.[17]

4. Latin WordNet and Latin Vallex

The LatinWordNet (LWN) [43] was initiated in the context of the MultiWordNet project [44], whose aim was to build a number of semantic networks for specific languages aligned with the synsets of the Princeton WordNet (PWN) [45]. Unfortunately, the automatic process employed to set up such an alignment resulted in a dataset that is at the same time largely incomplete (i.e. lacking a number of crucial lemmas e.g. *amo* "to love") and inaccurate, especially due to the presence of various modern senses inherited from MultiWordNet.

---

[7]To connect the entries of lexical resources as well as the lemmatized tokens of annotated corpora to the LiLa collection of lemmas, we perform a simple string match between the lemmas in the resource to connect and those in the LiLa collection. Ambiguous links, which happen when one lemma in the resource is connected to more than one lemma in the LiLa collection, are disambiguated manually. Missing links are solved by including the missing lemmas in LiLa. The procedure is detailed with reference to the *Index Thomisticus* Treebank in [19].

[8]https://lila-erc.eu/data/corpora/ITTB/id/corpus.

[9]https://lila-erc.eu/data/corpora/DanteSearch/id/corpus;   https://dantesearch.dantenetwork.it/.

[10]https://lila-erc.eu/data/corpora/Querolus/id/citationUnit/QuerolussiveAulularia.

[11]https://lila-erc.eu/data/lexicalResources/BrillEDL/Lexicon.

[12]https://lila-erc.eu/data/lexicalResources/LatinAffectus/Lexicon.

[13]https://lila-erc.eu/data/lexicalResources/IGVLL/Lexicon.

[14]http://lila-erc.eu/data/lexicalResources/LatinWordNet/Lexicon.

[15]https://lila-erc.eu/data/lexicalResources/LatinVallex/Lexicon.

[16]https://lila-erc.eu/data/lexicalResources/WFL/Lexicon.

[17]https://github.com/CIRCSE.

Before its inclusion in LiLa, LWN counted 8,973 synsets and 9,124 lemmas. These are currently undergoing substantial revision to refine and extend its contents.[18] There are currently 1,424 fully reviewed entries in LiLa, for a total of 2,809 unique synsets. Synset are found or checked against two main Classical and Late Latin dictionaries [29] [46]. For each sense found in the dictionaries, one or more corresponding synsets are extracted from the 3.0 version of Princeton WordNet [9]. For example, the Latin verb *concordo* has the following senses:

- "to be in good terms, be friendly, live in harmony (with someone)";
- "to be in agreement, harmonise, agree";
- "to bring about harmony/an harmonious relationship (between things), bring into union".

Thereby, the following synsets have been chosen for *concordo*:

- 02700104-v "go together";
- 02657219-v "be compatible, similar or consistent; coincide in their characteristics";
- 00805376-v "be in accord; be in agreement";
- 01035530-v "achieve harmony of opinion, feeling, or purpose";
- 00482473-v "bring into consonance or accord".

Each of these are then linked to a valency frame in the valency lexicon Latin Vallex (LV).

LV [41] was originally developed while performing the semantic annotation of two Latin treebanks, namely the *Index Thomisticus* Treebank, which includes works of Thomas Aquinas [47], and the Latin Dependency Treebank, featuring works of different authors of the Classical era [48]. All valency-capable lemmas occurring in the semantically annotated portion of the two treebanks are assigned one lexical entry and one valency frame in LV.

The structure of LV resembles that of the valency lexicon for Czech PDT-VALLEX [10]. On the topmost level, the lexicon is divided into lexical entries. Each entry consists of a sequence of frame entries relevant for the lemma in question. A frame entry contains a sequence of frame slots, each corresponding to one argument of the given lemma. Each frame slot is assigned a semantic role. The set of semantic roles is the same used for the semantic annotation of the PDT [49]. Since the development of the lexicon is directly related to the annotation of the texts in the PDT, the surface form of the semantic roles run across during the annotation process is recorded as well.

In view of its extension and linking to LiLa, a different choice has been made in regards to the inner structure and theoretical principles of LV. In order to increase the lexical coverage of LV, the writing of the valency frames was disassociated from the treebank annotation process and valency is now defined on the basis of senses. For each sense, a valency frame is established intuitively, listing only its obligatory complements. This process involves finding a valency frame for each sense of the dictionary headword, as there might be differences in the number and/or type of arguments for different senses.

Since senses of words in LiLa are represented as PWN synsets evoked by LWN lexical entries, each (valency-bearing) synset is linked to a valency frame of LV, thus

---

[18]For an evaluation of the original content in LWN, see [40].

interlinking the two resources (see Section 5.1). The job is currently being performed manually, the valency frames included in the first version of LV have been updated, cleaned or rectified, and applied to each valency-bearing synset. Currently, 1,064 lexical entries have been annotated, for a total of 9,806 valency frames, while 1,424 entries of the LWN have been checked and revised manually.

5. Modeling Valency in LiLa

5.1. Ontolex and PreMOn

In order to provide a common infrastructure to link the different lexical and textual resources using lemmatization as the connecting point, the LiLa KB adopts the *Ontolex-Lemon* ontology to model information of its comprehensive collection of Latin lemmas. *Ontolex-Lemon* [23] is a de-facto standard for the description of lexical entries. Particularly relevant for the aims of the projects is the property *canonical form*, as defined in the ontology, that allows us to express the relation between an entry in any given lexical resource and a lemma in the LiLa collection.

The core properties and classes of *Ontolex* are sufficiently expressive to account for the relations between words, senses and synsets as defined in WN. The meaning of a lexical entry is captured by expressing the relation to either a denoted entity or an evoked lexical concept in an ontology. An instance of the class Lexical Sense is used to reify this relation. Following the model of a complete publication of the PWN as LLOD, LiLa now includes all the 1,424 entries of the manually revised LWN.[19]

While a number of extensions of *Ontolex* allow for the expression of many properties of the lexical items, including the syntactic frames and their elements, the ontology is not well suited to conveyexpress the notion of a predicate structure of semantic roles. The *Predicate Model for Ontologies* (PreMOn) builds also on *Ontolex*, but is explicitly designed to provide a description of the predicate structure and of the semantic roles connected to each lexical entry. At the same time, it also allows to map different semantic descriptions of any given word (such as a predicate structure and a link to a WN synset) to each other. This feature makes it ideally suited to represent both the structure of the valency frames and their connection to the senses described in the LWN.

PreMOn is based on a core module, whose main elements are the Semantic Class and Semantic Role classes. The former represents the the semantic classes from the various predicate models; thus, for examplinstance, rolesets from PropBank and frames from FrameNet are all instances of semantic classes. The different sub-classes of this general class, however, can be further specified in dedicated submodels, where the terminology and the relations that are peculiar to each specific project can also be defined.

5.2. The Vallex Submodule

To properly capture the structure of the valency frames in LV, we created a submodule of *PreMOn* that introduces a series of new subclasses and subproperties (which are prefixed with the namespace pmolv in what follows). The structure of the LV submodule is

---

[19]Metadata and a list of the entries can be browsed at: http://lila-erc.eu/data/lexicalResources/ LatinWordNet/Lexicon.

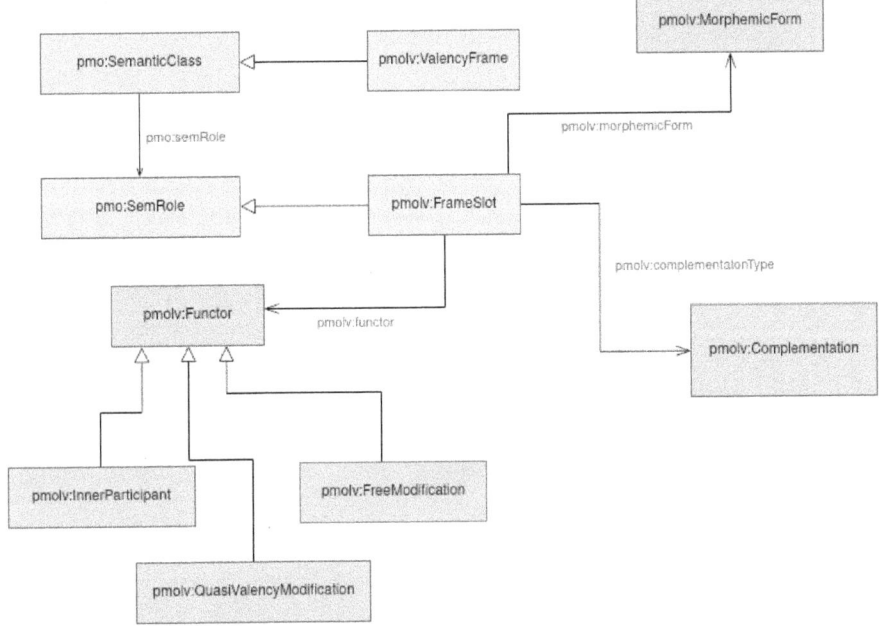

Figure 2. The Latin Vallex submodule for *PreMOn*.

illustrated in Fig. 2. We define the valency frame as a subclass of `pmo:SemanticClass`; each different frame of any given entry in our lexicon is an instance of this class. The arguments involved in the valency frames of LV, called *frame slots*, are treated as a subclass of `pmo:SemRole`. These slots, which, as it is mandated for *PreMOn*'s semantic roles, are defined locally to each semantic class, correspond to the so-called "functors" (i.e. semantic values of syntactic dependency relations) of the Functional Generative Description [49], which are classified into the three main categories of inner participants, free modifications, and quasi-valency modifications [49] [50]. We also use the `pmolv:complementationType` property to distinguish between obligatory and optional modification. Although the morphemic form, i.e. the morpho-syntactic realization of the role used in language, is not expressed in LV, the submodule identifies one property and one class to specify this information.

5.3. Mapping between Valency Frames and Synsets

PreMOn allows users to map pairs of words and predicate structure from different predicate models (e.g. from PropBank and FrameNet) to each other. In order to express this link, the core module defines a special reification of the relation between a given semantic class and a lexical entry, called "Conceptualization". Mapping itself is performed with instances of the class `pmo:Mapping`, which is defined as a set of conceptualizations, semantic classes, or semantic roles. Thus, in the *PreMOn* data, words-synsets pairs are matched with the predicate analyses from resources like PropBank and VerbNet by means of mapping instances linking the corresponding conceptualizations.[20]

---

[20]The mapping at the following address, for instance, links the conceptualization between the verb "to leave out" and synset 200616690-v to the one between the same verb and the class `neglect-75.1` for VerbNet:

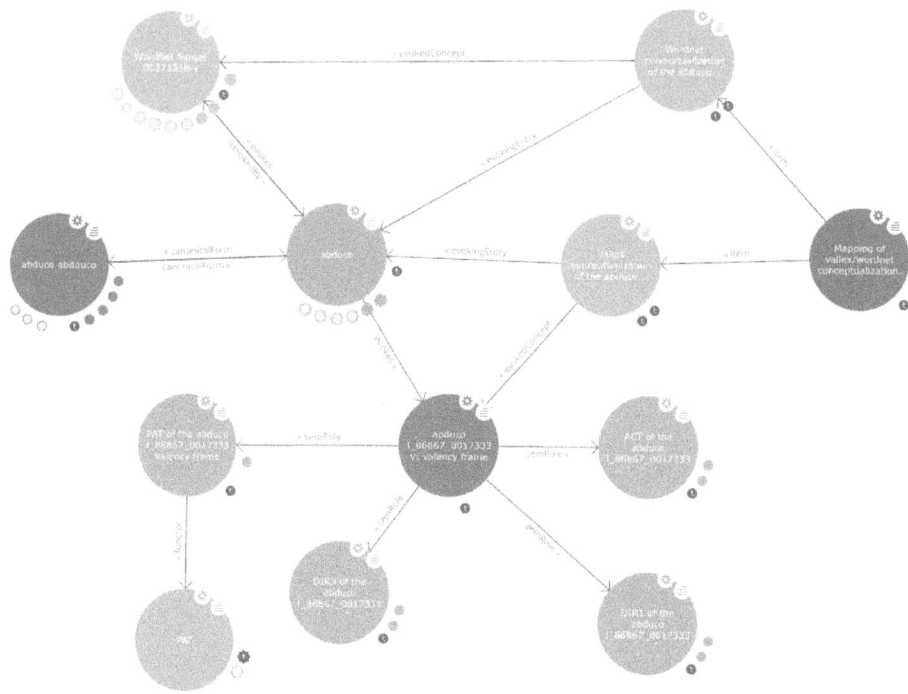

Figure 3. The verb *abduco* from the Latin Vallex and WordNet in LiLa.

The version of LV included in LiLa adopts the same approach to connect valency frames and senses from the LWV. Fig. 3 represents the predicate structure and one of the WN links for the Latin verb *abduco*, in the sense "to take away, to remove".[21] A mapping instance (furthest node on the right, in the figure) holds together the two conceptualizations, that connect the verb to, respectively, synset 00173338-v of WN[22] and a valency frame for that specific sense.[23]

The valency frame requires four (obligatory) frame slot, whose roles are filled by the functors: ACT (generally, the Actor), PAT (generally, the Patient),[24] DIR1 (Direction From) and DIR3 (Direction To). Note that in the figure only the link between the semantic role for PAT and the functor is shown.

5.4. Querying Interlinked Lexical and Textual Resources

As an example of the benefits of interoperability between different resources enabled by the Linked-Data approach to the publication of the joint LWN and LV data, we consider

---

http://premon.fbk.eu/resource/sense-Ep7UGYgbEXbB3B2uGhZamc.

[21]Following the habit of Latin lexicography, the 1st person singular of active present indicative is conventionally chosen as the citation form for verbs.

[22]See http://wordnet-rdf.princeton.edu/pwn30/00173338-v.

[23]The frame is: http://lila-erc.eu/data/lexicalResources/LatinVallex/id/Conceptualization/co-val-1_86867_00173338-v.

[24]It must be kept in mind that, in the PDT-VALLEX formalism, the first arguments are subject to the "argument shift" [49, sec. 6.2.1.4], and are always labeled ACT, PAT and EFF, regardless of their semantic value.

Table 1. Synsets associated with tetravalent verbs in LV (5 with highest nr. of lexical entries associated in LWN).

Synset	Gloss	Nr. Entries
00173338-v	remove something concrete, as by lifting, pushing, or taking off, or remove something abstract	13
01354673-v	connect, fasten, or put together two or more pieces	10
01494310-v	put into a certain place or abstract location	10
02304982-v	get or gather together	9
00179311-v	take out or remove	9

Table 2. Most frequent tetravalent verbs in the *Index Thomisticus* Treebank (ITTB) and in *DanteSearch* (DS).

Corpus	Verb	Freq.
	compono	423
ITTB	confero	300
	committo	136
	confero	60
DS	expello	32
	committo	28

a couple of complex queries that span over several resources. At present, the majority of valency frames in LV has two argument slots (5,505, i.e. 66% of the frames). The highest value of obligatory arguments is 4, a number that is required by 55 frames (0.6%).

The mapping between LV and the LWN allows for an easy investigation on the semantics of these verbs. By querying the SPARQL endpoint of LiLa,[25] it is possible to list the synsets that are mapped with the 55 valency frames that require 4 arguments. Table 1 lists the top five synsets associated with tetravalent verbs, ranked by the number of lexical entries associated to them.

LiLa's connections via lemmatization enables also to scrutinize, at least in a preliminary survey, the distribution of these tetravalent verbs in the linked corpora. The three most frequent verbs that have at least one 4-argument frame in the *Index Thomisticus* Treebank and *DanteSearch* are reported in Table 2. It must be kept in mind, however, that the raw frequencies reported in the table do not distinguish between the multiple valency frame associated with each verb; thus, the 300 and 60 occurrences of the verb *confero* "to bring, to carry together" might be instances of any of the 32 valency frames associated with it.[26] Only with a corpus enhanced with word-sense disambiguation it will be possible to distinguish between them.

6. Conclusions

In this paper we described how we modeled the contents of a valency lexicon for Latin strictly connected to a WordNet, to interlink it with other linguistic resources for Latin in a Knowledge Base built upon LLOD principles.

---

[25]https://lila-erc.eu/sparql.
[26]Translations of the Latin verbs in Table 2 beside *confero*: *committo* "to bring together, to join", *compono* "to bring together, to collect", *expello* "to drive out".

The modeling was performed by building a specific submodule of the *PreMOn* Linked Data resource for representing predicate-based lexical resources. In particular, the OWL ontology provided by *PreMOn* was used for modeling the valency frames and the semantic roles adopted in the Latin valency lexicon. We reused (and extended) an already existing vocabulary to meet one the main tenets of the LLOD world, where distributed linguistic data, metadata and resources are made interoperable just thanks to the fact that they are represented through common data categories and ontologies maintained by the large and active LLOD community.

Although the LiLa Knowledge Base aims first of all to interlink the available linguistic resources for Latin, by grounding on standard LLOD modules, it also wants to represent a reference architecture for the publication of the several (kinds of) resources that were developed for many languages over the last decades.

Thanks to LiLa, a number of linguistic resources for Latin are already made interoperable. The inclusion of a valency lexicon, with entries shared with a manually checked subset of the Latin WordNet, is a major achievement for the Knowledge Base and, hopefully, for the entire community interested in accessing and using linguistic resources for Latin, as it enhances the queries that can be performed on the textual resources connected to LiLa with lexical semantic information. In such respect, one of the near future objectives of the LiLa project is to include a reference Latin-English dictionary in the Knowledge Base [46], while continuing to enlarge the number of corpora that are made interoperable thanks to their connection to LiLa.

References

[1] Fillmore CJ. Frame semantics and the nature of language. Annals of the New York Academy of Sciences: Conference on the origin and development of language and speech. 1976;280(1):20–32.
[2] Ágel V, Fischer K. Dependency grammar and valency theory. In: Heine B, Narrog H, editors. The Oxford Handbook of Linguistic Analysis. Oxford University Press; 2009. p. 225–258.
[3] Tesnière L. Éléments de syntaxe structurale. Paris: Klinksieck; 1959.
[4] Panevová J. In favour of the argument-adjunct distinction (from the perspective of FGD). Prague Bulletin of Mathematical Linguistics. 2016;106(1):21–30.
[5] Kingsbury P, Palmer M. From TreeBank to PropBank. In: Proceedings of the Third International Conference on Language Resources and Evaluation (LREC 2002). Las Palmas: European Language Resources Association (ELRA); 2002. p. 1989–1993.
[6] Meyers A, Reeves R, Macleod C, Szekely R, Zielinska V, Young B, et al. The NomBank Project: An Interim Report. In: Proceedings of the Workshop Frontiers in Corpus Annotation at HLT-NAACL 2004. Boston: Association for Computational Linguistics; 2004. p. 24–31.
[7] Schuler KK. VerbNet: A broad-coverage, comprehensive verb lexicon [Dissertation]. University of Pennsylvania. Philadelphia; 2005. Available from: https://repository.upenn.edu/dissertations/AAI3179808.
[8] Baker CF, Fillmore CJ, Lowe JB. The Berkeley FrameNet Project. In: 36th Annual Meeting of the Association for Computational Linguistics and 17th International Conference on Computational Linguistics, Volume 1. Montreal, Quebec, Canada: Association for Computational Linguistics; 1998. p. 86–90.
[9] Miller GA. WordNet: a lexical database for English. Communications of the ACM. 1995;38(11):39–41.
[10] Hajic J, Panevová J, Urešová Z, Bémová A, Kolárová V, Pajas P. PDT-VALLEX: Creating a large-coverage valency lexicon for treebank annotation. In: Proceedings of the second workshop on treebanks and linguistic theories (TLT). Växjö: Växjö University Press; 2003. p. 57–68.
[11] Palmer M. Semlink: Linking PropBank, VerbNet, FrameNet. In: Proceedings of the generative lexicon conference. Pisa: Association for Computational Linguistics; 2009. p. 9–15.
[12] Pazienza MT, Pennacchiotti M, Zanzotto FM. Mixing WordNet, VerbNet and PropBank for studying verb relations. In: Proceedings of the Fifth International Conference on Language Resources and

Evaluation (LREC 2006). Genoa, Italy: European Language Resources Association (ELRA); 2006. p. 1372–1377.

[13]   Shi L, Mihalcea R. Putting pieces together: Combining FrameNet, VerbNet and WordNet for robust semantic parsing. In: Gelbukh A, editor. International conference on intelligent text processing and computational linguistics. Berlin and Heidelberg: Springer; 2005. p. 100–111.

[14]   Corcoglioniti F, Rospocher M, Aprosio AP, Tonelli S. PreMOn: a lemon extension for exposing predicate models as Linked Data. In: Proceedings of the Tenth International Conference on Language Resources and Evaluation (LREC'16); 2016. p. 877–884.

[15]   Hlaváčková D. The relations between semantic roles and semantic classes in VerbaLex. In: Sojka P, Horák A, editors. Proceedings of Recent Advances in Slavonic Natural Language Processing (RASLAN 2007). Brno: Masaryk University; 2007. p. 97–101.

[16]   Hajič J, Holub M, Hučínová M, Pavlík M, Pecina P, Straňák P, et al. Validating and Improving the Czech WordNet via Lexico-Semantic Annotation of the Prague Dependency Treebank. In: Proceedings of the 4th International Conference On Language Resources And Evaluation (LREC). Lisbon: European Language Resources Association; 2004. p. 25–30.

[17]   Vetulani Z, Kochanowski B. "PolNet - Polish WordNet" project: PolNet 2.0 - a short description of the release. In: Proceedings of the Seventh Global Wordnet Conference. Tartu, Estonia: University of Tartu Press; 2014. p. 400–404.

[18]   Passarotti M, González Saavedra B, Onambélé Manga C. Somewhere between valency frames and synsets. Comparing Latin Vallex and Latin WordNet. In: Bosco C, Zanzotto FM, editors. Proceedings of the Second Italian Conference on Computational Linguistics CLiC-it 2015. Torino: Accademia University Press; 2015. p. 221.

[19]   Passarotti M, Mambrini F, Franzini G, Cecchini FM, Litta E, Moretti G, et al. Interlinking through Lemmas. The Lexical Collection of the LiLa Knowledge Base of Linguistic Resources for Latin. Studi e Saggi Linguistici. 2020;58(1):177–212.

[20]   Berners-Lee T, Hendler J, Lassila O. The semantic web. Scientific american. 2001;284(5):34–43.

[21]   Chiarcos C, Sukhareva M. Olia – ontologies of linguistic annotation. Semantic Web. 2015;6(4):379–386.

[22]   Chiarcos C, Fäth C. CoNLL-RDF: Linked Corpora Done in an NLP-Friendly Way. In: Gracia J, Bond F, McCrae JP, Buitelaar P, Chiarcos C, Hellmann S, editors. Language, Data, and Knowledge. Cham, Switzerland: Springer; 2017. p. 74–88.

[23]   McCrae JP, Bosque-Gil J, Gracia J, Buitelaar P, Cimiano P. The OntoLex-Lemon Model: Development and Applications. In: Electronic lexicography in the 21st century. Proceedings of eLex 2017 conference. Brno, Czech Republic: Lexical Computing CZ s.r.o.; 2017. p. 587–597.

[24]   Bird S, Liberman M. A formal framework for linguistic annotation. Speech communication. 2001;33(1-2):23–60.

[25]   Lassila O, Swick RR. Resource Description Framework (RDF) Model and Syntax Specification; 1998. Available from: https://www.w3.org/TR/1999/REC-rdf-syntax-19990222/.

[26]   Sprugnoli R, Passarotti M, Cecchini FM, Pellegrini M. Overview of the EvaLatin 2020 Evaluation Campaign. In: Proceedings of LT4HALA 2020 - 1st Workshop on Language Technologies for Historical and Ancient Languages. Marseille, France: European Language Resources Association (ELRA); 2020. p. 105–110. Available from: https://www.aclweb.org/anthology/2020.lt4hala-1.16.

[27]   Passarotti M, Budassi M, Litta E, Ruffolo P. The Lemlat 3.0 Package for Morphological Analysis of Latin. In: Bouma G, Adesam Y, editors. Proceedings of the NoDaLiDa 2017 Workshop on Processing Historical Language. vol. 133. Gothenburg: Linköping University Electronic Press; 2017. p. 24–31.

[28]   Georges KE, Georges H. Ausführliches lateinisch-deutsches Handwörterbuch. Hannover: Hahn; 1913.

[29]   Glare PG. Oxford Latin Dictionary. Oxford: Oxford University Press; 1982.

[30]   Gradenwitz O. Laterculi vocum Latinarum: voces Latinas et a fronte et a tergo ordinandas. Leipzig: Hirzel; 1904.

[31]   Budassi M, Passarotti M. Nomen Omen. Enhancing the Latin Morphological Analyser Lemlat with an Onomasticon. In: Proceedings of the 10th SIGHUM Workshop on Language Technology for Cultural Heritage, Social Sciences, and Humanities. Berlin, Germany: Association for Computational Linguistics; 2016. p. 90–94.

[32]   Cecchini FM, Passarotti M, Ruffolo P, Testori M, Draetta L, Fieromonte M, et al. Enhancing the Latin Morphological Analyser LEMLAT with a Medieval Latin Glossary. In: Proceedings of the Fifth Italian Conference on Computational Linguistics (CLiC-it 2018). Torino: aAccademia University Press; 2018.

p. 87–92.

[33] Cecchini FM, Passarotti M, Marongiu P, Zeman D. Challenges in Converting the Index Thomisticus Treebank into Universal Dependencies. In: Proceedings of the Second Workshop on Universal Dependencies (UDW 2018). Brussels, Belgium: Association for Computational Linguistics; 2018. p. 27–36.

[34] Cecchini FM, Sprugnoli R, Moretti G, Passarotti M. UDante: First Steps Towards the Universal Dependencies Treebank of Dante's Latin Works. In: Seventh Italian Conference on Computational Linguistics. Bologna: CEUR-WS. org; 2020. p. 1–7.

[35] Vaan Md. Etymological Dictionary of Latin: and the other Italic Languages. Leiden and Boston: Brill; 2008. Available from: `https://brill.com/view/title/12612`.

[36] Mambrini F, Passarotti M. Representing Etymology in the LiLa Knowledge Base of Linguistic Resources for Latin. In: Proceedings of the 2020 Globalex Workshop on Linked Lexicography. Marseille, France: European Language Resources Association; 2020. p. 20–28.

[37] Sprugnoli R, Moretti G, Passarotti M. Towards the Modeling of Polarity in a Latin Knowledge Base. In: Adamou A, Daga E, Meroño-Peñuela A, editors. WHiSe 2020 Workshop on Humanities in the Semantic Web 2020. Heraklion, Greece: CEUR; 2020. p. 59–70.

[38] Saalfeld GAEA. Tensaurus Italograecus: ausführliches historisch-kritisches Wörterbuch der griechischen Lehn- und Fremdwörter im Lateinischen. C. Gerold's Sohn; 1884.

[39] Franzini G, Zampedri F, Passarotti M, Mambrini F, G. Græcissâre: Ancient Greek Loanwords in the LiLa Knowledge Base of Linguistic Resources for Latin. In: Monti J, Dell'Orletta F, Tamburini F, editors. Proceedings of the Seventh Italian Conference on Computational Linguistics. Bologna, Italy, March 1-3, 2021. Bologna: CEUR-WS.org; 2020. p. 1–6.

[40] Franzini G, Peverelli A, Ruffolo P, Passarotti M, Sanna H, Signoroni E, et al. Nunc Est Aestimandum. Towards an evaluation of the Latin WordNet. In: Bernardi R, Navigli R, Semeraro G, editors. Sixth Italian Conference on Computational Linguistics (CLiC-it 2019). Bari, Italy: CEUR-WS.org; 2019. p. 1–8.

[41] Passarotti M, Saavedra BG, Onambele C. Latin Vallex. A Treebank-based Semantic Valency Lexicon for Latin. In: Proceedings of the Tenth International Conference on Language Resources and Evaluation (LREC 2016). Portorož, Slovenia: European Language Resources Association (ELRA); 2016. p. 2599–2606.

[42] Litta E, Passarotti M, Mambrini F. The Treatment of Word Formation in the LiLa Knowledge Base of Linguistic Resources for Latin. In: Proceedings of the Second International Workshop on Resources and Tools for Derivational Morphology. Prague, Czechia: Charles University, Faculty of Mathematics and Physics, Institute of Formal and Applied Linguistics; 2019. p. 35–43. Available from: `https://www.aclweb.org/anthology/W19-8505`.

[43] Minozzi S. The Latin WordNet project. In: Anreiter P, Kienpointner M, editors. Latin Linguistics Today. Akten des 15. Internationalen Kolloquiums zur Lateinischen Linguistik. Innsbruck: Institut für Sprachen und Literaturen der Universität Innsbruck; 2010. p. 707–716.

[44] Pianta E, Bentivogli L, Girardi C. MultiWordNet: developing an aligned multilingual database. In: Proceedings of the First International Conference on Global WordNet. Mysore, India: Global WordNet Association; 2002. p. 293–302. Available from: `http://multiwordnet.fbk.eu/paper/MWN-India-published.pdf`.

[45] Fellbaum C. WordNet. In: Chapelle C, editor. The Encyclopedia of Applied Linguistics. Wiley Online Library; 2012. .

[46] Lewis CT, Short C. A Latin Dictionary. Oxford: Clarendon Press; 1879.

[47] Passarotti M. The Project of the Index Thomisticus Treebank. Digital Classical Philology. 2019;10:299–320.

[48] Bamman D, Crane G. The Design and Use of a Latin Dependency Treebank. In: TLT 2006: Proceedings of the Fifth International Treebanks and Linguistic Theories Conference; 2006. p. 68–78.

[49] Mikulová M, Bémová A, Hajic J, Hajičová E, Kolářová V, Kučová L, et al. Annotation on the tectogrammatical layer in the Prague Dependency Treebank. Annotation manual. Prague: UFAL; 2006. 30. Available from: `https://ufal.mff.cuni.cz/pdt2.0/doc/manuals/en/t-layer/pdf/t-man-en.pdf`.

[50] Lopatková M, Žabokrtský Z, Benešová V. Valency Lexicon of Czech verbs VALLEX 2.0. Prague: UFAL; 2006. TR-2006-34. Available from: `https://ufal.mff.cuni.cz/~lopatkova/literatura/06-TR-vallex-2.0.pdf`.

Further with Knowledge Graphs. M. Alam et al. (Eds.)
AKA Verlag and IOS Press, 2021
doi:10.3233/SSW210033

NEST: Neural Soft Type Constraints to Improve Entity Linking in Tables

Vincenzo CUTRONA [a,1], Gianluca PULERI [a], Federico BIANCHI [b],
Matteo PALMONARI [a]

[a] *University of Milano - Bicocca, Milan, Italy*
[b] *Bocconi University, Milan, Italy*

Abstract. Matching tables against Knowledge Graphs is a crucial task
in many applications. A widely adopted solution to improve the precision
of matching algorithms is to refine the set of candidate entities by their
type in the Knowledge Graph. However, it is not rare that a type is
missing for a given entity. In this paper, we propose a methodology
to improve the refinement phase of matching algorithms based on type
prediction and soft constraints. We apply our methodology to state-of-
the-art algorithms, showing a performance boost on different datasets.

Keywords. Table to KG matching, Type constraints, Soft constraints

1. Introduction

Linking values occurring in a table to entities in a Knowledge Graph (KG) is
a critical task for Semantic Table Interpretation (STI). The task is crucial for
several downstream applications, including the transformation of tabular data
into a KG, question answering over web tables, and KG completion, and it has
collected a lot of attention in last years [1,2]. In STI, entity linking is referred
to as Cell Entity Annotation (CEA), where other tasks are performed at the
same time to annotate columns with entity *types* (CTA) and *properties* (CPA) in
order to interpret the table schema into the graph-based model of the reference
KG. The CEA, CTA, and CPA tasks are interlinked and can mutually inform
each other; for example, entity-level annotations can suggest or provide evidence
for type and property-level annotations, while type-level annotations may help
disambiguation for entity-level annotations. Approaches addressing all the STI
tasks usually implement complex pipelines to collect and propagate the evidence
across tasks. A CEA algorithm is expected to disambiguate the textual values
in a cell, referred to as *labels* from now on, after retrieving a set of candidate
entities from the KG. As a result, the algorithm can decide whether to establish
a link for the label, *i.e.*, to annotate the cell with an entity from the KG, or
leave it not linked. Different benchmarks have shown that algorithms perform

---

[1]Corresponding Author. E-mail: vincenzo.cutrona@unimib.it

linking effectively when tables are small and labels are characterized by no or low ambiguity. However, the performance drops dramatically as soon as labels are ambiguous and the tables dimension increases, thus novel datasets have been developed with the objective of challenging algorithms to properly deal with both ambiguity and large tables [2,3]. Algorithms must tackle these challenges and improve their performance in settings covering relevant application scenarios.

In this paper we focus on how the entity type information can be better exploited to support CEA pipelines. Indeed, entity type plays a key role in CEA, with column-wise coherence of the entity types being a characterizing feature of table semantics; however, type information explicitly stored in KGs is known to be imperfect and incomplete [4], but this aspect is often overlooked by CEA algorithms, which assume KGs to be complete [5].

We found two patterns used by CEA algorithms available in the literature that can be improved by better handling entity types: (i) *Filtering by type*, where types associated to a column are used as hard constraints to filter out candidate entities having different types; (ii) *Ranking by distributed entity representations similarity*, where distributed representations of entities (*i.e.*, entity embeddings) are used to compute the similarity between candidates for different labels in order to support the disambiguation. These patterns are, for example, core mechanisms used by a state-of-the-art algorithms such as FactBase, EmbeddingsOnGraph, and their hybrid combinations [6], T2K [7], TableMiner+ [8], but also in more recent approaches tailored on STI challenge data [5,9,10].

We propose to use neural models for type prediction and type representation to improve the above-mentioned mechanisms, by enriching the type information used in existing pipelines in a modular fashion. A first approach, *Type enrichment for filtering by type*, enriches the types of candidate entities with types predicted by a neural network. A second approach, *Type enrichment for ranking by distributed entity representations similarity*, extends entity embedding with distributed representations of types, making similarity more aware of entity types. The two approaches can be combined and we propose to enrich entity embeddings with the type predicted by a neural model. Both approaches capture a similar principle in orthogonal ways, that is, to implement soft type-based constraints to improve entity disambiguation, from which the name NEST was given to the proposed methodology, as further explained in Section 4. As for type prediction, we test two different models using respectively textual descriptions and entity embeddings trained over the KG as input for the prediction.

To test our methodology we conduct experiments on datasets that have been used in previous work, or have been published to make disambiguation more challenging. In our experimental settings, we apply the methodology to a selected pool of state-of-the-art algorithms [6] that we chose because of their performance and because they are more prone to handle large tables, general enough to be applied to different settings and not based on specific assumptions tailored to a specific challenge. However, our novel methodology potentially applies to almost every algorithm that uses a filtering or ranking strategy based on the entity typing. Results suggest that the soft constraint principle significantly improves approaches based on similarity computed using entity embeddings and improves approaches based on filtering by type when the types of the correct entities are not completely coherent (by the construction of the dataset).

The rest of the paper is organized as follows: Section 3 describes the need for soft type-based constraints for entity disambiguation also introducing the key terminology. Section 4 describes NEST, the two type enrichment strategies and two neural models for type prediction. In Section 5 we evaluate NEST while in Section 2 we discuss related work. In Section 6 we report conclusive remarks.

2. Related Work

The growing interest of the Semantic Web community is witnessed by the creation in 2019 of the SemTab challenge [1], aimed at standardizing the evaluation of table annotation algorithms. Among the participant systems, we mention MTab [5], which applied a majority voting strategy to select the best candidate in a pool, Tabularisi [11], which created a feature space from the lookup service results using TF-IDF, and DAGOBAH [9], which is based on entity embeddings and K-means clustering. However, these systems are tailored to the challenge specifications, lacking generality. Indeed, the performance of these approaches are computed without considering the knowledge gap because the list of cells to annotate is given as input within SemTab, disregarding the decision making phase. Moreover, algorithms like MTab relied on a brute force strategy which raises the computational cost, hindering its adoption in real-world scenarios. We remark that FactBase and EmbeddingsOnGraph do not have these shortcomings.

Other unsupervised entity matching approaches adopt an iterative method that combines schema and entity matching. T2K [7] brought outstanding improvements in the state-of-the-art and inspired different systems [8,10]. The disambiguation component in the aforementioned approaches is dependant on the type-based constraints, which are assumed as hard constraints. None of the existing approaches explicitly addresses the problem of relaxing hard constraints, highlighting the novelty of NEST. Moreover, to the best of our knowledge, NEST is the first methodology that focuses on improving the use of types for entity disambiguation using neural models to predict the type of candidate entities. ColNet [12] is a supervised system based on convolutional neural networks to predict column types and it is limited to predicting only 17 types.

The work in [13] used a graphical model and a collective classification technique to optimize a global coherence score for a set of entities in a table. The approach requires collecting tables to train the underlying model. Similarly to our work, the authors tried to remove hard type constraints from the matching process, but they did not exploit the type assertion axioms in the KG, preferring to encode the type into features based on entity co-occurrence statistics. A very recent work demonstrated how language models can be exploited to solve many table understanding tasks [14]. Nonetheless, the authors did not exploit the information contained in the KG and required the use tables during pre-training.

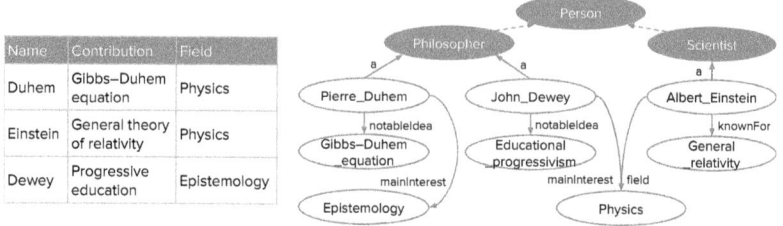

Name	Contribution	Field
Duhem	Gibbs–Duhem equation	Physics
Einstein	General theory of relativity	Physics
Dewey	Progressive education	Epistemology

Figure 1. A table containing data about philosophers of science (1900–1930) from Wikipedia, and a subgraph of the DBpedia KG. Dark nodes are types from the DBpedia Ontology and dashed lines represent subsumption axioms.

3. Entity Linking in Tables and Entity Types

The CEA task is defined as in Section 1.

Most algorithms exploit context information to support the disambiguation, looking at values occurring on the same column or row of the cell to annotate. The cell i, j refers to cell in the ith row and jth column, respectively indicated also as R_i and C_j. In STI it is assumed that some columns contain entity mentions while others do not. Some approaches and datasets even use a stronger *one-entity-per-row* assumption, *i.e.*, that only one column contains cells to annotate, which means that each row describes only one entity [7], but this assumption is not realistic in several application scenarios and is discarded in recent datasets [1]. When we are trying to annotate a cell i, j we refer to the column C_j as to the entity column and to all other columns as context columns, we refer to its label as to $label_{i,j}$ (while for sake of clarity we will use *value* to refer to the content of cells in the context columns).

We assume that the reader is familiar with KGs, for which we only introduce the terminology used in this paper. A KG describes entities with a set of (entity-related) facts that we express in a simple predicate logic notation. If e is an entity identifier, $P(e, v)$ or $P(v, e)$ are facts relating e to v with a property P, which represents a relation; for $P(e, v)$, v can be an entity identifier, a type identifier (or class identifier) or any literal. The set of *direct types* of an entity is defined by facts stored in the KG. An entity can have zero, one or more direct types. Types are connected by a subclass relation, which supports type inheritance.

To discuss the role that types play in CEA, we use the example depicted in Figure 1. First, we remark the ambiguity of the labels: *e.g.*, if we search for Dewey in DBpedia we retrieve two persons, John Dewey, the philosopher, and a librarian, plus several other entities of different types. Einstein also returns entities of different types.

Second, we can expect type-wise coherence in each column, in this case, philosophers, but we cannot expect that the classification of the table perfectly matches the classification in the KG (in some cases the list of direct types may be simply incomplete). The DBpedia entity `Albert Einstein` is assigned only with the type `Scientist`, even if his thoughts have been appreciated also from a philosophical point of view.[2] Filtering out candidates by using the column

---

[2] https://en.wikipedia.org/wiki/List_of_philosophers_of_science

type `Philosopher` as a hard constraint will lead to discard the entity `Albert Einstein`. Some algorithms resort to use a more generic type, which is superclass of the types associated with all or some entities (in this case, it would be `Person`), but as a drawback, they have to deal with a much larger set of candidates; for example, 34 entities of type `Person` in DBpedia contains the term "Einstein" in their label, 2 of which are of type `Scientist`.

CEA algorithms usually combine three main operations into complex pipelines:

1. **Candidates retrieval**, where some value in the table, usually the label of the cell to annotate, is matched against the facts of the KG; this operation returns a - possibly empty - set of *candidate entities*.
2. **Ranking**, where candidate entities are ranked according to some criterion, which may combine matching scores (*e.g.*, retrieval function), other scores, filters, and more sophisticated mechanisms.
3. **Decision making**, where the collected evidence drives the decision whether to link or not, and, in the first case, which entity consider as the annotation.

The combination of ranking and decision making are the core of a disambiguation algorithm. Filters over candidates and scoring used in ranking can contribute to decision making: if after filtering the ranked list of candidates is not empty, the top candidate can be selected for the annotation, otherwise the cell is not annotated. Other decision making strategies can use thresholds; however, it is difficult to apply thresholds over scores that are not bound, which is typical for scores returned by matching functions powered by search engines and available *lookup* services; search engines, on the other side, offer very efficient search over the vast amount of information stored in KGs. As a results, *lookup services* usually combine string similarity, document frequencies (*e.g.*, Lucene-based scores), and even other aspects like popularity (the DBpedia Lookup Service[3] exploits entity popularity measures, *i.e.*, inlinks pointing at the candidate). These considerations make filters and scoring particularly relevant. In this paper, we focus on type-based filters, and on the entity similarity used for scoring the candidates. As anticipated in Section 1, we believe that algorithms proposed by [6] provide state-of-the-art solutions in terms of trade-off among generality, performance, and scalability (see Section 2 for a more detailed discussion of related work).

3.1. Linking pipelines in FactBase and EmbeddingsOnGraph

Before explaining how the proposed methodology can support the selected CEA pipelines [6], we prefer to discuss these approaches with sufficient amount of details in such a way to ease the understanding of our methodology and its evaluation, as well as to make this work self-contained, favoring the replicability.

---

[3] https://wiki.dbpedia.org/lookup

FactBase   The algorithm works column-wise, *i.e.*, it examines all the cells of an entity column, it exploits direct entity types for filtering on candidates (filter by type) as well as representative language tokens (filter by token), and uses the values in the other columns to match facts in the KG and expand the set of candidates. It implements a pipeline that consists of a preliminary step and three entity annotation steps:

- *Candidates retrieval and schema-level annotation.* All the labels in the entity column are looked up in the index returning, for each label, a list of candidates ordered by the lookup service score. For each label, the algorithm looks at its top ranked candidate to extract (from the KG) its direct types and its textual description, which is processed (*e.g.*, stop words are discarded) to return a set of tokens. Given all the entity types and description tokens extracted for all the labels in the column, the k-most frequent types (in the original work, k = 5) and the most frequent token in the information extracted for all the labels are associated to the column, thus returning a set of *column types* and one *column token*. The algorithm then uses unambiguous labels, *i.e.*, labels for which one unique candidate is found, to understand which columns in the table describe *facts* about the entities that are also present in the KG. Given the entity column C_j under evaluation, it tries to annotate a context column C_k with a KG property P that describes the relation between the labels in the entity column and the values in the context columns. When a context column C_k is annotated with a property P also used in the KG, a fact $P(label_{i,j}, value_{i,k})$ can be extracted from the ith row of the table and used to look up more candidates, and, in particular, all those entities x for which the fact $P(x, value_{i,k})$ is part of the KG, thus expanding the set of candidates for a given label. To choose the properties to annotate some of the context columns, the algorithm picks each unambiguous label in the C_j column and, for each context column C_k, matches the pair $(label_{i,j}, value_{i,k})$ against all the indexed facts. A property P is chosen to annotate a context column if it matches facts extracted from at least n different rows (the original work heuristically set n = 5) that have unambiguous labels. If more properties satisfy this constraint, the most frequent property is selected. We refer to this property as to the *context column property*. As a consequence of this step, the entity column under attention is annotated with a set of its (five) column types and its most frequent token, while some context columns are annotated with a property.
- *Annotation by lookup - for unambiguous labels.* Unambiguous labels found in the previous step are annotated with their unique candidate entity.
- *Annotation by strict lookup for ambiguous labels*: this step refines the candidates list of ambiguous labels for which more than one candidate was found, by filtering out candidates that have types that differ from the entity column types *and* a description that does not contain the most frequent token. The label is annotated with the candidate with the highest score.
- *Loose lookup for labels without candidates*: this step looks for new candidates for the labels which annotation is still missing; given the context columns annotated in the first step with a property, this step retrieves as

candidates all the entities that match some of the indexed facts of the KG, as explained in the preliminary step. The new set of candidates is then ranked based on the edit distance between the entity name and the label in the entity column. The first candidate is used to annotate the label in current cell.

EmbeddingsOnGraph   The algorithm can work column-wise, row-wise or table-wise. It does not apply any filter by type mechanism and is based on the construction of a disambiguation graph like several approaches also applied to named entity linking [15]. We describe the column-wise approach that was tested in the original algorithm,[4] and we use in our experiments. A set of candidates is retrieved for each label in the entity column by selecting the best m matches using a char-level trigram similarity with a threshold σ (where $m = 8$ and $\sigma = 0.82$ in the original paper). All the candidate entities for each label represent the nodes of the disambiguation graph; each node has i) a *prior* probability, which is based on the degree (in links + out links) of the corresponding DBpedia page (see the original paper for details), and ii) an embedding that represent the entity. Each pair of candidates from different sets is connected by an edge, which is weighted by the cosine similarity of the respective embeddings. Finally, the priors are updated by executing PageRank on the constructed graph; the candidate with the highest score in each set is chosen for the annotation.

HybridI/HybridII   The hybrid models sequentially combine the baselines; HybridI executes FactBase first, then annotates cells without an annotation with using EmbeddingsOnGraph; HybridII works in the other way around.

4. NEST: Candidate Selection with Soft Type Constraints

NEST (NEural Soft Type Constraints) is a methodology to replace hard constraints based on entity types adopted in CEA pipelines. The methodology relies on distributed representations of entities, *i.e.*, entity embeddings, which can be computed with different approaches [16]. We consider two strategies to include soft type constraints, addressing two patterns used in previous work and, especially, in the unsupervised state-of-the-art algorithms described in Section 3:

- the first strategy, *type enrichment for filtering by type*, combines direct types with types predicted by a neural model to refine type-based filtering. The neural model relies on distributed representations of entities for type prediction. Given an input vector representing an entity, a neural network returns a probability distribution over the possible entity types. The distribution can be used to select a list of most probable types according to

---

[4]The approach used in the original work was not explicitly stated. The table-wise approach combines richer information but at the price of scalability for large tables with thousands of rows; the row-wise approach demands for embedding that maximizes the relatedness between entities, like the ones used in the original work, while the column-wise approach should exploit embeddings which maximize the type coherence between similar entities. These aspects are not discussed in [6], but we suppose the original algorithm works column-wise because it has been tested only on datasets featuring tables with at most one entity column.

the network, which can enrich (or refine) the set of direct types, *e.g.*, by predicting the type `Philosopher` for `Albert Einstein`. This strategy will be demonstrated by applying it to the `FactBase` algorithm.

- the second strategy, *type enrichment for ranking by distributed entity representations similarity*, starts from the consideration that entity embeddings are particularly useful to evaluate entity similarity, and evaluating the similarity between candidate entities in a same column helps entity disambiguation like in the `EmbeddingsOnGraph` algorithm. However, the type-level characterization is not explicitly featured in popular entity embeddings, *e.g.*, RDF2Vec. To feature type-level information more explicitly in the embeddings, we rely on type embeddings [17], *i.e.*, distributed representations of entity types: given the vector of an entity **e** and the vector of its type **t**, the two vectors are concatenated generating a final representation, a *typed entity embedding*, in a vector space where entities that share the same types are closer [17]. In this way, the type-parts of the concatenated vectors induce a sort of *soft* (type) constraint over the selected annotations. For example, if the vector `Philosopher` is concatenated to the vector of `Albert Einstein`, this candidate entity will be more similar to other entities of type `Philosopher`; otherwise, since `Philosopher` and `Scientist` are similar in the type space, even if we concatenate the vector `Scientist`, the similarity between `Albert Einstein` and other philosophers will not be penalized too much.

A clear advantage of NEST is its modularity. The two methods can be used jointly and also integrated into different pipelines with near to zero engineering disruption. Different entity and type embeddings and different type prediction models can be adopted for NEST. For type embeddings, we use Type2vec [17], a model inspired by distributional semantics that does not require expressive and rich ontologies. Type2Vec embeddings are obtained by annotating a text with entities, replacing the entities with their direct type and then applying Word2Vec [18] to generate the embeddings. In Section 4.1 we describe two neural prediction models working with different source of information, while in Section 4.2 we explain in detail how we featured these strategies into algorithms by [6] to demonstrate their effectiveness.

4.1. Type Prediction Models

The two Deep Neural Networks (DNNs) introduced for type prediction are depicted in Figure 2 and take as input embeddings generated with different models. The first one uses embeddings generated with RDF2Vec [19], which creates a virtual document containing random walks over a KG and then applies Word2Vec on this document. The second one uses entity embeddings generated from textual descriptions using Bidirectional Encoder Representations from Transformers (BERT) [20], which has shown strong performance over several downstream tasks in different languages [21]. Thus, for generating BERT Entity Embeddings (BERT EE), we collect DBpedia abstracts, and for each entity, we extract token

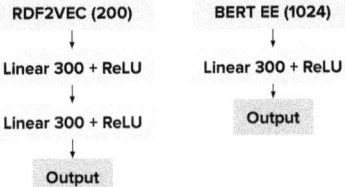

Figure 2. The two architectures used in this paper, numbers describe layer size.

embeddings from its abstract with BERT,[5] and then we represent the entity with the average vector of the token embeddings of its abstract.

The architectures have been selected with respect to the performances obtained at validation time and we use early stopping to prevent overfitting. Both DNNs are trained to reduce the categorical cross-entropy loss. To predict the type of an entity, NEST implements a classifier modeled as a straightforward DNN, which learns to map entities with similar embeddings to the same type. As an example, we obtain that the entity `Albert Einstein`, whose embedding is similar to the embeddings of other scientists and philosophers, has an high probability of being of type `Scientist` and of type `Philosopher`. While architecturally simple, the DNNs in NEST can be trained quickly with already available data and it does not require sophisticated hardware to be trained. This increases the applicability of the methods to different KGs.

4.2. NEST-enriched algorithms

FactBaseST Since FactBase uses the column types and the column token to filter out the retrieved candidates, we enhance this algorithm by exploiting the neural type prediction models, trained and executed over DBpedia (see details below), instead of relying only on the direct types from the KG. The usage of predicted types in FactBaseST aims to capture two intertwined intuitions: (i) Predicted types for all entities in a column can provide additional evidence to determine the correct column types thus reducing the set of column types used as filters subsequently; (ii) By enriching the set of types associated with a candidate entity (*e.g.*, by adding the type `Philosopher` to `Albert Einstein`), the filters applied to individual candidates are softened and become less sensitive to missing type information or mismatches between the intended conceptualization in the table column and the classification in the KG. More precisely, these intuitions are captured as follows:

- The set of column types extracted from the KG is refined by retaining only types predicted also by the neural type prediction model (if any, otherwise, direct types are preserved). The set of predicted types used in this refinement consists of the h most frequent types among all the most likely types predicted for each candidate. We chose $h = 5$ as for the column types.

---

[5]BERT has a limit on the number of input tokens, if the sentence we pass to it contains more tokens, the rest is ignored.

- The set of types associated with each individual candidate is extended by considering also the two most likely types predicted for the candidate. We consider only the first two predicted types because we found that this reflects the average number of different direct types in DBpedia, for the entities that have more than one direct type.

By considering the two neural type prediction models described in Section 4, we implemented two versions of FactBaseST:

- FactBaseST-R2V uses the DNN based on RDF2vec to predict types. The network has been trained using 200-dimensional vectors of ~200k DBpedia entities as input [19] (1000 samples per type); we removed those types with less than 1000 instances to reduce variability (*e.g.*, BowlingLeague and MouseGene), resulting in 236 different predictable types. This network does not exploit the textual description of entities, thus it can be applied to almost every KGs. This DNN has shown remarkable performance, surpassing 0.90 in accuracy score both on the training and on the validation set (that is run 20% of the data, we use early stopping on the validation loss with a patience[6] equal to 4) on the type prediction task.
- FactBaseST-A2V, uses the DNN based on BERT EE to predict types, which is suitable for a KG that includes a textual description of its entities. We trained the DNN in FactBaseST-A2V with embeddings generated by feeding a pre-trained large BERT model (1024-dimensional vectors) with abstracts of DBpedia entities. Like above, we sampled 1000 samples per type removing those types with less than 1000 instances, but we also had to remove from the training set the entities without an abstract, resulting in 228 different predictable types. This DNN scores slightly above 0.90 in accuracy score on the type prediction task (same conditions as above).

EmbeddingsOnGraphST   This algorithm is an extension of EmbeddingsOnGraph and differs only in the - small but conceptually relevant - difference that *typed entity embeddings* are used to computed the similarity instead of plain entity embeddings. We remind that this mechanism makes entities with similar predicted types have a higher cosine similarity; as a consequence, when the PageRank is computed, the weight of edges between entities of the same type increases while the weight of edges between entities of different types decreases further, thus implementing the soft constraint over the similarity that we aimed to capture.

HybridIST/HybridIIST   The algorithms jointly apply FactBaseST and EmbeddingsOnGraphST (as for their original implementations), generating the variants HybridIST-R2V, HybridIST-A2V, HybridIIST-R2V, HybridIIST-A2V.

5. Experiments and Results

Our experiments can be replicated using the documented code we release.[7]

---

[6]Maximum number of epochs with no improvement before stopping the training.

[7]Source code available at https://github.com/vcutrona/nest.

Table 1. Profiles of benchmark datasets.

Dataset	Cols (avg)	Rows (avg)	Matches	Entities	Cols with matches (avg)	Tables
T2D	1,153 (4.95)	28,333 (121.60)	26,124	13,785	233 (1.00)	233
ST19-R4	3,564 (4.36)	51,249 (62.73)	107,352	53,007	1,732 (2.12)	817
2T	802 (4.46)	194,438 (1080.21)	663,656	15,997	540 (3.00)	180

We recreated the SemTab 2019 environment for the CEA task, thus we used DBpedia 2016-10 as the target KG and we scored the algorithms using the *macro* Precision (P), Recall (R), and F1-score (F1) metrics [1].

Datasets   In our experiments we considered three datasets (Table 1):

- T2D [7] is a small dataset with only limited contents, but still represent a reference dataset in the literature; we also used it to better observe the impact of the adaptation we made while re-implementing the original algorithms. We did not use the other datasets tested with the original algorithms (Limaye [13] and Wikipedia [6]) because Limaye has a profile similar to the T2D one, but with smaller tables and less columns to annotate; Wikipedia features only very small tables (23 cells in average to annotate for each column), and anyway it has been partially included in the SemTab dataset.

- ST19-R4 is part of SemTab 2019 [1]. This dataset is the only one in SemTab that contains only non-trivial cases.[8] More importantly, ST19-R4 has been built using a generator, which constructs tables by querying DBpedia. Each table has one class as the main topic, and the other columns are filled with values of a predefined pool of properties of each instance. The generator ensures that the type of the object property matches the expected range in the ontology [1]. Thus, the problem we are addressing in this paper has been artificially removed from ST19-R4. As an example, in a table about `Film`, the actor `Arnold Schwarzenegger`, typed as `OfficeHolder` in DBpedia, will be filtered out from the results of the property `starring`, which has range `Actor`. For this reason, NEST is not expected to improve the results on ST19-R4, making it a good resource to study the possible negative impact of applying NEST to algorithms.

- Tough Tables (2T) [3] features ambiguous and noisy tables that resemble real-world cases. 2T has been included in the last round of SemTab 2020, showing that its high ambiguity makes it harder than any other dataset.[9]

Algorithms   To demonstrate the generality of NEST, we looked for algorithms in literature to use in our experiments. However, just a few CEA algorithms are open-source, with some limitations (*e.g.*, MantisTable [10] has scalability issues;

---

[8]The performance obtained in SemTab 2019 for this dataset were high, also thanks to hardcoded workarounds adopted by the participants [22] that we did not implement.

[9]Performance with the Wikidata version of 2T is dramatically reduced for all the systems that participated in the SemTab 2020 challenge [2].

the repository of CSV2KG [22] is incomplete. Authors of the best performing systems in SemTab 2019 (MTab [5], Tabularisi [11], and CSV2KG [22]) reported that their systems were not ready to be released.

Thus, in our experiments we applied NEST to the algorithms described in Section 4 because they employ the filtering and ranking strategies we want to test with NEST, and can scale reasonably (*i.e.*, annotating selected datasets takes a few hours). The source code of these algorithms is not available, but they are partially reproducible since they have been explained in detail [6]. We tested our re-implemented versions on T2D - used in the original work - observing low performance compared with the original results.[10] In our opinion, the performance decrease is due to the following factors:

- In the original work, the private *FactBase* index was used; the index included documents from Wikipedia, WikiData and DBpedia (not provided). Thus, we generated a new ElasticSearch index containing entities from DBpedia, their labels,[11] and their anchor texts from Wikipedia. We preferred to not include Wikidata in our index to reduce the amount of total memory needed to store it.
- Within FactBase, the *description* field of WikiData entities is crucial for the candidate disambiguation phase. The corresponding property of this field in DBpedia is dct:description, which however is missing for many entities (*e.g.*, Milan). We resembled it by analyzing the DBpedia short abstracts, which leads to different descriptions.
- The queries to the index are not publicly available, thus it is not possible to either reuse the same strategies (*e.g.*, fuzzy match) or apply the same parameters (*e.g.*, max edit distance in fuzzy search).
- We used the RDF2Vec vectors (uniform model from [19]) in EmbeddingsOnGraph, which differ from the embeddings used in the original work.

Given the above limitations, we managed to replicate the disambiguation pipelines of the original algorithms, while the lookup search is suboptimal.

The original algorithms annotate rows, based on the one entity per cell assumption. We provided a generalization of the algorithms by exploiting their column-wise nature: we can annotate tables with multiple entity columns by considering one entity column at a time, and setting the other as context columns, thus annotating individual cells instead of entire rows.

For our experiments, we modified the original EmbeddingsOnGraph algorithm to avoid scalability issues; in fact, running EmbeddingsOnGraph on a table with 5000 rows will lead to the creation of a disambiguation graphs with 40k nodes in the worst case (if all the top-8 candidates for each label are distinct) and ~800M edges. The disambiguation graph is a k-partite graph; thus the maximum number of edges is $\frac{n^2(k-1)}{2k}$ in the worst case. We thus split big tables in chunks of 500 rows each to execute the algorithm on large tables.

---

[10]A proper comparison is not possible because we computed the macro P, R, and F1 (as in SemTab), while the original work reported their micro versions. We report the original scores to help the reader in quantifying the gap: FactBase (P: 0.88, R: 0.78, F1: 0.83); EmbeddingsOnGraph (P: 0.86, R: 0.77, F1: 0.81).

[11]We also include the labels from the DBpedia Lexicalization datasets.

Table 2. Results for benchmark datasets. ♣ identifies our algorithms. Highlighted, best result for each dataset; bold text, best results for each algorithm.

Method	T2D			ST19-R4			2T		
	P	**R**	**F1**	**P**	**R**	**F1**	**P**	**R**	**F1**
EmbeddingsOnGraph	0.782	0.723	0.751	0.483	0.470	0.477	0.293	0.245	0.267
EmbeddingsOnGraphST ♣	**0.811**	**0.751**	**0.780**	**0.540**	**0.526**	**0.533**	**0.378**	**0.316**	**0.344**
FactBase	**0.791**	0.635	0.704	**0.745**	**0.465**	**0.573**	0.365	0.185	0.246
FactBaseST-R2V ♣	0.789	**0.638**	**0.706**	0.731	0.454	0.560	**0.434**	**0.241**	**0.309**
FactBaseST-A2V ♣	0.783	**0.638**	0.703	0.735	0.458	0.565	0.374	0.216	0.274
HybridI	0.756	0.740	0.748	0.530	0.526	0.528	0.275	0.231	0.251
HybridIST-R2V ♣	**0.766**	**0.751**	**0.759**	0.549	0.544	0.546	**0.355**	**0.299**	**0.324**
HybridIST-A2V ♣	0.762	0.746	0.754	**0.551**	**0.547**	**0.549**	0.317	0.266	0.289
HybridII	0.758	0.742	0.750	0.488	0.484	0.486	0.295	0.248	0.270
HybridIIST-R2V ♣	**0.784**	**0.768**	**0.776**	**0.544**	**0.540**	**0.542**	0.380	**0.319**	**0.347**
HybridIIST-A2V ♣	**0.784**	**0.768**	**0.776**	**0.544**	**0.540**	**0.542**	0.380	**0.319**	**0.347**

We remark here that the gap in the algorithms performance does not impact on our analysis, which is fair over the different models.

5.1. Results

Table 2 confirms that the use of NEST can improve state-of-the-art matching pipelines. As expected, applying NEST to EmbeddingsOnGraph increases the F1 score in all our tests (T2D: +2.9%; ST19-R4: +5.6%; 2T: +7.7%) because using typed entity embedding strengthens the similarity between entities of the same type; as a result, since EmbeddingsOnGraph is a column-wise approach, the typed entity embeddings can guarantee a higher column type coherence, which was completely disregarded in the original work. Also considering the improvement brought by the application of NEST, results on 2T are still poor. The main reasons are that i) the candidate retrieval phase is based only on the trigram similarity and uses a high threshold, returning a small set of candidates, and ii) the *priors* used to initialize PageRank are based on the entity popularity, which rewards popular entities in almost the cases, but 2T contains tables with many homonyms, which often do not link to the most popular mentioned entity.

FactBase does not benefit a lot from NEST when annotating T2D and ST19-R4, while its contribution is more valuable on 2T. We observe similar results for FactBaseST-R2V and FactBaseST-A2V, showing that the type information can be predicted alternatively from textual and factual descriptions, when both are available. However, we did not have enough evidence to prefer one source over the other for similar KGs. The performance on T2D are in line with the one achieved by the original algorithm (< 1%): the recall slightly increases, while the precision drops a bit; this is the expected behaviour, since types in T2D are homogeneous in each column; furthermore, tables in T2D are mainly collected from Wikipedia, the same source used to create DBpedia, so there is an overlap between the information in Wikipedia and the entity representations in the KG. If there is a mismatch, like the example of `Albert Einstein` in Section 3, NEST helps increasing the performance, but in all the other cases, considering the secondary type of an entity may add noise into the matching pipeline. This effect is amplified in ST19-R4, where we knew in advance that there was a perfect match between the content of the tables and the type information in DBpedia. Interestingly, the performance drop is limited (−1% in P and R), proving that NEST does not critically affect the original performance; moreover, the small loss on this specific dataset is balanced by the consistent gain in all the other settings where the artificial removal of this problem does not occur. We observe that the standard `FactBase` pipeline underperforms on 2T, mainly because the candidate retrieval step is not able to deal with the values in 2T tables, which are ambiguous and perturbed with typos. However, using NEST to relax the type-based filtering leads to a valuable performance increase (+6.3% and +2.8% for `FactBaseST-R2V` and `FactBaseST-A2V` respectively), helping the algorithm to disambiguate the higher number of candidates. Hybrid methods improve the recall of their main method at cost of precision. Results of `HybridII`-based algorithms are higher[12] thanks to the better performance of their main `EmbeddingsOnGraphST` method.

6. Conclusions and Future Work

In this paper we presented NEST, a novel methodology to include soft type-based constraints into an entity matching pipeline. NEST is modular and can be applied with nearly zero effort. Our experimental campaign shows how state-of-the-art algorithms can benefit from the use of NEST, testing different NEST-improved algorithms on benchmark datasets with different profiles. In our experiments, we used DBpedia as target KG, and we expect NEST achieving similar results on KGs with a similar type hierarchy granularity (which is a typical size in entity linking in tables). As future work, we plan to investigate the application of soft constraints to matching algorithms that target KGs with a more fine-grained type hierarchy (also by many order of magnitude, like YAGO); in this scenario, training a type prediction model could be challenging. Also, we are interested in finding more insights about possible error patterns, studying if the prediction models are biased towards specific types. Finally, we want to investigate the effects of replacing the prediction models with more complex models [4], and relaxing filters for entities linked on the same row, so that to increase their relatedness.

References

[1] Jiménez-Ruiz E, Hassanzadeh O, Efthymiou V, Chen J, Srinivas K. SemTab 2019: Resources to Benchmark Tabular Data to Knowledge Graph Matching Systems. In: ESWC. vol. 12123 of Lecture Notes in Computer Science; 2020. p. 514-30.
[2] Jiménez-Ruiz E, Hassanzadeh O, Efthymiou V, Chen J, Srinivas K, Cutrona V. Results of SemTab 2020. In: SemTab 2020@ISWC. vol. 2775 of CEUR Workshop Proceedings; 2020. p. 1-8.

---

[12]Results in Table 2 show equal performance, but it is an effect due to the rounding.

[3]   Cutrona V, Bianchi F, Jiménez-Ruiz E, Palmonari M. Tough Tables: Carefully Evaluating Entity Linking for Tabular Data. In: ISWC. vol. 12507 of Lecture Notes in Computer Science; 2020. p. 328-43.

[4]   Melo A, Völker J, Paulheim H. Type Prediction in Noisy RDF Knowledge Bases Using Hierarchical Multilabel Classification with Graph and Latent Features. Int J Artif Intell Tools. 2017;26(2).

[5]   Nguyen P, Kertkeidkachorn N, Ichise R, Takeda H. MTab: Matching Tabular Data to Knowledge Graph using Probability Models. In: SemTab@ISWC. vol. 2553 of CEUR Workshop Proceedings; 2019. p. 7-14.

[6]   Efthymiou V, Hassanzadeh O, Rodriguez-Muro M, Christophides V. Matching Web Tables with Knowledge Base Entities: From Entity Lookups to Entity Embeddings. In: ISWC. vol. 10587 of Lecture Notes in Computer Science; 2017. p. 260-77.

[7]   Ritze D, Lehmberg O, Bizer C. Matching HTML Tables to DBpedia. In: WIMS; 2015. p. 10:1-10:6.

[8]   Zhang Z. Effective and efficient Semantic Table Interpretation using TableMiner^{+}. Semantic Web. 2017;8(6).

[9]   Chabot Y, Labbé T, Liu J, Troncy R. DAGOBAH: An End-to-End Context-Free Tabular Data Semantic Annotation System. In: SemTab@ISWC. vol. 2553 of CEUR Workshop Proceedings; 2019. p. 41-8.

[10] Cremaschi M, Paoli FD, Rula A, Spahiu B. A fully automated approach to a complete Semantic Table Interpretation. Future Gener Comput Syst. 2020;112.

[11] Thawani A, Hu M, Hu E, Zafar H, Divvala NT, Singh A, et al. Entity Linking to Knowledge Graphs to Infer Column Types and Properties. In: SemTab@ISWC. vol. 2553 of CEUR Workshop Proceedings; 2019. p. 25-32.

[12] Chen J, Jiménez-Ruiz E, Horrocks I, Sutton C. Colnet: Embedding the semantics of web tables for column type prediction. In: AAAI; 2019. p. 29-36.

[13] Bhagavatula CS, Noraset T, Downey D. TabEL: Entity Linking in Web Tables. In: ISWC. vol. 9366 of Lecture Notes in Computer Science; 2015. p. 425-41.

[14] Deng X, Sun H, Lees A, Wu Y, Yu C. TURL: Table Understanding through Representation Learning. Proc VLDB Endow. 2020;14(3):307-19.

[15] Moro A, Raganato A, Navigli R. Entity Linking meets Word Sense Disambiguation: a Unified Approach. TACL. 2014;2.

[16] Ji S, Pan S, Cambria E, Marttinen P, Yu PS. A survey on knowledge graphs: Representation, acquisition and applications. arXiv:200200388 preprint. 2020.

[17] Bianchi F, Palmonari M, Nozza D. Towards encoding time in text-based entity embeddings. In: ISWC. vol. 11136 of Lecture Notes in Computer Science; 2018. p. 56-71.

[18] Mikolov T, Sutskever I, Chen K, Corrado GS, Dean J. Distributed representations of words and phrases and their compositionality. NIPS. 2013;26.

[19] Ristoski P, Rosati J, Di Noia T, De Leone R, Paulheim H. RDF2Vec: RDF Graph Embeddings and Their Applications. Semantic Web Journal. 2018.

[20] Devlin J, Chang MW, Lee K, Toutanova K. BERT: Pre-training of Deep Bidirectional Transformers for Language Understanding. In: NAACL-HLT; 2019. p. 4171-86.

[21] Nozza D, Bianchi F, Hovy D. What the [mask]? making sense of language-specific BERT models. arXiv:200302912 preprint. 2020.

[22] Vandewiele G, Steenwinckel B, Turck FD, Ongenae F. CVS2KG: Transforming Tabular Data into Semantic Knowledge. In: SemTab@ISWC. vol. 2553 of CEUR Workshop Proceedings; 2019. p. 33-40.

Further with Knowledge Graphs. M. Alam et al. (Eds.)
AKA Verlag and IOS Press, 2021
© 2021 Akademische Verlagsgesellschaft AKA GmbH, Berlin
doi:10.3233/SSW210034

Raising Awareness of Data Sharing Consent Through Knowledge Graph Visualisation

Christof BLESS [a,1], Lukas DÖTLINGER [a], Michael KALTSCHMID [a],
Markus REITER [a], Anelia KURTEVA [a], Antonio J. ROA-VALVERDE [a],
Anna FENSEL [a,b]

[a] *Semantic Technology Institute (STI) Innsbruck, Department of Computer Science, University of Innsbruck, Innsbruck, Austria*
[b] *Wageningen University and Research, Wageningen, the Netherlands*

Abstract. Knowledge graphs facilitate systematic large-scale data analysis by providing both human and machine-readable structures, which can be shared across different domains and platforms. Nowadays, knowledge graphs can be used to standardise the collection and sharing of user information in many different sectors such as transport, insurance, smart cities and internet of things. Regulations such as the GDPR make sure that users are not taken advantage of when they share data. From a legal standpoint it is necessary to have the user's consent to collect information. This consent is only valid if the user is aware about the information collected at all times. To increase this awareness, we present a knowledge graph visualisation approach, which informs users about the activities linked to their data sharing agreements, especially after they have already given their consent. To visualise the graph, we introduce a user-centred application which showcases sensor data collection and distribution to different data processors. Finally, we present the results of a user study conducted to find out whether this visualisation leads to more legal awareness and trust. We show that with our visualisation tool data sharing consent rates increase from 48% to 81.5%.

Keywords. Knowledge Graph Visualisation, User Interface, GDPR, Consent, Legal Awareness, Comprehension

1. Introduction

Collecting information about how users consume a service is crucial for the service usage understanding and improvement of its quality. Taking the automotive field as example, the more drivers agree to send usage data from their cars, the more value the data analysis will generate and better services will be offered. However, the success of campaigns for collecting user data is highly dependent on requesting and receiving informed consent for sensor data sharing. It is debatable whether

---

[1]Corresponding Author: Christof Bless, E-mail: christof.bless@sti2.at.

current consent gathering methods really make clear for users what happens in the background once consent is given. According to [1], users tend to agree to most consent requests they are confronted with. Reading through all the agreement specifications is time-consuming. Often such agreements are written in a complex language typical of legal documents. In most cases users try to get through the consent procedure as fast as possible and are not aware of the implications. For this reason most users who give their consent to data sharing agreements do so without understanding many details of the contract. Bechmann [2] defines this as a "culture of blind consent", implying that having one's consent is not equivalent to having awareness.

This paper presents an approach to visualise consent decisions (i.e. what happens to an individual's data after consent is given) in the domain of vehicle sensor data sharing. The work is part of the CampaNeo project[2], which focuses on vehicle sensor data sharing based on individuals' informed consent as defined by the General Data Protection Regulation (GDPR)[3]. Under GDPR, data processing can only start once an agreement, which GDPR defines as consent, has been set in place. Further, consent has to be freely given, specific, informed and unambiguous (Rec. 32). In order to have informed consent, individuals need to be presented with information about what data is requested, for what purposes it will be used, how it will be processed and by whom (Rec. 32). The GDPR has had a major impact on the way companies deal with personal data, since it has come into effect in May 2018. For many companies adhering to the regulation is not only important to prevent costly legal affairs but also to retain their reputation.

With GDPR compliance in mind, the CampaNeo project aims to create a system that collects and distributes sensor data generated by vehicles with the help of semantic technology, namely knowledge graphs, which can provide a transparent, traceable and centralised record of user data and contractual meta-data (e.g. consent status). On the technical side, knowledge graphs are a state-of-the-art solution for building versatile, explainable and machine-readable data modelling solutions [3][4][5]. Through the use of semantic technologies one can ensure a standardised way of collecting and storing sensor data independently of proprietary formats of different vehicle manufacturers. Knowledge graphs provide the needed level of interpretability due to their ability to represent data in both human and machine-readable formats thus being a suitable solution for representing data sharing between multiple entities.

We introduce a new visualisation which portrays certain aspects of the knowledge graph, mainly how data is processed after consent is given. The visualisation aims to raise individuals' awareness of what it means to consent and the implications that follow. With the help of the visualisation users can inspect data sharing activities at any time after consent was given. We believe that visualisations help end users understand how their data is being shared, with less effort than by reading agreement specifications in textual format, which is the prevalent status quo [6]. Our research focuses on increasing the awareness of data sharing processes through visualisation and has set to answer the following two questions:

---

[2]https://projekte.ffg.at/projekt/3314668
[3]http://data.europa.eu/eli/reg/2016/679/oj

1. Are users more willing to share their data if they are fully informed on what exactly they are sharing, when they are sharing it and with whom exactly they are sharing it?
2. Do data visualisations improve comprehension of consent?

The paper is structured as follows. Section 2 presents related work. Section 3 describes the followed methodology. The architecture and implementation details can be found in Section 4. Section 5 presents the evaluation methodology and the discussion of the results. Finally, conclusions and future work are addressed in Section 6.

2. Related Work

The main aims of imposing GDPR when dealing with the data of European citizens is to ensure transparency of data processing and to make individuals aware of their rights and the implications of giving consent. Individuals should be aware of both the upsides, such as cost benefits or optimized applications and the downsides, such as possible discrimination, spam or even identity theft.

Several studies [2][7][8] have confirmed that, having consent and making individuals aware of the actual meaning of the consent are two different tasks.

Bechmann [2] compares existing regulations and consent practises that are adopted by social media platforms such as Facebook and notes that the need for user convenience has turned the culture of consent into "a blind, non-informed consent culture". The qualitative study done among Danish students showed that none of the participants had read the privacy policies before directly providing consent for their data to be used and shared. The same issue is confirmed by Joergensen [7], who conducts a survey with 58 high school students aimed at understanding users' perception of data privacy and consent with regards to social media participation. The findings showed that the participants are unaware of their privacy rights and what happens to their data.

In their survey on the economics of privacy, Acquisti et al. [8] show that new technologies are needed to support users in making complex privacy choices, such as giving consent to data processing. Naeini et al. [9] conduct a large study with more than 1000 participants on privacy expectations and preferences in the internet of things domain. They conclude that participants want to be informed about various details of data collection, such as what the data is used for and how long it will be stored.

Information arising in different phases of a consent agreement can be described in a "consent life-cycle" consisting of the four stages request, comprehension, decision and use [10]. Kurteva et al. [10] argue that it is useful to have a semantic model (i.e. a machine-readable ontology) of the whole consent life-cycle. Further, the semantic model can be visualised at every stage to make the process more transparent to users. Especially the visualisation of the "use" stage of consent is something current consent visualisations are mostly lacking. Meanwhile, as pointed out by the surveys, users should be able to get information on their consent contract continually and not just at the time of giving consent. Only then, users can become and stay aware of data processing and privacy implications.

A possible way to help users achieve more awareness over their data sharing activities is through different types of data visualisations. Visual elements such as images, graphs, icons and schemas have proven to be easier to comprehend than text [11][12][13][14]. In recent years there have been several attempts to design applications that implement a transparent visualisation of data sharing mechanisms [15][16][17]. Raschke et al. [15] built a dashboard to visualise data sharing activities and give consent approval and withdrawal functionality. The dashboard is a single page application with a vertical timeline listing the different types of actions. The authors evaluated the tool with a set of tasks for participants to complete. The evaluation showed that the tool was still not making users completely aware as even expert users found it hard to answer questions about their data privacy based on the information available from the dashboard.

The issue of consent awareness is also addressed by Drozd and Kirane in CoRe [16] and CURE [17] user interfaces (UIs), which present users a graphical visualisation of a consent request. The CoRe UI displays a graph that shows what data is sent out, where it is stored, the type of processing that is done on it and which third party companies it is to be shared with. The evaluation of both UIs showed that individuals found the graphical visualisation of a consent request and the provided personalisation of consent useful and helpful. The research of Drozd and Kirrane [16][17] showed that visualisations such as graphs can be used for easing individuals' comprehension of what it means to consent and the implications that follow. Angulo et al. [18] propose a data sharing transparency visualisation, which shows a user-centred network graph connecting shared data artifacts with websites and third-party companies. Similarly to the work in [16] and [17], Angulo et al. [18] showed that individuals find visualisations of a data sharing processes helpful when trying to comprehend what is happening to their data. However, the research also showed that how information is organised on the screen can affect interactions (i.e. slower user interactions when data is not well organised) [18].

Many tools which try to bring GDPR awareness to data owners still have problems with user acceptance. Complex designs such as [16] and [17] can cause issues such as information overload [19], which can occur when one is presented with information written in formal legal language [20]. The current solutions for requesting consent in compliance with GDPR are somewhat effective in achieving their task of requesting informed consent. CoRe and CURE UIs present detailed consent requests but do not show what happens after consent is given. On the other hand, the visualisation of Angulo et al. [18] focuses on the actual process of data sharing but not in the context of consent.

Knowledge graph visualisation tools such as WebOWL [21], Ontosphere[4], OntoGraph[5], Isaviz[6] provide information visualisation with different graphs but are focused on users with expert knowledge in the field of the Semantic Web. Surveys such as [22] provide a detailed overview of existing graph designs and tools, which could be reused and adapted for data sharing consent.

---

[4]http://ontosphere3d.sourceforge.net
[5]https://protegewiki.stanford.edu/wiki/OntoGraf
[6]https://www.w3.org/2001/11/IsaViz/

In Bikakis et al. [23], the authors use a a hierarchical type of visualisation as it could help prevent overloading the user with information that is not essential. The authors claim that this visualisation could further be used with large data sets and still perform well. The proposed model takes into consideration the needs of non-expert users and provides them with interactivity and flexibility. A hierarchical layout of graph visualisation is therefore also fitting for the purpose of visualising consent.

Considering the findings from [16][17][15][18], research such as [24][25][26][27][9] and existing knowledge visualisation solutions such as the ones mentioned in this section, we propose an alternative visualisation approach, which focuses on raising legal awareness of the implications of giving consent by showing the data processing that takes place *after* consent is given.

3. Methodology

The aim of this work is to facilitate the handling of consent data by using data visualisation techniques in order to raise individuals' comprehension of consent. To achieve this, we (i) determined the different user requirements of the application in the vehicle sensor data domain, (ii) reviewed existing linked data visualisation solutions that focus on consent, (iii) produced wireframes and (iv) implemented the solution. The use case that we followed are vehicle owners who want to check details of their data sharing activities after having consented to it.

We designed the first prototype of the visualisation using wire-framing techniques [28]. The UI design follows design principles such as the 'Gestalt' laws of grouping [29] and linked data visualisation techniques (e.g. using different visualisation elements such as icons, charts and graphs) as presented in [26]. Having in mind the findings in [16][17][18] regarding the usefulness of graphs for consent visualisation, we selected graphs as our main visualisation element. We reviewed different graph layouts as presented in [22] and the ones available in the D3.js Gallery[7] itself, which could be suitable for our work. A star layout was selected due to its simplicity and intuitive representation of data flows. Additionally, we used particle flow animations to add a sense of direction to parts of the visualisation (e.g. visualise data flow between the users and their campaigns).

Once the wireframing stage was complete the implementation of the solution began. The D3.js[8] library was used for implementing the graph visualisation of data and the data flows. The data itself was queried from the CampaNeo knowledge graph[9], which is stored in the GraphDB[10] graph database. Details about the design decisions and the implementation are presented in Section 4.

---

[7]https://observablehq.com/@d3/gallery
[8]https://d3js.org
[9]https://github.com/STIInnsbruck/CampaNeoViz/blob/main/CampaNeoOntology_rdfxml.owl
[10]https://graphdb.ontotext.com

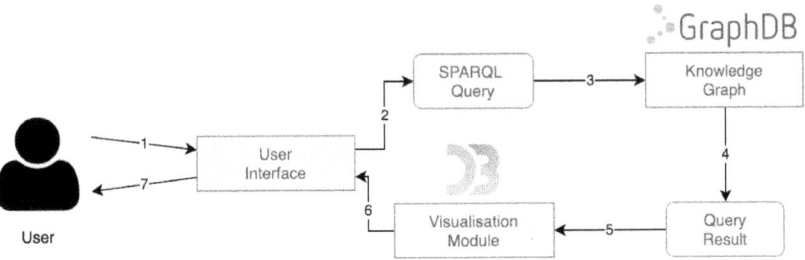

Figure 1. System Architecture

4. Implementation

The goal of the implementation is to visualise the flow of data from a user's car to third-party companies on small to medium displays (e.g. tablet, smartphone or the car's built-in infotainment system). The user can get an overview on what data is shared with organisations like governmental agencies, universities or data processing companies, who collect high amounts of data with the aim of solving problems related to mobility and transport. The visualisation focuses on highlighting the data streams, so the user can get information about the type of data that is shared, at what intervals it is sent out and who the receiving party is.

In CampaNeo, data is requested via specific campaigns, which must be approved by the user. Following the GDPR, campaigns must state exactly what the purpose of their data collection is and what type of processing they plan to do on it. For example, a campaign dedicated to enhance traffic flow around a city can collect GPS location and speed data from a large number of cars. This data can then help optimise traffic guidance and speed constraints on the roads, which leads to less congested roads and time savings for drivers. We have built a first prototype as a web application, which allows users to access their data sharing (based on the given informed consent) from any device. The source code is publicly available at `https://github.com/STIInnsbruck/CampaNeoViz`.

Figure 1 shows an overview of the main components of the web application. The user interacts with the User Interface at the front-end of the application (step 1). The interface captures the user's intention and initiates the process for retrieving the required data. This is achieved by sending a SPARQL query (Listing 1) to the back-end (steps 2 and 3). As depicted in the figure, the main component of the back-end is the graph database, which is used to store the consent data as a knowledge graph. For this specific implementation we have used an instance of GraphDB, which offers multiple APIs for querying the database, including RDF4J and SPARQL. Since we rely on SPARQL queries, the front-end is totally decoupled from the back-end, and we could replace the data store later if necessary.

Once the result of the SPARQL query is retrieved (step 4), it is passed to the Visualisation Module (step 5). This module is implemented using D3.js, a JavaScript library for manipulating data driven documents. The Visualisation Module prepares the data for the User Interface depending on the specific screen selected by the user (step 6).

In the following, we describe the User Interface in further detail. We then show how the consent data has been modelled in the knowledge graph and how this is consumed by the web application.

4.1. User Interface

The goal of the CampaNeo project is to facilitate the collection of campaign-based data with a focus on the data ownership of vehicle owners and the traceability of data processing. Figure 2 shows the entry point of the web application. This

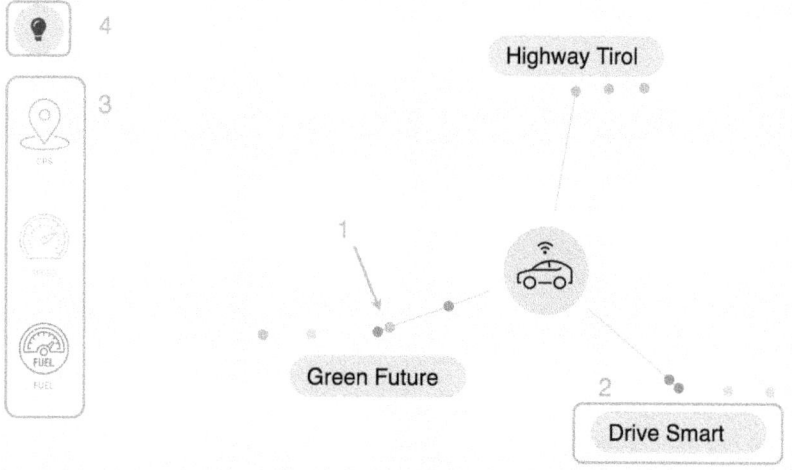

Figure 2. Data processing visualisation after consent is granted. Highlighted are: Flow of information chunks from data owner to data processor campaigns (1), example of a CampaNeo campaign (2), data type legend (3) and light/dark mode switch (4).

screen represents a dashboard that helps visualising all campaigns related to the user once consent is granted.

Campaigns are represented by a rounded rectangle with the corresponding campaign name. The round particles next to each campaign represent data that the user is sharing with the organisation behind the campaign. They are colour-coded to give additional information on the type of data that is sent, e.g. fuel consumption, speed or the GPS location of the car. To make this even more clear, shared data packets are visualised as moving particles between the nodes. This feature gives the visualisation a sense of directional flow and helps users to see at one glance what kind of data they are sharing and at what rate. The meaning of the different colours is encoded in a legend on the left side of the screen.

Further details about a specific campaign can be accessed after clicking on any campaign title (labeled as 2 in Figure 2). Figure 3 shows a screenshot of the campaign details interface. Here we rely on a time series to display the data sharing events according to their timestamp. Additional information about the sensor that retrieved the data and the final organisations is shown.

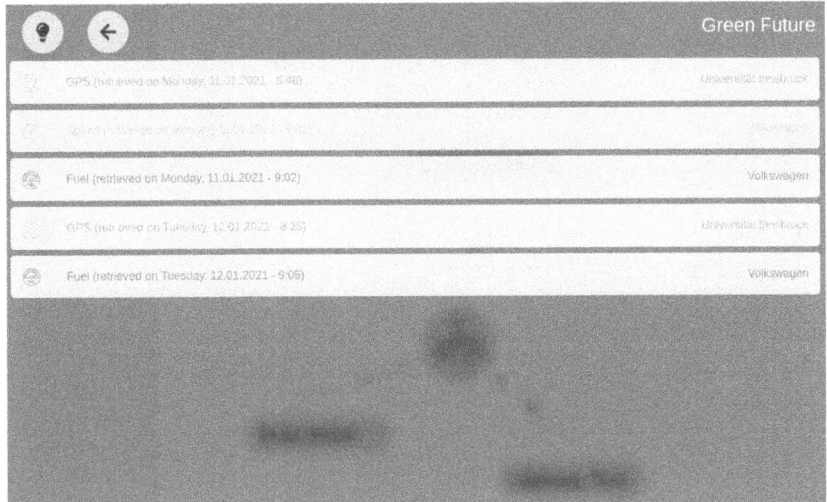

Figure 3. Detailed information for a given campaign

4.2. Knowledge Graph Data Model

We modelled the data shown in the visualisation using a knowledge graph (built with Protégé[11] and stored in GraphDB), which represents informed consent as defined by the GDPR (Art 4.). The knowledge graph represents campaigns and their consent status (given, not given, withdrawn, expired) and purpose, specific vehicle sensor data e.g. GPS location, data provider, data processor, data controller and third-party organisations involved in the data processing.

The knowledge graph reuses the following ontologies: GConsent[12], namely the classes *Consent* and *Status*, Semantic Sensor Network Ontology (SSN)[13] for defining sensor data types and the Financial Business Ontology (FIBO)[14] for representing contracts and agreements. Currently the knowledge graph consists of 425 axioms, 34 classes, 50 object properties and 23 data properties.

The knowledge graph models the data sharing campaigns and the consent relations to users. Associated with a campaign are also the data packets that were retrieved during the duration of consent. Data packets consist of the retrieval time, content and the third-party processors who requested it. Further, they are categorised into well-defined data types such as GPS coordinates, speed, or fuel consumption.

Listing 1 shows the SPARQL query that is used for retrieving the visualisation data for the example user "user1". In the visualisation each of the data packets retrieved in the query will be represented by a small particle moving from the user to the data processor. Additional information about the data packets like the retrieval time and the data processor can be inspected upon interaction with the campaign node or the data stream.

---

[11]https://protege.stanford.edu
[12]http://openscience.adaptcentre.ie/ontologies/GConsent/docs/ontology
[13]https://www.w3.org/TR/vocab-ssn/
[14]https://spec.edmcouncil.org/fibo/

Listing 1: SPARQL query sent to the knowledge graph

```
PREFIX : <http://www.semanticweb.org/ontologies/CampaNeo#>
PREFIX rdfs: <http://www.w3.org/2000/01/rdf-schema#>
SELECT ?campaign_name ?data_type ?retrieval_time
?institution_name
WHERE {
    ?campaignnode a :Campaign .
    ?campaignnode :hasConsentBy :user1 .
    ?campaignnode rdfs:label ?campaign_name .
    ?data :wasRetrievedByCampaign ?campaignnode .
    ?data :hasDataType ?data_type .
    ?data :wasRetrievedAtTime ?retrieval_time .
    ?data :isRequestedBy ?institution .
    ?institution rdfs:label ?institution_name .
}
```

5. Evaluation and Results

To assess the usefulness of our data sharing visualisation tool, we conducted a user test. The following section explains the methodology that we applied, to find out whether we can increase data sharing consent awareness of the test users. After that, we present the results of the user test. The questionnaire and results are available online[15].

5.1. Evaluation Methodology

For the user tests we provided the web application described in the previous section. Figure 4 gives an overview of the evaluation procedure. The tests could be performed on desktop computers, laptops or other mobile devices. The test subject needed a thorough introduction into the scenario since the use case of the application is very specific. For example, the participants had to understand that this visualisation only shows campaigns which they had already given their consent to.

After the introduction and demographic survey, we asked questions related to data privacy comprehension of the participants, before presenting the visualisation. This allowed us to assess the prior knowledge of participants and to measure the hypothetical improvement of comprehension and trust through the visualisation, by comparing to answers of the same questions after the test.

After the first questions, we revealed the visualisation to the test subjects. They were presented with a series of simple to slightly complex tasks, beginning with interface interaction and basic comprehension. Later we asked them questions which led them to aggregate different information from the visualisation. During the evaluation the test subjects were observed in real time through screen

---

[15]https://github.com/STIInnsbruck/CampaNeoViz/tree/main/evaluation

sharing. Using the "think aloud" method, they informed the tester regularly about their thoughts, i.e. what they wanted to achieve next and where they expected to find a specific information in the application.

After the task solving period, the subjects were asked to fill out a question-naire, in which they rated their experience and explained problems they had or gave suggestions for improvements. We tested the potential improvement in com-

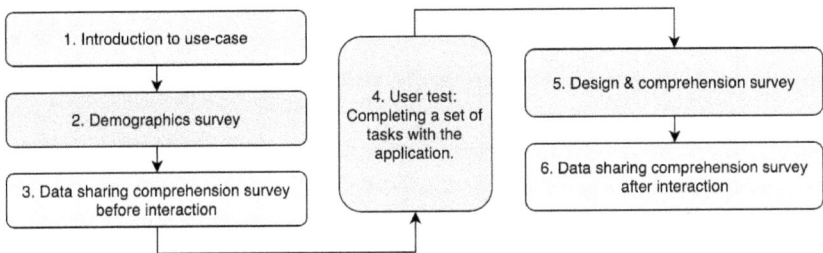

Figure 4. Evaluation flow with the different steps of the user study

prehension and awareness of GDPR rights by asking the users if they felt more confident in their knowledge of data sharing and observed the difference in their stance on data privacy before and after the test, as described above.

5.2. Results

The evaluation took place over the course of a week and comprised user tests with 27 participants. The age groups were evenly distributed between 16 and 50+ years. All participants assessed themselves to be competent with internet surfing and most stated that they spend more than 4 hours a day on the internet, which shows that they have probably already come into contact with data sharing agreements in the form of website cookies or similar requests. 80% of the test users claimed to have a valid driver's license. 40% of the participants drive daily and use the car as their main mean of transport.

In the testing phase we noticed that the test users had no problems solving the tasks, that were given to them. There were only a few exceptions, where tasks couldn't be solved without help. The users understood the interface by mostly relying on their intuitions and recognition of symbols.

After the practical tasks, the participants rated the overall design of the application with a mean score of 3.4 on a scale from 1 to 4. Also, they were asked to choose from a set of adjectives, which they found to be describing the interaction with the application best. Among the most chosen ones were "organised" (74%), "innovative" (70.3%) and "effective" (44.3%). The more negatively associated adjectives like "complex", "hard to use" and "useless" were only selected by two people at most. The good general impression test users had with the application was further strengthened by the fact that 74.1% of the participants stated they were "very satisfied" with the user interface.

When looking at the rated understandability, we saw that 76.5% of the par-ticipants said that the application improved their understanding of what happens to their personal data, showing a clear increase in the users awareness of the data sharing process. Before starting the test with the tool, the participants were asked if they trust companies in the European Union (EU) to respect their data privacy, which the majority answered with "yes" or "probably" (combined 59.2%). The remaining 40.8% of the participants were more sceptical about GDPR adherence of companies or were not even aware of the GDPR. After the test with the visualisation, 40% of the sceptics changed their mind on this particular question, gaining trust in the regulations. At the same time 28% of the people who trusted companies in the EU before the test, felt less secure after the test.

1. Would you agree to share vehicle data like GPS location, speedometer data or fuel gauge readings with certain companies?

2. Would you agree to share vehicle data like GPS location, speedometer data or fuel gauge readings, if you had the tool available to control the sharing activities?

Figure 5. Results of the user evaluation concerning vehicle data sharing. The questions were asked before (1) and after (2) the participants' interaction with the tool.

After finishing the test we asked again if the participants were willing to share vehicle data like GPS location, speedometer data or fuel gauge readings, if they had the tested tool at their disposal. Before having seen the visualisation, 48% of the participants claimed they would share at least selected types of data with campaigns on CampaNeo. After the interaction with the tool, 85.2% of the participants stated that they would possibly share their vehicle data, if they had the tool to control the sharing activities (see Figure 5).

Further we asked the participants: "If such a tool were available to you in any service or application, would you share selected data with a company or institution?". To this 81.5% said "Yes", "possibly" or "possibly, rather than without the tool". Before the test we had asked: "Are you willing to send your user data to companies or institutions, so they can improve user experience more efficiently?". Only 48% of the users responded positively before they had interacted with the visualisation. This indicates that the general approach of our visualisation would also be desirable to users outside of the vehicle sensor data scenario.

6. Conclusion

This paper proposes an application and associated design approaches to visualise data sharing activities after consent was received by a data owner. We built a tool for the scenario of vehicle sensor data sharing. The visualisation shows an overview of the data sharing campaigns which have user consent. A particle stream animation lets users oversee data sharing activities with one glance. A more detailed overlay is designed to present the user all the organisations behind the data sharing campaigns and the detailed data retrievals in a time series.

The conclusion was drawn from a user case study, which was designed to find out whether the visualisation is helpful to improve the comprehension of data privacy rights. The results showed that 40% of the test candidates, who did not believe that companies in the EU were respecting an individual's data privacy, changed their mind after the test with the visualisation tool. They were afterwards more convinced that user data of EU citizens can not be gathered without consent.

The work shows that the availability of the presented tool can increase consent rates for data sharing campaigns in the automotive sector from 48% to 81%. In the user test, we asked test users whether they can imagine using this tool for any kind of data sharing. More than 40% of the test users stated that they would be more likely to share different kinds of user data in services and applications they use, if they had such a tool. We can therefore conclude that there is a clear need for better visualisation of data sharing streams. Furthermore, the case study shows that users feel more comfortable sharing data, if they can easily oversee the exact activities in a visualisation tool.

Since this is the first design iteration of this tool, the collected feedback ideas and comments will be implemented in future iterations to enhance the interface. Further, the visualisation will be integrated into a bigger application which presents data sharing campaigns and handles consent management. Once the next prototype is built, another user test with a bigger sample group will be scheduled.

Acknowledgements

This research is supported by the CampaNeo project funded by FFG (grant 873839) as well as the smashHit EU project funded under Horizon 2020 (grant 871477). We would like to thank Nils Henke, Timo Graen and Philip Matesanz from Volkswagen AG for their feedback regarding the evaluation setup.

References

[1] Borgesius FZ. Informed Consent: We Can Do Better to Defend Privacy. 35th International Conference on ICT Systems Security and Privacy Protection. 2015;13:103-7.

[2] Bechmann A. Non-Informed Consent Cultures: Privacy Policies and App Contracts on Facebook. Journal of Media Business Studies. 2014;11(1):21-38.

[3] Fensel D, Simsek U, Angele K, Huaman E, Kärle E, Panasiuk O, et al. Knowledge Graphs: Methodology, Tools and Selected Use Cases. Springer International Publishing; 2020.

[4] Hogan A, Blomqvist E, Cochez M, D'amato C, de Melo G, Gutiérrez C, et al. Knowledge graphs. Communications of the ACM. 2020;64:96-104.

[5] Ji S, Pan S, Cambria E, Marttinen P, Yu PS. A Survey on Knowledge Graphs: Representation, Acquisition and Applications. IEEE Transactions on Neural Networks and Learning Systems. 2021.

[6] McDonald AM, Cranor L. The Cost of Reading Privacy Policies. A Journal of Law and Policy for the Information Society. 2009.

[7] Joergensen RF. The unbearable lightness of user consent. Internet Policy Review. 2014;3(4).

[8] Acquisti A, Taylor C, Wagman L. The Economics of Privacy. Journal of Economic Literature. 2016 June;54(2):442-92.

[9] Naeini PE, Bhagavatula S, Habib H, Degeling M, Bauer L, Cranor LF, et al. Privacy Expectations and Preferences in an IoT World. In: Thirteenth Symposium on Usable Privacy and Security (SOUPS 2017). Santa Clara, CA: USENIX Association; 2017. p. 399-412.

[10] Kurteva A, Chhetri TR, Pandit HJ, Fensel A. Consent Through the Lens of Semantics: State of the Art Survey and Best Practices. Semantic Web – Interoperability, Usability, Applicability. 2021.

[11] Passera S. Enhancing Contract Usability and User Experience Through Visualization - An Experimental Evaluation. In: 16th International Conference on Information Visualisation; 2012. p. 376-82.

[12] Passera S, Haapio H. Transforming contracts from legal rules to user-centered communication tools: a human-information interaction challenge. Communication Design Quarterly Review. 2013;1:38-45.

[13] Passera S, Haapio H, Curtotti M. Making the Meaning of Contracts Visible – Automating Contract Visualization. In: Proceedings of the 17th International Legal Informatics Symposium IRIS; 2014. p. 443–450.

[14] Rossi A, Palmirani M. A Visualization Approach for Adaptive Consent in the European Data Protection Framework. In: 2017 Conference for E-Democracy and Open Government (CeDEM); 2017. p. 159-70.

[15] Raschke P, Küpper A, Drozd O, Kirrane S. Designing a GDPR-Compliant and Usable Privacy Dashboard. In: Privacy and Identity Management. The Smart Revolution. Springer, Cham; 2018. p. 221-36.

[16] Drozd O, Kirrane S. I Agree: Customize Your Personal Data Processing with the CoRe User Interface. Trust, Privacy and Security in Digital Business. 2019:17-32.

[17] Drozd O, Kirrane S. Privacy CURE: Consent Comprehension Made Easy. In: 35th International Conference on ICT Systems Security and Privacy Protection; 2020. p. pp. 1-14.

[18] Angulo J, Fischer-Hübner S, Pulls T, Wästlund E. Usable Transparency with the Data Track: A Tool for Visualizing Data Disclosures. In: Proceedings of the 33rd Annual ACM Conference Extended Abstracts on Human Factors in Computing Systems. CHI EA '15; 2015. p. 1803–1808.

[19] Gross BM. The Managing of Organizations: The Administrative Struggle. The ANNALS of the American Academy of Political and Social Science. 1965;360(1):197-8.

[20] Mellinkoff D. The language of the law. Wipf and Stock Publishers; 2004.

[21] Batzios A, Mitkas PA. WebOWL: A Semantic Web search engine development experiment. Expert Systems with Applications. 2012;39(5):5052-60.

[22] Dadzie AS, Rowe M. Approaches to visualising Linked Data: A survey. Semantic Web. 2011;2:89-124.

[23] Bikakis N, Skourla M, Papastefanatos G. rdf: SynopsViz - A Framework for Hierarchical Linked Data Visual Exploration and Analysis. In: The Semantic Web: ESWC 2014 Satellite Events. vol. 8798; 2014. p. 292-7.

[24] Brunetti JM, Auer S, García R. The Linked Data Visualization Model. In: Proceedings of the 2012th International Conference on Posters & Demonstrations Track - Volume 914. ISWC-PD'12; 2012. p. 5–8.

[25] Helmich J, Potoček T, Klímek J, Nečaský M. Towards Easier Visualization of Linked Data for Lay Users. In: Proceedings of the 7th International Conference on Web Intelligence, Mining and Semantics. WIMS '17; 2017. p. 1-10.

[26] Po L, Bikakis N, Desimoni F, Papastefanatos G. Linked Data Visualization: Techniques, Tools, and Big Data. Synthesis Lectures on Semantic Web: Theory and Technology. 2020;10(1):1-157.

[27] Kurteva A, De Ribaupierre H. Interface to Query and Visualise Definitions from a Knowledge Base. In: International Conference on Web Engineering. Springer, Cham; 2021. p. 3-10.

[28] Hamm MJ. Wireframing Essentials: An introduction to user experience design. Packt Publishing; 2014.

[29] Banerjee JC. Gestalt Theory of Perception. Encyclopaedic Dictionary of Psychological Terms. 1994:107–109.

Further with Knowledge Graphs. M. Alam et al. (Eds.)
AKA Verlag and IOS Press, 2021
© 2021 Akademische Verlagsgesellschaft AKA GmbH, Berlin
This article is published online with Open Access by IOS Press and distributed under the terms
of the Creative Commons Attribution License 4.0 (CC BY 4.0).
doi:10.3233/SSW210035

Facade-X:
An Opinionated Approach to SPARQL Anything

Enrico Daga[1] [0000−0002−3184−5407], Luigi Asprino[2] [0000−0003−1907−0677],
Paul Mulholland[1] [0000−0001−6598−0757], and Aldo Gangemi[3] [0000−0001−5568−2684]

[1] The Open University (United Kingdom) {enrico.daga,paul.mulholland}@open.ac.uk
[2] University of Bologna (Italy) luigi.asprino@unibo.it
[3] Consiglio Nazionale delle Ricerche (CNR) aldo.gangemi@cnr.it

Abstract. The Semantic Web research community understood since its beginning how crucial it is to equip practitioners with methods to transform non-RDF resources into RDF. Proposals focus on either engineering content transformations or accessing non-RDF resources with SPARQL. Existing solutions require users to learn specific mapping languages (e.g. RML), to know how to query and manipulate a variety of source formats (e.g. XPATH, JSON-Path), or to combine multiple languages (e.g. SPARQL Generate). In this paper, we explore an alternative solution and contribute a general-purpose meta-model for converting non-RDF resources into RDF: *Facade-X*. Our approach can be implemented by overriding the SERVICE operator and does not require to extend the SPARQL syntax. We compare our approach with the state of art methods RML and SPARQL Generate and show how our solution has lower learning demands and cognitive complexity, and it is cheaper to implement and maintain, while having comparable extensibility and efficiency.

Keywords: SPARQL · Meta-model · Re-engineering

1 Introduction

Knowledge graphs have nowadays a key role in domains such as enterprise data integration and cultural heritage. However, domain applications typically deal with heterogeneous data objects. Therefore, ontology engineers develop knowledge graph construction pipelines that include the transformation of different types of content into RDF. Typically, this is achieved by using tools that act as mediators between the data sources and the needed format and data model [12]. Alternatively, dedicated software components implement ad-hoc transformations from custom formats to a multiplicity of ontologies relevant to the domain [4]. We place our research under the context of the EU H2020 SPICE project, which aims at developing a linked data infrastructure for integrating and leveraging museum collections using multiple ontologies covering sophisticated aspects of citizen engagement initiatives [4]. Museum collections come in a variety of data objects, spanning from public websites to open data sets. These include metadata

---

[4] SPICE Project: https://spice-h2020.eu

summaries as CSVs, record details as JSON files, and binary objects (e.g. artwork images), among others. The semantic lifting of such a variety of resources can be a serious bottleneck for the project activities. Several languages have been developed to either engineer content transformation (e.g. RML) or extending the SPARQL query language to access non-RDF resources (e.g. SPARQL Generate). However, existing solutions require Semantic Web practitioners to learn a mapping language, or even combine multiple languages, for example requiring to use XPath for XML transformations. In addition, these require Semantic Web practitioners to know the details of the original format (e.g. XML) as well as the target domain ontology.

In this paper, we don't propose a new language. Instead, we aim at reducing the effort of Semantic Web practitioners in dealing with heterogeneous data sources by providing a generic, domain-independent meta-model as a *facade* to wrap the original resource and to make it query-able *as-if* it was RDF. Specifically, we contribute a meta-model and associated algorithm for accessing non-RDF resources as RDF: *Facade-X*. Our approach can be implemented by overriding the SERVICE operator and does not require to extend the SPARQL syntax. We compare our approach with the state of art methods RML and SPARQL Generate, and show how our solution has lower learning demands and cognitive complexity, and it is cheaper to implement and maintain, while having comparable extensibility and efficiency (in our naive implementation).

In the next section we analyse the key requirements, building also on the work of [15]. In Section 3 we describe our approach for adopting *facades* for re-engineering resources into RDF and give a formal definition of *Facade-X*. Section 4 is dedicated to the prototype implementation of the approach in a software named SPARQL Anything. Related work is discussed in Section 5. We compare our approach with state of art methods (RML and SPARQL Generate) in Section 6, before concluding our paper in Section 7.

2   Requirements

The motivation for researching novel ways to transform non-RDF resources into RDF comes from the scenarios under development in the EU H2020 project SPICE: Social Cohesion, Participation, and Inclusion for Cultural Engagement. In this project, a consortium of eleven partners collaborate in developing novel ways for engaging with cultural heritage, relying on a *linked data* network of resources from museums, social media, and businesses active in the cultural industry. However, the majority of resources involved are not exposed as Linked Data but are released, for example, as CSV, XML, JSON files, or combinations of these formats. In addition, the research activity aims at the design of task-oriented ontologies, producing multiple semantic *viewpoints* on the resources and their metadata. It is clear how the effort required for transforming resources could constitute a significant cost to the project. In the absence of a strategy to cope with this diversity, content transformation may result in duplication of effort and become a serious bottleneck. Table 1 provides a summary of the requirements. The main requirement is the ability to support users in transforming existing

Table 1: Requirements

Requirement	Description
Transform	Transform several sources having heterogeneous formats
Query	Query resources having heterogeneous formats
Binary	Support the transformation of binary formats
Embed	Support the embedding of content in RDF
Metadata	Support the extraction of metadata embedded in files
Low learning demands	Minimise the tools and languages that need to be learned
Low complexity	Minimise complexity of the queries
Meaningful abstraction	Enable focus on data structures rather than implementation details
Explorability	Enable data exploration without premature commitment to a mapping, in the absence of a domain ontology.
Workflow	Integrate with a typical Semantic Web engineering workflow
Adaptable	Be generic but flexible and adaptable
Sustainable	Inform into a software that is easy to implement, maintain, and does not have evident efficiency drawbacks
Extendable	Support the addition of an open set of formats

non-RDF resources having heterogeneous formats (Transform). In addition, the solution should be able to support cases in which practitioners only need to interrogate the content (Query). A valid approach should be able to cope with binary resources as well as textual formats (Binary). In the cultural heritage domain, metadata files are typically associated to repositories of binary content such as images in various formats. Applications may need to transfer data and metadata in a single operation, embedding the binary content in a data value (Embed) and extracting metadata (Metadata) from the file (from EXIF annotations).

We consider requirements related to usability and adoption. The approach should ideally limit the number of new languages and tools that need to be learned in order to transform and use non-RDF resources (Low learning demands). This can be expected to both encourage adoption and reduce the learning curve for new users. The code that the user is required to develop in order to access the resources should be as simple as possible (Low complexity). The approach should provide the user with a meaningful level of abstraction, enabling them to focus on the the structure of the data (e.g. data rows and hierarchies) rather than the details of how the structure has been implemented (Meaningful abstraction). The approach should support an exploratory way of working in which the user does not have to prematurely commit to a domain ontology before they come to understand the data representation that they require (Explorability). The resulting technology should be easily combined with typical Semantic Web engineering workflow (Workflow). This requirement, already mentioned in [15], is interpreted considering that the solution should rely as much as possible on already existing technologies typically used by our domain users. The approach should allow for a technical solution that is generic but easily `Adaptable` to user tasks, for example, supporting symbol manipulation, variable assignments, and data type manipulation.

Finally, we look into requirements of software engineering. The approach should be `Sustainable` and inform a software that is easy to implement on top of existing Semantic Web technologies, easy to maintain, and does not have efficiency drawbacks compared to alternative state of the art solutions. Ultimately, the system should be easy to extend (`Extendable`) to support an open ended set of formats.

3 An Opinionated Approach

We introduce a novel approach to interrogate non-RDF resources with SPARQL. Our opinion is that the task of transforming resources into RDF should be decoupled in two very different operations: (a) re-engineering, and (b) remodelling. We define *re-engineering* as the task of transforming resources minimising domain considerations, focusing on the meta-model. Instead, remodelling is the transformation of *domain knowledge*, where the original domain model is reframed into a new one, whose main objective is to add semantics. From this perspective, we propose to solve the re-engineering problem automatically and delegating the remodelling to the RDF-aware user. *How to use RDF to access heterogeneous source formats?* We rely on the notion of *facade* [14] as *"an object that serves as a front-facing interface masking more complex underlying or structural code "*[5]. Applied to our problem, a facade acts as a generic meta-model allowing (a) to inform the development of transformers from an open ended set of formats, and (b) to generate RDF content in a consistent and predictable way. In what follows, we describe a generic approach that can be used to develop facade-based connectors to heterogeneous file formats. After that, we introduce Facade-X, which is the first of these interfaces, and describe how our facade maps to RDF. Finally, we design a method to inject facades into SPARQL engines. To support the reader, we introduce a guide scenario reusing the data of the Tate Gallery collection, published on GitHub[6]. The repository contains CSV tables with metadata of artworks and artists and a set of JSON files with details about each catalogue record, for example, with the hierarchy of archive subjects. The file `artwork_data.csv` includes metadata of the artworks in the collection such as `id`, `artist`, `artistId`, `title`, `year`, `medium`, and references two external resources: a JSON file with the artwork `subjects` headings and a link to a JPG `thumbnail` image. Our objective is to serve this content to the Semantic Web practitioners for exploration and reuse.

3.1 Resources, data sources, and facades

In this section we give a formal definition of the three components of our approach: resources, data sources, and facades. In addition, we describe how an algorithm can apply these concepts for re-engineering resources in RDF.

---

[5] See also The Facade Design Pattern: https://en.wikipedia.org/wiki/Facade_pattern (accessed 15/12/2020).

[6] Tate Gallery collection metadata: https://github.com/tategallery/collection.

We consider a *resource* anything accessible from a URL and distinguish it from its content, that we name *data source*. The file `artwork_data.csv`[7] and the image $N04858\_8.jpg$ are resources and the CSV and JPG content are data sources. We assume that a resource contains at least one data source[8]. A data source can be named with the URL or have a different name[9]. We introduce the following predicates and associated axioms, in predicate logic:

1 $Resource(r)$ $DataSource(ds)$ $Name(n)$ $includes(r, ds)$ $hasName(ds, n)$
2 $\forall r.Resource(r) \rightarrow \exists ds.includes(r, ds) \wedge DataSource(ds)$
3 $\forall ds.DataSource(ds) \rightarrow \exists n.hasName(ds, n) \wedge Name(n)$
4 $\forall ds.DataSource(ds) \rightarrow \exists r.Resource(r) \wedge includes(r, ds)$
5 $\forall ds_1 \forall ds_2 \forall n \forall r.$
6 $includes(r, ds_1) \wedge includes(r, ds_2) \wedge hasName(ds_1, n) \wedge hasName(ds_2, n) \rightarrow ds_1 = ds_2$
7 $\forall ds \forall n_1 \forall n_2.hasName(ds, n_1) \wedge hasName(ds, n_2) \rightarrow n_1 = n_2$

In addition, we refer to two additional concepts: RDF Graph and RDF Dataset, as specified by RDF 1.1 [3]. We now describe how an algorithm can apply facades to resources to derive RDF datasets capable of answering a given query[10]. Let Q be the set of all possible queries, G the set of all possible graphs, N the set of all possible graph names, R the set of all possible resources and DS the set of all data sources (found in the resources). We define: *(i)* D as a collection of named graphs (i.e. $D \subseteq N \times G$); *(ii)* A (i.e. the algorithm) as a function that given a resource ($r \in R$), a facade function ($f \in F$), and a query ($q \in Q$), returns a collection of named graphs including the graphs required to answer the query (i.e. one of the possible subsets of $N \times G$); *(iii)* F is a set of functions where each $f \in F$ associates a data source from the resource ($ds \in DS$) and a query ($q \in Q$) with a graph $g \in G$, according to a facade. A and F can be formally defined as follows:

$$A : R \times F \times Q \rightarrow 2^{N \times G} \qquad\qquad F = \{f | f : DS \times Q \rightarrow G\}$$

Additionally, given a query $q \in Q$, a resource $r \in R$ and its data sources $ds \in DS$, we define: *(i)* $g^*_{ds,q} \in G$ as the graph which contains the minimal (optimal) set of triples required to answer q on ds; *(ii)* $D^*_{r,q} = \{(n, g^*_{ds,q}) | includes(r, ds)$ and $n \in N$ and $g^*_{ds,q} \in G\}$ as the collection of minimal set of triples required to answer q on r. It is worth noticing that given a query and a resource neither A nor any $f \in F$ has to return an optimal response (i.e. $D^*_{r,q}$ and $g^*_{ds,q}$), but they can return any super set of the optimum (i.e. any $g \in G$ such that $g^*_{ds,q} \subseteq g$). We don't make any commitment on the underlying implementation of the facade with respect to the resource/data sources, apart from assuming that the resulting dataset will be sufficient, but not necessarily optimal, for answering the query.

---

[7] Available at https://raw.githubusercontent.com/tategallery/collection/master/artwork_data.csv

[8] In principle, a resource may include multiple data sources, for example, an Excel spreadsheet may include several sheets.

[9] Although resources and data sources can be named with the same string (URL), we consider them different entities in our model.

[10] Note that we are not enforcing a specific algorithm, although we implement one in our experimental evaluation.

3.2   Facade-X

We base the design of Facade-X on the distinction between containers and values. Specifically, we define a *container* as a set of uniquely identifiable *slots*, each one of them including either another container or a data *value*. Slot identifiers (*keys*) can be either XSD strings (*StringKey*) or XSD positive integers (*NumberKey*). The predicate *Key* is a reification of either an integer or a string, while the predicate *Value* reifies a string only. Containers can optionally be qualified by a *type*. In Facade-X, data sources are referred to as *root* containers. We specify our facade in predicate logic as follows:

1	$Root(c0)$ $Container(c1)$ $Slot(s1)$ $Key(n)$
2	$StringKey(n)$ $NumberKey(n)$ $Value(v1)$ $Type(t)$
3	$\forall k.StringKey(k) \rightarrow Key(k)$
4	$\forall k.NumberKey(k) \rightarrow Key(k)$
5	$\neg \exists k.NumberKey(k) \wedge StringKey(k)$
6	$\forall\ c.Root(c) \rightarrow Container(c)$

In addition, we define relations between the model components, including definitions of domain and range:

1	$hasSlot(c,s)$ $hasType(c,t)$ $hasKey(s,k)$
2	$hasContainer(s,c)$ $hasValue(s,v)$
3	$\forall(x,y).hasSlot(x,y) \rightarrow Container(x) \wedge Slot(y)$
4	$\forall(x,y).hasType(x,y) \rightarrow Container(x) \wedge Type(y)$
5	$\forall(x,y).hasKey(x,y) \rightarrow Slot(x) \wedge Key(y)$
6	$\forall(x,y).hasContainer(x,y) \rightarrow Slot(x) \wedge Container(y)$
7	$\forall(x,y).hasValue(x,y) \rightarrow Slot(x) \wedge Value(y)$

We define a set of axioms describing additional properties of the meta-model. Only containers can have a type (but they don't have to), and there can only be one root container. A slot can have either one container or one value and cannot have both. A slot can be member of one container only and slots of a container are uniquely identified by their key:

1	$\forall(x,y).Root(x) \wedge Root(y) \rightarrow x = y$
2	$\neg \exists(x,y,z).hasContainer(x,y) \wedge hasValue(x,z)$
3	$\forall(x,y,z).hasContainer(x,y) \wedge hasContainer(x,z) \rightarrow y = z$
4	$\forall(x,y,z).hasValue(x,y) \wedge hasValue(x,z) \rightarrow y = z$
5	$\forall(x,y,z).hasSlot(x,y) \wedge hasSlot(z,y) \rightarrow x = z$
6	$\forall(c,s1,s2p,n).hasSlot(c,s1) \wedge hasSlot(c,s2) \wedge hasKey(s1,n) \wedge hasKey(s2,n) \rightarrow s1 = s2$

The data from our guide scenario can be represented as follows:

1	$Root(ds)$
2	$StringKey(id)$ $StringKey(artist)$ $StringKey(artistId)$ $StringKey(title)$
3	$hasSlot(ds,s1)$ $hasKey(s1, IntegerKey(1))$ $hasContainer(s1,r1)$
4	$hasSlot(r1,r1s1)$ $hasKey(r1s1,id)$ $hasValue(r1s1,"1035")$
5	$hasSlot(r1,r1s2)$ $hasKey(r1s2,artist)$ $hasValue(r1s2,"Blake\ Robert")$
6	$hasSlot(r1,r1s3)$ $hasKey(r1s3,artistId)$ $hasValue(r1s3,"38")$
7	$hasSlot(r1,r1s4)$ $hasKey(r1s4,title)$ $hasValue(r1s4,"A\ Figure\ Bowing\ ...")$ [...]

Finally, we define mapping rules to RDF, where properties are built using string keys and resources can be either blank nodes or named IRIs[11]:

---

[11] The system may allow users to define their own namespace, or reuse the name of the *ds*, and leave to the underlying machinery to mint IRIs.

$$1 \quad Root(ds) \xrightarrow{f} Triple(Resource(ds), rdf : type, fx : Root)$$

$$2 \quad hasSlot(c, s) \wedge hasKey(s, k) \wedge StringKey(k) \wedge hasContainer(s, c1)$$

$$3 \quad \xrightarrow{f} Triple(Resource(c), Property(k), Resource(c1))$$

$$4 \quad hasSlot(c, s) \wedge hasKey(s, k) \wedge IntegerKey(k) \wedge hasContainer(s, c1)$$

$$5 \quad \xrightarrow{f} Triple(Resource(c), ContainerMembershipProperty(k), Resource(c1))$$

$$6 \quad hasSlot(c, s) \wedge hasKey(s, k) \wedge StringKey(k) \wedge hasValue(s, v)$$

$$7 \quad \xrightarrow{f} Triple(Resource(c), Property(k), Literal(v))$$

$$8 \quad hasSlot(c, s) \wedge hasKey(s, k) \wedge IntegerKey(k) \wedge hasValue(s, v)$$

$$9 \quad \xrightarrow{f} Triple(Resource(c), ContainerMembershipProperty(k), Literal(v))$$

$$10 \quad hasType(c, t) \xrightarrow{f} Triple(Resource(c), rdf : type, Resource(t))$$

Our model maps into an RDF that mixes *lists*, *type* statements, and *key-value* pairs. Recent work suggests good practices for developing lists in RDF that are efficient to query [5, 6], favouring container membership properties over nested structures to represent lists. We define two namespaces, one for the primitive entity Root and another for minting properties from keys[12]. The Facade-X RDF vocabulary is published at http://sparql.xyz/facade-x/ns/. The above mappings produce the following *Facade-X RDF*, from our example scenario:

```
1  @prefix fx: <http://sparql.xyz/facade-x/ns/>.
2  @prefix rdf: <http://www.w3.org/1999/02/22-rdf-syntax-ns#>.
3  @base <http://sparql.xyz/facade-x/data/>.
4  [] a fx:Root ;
5     rdf:_1 [:id "1034"; :artist "Blake Robert"; :artistId "38"; ...
6     rdf:_2 [:id "16216"; :artist "Williams Terrick" :artistId "2149"; ...
7     rdf:_3 [:id "12086"; :artist "Pissarro Lucien" :artistId "1777"; ...
8     ...
```

3.3 Using facades in SPARQL

The algorithm in Section 3.1 requires as input a URL and returns an RDF dataset as output. We propose to *overload* the SPARQL SERVICE operator by defining a custom URI-schema, based on the protocol x-sparql-anything:, which is intended to behave as a *virtual* remote endpoint. The related URI-schema supports an open-ended set of parameters specified by the facade implementations available. Options are embedded as key-value pairs, separated by comma. Implementations are expected to either guess the source type from the resource locator or to obtain an indication of the type from the URI schema, for example, with an option "mime-type":

x−sparql−anything:mime−type=application/json; charset=UTF−8,location=...

Following our example scenario, users can write a query and select metadata from the CSV file, as well as embed the content of remote JPG thumbnails in the RDF. Multiple SERVICE clauses may integrate data from more files, for example, the JSON with details about artwork subjects. We leave the content of the CONSTRUCT section to be filled by the ontology engineer:

---

[12] Not all strings are valid IRI local names. Implementations will need to apply heuristics to cope with corner cases in CSV or JSON keys.

```
1   PREFIX fx:  <http://sparql.xyz/facade-x/ns/>
2   PREFIX xyz: <http://sparql.xyz/facade-x/data/>
3   PREFIX rdf: <http://www.w3.org/1999/02/22-rdf-syntax-ns#>
4   CONSTRUCT {
5       [...] # Amazing ontology here
6   } WHERE {
7       BIND (IRI(CONCAT(STR(tate:), "artwork-", ?id )) AS ?artwork) .
8       BIND (IRI(CONCAT(STR(tate:), "artist-", ?artistId )) AS ?artist) .
9       SERVICE <x-sparql-anything:csv.headers=true,location=file:./
            artwork_data.csv> {
10          []  xyz:id ?id ;                  xyz:artist ?artistLabel ;
11              xyz:accessionId ?accId ;      xyz:artistId ?artistId ;
12              xyz:title ?title;             xyz:medium ?medium ;
13              xyz:year ?year ;              xyz:thumbnailUrl ?thumbnail .
14      }
15      # JPEG Thumbnail from the Web
16      BIND (IRI(CONCAT("x-sparql-anything:location=", ?thumbnail )) AS ?
            embedJPG ).
17      SERVICE ?embedJPG { [] rdf:_1 ?imageInBase64 }.
18      # JSON File with subjects
19      BIND (IRI(CONCAT("x-sparql-anything:file:./artworks/", ?accId )) AS ?
            subJSON ).
20      SERVICE ?subJSON { [ xyz:id ?subjectId ; xyz:name ?subjectName ] }.
21  }
```

4   Implementation to SPARQL Anything

In this section we describe SPARQL Anything which is meant to provide a proof-of-concept of our approach. SPARQL Anything implements a stack of transformers mapped to media types and file extensions. The framework allows the addition of an open-ended set of transformers as Java classes. During execution, a query manager intercepts usage of the SERVICE operator and in case the endpoint URI has the x-sparql-anything protocol, it parses the URI extracting the resource locator and parameters. Default parameters are: mime-type, locator, namespace (to be used when defining RDF resources), and root (to use as the IRI of the root RDF resource, instead of a blank node), and metadata. SPARQL Anything will project an RDF dataset during query execution including the data content and optionally a graph named http://sparql.xyz/facade-x/data/metadata, including file metadata extracted from image files (also in Facade-X). Specific formats may support specific parameters. For example, the Text triplifier supports a regular expression to be used by a tokenizer that splits the content in a list of strings (defaults to the space character). Similarly, the CSV triplifier allows to specify whether to use the first row as headers or only use column indexes. More information on the currently supported formats can be found in the project page[13].

We validated the generality of Facade-X as a meta-model with relation to the triplifiers currently implemented in SPARQL Anything. We already considered CSV in the guide example. The following JSON example, also derived from the Tate Gallery open data, can be mapped to our model as in the associated listing.

```
1   { "fc": "Kazimir Malevich",
2       "id": 1561,
```

---

[13] http://github.org/sparql-anything/sparql-anything.

```
3    "places": [
4      { "name": "Ukrayina", "type": "nation" },
5      { "name": "Moskva, Rossiya", "type": "inhabited_place" }
6    ]}
7
```

8 $Root(malevic)$
9 $StringKey(fc)StringKey(id)StringKey(places)StringKey(name)StringKey(type)$
10 $NumberKey(1)NumberKey(2)$
11 $hasSlot(malevic, s_{fc}) \wedge hasKey(s_{fc}, fc) \wedge hasValue(s_{fc}, "KazimirMalevich")$
12 $hasSlot(malevic, s_{id}) \wedge hasKey(s_{id}, id) \wedge hasValue(s_{id}, 1561)$
13 $hasSlot(malevic, s_{places}) \wedge hasKey(s_{places}, places) \wedge hasContainer(s_{places}, c_{places})$
14 $hasSlot(c_{places}, s_{place/1}) \wedge hasKey(s_{place/1}, 1) \wedge hasContainer(s_{place/1}, ukraina)$
15 $hasSlot(ukraina, s_{ukr/name}) \wedge hasKey(s_{ukr/name}, name) \wedge$
16      $hasValue(s_{ukr/name}, "Ukrayina")$
17 $hasSlot(ukraina, s_{ukr/type}) \wedge hasKey(s_{ukr/type}, type) \wedge hasValue(s_{ukr/type}, "nation")$
18 $hasSlot(c_{places}, s_{place/2}) \wedge hasKey(splace/2, 2) \wedge hasContainer(s_{place/2}, moskva)$
19 $hasSlot(moskva, s_{mos/name}) \wedge hasKey(s_{mos/name}, name) \wedge$
20      $hasValue(s_{mos/name}, "Moskva, Rossiya")$
21 $hasSlot(moskva, s_{mos/type}) \wedge hasKey(s_{mos/type}, type) \wedge$
22      $hasValue(s_{mos/type}, "inhabited\_place")$

Finally, we show how an excerpt from a catalogue record in XML, can be interpreted with our Facade-X (this also applies to HTML):

```
1    <OGT hint="OGGETTO">
2      <OGTD hint="Definizione">reperti antropologici ...</OGTD>
3      <OGTT hint="Tipologia">reperto osteo-dentario</OGTT>
4      ...
5
```

6 $Root(ogt) \wedge hasType(record, "OGT")$
7 $Container(ogtd) \wedge hasType(ogtd, "OGTD")$
8 $Container(ogtt) \wedge hasType(ogtt, "OGTT")$
9 $StringKey(hint)$
10 $NumberKey(1)NumberKey(2)$
11 $hasSlot(ogt, s_1) \wedge hasKey(s_1, 1) \wedge hasValue(s_1, ogtd)$
12 $hasSlot(ogt, s_2) \wedge hasKey(s_2, 2) \wedge hasValue(s_2, ogtt)$
13 $hasSlot(ogt, s_{hint}) \wedge hasKey(s_{hint}, hint) \wedge hasValue(s_{hint}, "OGGETTO")$
14 ...

5 Related Work

Related work includes semantic web approaches to content re-engineering, approaches to extending the functionalities of SPARQL, and research on end-user development and human interaction with data.

In ontology engineering, non-ontological resource re-engineering refers to the process of taking an existing resource and transforming it into an ontology [21]. These family of approaches integrate resource transformation within the methodology, where domain knowledge plays a central role. Triplify [2] is one of the first tools aiming at converting sources into RDF in a domain independent way. The approach is based on mapping HTTP URIs to ad-hoc database queries, and rewriting the output of the SQL query into RDF. Other tools are based on the W3C Direct Mapping recommendation [20] for relational databases. Systems are available for automatically transforming data sources of several formats into RDF (Any23[14], JSON2RDF[15], CSV2RDF[16] to name a few). A recent survey

---

[14] http://any23.apache.org/
[15] https://github.com/AtomGraph/JSON2RDF
[16] http://clarkparsia.github.io/csv2rdf/

lists systems to lift tabular data [9]. While these tools have a similar goal (i.e. enabling the user to access the content of a data source as if it was in RDF), the (meta)model used for generating the RDF data highly depends on the input format. All these approaches are not interested in the requirement of providing a common useful abstraction to heterogeneous formats. A long history of mapping languages for transforming heterogeneous files into RDF can be considered superseded by RML [8], including a number of approaches for ETL-based transformations [1]. We consider RML as representative of general data integration approaches such as OBDA [24]. This family of solutions are based on a set of declarative mappings. The mapping languages incorporate format-specific query languages (e.g. SQL or XPath) and require the practitioner to have deep knowledge not only of the input data model but also of standard methods used for its processing. Recent work acknowledges how these languages are built with machine-processability in mind [13] and how defining or even understanding the rules is not trivial to users.

We survey approaches to extend SPARQL. A standard method for extending SPARQL is by providing custom functions[17], or by using so-called *magic* properties. This approach defines custom predicates to be used for instructing specific behaviour at query execution. SPARQL-Generate [15] introduces a novel approach for performing data transformation from heterogeneous sources into RDF by extending the SPARQL syntax with new operators [15]: GENERATE, SOURCE, and ITERATOR. Custom functions perform ad-hoc operations on the supported formats, for example, relying on XPath or JSONPath. Other approaches extend SPARQL *without* changes to the standard syntax. BASIL [7] allows to define parametric queries by enforcing a convention in SPARQL variable names. As a result, SPARQL query templates can be processed with standard query parsers. `grlc` decorates the query with execution metadata declared in comments [17]. SPARQL Micro-service [18] provides a framework that, on the basis of API mapping specification, wraps web APIs in SPARQL endpoints and uses JSON-LD profile to translate the JSON responses of the API into RDF. In this paper, we follow a similar, minimalist approach and extend SPARQL by *overriding* the behaviour of the SERVICE operator. We compare our proposal with SPARQL Generate and RML in detail in the evaluation section.

The proposed approach relates to research on end-user development and human interaction with data. End-user development is defined by [16] as *"methods, techniques, and tools that allow users of software systems, who are acting as non-professional software developers, at some point to create, modify or extend a software artefact"*. Many SPARQL users fall into the category of end-user developer. In a survey of SPARQL users, [22] found that although 58% came from the computer science and IT domain, other SPARQL users came from non-IT areas, including social sciences and the humanities. Findings in this area [19] suggest

---

[17] ARQ provides a library of custom functions for supporting aggregates such as computing a standard deviation of a collection of values. ARQ functions: https://jena.apache.org/documentation/query/extension.html (accessed 15/12/2020).

that the data with which users work is more often primarily list-based and/or hierarchical rather than tabular. For example, [11] proposes an alternative formulation to spreadsheets in which data is represented as *list-of-lists*, rather than tables. Our proposal goes in this direction and accounts for recent findings in end-user development research.

6 Evaluation

We conduct a comparative evaluation of SPARQL Anything with respect to the state of art methods RML and SPARQL Generate. First, we analyse in a quantitative way the cognitive complexity of the frameworks. Second, we conduct a performance analysis of the reference implementations. Finally, we discuss the approaches in relation to the requirements elicited in Section 2. Competency questions, queries, experimental data, and code used for the experiment are available on the GitHub repository of the SPARQL Anything project[18].

Cognitive Complexity Comparison. We present a quantitative analysis on the cognitive complexity of SPARQL Anything, SPARQL Generate and RML frameworks. One effective measure of complexity is the number of distinct items or variables that need to be combined within a query or expression [10]. Such a measure of complexity has previously been used to explain difficulties in the comprehensibility of Description Logic statements [23]. Specifically, we counted the number of tokens needed for expressing a set of competency questions. We selected four JSON files from the case studies of the SPICE project where each file contains the metadata of artworks of a collection. Each file is organised as a JSON array containing a list of JSON objects (one for each artwork). This simple data structure avoids favouring one approach over the others. Then, an analysis of the schema of the selected resources allowed us to define a set of 12 competency questions (CQs) that were then specified as SPARQL queries or mapping rules according to the language of each framework, in particular: (i) 8 CQs (named q1-q8), aimed at retrieving data from the sources, were specified as SELECT queries (according to SPARQL Anything and SPARQL Generate); (ii) 4 CQs (named q9-q11), meant for transforming the source data to RDF, were expressed as CONSTRUCT queries (according to SPARQL Anything and SPARQL Generate) or as mapping rules complying with RML. These queries/rules intend to generate a blank node for each artwork and to attach the artwork's metadata as dataproperties of the node. Finally, we tokenized the queries (by using "(){},;\n\t\r␣ as token delimiters) and we computed the total number of tokens and the number of distinct tokens needed for each queries. By observing the average number of tokens per query we can conclude that RML is very verbose (109.75 tokens) with respect to SPARQL Anything (26.25 tokens) and SPARQL Generate (30.75 tokens) whose verbosity is similar (they differ of the ∼6.5%). However, the average number of *distinct* tokens per query shows that SPARQL Anything requires less cognitive load than other frameworks. In

---

[18] https://github.com/spice-h2020/SPARQL Anything/tree/main/experiment

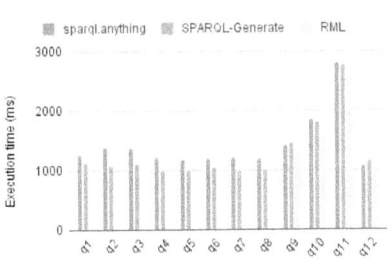

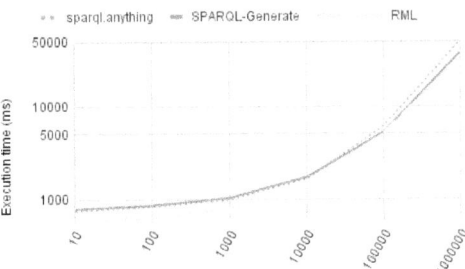

(a) Execution time per query.   (b) Execution time with increasing input size.

Fig. 1: Analysis of the the execution time.

Table 2: Formats supported by RML, SPARQL Generate, and SPARQL Anything.

	JSON	CSV	HTML	Bin.	XML	RDB	Text	Embed	Meta.	Spread.
RML	✓	✓	✓		✓	✓	✓			
SPARQL-Generate	✓	✓	✓	✓	✓	✓	✓			
SPARQL Anything	✓	✓	✓	✓	✓		✓	✓	✓	✓

fact, while SPARQL Anything required 18.25 distinct tokens, SPARQL Generate needed 25.5 distinct tokens (∼39.72% more) and RML 45.25 distinct tokens (∼150% more).

Performance Comparison. We assessed the performance of three frameworks in generating RDF data. All of the tests described below were run three times and the average time among the three executions is reported. The tests were executed on a MacBook Pro 2020 (CPU: i7 2.3 GHz, RAM: 32GB). Figure 1a shows the time needed for evaluating the SELECT queries q1-q8 and for generating the RDF triples according to the CONSTRUCT queries/mapping rules q9-q12. The three frameworks have comparable performance. We also measured the performance in transforming input of increasing size. To do so, we repeatedly concatenated the data sources in order to obtain a JSON array containing 1M JSON objects and we cut this array at length 10, 100, 1K, 10K and 100K. We ran the query/mapping q12 on these files and we measured the execution time shown in Figure 1b. We observe that for inputs with size smaller than 100K the three frameworks have equivalent performance. With larger inputs, SPARQL Anything is slightly slower than the others. The reason is that, in our naive implementation, the data source is completely transformed and loaded into a RDF dataset in-memory, before the query is evaluated. However, implementations could *stream* the triples during query execution, or transform the optimal triple set for the query solution, thus achieving better performance on large input. However, we leave this optimisations to future work.

Requirements satisfaction and discussion We discuss the requirements introduced in Section 2.

Transform, Binary, Embed, and **Metadata.** All the frameworks support users in transforming heterogeneous formats with few differences (a comparison is provided in Table 2). Currently, SPARQL Anything and SPARQL-Generate cover the largest set of input formats. SPARQL-Generate however does not support embedding content (**Embed**) and extracting metadata from files (**Metadata**). Both features are not supported by RML, which doesn't support plain text as well. SPARQL Anything allows users to query spreadsheets, but it is not able to handle relational databases yet[19]. SPARQL Anything is the only tool supporting the extraction of metadata and the embedding of binary content.

Query. In terms of query support, while RML requires data to be transformed first and then uploaded to a SPARQL triple store, SPARQL Anything and SPARQL-Generate enable users to query resources directly.

Low learning demands. SPARQL Generate uses an extension to SPARQL 1.1 to transform source formats into RDF. RML provides an extension to the R2RML vocabulary in order to map source formats into RDF. Therefore either a SPARQL extension or a new mapping language has to be learned to perform the translation. In the case of Facade-X, no new language has to be learned as data can be queried using existing SPARQL 1.1 constructs.

Low complexity. Complexity can be measured as the number of distinct items or variables that need to be combined with the query. In experiments, Facade-X is found to perform favourably in comparison to SPARQL Generate and RML.

Meaningful abstraction. Differently from RML and SPARQL-Generate, which require users to be knowledgeable of the source formats and their query languages (e.g. XPath, JSONPath etc.), Facade-X users can access a resource *as if* it was an RDF dataset, hence the complexity of the non-RDF languages is completely hidden to them. The cost for this solution is limited to the users which are required to *explore* the facade that is generated and tweak the configuration via the Facade-X IRI schema.

Explorability. With SPARQL Generate and RML, the user needs to commit to a particular mapping or transformation of the source data into RDF. However, the data representation required to carry out a knowledge intensive task often emerges from working with data and cannot be wholly specified in advance (this is a crucial requirement of our project SPICE). By distinguishing the processes of re-engineering and re-modelling, Facade-X enables the user to avoid prematurely committing to a mapping and rather focus on querying the data within SPARQL, in a domain-independent way.

Workflow. All the technologies considered can in principle be integrated with a typical Semantic Web engineering workflow. However, while we cannot assume that Semantic Web experts have knowledge of RML, XPath, and SPARQL Generate, we can definitely expect knowledge of SPARQL.

Adaptable. All technologies provide a flexible set of methods for data manipulation, sparql.aything relying on plain SPARQL. We make the assumption that

---

[19] However, relational tables can be mapped using an approach similar to CSV and spreadsheets tables. A dedicated component is currently being developed.

SPARQL itself is enough for manipulating variables, content types, and RDF structures. It is an interesting, open research question to investigate content manipulation patterns in the various languages and compare their ability to meet user requirements.

Extendable and Sustainable. Our approach can be implemented within existing SPARQL query processors with minimal development effort. Extending SPARQL Anything requires to write a component that exposes a data source format as Facade-X. Facade-X does not need to be encoded in the software but serves as a reference for mapping an open ended set of formats. In contrast, extending SPARQL Generate and RML requires extending the user toolkit to handle the specificity of the formats, exposing to users new functions for querying, filtering, traversing, and so on. In addition, our approach leads to a more sustainable codebase. To give evidence of this statement, we use the tool cloc[20] to count the lines of Java code required to implement the core module of SPARQL Generate in Apache Jena (without considering format-specific extensions[21]) and the RML implementation in Java[22]. SPARQL Generate and RML require developing and maintaining 12280 and 7951 lines of Java code, respectively. We developed the prototype implementation of SPARQL Anything with 3842 lines of Java code, including all the currently supported transformers.

7 Conclusions

In this paper, we presented an opinionated approach for making non-RDF resources query-able with SPARQL. We contributed a general approach to apply *facades* to content re-engineering and a specific instance of this approach, Facade-X, which defines a general meta-model akin to a *list-of-lists*. We compared our approach with the state of art methods RML and SPARQL Generate and demonstrated how our solution has lower learning demands and cognitive complexity, and it is cheaper to implement and maintain, while having comparable extensibility. Next, we will extend the range of supported formats of SPARQL Anything, including relational databases, Microsoft Office files, and binary content other then images. The approach does not enforce a specific algorithm and leaves open the opportunity of developing alternative strategies for performance optimisation, considering the specificity of the resources, the complexity of the queries, and the computational resources available. Moreover, we will perform a user study for investigating the cognitive implications of using Facade-X as a meta-model with respect to arbitrary RDF, and compare the tools in terms of expressivity and ability to meet user requirements. Finally, other *facades* can be designed as well. It is an interesting research question to investigate content manipulation patterns in alternative facades and evaluate their benefit for content exploration and transformation.

---

[20] cloc: https://github.com/AlDanial/cloc (accessed 15/12/2020).

[21] For SPARQL Generate, we only considered the code included in the submodule sparql-generate-jena.

[22] RMLMapper: https://github.com/RMLio/rmlmapper-java.

Acknowledgements   The research has received funding from the European Union's Horizon 2020 research and innovation programme through the project SPICE - Social Cohesion, Participation, and Inclusion through Cultural Engagement (Grant Agreement N. 870811), https://spice-h2020.eu, and the project Polifonia: a digital harmoniser of musical cultural heritage (Grant Agreement N. 101004746), https://polifonia-project.eu.

References

1. Arenas-Guerrero, J., Scrocca, M., Iglesias-Molina, A., Toledo, J., Pozo-Gilo, L., Dona, D., Corcho, O., Chaves-Fraga, D.: Knowledge graph construction: An etl system-based overview. ESWC 2021 Workshop KGCW (Submission) (2021)
2. Auer, S., Dietzold, S., Lehmann, J., Hellmann, S., Aumueller, D.: Triplify: lightweight linked data publication from relational databases. In: Proceedings of the 18th international conference on World wide web. pp. 621–630 (2009)
3. Cyganiak, R., Wood, D., Lanthaler, M.: RDF 1.1 concepts and abstract syntax. W3C recommendation, W3C (Feb 2014), https://www.w3.org/TR/2014/REC-rdf11-concepts-20140225/
4. Daga, E., d'Aquin, M., Adamou, A., Brown, S.: The open university linked data–data. open. ac. uk. Semantic Web **7**(2), 183–191 (2016)
5. Daga, E., Meroño-Peñuela, A., Motta, E.: Modelling and querying lists in RDF. A pragmatic study. In: Proceedings of the QuWeDa 2019: 3rd Workshop on Querying and Benchmarking the Web of Data co-located with 18th International Semantic Web Conference (ISWC 2019), Auckland, New Zealand, October 26-30, 2019. CEUR-WS.org (2019)
6. Daga, E., Meroño-Peñuela, A., Motta, E.: Sequential linked data: the state of affairs. Semantic Web (2021)
7. Daga, E., Panziera, L., Pedrinaci, C.: A basilar approach for building web apis on top of sparql endpoints. In: CEUR Workshop Proceedings. vol. 1359, pp. 22–32 (2015)
8. Dimou, A., Vander Sande, M., Colpaert, P., Verborgh, R., Mannens, E., Van de Walle, R.: Rml: a generic language for integrated rdf mappings of heterogeneous data. In: 7th Workshop on Linked Data on the Web (2014)
9. Fiorelli, M., Stellato, A.: Lifting tabular data to rdf: A survey. Metadata and Semantic Research **1355**, 85 (2021)
10. Halford, G.S., Andrews, G.: : The development of deductive reasoning: How important is complexity? Thinking & Reasoning **10**(2), 123–145 (2004)
11. Hall, A.G.: The Lish: A Data Model for Grid Free Spreadsheets. Ph.D. thesis, The Open University (2019)
12. Haslhofer, B., Isaac, A.: data. europeana. eu: The europeana linked open data pilot. In: International Conference on Dublin Core and Metadata Applications. pp. 94–104 (2011)
13. Heyvaert, P., De Meester, B., Dimou, A., Verborgh, R.: Declarative rules for linked data generation at your fingertips! In: European Semantic Web Conference. pp. 213–217. Springer (2018)
14. Johnson, R., Vlissides, J.: Design patterns. Elements of Reusable Object-Oriented Software Addison-Wesley, Reading (1995)
15. Lefrançois, M., Zimmermann, A., Bakerally, N.: A sparql extension for generating rdf from heterogeneous formats. In: European Semantic Web Conference. pp. 35–50. Springer (2017)

16. Lieberman, H., Paternò, F., Klann, M., Wulf, V.: End-user development: An emerging paradigm. In: End user development, pp. 1–8. Springer (2006)
17. Meroño-Peñuela, A., Hoekstra, R.: grlc makes github taste like linked data apis. In: European Semantic Web Conference. pp. 342–353. Springer (2016)
18. Michel, F., Faron-Zucker, C., Corby, O., Gandon, F.: Enabling automatic discovery and querying of web apis at web scale using linked data standards. In: Companion Proceedings of The 2019 World Wide Web Conference. pp. 883–892 (2019)
19. Panko, R.R., Aurigemma, S.: Revising the panko–halverson taxonomy of spreadsheet errors. Decision Support Systems **49**(2), 235–244 (2010)
20. Prud'hommeaux, E., Arenas, M., Bertails, A., Sequeda, J.: A direct mapping of relational data to RDF. W3C recommendation, W3C (Sep 2012), https://www.w3.org/TR/2012/REC-rdb-direct-mapping-20120927/
21. Villazón-Terrazas, B.C., Suárez-Figueroa, M., Gómez-Pérez, A.: A pattern-based method for re-engineering non-ontological resources into ontologies. International Journal on Semantic Web and Information Systems (IJSWIS) **6**(4), 27–63 (2010)
22. Warren, P., Mulholland, P.: Using sparql–the practitioners' viewpoint. In: European Knowledge Acquisition Workshop. pp. 485–500. Springer (2018)
23. Warren, P., Mulholland, P., Collins, T., Motta, E.: Making sense of description logics. In: Proceedings of the 11th International Conference on Semantic Systems. pp. 49–56 (2015)
24. Xiao, G., Calvanese, D., Kontchakov, R., Lembo, D., Poggi, A., Rosati, R., Zakharyaschev, M.: Ontology-based data access: A survey. International Joint Conferences on Artificial Intelligence (2018)

Further with Knowledge Graphs. M. Alam et al. (Eds.)
AKA Verlag and IOS Press, 2021
© 2021 Akademische Verlagsgesellschaft AKA GmbH, Berlin
This article is published online with Open Access by IOS Press and distributed under the terms
of the Creative Commons Attribution License 4.0 (CC BY 4.0).
doi:10.3233/SSW210036

Literal2Feature: An Automatic Scalable RDF Graph Feature Extractor

Farshad BAKHSHANDEGAN MOGHADDAM [a,1], Carsten DRASCHNER [a],
Jens LEHMANN [a], and Hajira JABEEN [b]

[a] *SDA Research Group, University of Bonn, Bonn, Germany*
[b] *University of Cologne, Cologne, Germany*

Abstract. The last decades have witnessed significant advancements in terms of data generation, management, and maintenance. This has resulted in vast amounts of data becoming available in a variety of forms and formats including RDF. As RDF data is represented as a graph structure, applying machine learning algorithms to extract valuable knowledge and insights from them is not straightforward, especially when the size of the data is enormous. Although Knowledge Graph Embedding models (KGEs) convert the RDF graphs to low-dimensional vector spaces, these vectors often lack the explainability. On the contrary, in this paper, we introduce a generic, distributed, and scalable software framework that is capable of transforming large RDF data into an explainable feature matrix. This matrix can be exploited in many standard machine learning algorithms. Our approach, by exploiting semantic web and big data technologies, is able to extract a variety of existing features by deep traversing a given large RDF graph. The proposed framework is open-source, well-documented, and fully integrated into the active community project Semantic Analytics Stack (SANSA). The experiments on real-world use cases disclose that the extracted features can be successfully used in machine learning tasks like classification and clustering.

Keywords. RDF Graph, Prepositionalization, Feature Extraction, Big Data, Distributed Computing, Scalable Analytics, SANSA

1. Introduction

With the rapidly growing amount of data available on the Internet, it becomes necessary to develop a set of tools to extract meaningful and hidden information from the online data. The Semantic Web enables a structural view of the existing data on the web and provides machine-readable formats [1] as the Resource Description Framework (RDF)[2]. RDF has been introduced by the World Wide Web Consortium[3] as a standard to model the real world in the form of entities and relations between them. RDF data are a collection of triples $< subject, predicate, object >$ which tend to have rich relationships, forming a potentially very large and complex graph-like structure. Figure 1 shows a sample RDF.

---

[1]Corresponding Author: Farshad Bakhshandegan Moghaddam, SDA Research Group, University of Bonn, Bonn, Germany; E-mail: farshad.moghaddam@uni-bonn.de

[2]https://www.w3.org/RDF/

[3]https://www.w3.org

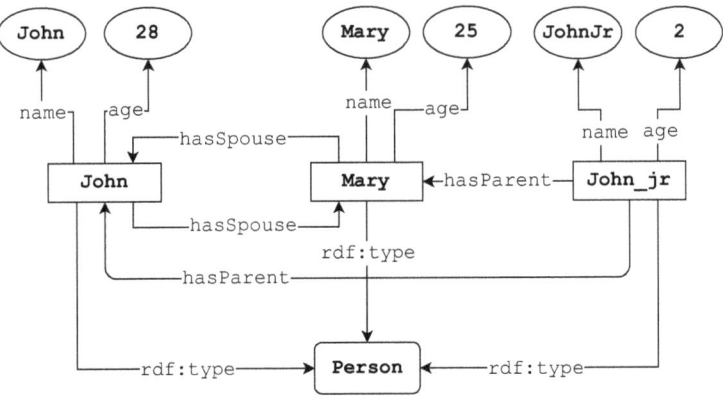

Figure 1. A Sample RDF Graph

Currently, many companies in the fields of science, engineering, and business, including bioinformatics, life sciences, business intelligence, and social networks, publish their data in the form of RDF [2][4,5]. In addition, the Linked Open Data Project initiative [3] helped the Semantic Web to gain even more attention in the past decade. Currently, the Linked Open Data (LOD) cloud comprises more than 10,000 datasets available online[6] using the RDF standard. Nowadays, RDF data can have sizes up to billions of triples[7].

Besides this, Machine Learning, a field of discovering how machines can perform tasks without being explicitly programmed to do so, is growing and finding its way in human daily life. Some prominent examples are autonomous driving, face detection, weather forecasting, etc. Recently with the rapid growth of computational power, training machine learning algorithms at scale is getting much more feasible. However, most of the well-known machine learning algorithms for classification, regression, and clustering need to work with a standard representation of data, i.e. a *feature matrix*. In this format, the data is mostly presented as a 2D matrix, in which rows present the data points and columns indicate the features. Normally, for supervised learning, one (or more) of the columns can be considered as a label (target) for the given row (data point).

Due to the complex graph nature of RDF data, applying standard machine learning algorithms to this data is cumbersome. Although there are efforts in the community to incorporate RDF graphs directly in the machine learning algorithms, they are mostly focused on the structural properties of RDF datasets [4,5,6,7] and offer limited support for RDF literals. Moreover, the challenges in the current big data era (limited computational resources) cause the traditional analytical approaches to mostly fail to operate on large-scale data.

Even though Knowledge Graph Embeddings (KGE) are getting popular as a paradigm to obtain low-dimensional feature representations of Knowledge Graphs (KG),

---

[4]http://www.openphacts.org
[5]https://ontop-vkg.org
[6]http://lodstats.aksw.org/
[7]https://www.w3.org/wiki/DataSetRDFDumps

most of them do not exploit literals in their learning process (an exception is [8] for numerical literal values). Moreover, the feature vectors obtained by KGE models are latent features, which are not explainable. Latent embeddings lose locatable information such as the numerical annotation stored in literals, e.g., *salary of colleagues, timestamp of buying a certain item, runtime of a movie.* The loss of such numeric or timestamp features in multi-modal knowledge graphs need to be avoided in many use cases, especially those that use RDF for data integration and exploiting such features.

To tackle the aforementioned issues, we propose Literal2Feature, a generic, distributed, and scalable software framework which is able to automatically transform a given RDF dataset to a standard feature matrix (also dubbed *Prepositionalization*) by deep traversing the RDF graph and extracting literals to a given depth. Literal2Feature enables the use of a wide range of machine learning algorithms for the Semantic Web community. The proposed method is able to extract features automatically by creating a SPARQL query to produce the feature matrix. All steps are performed automatically without human intervention (details in Section 3). In addition, Literal2Feature is integrated into the SANSA stack [9] and interacts with the different SANSA computational layers. This integration enables sustainability, as SANSA is an actively maintained project, and uses the community ecosystem (mailing list, issue trackers, continuous integration, web-site, etc.). In contrast to KGEs, our proposed approach successfully utilizes literals as extracted features and provides high-level explainability for each feature. Moreover, our approach enables ML practitioners to select the features of interest, based on learning objectives and scenarios.

To summarize, the main contributions of this paper are as follows:

- Introducing a distributed generic framework that can automatically extract semantic features from an RDF graph
- Integrating the approach into the SANSA stack
- Covering the code by unit tests, documenting it in Scala docs [10] and providing a tutorial [11]
- Making Literal2Feature and the framework open source and publicly available on Github[8]
- Evaluation of the results over multiple datasets on classification and clustering scenarios, and comparing it with similar approaches
- Empirical evaluation of scalability

The rest of the paper is structured as follows: The related work is discussed in Section 2. Literal2Feature workflow, and implementation are detailed in Section 3. The use-cases are discussed in Section 4. Section 5 covers the evaluation of the Literal2Feature and demonstrates the scalability. Finally, we conclude the paper in Section 6.

2. Related Work

This section presents prior related studies on Prepositionalization, Graph Embeddings, and Machine Learning on Semantic Data.

---

[8] https://github.com/SANSA-Stack/SANSA-Stack

Prepositionalization. In the recent years, a variety of approaches have been proposed for generating features from LOD. Many of these methods assume a manual design of the feature selection mechanism and in most situations these methods require the user to create a SPARQL query to retrieve the features. For instance, LiDDM [12] enables the users to specify SPARQL queries for retrieving features from RDF graphs that can be used in various machine learning algorithms. Similarly, an automatic feature generation approach is proposed in [13], where the user has to define the type of features in the form of SPARQL queries. Another approach, RapidMiner[9] *semweb* plugin [14] prepro-cesses RDF data using user-specified SPARQL queries, such that the data can be han-dled in RapidMiner. Another similar approach is FeGeLOD [15] and its successor, the RapidMiner Linked Open Data Extension [16]. FeGeLOD is an unsupervised approach for enriching data with features derived from LOD. This approach uses six unsupervised feature generation techniques to explore the data and fetches the features.

Our approach differs from the above-mentioned methods since it does not require any predefined SPARQL query to directly extract the features. Moreover, our approach can be scaled horizontally over a cluster of nodes to handle large amounts of data.

Graph Embeddings. Beside the above-mentioned classical methods, our work is also related to graph embeddings such as [17,18,19,20]. Although these approaches convert entities to dense vectors, however, their result is usually not explainable due to latent rep-resentations of entities. Moreover, most of them ignore literals in their learning process. RDF2Vec [17] is an approach for learning latent entity representations in RDF graphs. It first converts RDF graphs into sequences of graph random walks and Weisfeiler-Lehman graph kernels, and then adopts CBOW and Skip-gram models on the sequences to build entity representations. TransE [18] is a geometric model that assumes that the tail em-beddings are close to the sum of the head and relation embeddings, according to the cho-sen distance function. DistMult [19] is a matrix factorization model that allows all rela-tion embeddings to be diagonal matrices, which reduces the space of parameters to be learned and results in a relatively easy model to train. SimplE [20], like DistMult, forces the relation embeddings to be diagonal matrices but extends it by a) associating two dif-ferent embeddings, e_h and e_t with each entity e, depending on whether e is head or tail b) associating two distinct diagonal matrices, r and r_{-1}, with each relation r, expressing the relation in its normal and inverse direction.

Our approach differs from the KGE methods, as it only utilizes literals from knowl-edge graphs to generate the feature vectors while demonstrating a high-level of explain-ability and relatedness.

Machine Learning on Semantic Data. There are numerous centralized machine learning frameworks and algorithms for RDF data. For example, TensorLog [21] and ProPPR [4] are recent frameworks for efficient probabilistic inference in first-order logic. AMIE [5] and AMIE+ [22] learn association rules from RDF data. DL Learner [7] is a framework for inductive learning on the Semantic Web. [6] provides a review of statisti-cal relational learning techniques for knowledge graphs.

Although there are some efforts in the community to incorporate RDF data in machine learning pipelines, however, to the best of our knowledge, Literal2Feature is the first in a row which deeply extracts literals as a feature matrix from the RDF data in a distributed

---

[9]http://www.rapidminer.com/

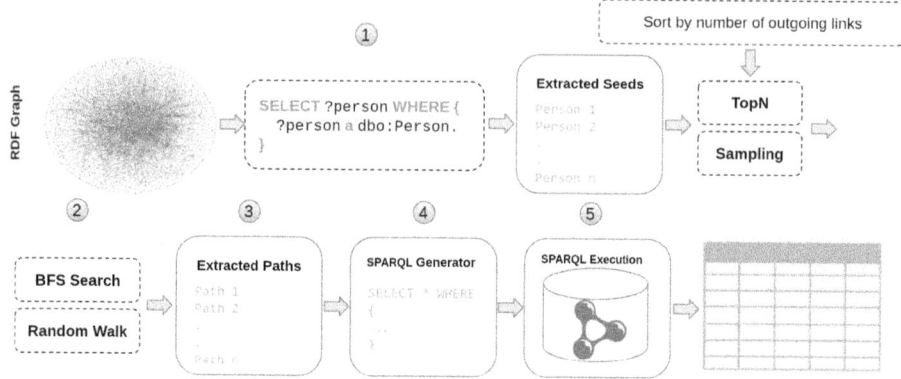

Figure 2. System Architecture Abstract Overview

and scalable manner. One may argue that these features can be extracted from the on-tologies as well [23]. However, it should be noted that 1) ontologies can be large and not fully used in the data 2) there may not be any ontologies associated with a given RDF data set.

3. Literal2Feature

In this section, we present the system architecture of Literal2Feature. The main goal of the framework is to retrieve literals for each entity based on the predefined graph depth. In other words, Literal2Feature, by deeply traversing the RDF graph, is able to gather literals for each entity up to a predefined level and consider them as a feature vector for the given entity. We believe that literals contain valuable information for each entity which can be used for any subsequent machine learning pipeline. Although other features such as a number of specific predicates (e.g. `foaf:knows` which can count the number of friends of each person) or existence of a type relation (e.g. a boolean value which is `True` if a specific type relation exists such as `rdf:type dbo:Person`) can also be retrieved from an RDF graph, however, in Literal2Feature, we neglect them and only focus on the literals.

Figure 2 shows the high-level system architecture overview. The core section of the framework consists of five main components: 1) Seed Generator 2) Graph Search 3) Path Extractor 4) SPARQL Generator 5) SPARQL Executor. Below, each part is discussed in more detail.

3.1. Components

3.1.1. Seed Generator Component

The input of the system is an RDF graph $\mathcal{G}$ and a set of RDF triples $\mathcal{T}$. The triples define the entities that the user is interested to generate features for. $\mathcal{T}$ will automatically for-mulate a `SELECT` SPARQL query which is used to generate only starting points for the deep search. In other words, this query specifies the entities for which the user is inter-ested to extract features for (e.g. in Figure 1, all the persons). By executing the `SELECT`

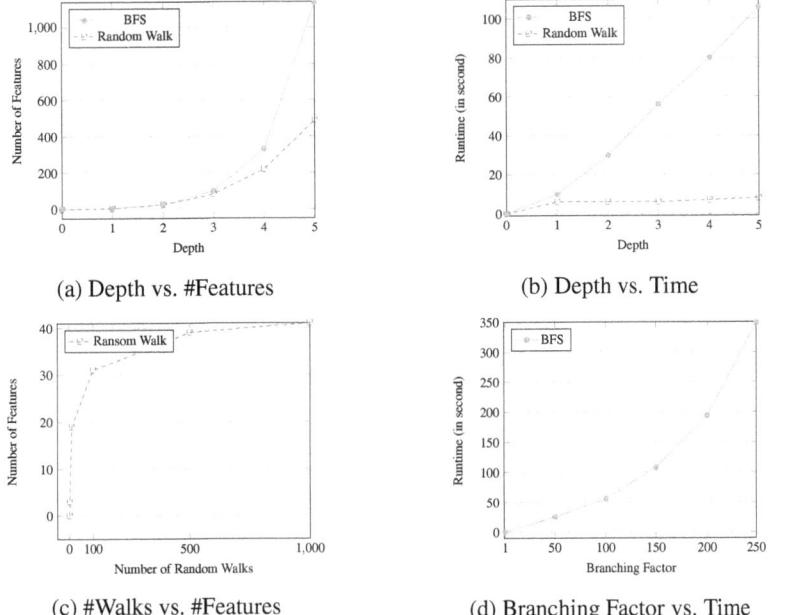

(a) Depth vs. #Features   (b) Depth vs. Time

(c) #Walks vs. #Features   (d) Branching Factor vs. Time

Figure 3. Impact of different factors on the runtime and the number of extracted features (a, b, and c are experimented on the Engie dataset (Section 5.1) and d on a synthetic data on a single machine)

query over the given RDF data, the starting points of search (seeds) are generated. These seeds are sorted based on the number of outgoing links. The higher the number of outgoing links, the higher chance of generating more features (see Section 3.1.2). To execute the query, Sparklify [24], a SANSA built-in distributed SPARQL executor is used.

3.1.2. Graph Search Component

The next step executes a graph search algorithm starting from the seed nodes. Without loss of generality, in this framework we use two different strategies, a) full graph search and b) approximated graph search. For the full graph search, we use Breadth-First Search (BFS) [25] to be able to traverse the entire graph. For the approximation, we use Random Walk model [26]. In both approaches, the user will have full control over the depth, the number of walks, and direction of the search (downward, upward). There is a relation between extracted feature completeness and the search execution time with the search strategy. Full graph search is able to extract all the existing features, but the execution time is higher than the random walk model. The three factors that have an impact on the number of extracted features and the execution time are a) the depth of search b) the average branching factor of nodes of the graph c) the number of random walks (only in the Random Walk model). Figure 3 depicts the impact of each factor. It can be seen that most of the parameters have an exponential impact on the full graph search. However, the Random Walk model depicts a linear and logarithmic behavior in terms of time and the number of extracted features.

Each search walk (regardless of the selected search method) generates a path and continues until one of the following conditions occurs:

- Reaching a node which is a literal node

• Exceeding the pre-configured length of the walk

3.1.3. Path Generator Component

By considering the nodes and edge labels (RDF entities and properties) we could generate property paths. Each properties path encodes all needed properties to reach a literal from the given seed node. For example, based on Figure 1, the sequence of `John_jr->hasParent->Mary->age` encodes the path which can fetch the "age of the mother of `John_jr`". Each walk of the search algorithm generates a properties path. Due to the probabilistic nature of the algorithms (in the Random Walk method) and repetition in the RDF graphs, there is a chance of having duplicated paths. The final output of this component is distinct properties paths.

3.1.4. SPARQL Generator Component

By gathering all property paths, ignoring the entities, and only keeping properties, each path is transformed automatically to a SPARQL query. For instance, the above-mentioned example will be transformed to `->hasParent->age` and then to the following SPARQL query (Listing 1, prefixes have been omitted for simplicity). Due to the data sparsity issue and as all the seeds may not have all the possible properties, each properties-path is wrapped with an `Optional` block to ensure the successful generation of the final result. To have explanatory names for the projected variables, the prefix part of each RDF property is omitted and after splitting based on underscore character, the last part of each property is selected and concatenated (see Listing 1). These names are human-readable and demonstrate explainability for each feature.

Listing 1: Sample result of the generated SPARQL query

```
SELECT ?person ?hasParent_age WHERE {
  ?person a Person.
  OPTIONAL {
    ?person hasParent ?parent.
    ?parent age ?hasParent_age.
  }
}
```

3.1.5. SPARQL Executor Component

After generating the SPARQL query based on the generated properties paths, we use the built-in SPARQL engine in SANSA to execute the query over the given RDF data. The result of this component is the desired feature matrix. Due to the structure of the graph, the SPARQL query may result in multiple rows for a single entity. Based on Figure 1, this behavior can be seen when we want to extract the age of a parent of `John_jr` as he has two parents. In such a case, one of the rows is selected randomly and kept for the subsequent machine learning pipeline. In future work, we plan to use other strategies for merging different rows by applying aggregator functions such as taking an average, median, etc.

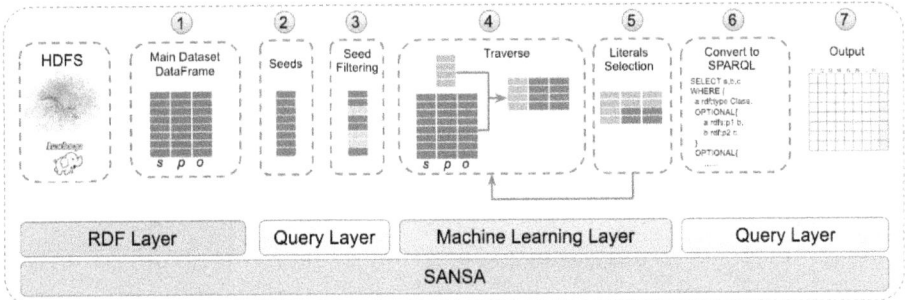

Figure 4. Literal2Feature Execution Pipeline (Best viewed in color)

3.2. Implementation

As the programming language of SANSA is Scala[10], we have selected this language and its APIs in Apache Spark to provide the distributed implementation of Literal2Feature. Moreover, we benefit from SANSA IO and Query layers. Technically, Literal2Feature can be divided into the following steps 1) Read RDF data as a data frame 2) generate seeds 3) filter seeds 4) traverse the graph by joining data frames up to a certain depth 5) select paths ending with literals 6) convert the paths to SPARQL 7) execute the SPARQL and output the result, as shown in Figure 4 which depicts the framework execution pipeline.

4. Use Cases

Literal2Feature is a generic tool that can be used in many use cases. To validate this, we develop use case implementations in several domains and projects.

PLATOON   Digital PLatform and analytic TOOls for eNergy (PLATOON[11]) is a Horizon 2020 Project aiming to deploy distributed/edge processing and data analytics technologies for optimized real-time energy system management in a simple way for the energy domain. PLATOON uses SANSA Stack as a generic data analytics framework in which Literal2Feature is an integral module in the pipeline. Literal2Feature makes it possible for non-experts to deduce the features and enrich their use case related data.

Engie   Engie SA[12] is a French multinational electric utility company that operates in the fields of energy transition, electricity generation and distribution, natural gas, nuclear, renewable energy, and petroleum. Together with Engie we are working on a dataset related to accidents that occurred in France. One of the major challenges is the prediction and classification of the accidents in an effective and scalable manner. In order to perform this task efficiently and effectively, Literal2Feature integrated into SANSA stack is an integral module for classification task.

---

[10]https://www.scala-lang.org/
[11]https://cordis.europa.eu/project/id/872592/de
[12]https://www.engie.com

5. Experimental Results

In this section, we present two sets of experiments to analyze different aspects of Literal2Feature. In the first experiment, the quality and usefulness of the extracted features will be analyzed over classification and clustering scenarios and in the second experiment, the scalability of the proposed framework will be investigated.

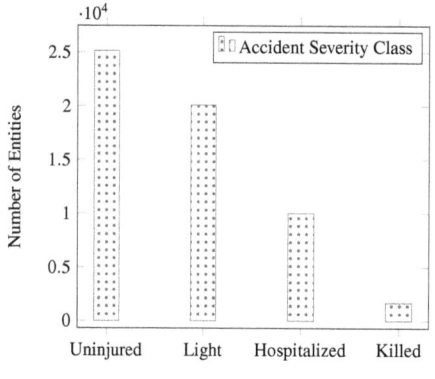

Figure 5. Entity Distribution (Accident Classification 1)

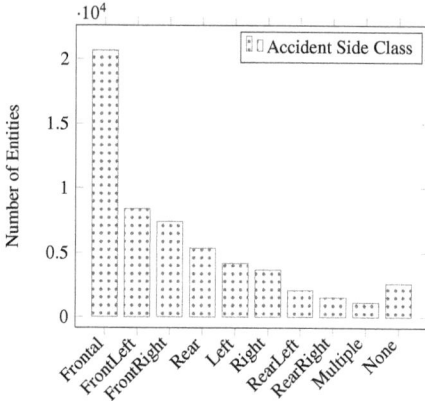

Figure 6. Entity Distribution (Accident Classification 2)

5.1. Experiment A: Assessment of the extracted Features

Literal2Feature can be used in many scenarios, from statistical analysis to classification and clustering. In this section, we analyze the quality of the extracted features for classification and clustering scenarios. To this end, two datasets have been exploited. Engie accident dataset[13] and Carcinogenesis dataset [27]. The accident dataset contains the data about accidents occurred in France in 2018. The Carcinogenesis dataset contains information about drug molecules and their features. An overview of the datasets is given in Table 1.

5.1.1. Classification

For the above-mentioned datasets, three classification scenarios have been defined as follows (all scenarios are multiclass single-label classification problem):

1- Accident classification based on how dangerous was an accident (4 classes).
2- Accident classification based on which side of the vehicle was shocked in the accident (10 classes).
3- Carcinogenic drugs classification (2 classes)

As a baseline for feature vectors, FeGeLOD [15], RDF2Vec [17], TransE [18], SimplE [20], and DistMult [19] are selected (KGEs are trained by OpenKE[14] on NVIDIA GeForce GTX 1080 Ti). For the learning algorithms, we selected Random Forest (RF), Logistic Regression (LR), Multi-Layer Perceptron (MLP), and XGBoost (XG)[28] to

---

[13]Can not be publicly published due to Intellectual Property concerns
[14]https://github.com/thunlp/OpenKE

Table 1. Dataset statistics (GT=Ground Truth)

Dataset	Format	#Triples	|GT|	Classification Scenario	Classes
Accident	N-Triple	5,961,107	57,783	How dangerous is an accident	4
				Which side of vehicle is shocked	10
Carcinogenesis	OWL	74,567	298	Is a drug carcinogenesis	2

Table 2. F1-Measure (macro) evaluation results

Approach		Accident Scenario 1	Accident Scenario 2	Carcinogenesis
FeGeLOD[15]	RF	0.17 ± 0.01	0.05 ± 0.001	0.59 ± 0.07
	LR	0.20 ± 0.02	0.05 ± 0.003	0.61 ± 0.06
	MLP	0.18 ± 0.01	0.05 ± 0.001	0.58 ± 0.07
	XG	0.18 ± 0.02	0.05 ± 0.004	0.58 ± 0.05
RDF2Vec[17]	RF	0.17 ± 0.004	0.05 ± 0.0001	0.41 ± 0.13
	LR	0.25 ± 0.02	0.07 ± 0.006	0.49 ± 0.12
	MLP	0.23 ± 0.02	0.09 ± 0.008	0.51 ± 0.18
	XG	0.23 ± 0.02	0.07 ± 0.006	0.42 ± 0.10
TransE[18]	RF	0.16 ± 0.001	0.05 ± 0.0001	0.52 ± 0.09
	LR	0.17 ± 0.002	0.05 ± 0.001	0.56 ± 0.06
	MLP	0.24 ± 0.006	0.08 ± 0.001	0.56 ± 0.06
	XG	0.24 ± 0.005	0.06 ± 0.001	0.51 ± 0.06
DistMult[19]	RF	0.22 ± 0.01	0.05 ± 0.0001	0.50 ± 0.06
	LR	0.22 ± 0.005	0.05 ± 0.001	0.53 ± 0.06
	MLP	0.26 ± 0.005	0.09 ± 0.004	0.54 ± 0.04
	XG	0.37 ± 0.04	0.09 ± 0.002	0.58 ± 0.05
SimplE[20]	RF	0.22 ± 0.01	0.05 ± 0.0001	0.45 ± 0.09
	LR	0.23 ± 0.003	0.05 ± 0.001	0.48 ± 0.04
	MLP	0.28 ± 0.004	0.09 ± 0.004	0.53 ± 0.04
	XG	0.36 ± 0.03	0.08 ± 0.003	0.50 ± 0.07
Literal2Feature	RF	0.37 ± 0.007	0.10 ± 0.01	0.57 ± 0.07
	LR	0.41 ± 0.002	0.12 ± 0.005	$\mathbf{0.62 \pm 0.08}$
	MLP	$\mathbf{0.46 \pm 0.006}$	$\mathbf{0.21 \pm 0.005}$	0.48 ± 0.07
	XG	0.38 ± 0.18	0.19 ± 0.07	0.53 ± 0.04

cover a range from decision trees to neural networks. As the accident dataset has imbalanced labels (see Figures 5,6), only F1-measure (macro) is reported. The results are summarised in Table 2. These experiments have been conducted on a single node with a Intel Core i5 CPU and 8GB of RAM. For FeGeLOD, its original default configurations have been preserved, and for KGEs the dimension of vectors has been set to 200. Moreover, all algorithms have been trained using 5-fold cross-validation.

The focus of this experiment is to show the quality of the extracted features and compare it with other approaches. As can be seen, in all cases the extracted features from our proposed framework yield a higher F1 score. For example, in Accident Scenario 1, Literal2Feature achieves 0.46 in comparison to 0.37 for DistMult. The same behavior can be observed in Accident Scenario 2. Here, Literal2Feature achieves 0.21, however, the F1 of all other baselines is less than 0.09. In the Carcinogenesis binary classification scenario, still, Literal2Feature outperforms other methods. Although in this case,

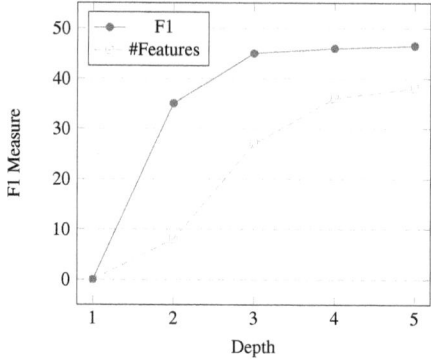

Figure 7. Depth Impact on the Classification Result and Number of Extracted Features

FeGeLOD results are comparable, FeGeLOD achieved 0.61 with 247 extracted features, however, Literal2Feature achieved 0.62 using only 8 extracted features. This reveals that the features extracted by Literal2Feature are more informative and useful.

As a hypothesis, the further we go deeper in the graph, the more likely to find features, but the less trust-worthy and less-relevant the features become. To prove it, we run the classification scenario on the Engie dataset with 4 classes (Accident Scenario 1) with MLP algorithm for the features in different depths. As shown in Figure 7, there is no significant change in F1 after step 3. It indicates that considering the features uptil the depth of 3 is sufficient and there is no need to consider farther features as it can increase the running time of the system without apparent gain.

5.1.2. Clustering

To evaluate the usefulness of the extracted features, we additionally designed a clustering scenario. However, as our datasets have no ground truth for the clustering scenario, we have used Silhouette Coefficient to measure the quality of the clustering results. The Silhouette Coefficient is defined for each sample and is composed of two scores: a: The mean distance between a sample and all other points in the same class. b: The mean distance between a sample and all other points in the next nearest cluster. The Silhouette Coefficient*s* for a single sample is then given as:

$$s = \frac{b - a}{max(a,b)} \tag{1}$$

The Silhouette Coefficient for a set of samples is given as the mean of the Silhouette Coefficient for each sample, and a higher Silhouette Coefficient score relates to a model with better defined clusters. We have selected K-Means to demonstrate clustering results and applied elbow-method to determine the optimal number of clusters, which is set to 4. Table 3 shows the result of the clustering.

As the result depicts, Literal2Feature achieved better clustering for the Engie dataset and obtained comparable results to RDF2Vec for the Carcinogenesis dataset, whereas TransE achieved the best clustering score. The reason why TransE achieves good results in clustering is that TransE is a geometric model and is trained using an objective function to keep the similar entities close.

Table 3. Silhouette Coefficient

	Engie	Carcinogenesis
RDF2Vec	0.004	0.263
TransE	0.113	**0.669**
SimplE	0.008	0.008
DistMult	0.006	0.009
Literal2Feature	**0.133**	0.247

Table 4. Synthetic Dataset Description

Dataset	#Seeds	Size	#Triples
DS 1	1	6.5 MB	127 K
DS 2	300	2.2 GB	38 M
DS 3	600	4.5 GB	76 M
DS 4	1200	9.1 GB	153 M
DS 5	2400	13 GB	306 M
DS 6	6000	47 GB	765 M

5.2. Experiment B: Scalability

In this experiment we evaluate the scalability of Literal2Feature by using different data sizes and varying cluster computing setups. To be able to have different sizes of datasets, we implemented an RDF data simulator which generates synthetic RDF graph based on the given depth, branching factor, and number of seeds. Table 4 lists the generated datasets and their characteristics. The branching factor is set to 50, depth to 3, and all literals lie at the leaf node to form a complete tree. Worth to mention that the German DBpedia size is 48GB with 336 M triples, however, as the branching factors of nodes are not fixed and equal in real datasets, we decided to do the experiments on synthetic data which requires more CPU and Memory consumption.

5.2.1. Scalability over number of cores

To adjust the distributed processing power, the number of available cores was regulated. In this experiment, *DS 4* is selected as a pilot dataset and the number of cores was increased starting from $2^2 = 4$ up to $2^7 = 128$. The experiments were carried out on a small cluster of 4 nodes (1 master, 3 workers): AMD Opteron(tm) CPU Processor 6376 @ 2300MHz (64 Cores), 256 GB RAM. Moreover, the machines were connected via a Gigabit network. All experiments are executed three times and the average value is reported in the results. Figure 8 shows the scalability over different computing cluster setups. It is clear that increasing the computational power horizontally, decreases the execution time. It should be noted that the runtime does not include the time for data ingestion from the Hadoop file system and SPARQL query execution as we used SANSA's internal SPARQL engine for SPARQL execution.

In the beginning, by doubling the number of cores, the execution time dramatically decreases almost with the factor of 2. However, by adding more cores, the execution time only slightly decreases. This behavior can be seen due to the overhead of shuffling data between nodes and network latency. The maximum speedup achieved is 6.3x.

5.2.2. Scalability over dataset size

To analyze the scalability over different datasets, we fix the computational power to 64 cores and run the experiments for all datasets introduced in Table 4. By comparing the runtime as shown in Figure 9, we note that the execution time does not increase exponentially. Hence, doubling the size of the dataset does not necessarily increase the execution time with the factor of 2. This behaviour is due to the available resources (memory) and partition size. On the other hand, as expected, it can be noted that the random walk consumes much lesser time as compared to full search, which requires comparatively more resources.

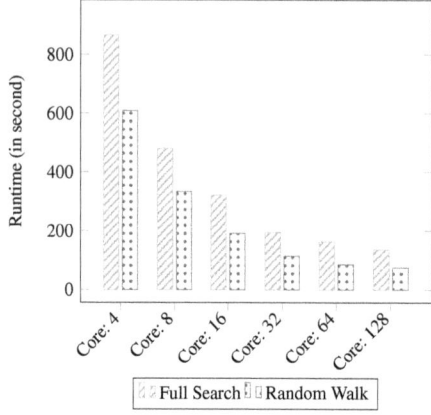 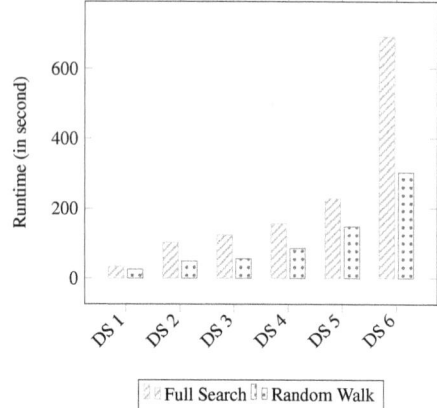

Figure 8. Processing Power Scalability on DS 4 Dataset

Figure 9. Sizeup performance evaluation over 64 Cores

6. Conclusion

In this paper, we introduce Literal2Feature, a generic distributed framework for transforming RDF data into a feature matrix, which can be used in many machine learning algorithms. By providing full control over different hyper-parameters, users will have a substantial level of flexibility in using the framework. Our experiments also showed that the framework can be used to analyze RDF data with existing statistical machine learning pipelines. Moreover, our experiments show that Literal2Feature can be successfully scaled over a cluster of nodes for large amount of data. In future, we plan to exploit more features such as graph topological structure, e.g. number of neighbors, type-related features, etc.. For multiple features with the same property path, we aim to test the application of aggregator functions like average or max, min, as discussed in Section 3.1.5.

Acknowledgment

This work was partly supported by the EU Horizon 2020 project PLATOON (Grant agreement ID: 872592)

References

[1] T. Berners-Lee, A roadmap to the Semantic Web, 1998.

[2] M. Schmachtenberg, C. Bizer and H. Paulheim, Adoption of the Linked Data Best Practices in Different Topical Domains, in: *The Semantic Web – ISWC 2014*, P. Mika, T. Tudorache, A. Bernstein, C. Welty, C. Knoblock, D. Vrandečić, P. Groth, N. Noy, K. Janowicz and C. Goble, eds, Springer International Publishing, Cham, 2014, pp. 245–260. ISBN ISBN 978-3-319-11964-9.

[3] C. Bizer, M.-E. Vidal and H. Skaf-Molli, *Linked Open Data*, in: *Encyclopedia of Database Systems*, Springer New York, New York, NY, 2018, pp. 2096–2101. ISBN ISBN 978-1-4614-8265-9.

[4] W.Y. Wang, K. Mazaitis and W.W. Cohen, Structure Learning via Parameter Learning., in: *CIKM*, ACM, 2014, pp. 1199–1208. ISBN ISBN 978-1-4503-2598-1.

[5] L. Galárraga, C. Teflioudi, K. Hose and F.M. Suchanek, Fast rule mining in ontological knowledge bases with AMIE+., *VLDB J.* **24**(6) (2015), 707–730.

[6] M. Nickel, K. Murphy, V. Tresp and E. Gabrilovich, A Review of Relational Machine Learning for Knowledge Graphs, *Proceedings of the IEEE* **104**(1) (2016), 11–33.
doi:10.1109/JPROC.2015.2483592.

[7] L. Bühmann, J. Lehmann and P. Westphal, DL-Learner - A framework for inductive learning on the
Semantic Web., *J. Web Semant.* **39** (2016), 15–24.

[8] A. Kristiadi, M.A. Khan, D. Lukovnikov, J. Lehmann and A. Fischer, Incorporating literals into knowledge graph embeddings, *arXiv preprint arXiv:1802.00934* (2018).

[9] J. Lehmann, G. Sejdiu, L. Bühmann, P. Westphal, C. Stadler, I. Ermilov, S. Bin, N. Chakraborty,
M. Saleem, A.-C.N. Ngonga and H. Jabeen, Distributed Semantic Analytics using the SANSA Stack, in:
Proceedings of 16th International Semantic Web Conference - Resources Track (ISWC'2017), Springer,
2017, pp. 147–155.

[10] Literal2Feature   ScalaDoc.   `https://sansa-stack.github.io/`
`SANSA-Stack/scaladocs/0.8.0/net/sansa_stack/ml/spark/utils/`
`FeatureExtractingSparqlGenerator$.html`.

[11] Literal2Feature   Tutorial.   `https://github.com/SANSA-Stack/SANSA-Stack/blob/`
`develop/sansa-ml/README.md`.

[12] V.N.P. Kappara, R. Ichise and O.P. Vyas, LiDDM: A Data Mining System for Linked Data, in:
WWW2011 Workshop on Linked Data on the Web, Hyderabad, India, March 29, 2011, CEUR
Workshop Proceedings, Vol. 813, CEUR-WS.org, 2011. `http://ceur-ws.org/Vol-813/`
`1dow2011-paper07.pdf`.

[13] W. Cheng, G. Kasneci, T. Graepel, D.H. Stern and R. Herbrich, Automated feature generation from
structured knowledge, in: *Proceedings of the 20th ACM Conference on Information and Knowledge
Management, CIKM 2011, Glasgow, United Kingdom, October 24-28, 2011*, ACM, 2011, pp. 1395–
1404. doi:10.1145/2063576.2063779.

[14] M.A. Khan, G.A. Grimnes and A. Dengel, Two pre-processing operators for improved learning from
semanticweb data, in: *First RapidMiner Community Meeting And Conference (RCOMM 2010)*, 2010.

[15] H. Paulheim and J. Fürnkranz, Unsupervised generation of data mining features from linked open data,
in: *2nd International Conference on Web Intelligence, Mining and Semantics, WIMS '12, Craiova, Ro-
mania, June 6-8, 2012*, ACM, 2012, pp. 31:1–31:12. doi:10.1145/2254129.2254168.

[16] P. Ristoski, C. Bizer and H. Paulheim, Mining the Web of Linked Data with RapidMiner, *J. Web Semant.*
35 (2015), 142–151. doi:10.1016/j.websem.2015.06.004.

[17] P. Ristoski and H. Paulheim, RDF2Vec: RDF Graph Embeddings for Data Mining, in: *The Semantic Web
- ISWC 2016 - 15th International Semantic Web Conference, Kobe, Japan, October 17-21, 2016, Proceedings, Part I*, Lecture Notes in Computer Science, Vol. 9981, 2016, pp. 498–514. doi:10.1007/978-
3-319-46523-4_30.

[18] A. Bordes, N. Usunier, A. Garcia-Durán, J. Weston and O. Yakhnenko, Translating Embeddings for
Modeling Multi-Relational Data, in: *Proceedings of the 26th International Conference on Neural Information Processing Systems - Volume 2*, NIPS'13, Curran Associates Inc., Red Hook, NY, USA, 2013,
pp. 2787–2795–.

[19] B. Yang, W. Yih, X. He, J. Gao and L. Deng, Embedding Entities and Relations for Learning and
Inference in Knowledge Bases, in: *3rd International Conference on Learning Representations, ICLR
2015, San Diego, CA, USA, May 7-9, 2015, Conference Track Proceedings*, Y. Bengio and Y. LeCun,
eds, 2015. `http://arxiv.org/abs/1412.6575`.

[20] S.M. Kazemi and D. Poole, SimplE Embedding for Link Prediction in Knowledge Graphs, 2018.

[21] W.W. Cohen, TensorLog: A Differentiable Deductive Database, *CoRR* **abs/1605.06523** (2016).

[22] L. Galárraga, C. Teflioudi, K. Hose and F.M. Suchanek, Fast rule mining in ontological knowledge bases
with AMIE+, *VLDB J.* **24**(6) (2015), 707–730. doi:10.1007/s00778-015-0394-1.

[23] F.Z. Smaili, X. Gao and R. Hoehndorf, Onto2Vec: joint vector-based representation of biological entities and their ontology-based annotations, *Bioinformatics* **34**(13) (2018), i52–i60.
doi:10.1093/bioinformatics/bty259.

[24] C. Stadler, G. Sejdiu, D. Graux and J. Lehmann, Sparklify: A Scalable Software Component for Efficient Evaluation of SPARQL Queries over Distributed RDF Datasets, in: *The Semantic Web - ISWC
2019 - 18th International Semantic Web Conference, Auckland, New Zealand, October 26-30, 2019,
Proceedings, Part II*, C. Ghidini, O. Hartig, M. Maleshkova, V. Svátek, I.F. Cruz, A. Hogan, J. Song,
M. Lefrançois and F. Gandon, eds, Lecture Notes in Computer Science, Vol. 11779, Springer, 2019,
pp. 293–308. doi:10.1007/978-3-030-30796-7_19.

[25] E.F. Moore, *The Shortest Path Through a Maze*, Bell Telephone System. Technical publications. monograph, Bell Telephone System., 1959.

[26] F. Xia, J. Liu, H. Nie, Y. Fu, L. Wan and X. Kong, Random Walks: A Review of Algorithms and Applications, *IEEE Transactions on Emerging Topics in Computational Intelligence* **4**(2) (2020), 95–107. doi:10.1109/TETCI.2019.2952908.

[27] P. Westphal, L. Bühmann, S. Bin, H. Jabeen and J. Lehmann, SML-Bench - A benchmarking framework for structured machine learning, *Semantic Web* **10**(2) (2019), 231–245.

[28] T. Chen and C. Guestrin, XGBoost: A Scalable Tree Boosting System, in: *Proceedings of the 22nd ACM SIGKDD International Conference on Knowledge Discovery and Data Mining*, ACM, 2016, pp. 785–794.

Further with Knowledge Graphs. M. Alam et al. (Eds.)
AKA Verlag and IOS Press, 2021
© 2021 Akademische Verlagsgesellschaft AKA GmbH, Berlin
This article is published online with Open Access by IOS Press and distributed under the terms
of the Creative Commons Attribution License 4.0 (CC BY 4.0).
doi:10.3233/SSW210037

LLOD-Driven Bilingual Word Embeddings Rivaling Cross-Lingual Transformers in Quality of Life Concept Detection from French Online Health Communities

Katharina ALLGAIER [a], Susana VERÍSSIMO [a], Sherry TAN [a1],
Matthias ORLIKOWSKI [a] and Matthias HARTUNG [a]

[a] *Semalytix GmbH, Bielefeld, Germany*
e-mail: {first.last}@semalytix.com

Abstract. We describe the use of Linguistic Linked Open Data (LLOD) to support a cross-lingual transfer framework for concept detection in online health communities. Our goal is to develop multilingual text analytics as an enabler for analyzing health-related quality of life (HRQoL) from self-reported patient narratives. The framework capitalizes on supervised cross-lingual projection methods, so that labeled training data for a source language are sufficient and are not needed for target languages. Cross-lingual supervision is provided by LLOD lexical resources to learn bilingual word embeddings that are simultaneously tuned to represent an inventory of HRQoL concepts based on the World Health Organization's quality of life surveys (WHOQOL). We demonstrate that lexicon induction from LLOD resources is a powerful method that yields rich and informative lexical resources for the cross-lingual concept detection task which can outperform existing domain-specific lexica. Furthermore, in a comparative evaluation we find that our models based on bilingual word embeddings exhibit a high degree of complementarity with an approach that integrates machine translation and rule-based extraction algorithms. In a combined configuration, our models rival the performance of state-of-the-art cross-lingual transformers, despite being of considerably lower model complexity.

Keywords. Multilingual Text Analytics, Linguistic Linked Open Data, Bilingual Word Embeddings, Cross-lingual Transformers, Health-related Quality of Life

1. Introduction

Increasingly, multilingual language resources are available as Linguistic Linked Open Data (LLOD) [1] which model relations between resources and include rich metadata with standardized, non-proprietary technologies – a trend which promises to lead to improved multilingual NLP systems. However, how to effectively utilize these resources is

---

[1] This author contributed to the results presented in this paper during an internship at Semalytix.

not self-evident, in particular for specialized domains. One example of such a domain are posts from online health communities, i.e., web fora and similar systems focused on health topics used by patients, caregivers and/or professionals in a wide range of languages. Online health communities are a relevant data source for a range of emerging application areas, such as public health monitoring or evidence generation for regulatory drug approval [2], which entail analysing patients' experiences beyond clinical trials. A central aspect of these so-called patient-reported outcomes is health-related quality of life (HRQoL) [3].

In this paper, we focus on classifying posts into categories derived from facets of HRQoL as described in the World Health Organization's quality of life surveys (WHO-QOL) [4], e.g., pain and discomfort, work capacity, financial resources. We approach the problem of predicting HRQoL facets across languages via a multitude of individual binary classifiers trained using a cross-lingual transfer learning framework based on bilingual lexica available as multilingual LLOD. The combination of LLOD and transfer learning is motivated by the flexibility required to predict a large number of HRQoL facets (we consider a total of 19 facets) in a multilingual setting: Transfer learning allows us to train classifiers for different languages based on training data in a single source language, without the need of additional annotated data for each target language. LLOD enables us to leverage a breadth of existing multilingual resources and infer lexica for additional language pairs using implicit links between resources. We demonstrate in the reported experiments that this not only a benefit in terms of flexibility, but also leads to improved performance for our cross-lingual transfer learning approach in comparison to a medical lexicon directly applicable to the evaluated language pair.

In more technical detail, our approach is based on word embeddings and cross-lingual supervision via token-level lexica (supervised bilingual word embeddings). Thus, the training procedure and resulting models are considerably less complex than state-of-the-art cross-lingual zero-shot models, which are based on contextualized representations learnt via pre-training transformer-based language models on massive multilingual corpora. Consequently, we present evaluation results comparing our approach to a language-model-based classifier for the case of transfer from English to French for detection of HRQoL facets in posts from online health communities. We find that our models, when combined with a baseline approach that integrates machine translation and rule-based extraction algorithms, are strong contestants to cross-lingual transformers.

2. Related Work

Given our focus on exploring the factors of effectively applying LLOD resources to cross-lingual transfer learning for text classification, we build on supervised approaches for learning bilingual word representations which are able to incorporate existing seed lexica (cf. [5]), but do not require additional supervision or resources, e.g. parallel or aligned corpora as in early work on cross-lingual transfer [6]. In particular, we adopt workflows for using LLOD in cross-lingual transfer learning based on task-informed, bilingual word embeddings (adopted from bilingual sentiment embeddings [7]) presented in [8] and apply them to a different target language (Spanish vs. French), a much more varied task (HRQoL aspect detection vs. sentiment analysis) and different text genre (online health community posts vs. medical experts' interview transcripts).

As our research questions imply the availability of applicable lexica, unsupervised or weakly supervised approaches for inducing bilingual word embeddings [9,10,11] are only indirectly relevant to our work. However, we plan to compare against them in future work, especially given that claims of comparable or even superior performance of unsupervised methods (e.g., [12]) have been called into question [13,14], in particular when evaluated on actual downstream tasks instead of bilingual lexicon induction [15].

Since the introduction of the Transformer neural architecture and pre-training via language modelling objectives on massive corpora, cross-lingual representations derived from these models, e.g. multilingual versions of BERT [16] or XLM-R [17], became state-of-the-art on a large number of multilingual problems. This comes, however, with a noticeable added cost in comparison to bilingual word embeddings in terms of model complexity and computational resources, especially during training (cf. [18]). We explore this performance-complexity trade-off by comparing our models based on bilingual word embeddings against a zero-shot cross-lingual classifier based on XLM-R.

Using indirect connections between translation lexica to automatically construct a bilingual lexicon via a pivot language goes at least back to [19]. Lexicon induction techniques using LLOD, and Apertium RDF in particular, were explored in [20,21].

3. Language- and Task-informed Cross-lingual Transfer Learning

Our approach to language- and task-informed transfer learning (LTTL) relies on the framework described in our previous work [8]. Using this architecture based on bilingual word embeddings [7], task-informed bilingual embedding spaces can be learned for any task which can be framed as text classification. Following this idea, we apply LTTL to HRQoL concept detection in this paper.

For training a task-specific model LTTL requires 1) monolingual word embeddings in both the source and target language, 2) ground-truth annotations in the source language, and 3) a bilingual dictionary that maps tokens from the source language to their translations in the target language (see Section 4). Annotations in the target language are required for evaluation only.

During training (Figure 1), word embeddings are looked up for the tokens in each document in the source-language annotated corpus and averaged in order to yield document representations a_S. A projection matrix M_S is trained to map a_S to a task-specific vector z_s, which is then passed to a softmax layer to derive the predicted label. By minimizing the cross-entropy loss between the predicted and the annotated labels, M_S and the parameters of the softmax layer are learnt to produce better task-specific predictions. Simultaneously, for every pair in the bilingual dictionary, we look up their word embeddings in the respective monolingual embedding space and project them using M_S and M_T (a corresponding matrix in the target language), respectively. Both matrices are jointly optimized to minimize the Euclidean distance between the projected embeddings in a shared bilingual embedding space, so that the projections from the target language are as close as possible to the projections from the source language for which monolingual task-specific supervision is available.

When using a trained LTTL model to classify a target-language document (Figure 2), we apply the same steps as during training based on target-language embeddings (embedding lookup, averaging, projection, prediction using the softmax layer). The projection

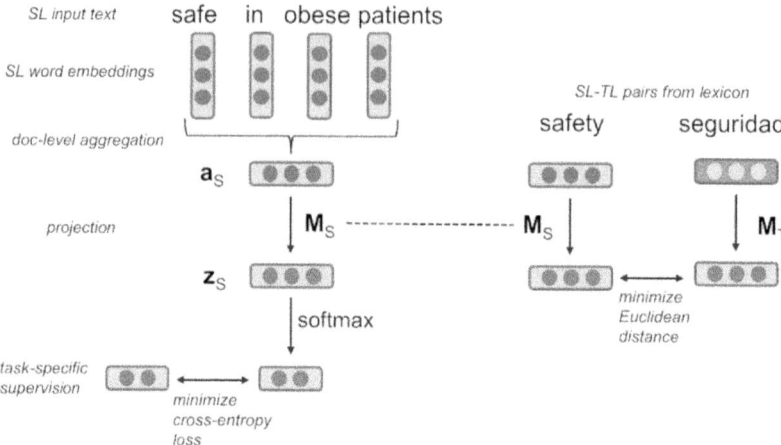

Figure 1. Training LTTL on a source-language (SL) annotated corpus and a source-language to target-language (TL) bilingual lexicon using TL and SL word embeddings to represent individual tokens

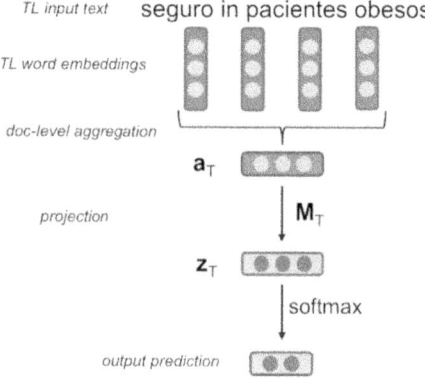

Figure 2. Predictions with LTTL on target-language (TL) text using TL word embeddings to represent individual tokens

step, however, is calculated using the matrix M_T which was optimized to project target-language embeddings close to the projections from the task-informed, source-language projection matrix M_S.

4. Language Resources

In this section we describe the relevant lexical resources used in LTTL. A detailed description of the LLOD pipeline used to generate these resources and the individual processing steps involved is presented in [8]. While our focus is on Apertium RDF as a bilingual lexicon in this paper, these workflows have the potential of growing the LLOD cloud over time both in terms of data volume and richness of available resources.

4.1. Bilingual Translation Dictionaries

The bilingual lexica used in our experiments contain word-level translation pairs from a source to a target language. Lexica vary in terms of vocabulary size, the type of knowledge provided, origin, and purpose. In our experiments, we selected lexica according to the criteria of domain- and task specificity. Accordingly, broad-coverage, open-domain and medical lexica were used as described below. We deduplicated entries in all lexica during pre-processing.

Apertium lexica[2] are very comprehensive open-domain, broad-coverage lexica. Originally, this resource was generated for an open-source machine translation platform [22]. Apertium lexica used in our work were converted into RDF using the FINTAN platform [23] and published as linked data. These lexica contain entries annotated as nouns, proper nouns, verbs, adjectives and adverbs.

MeSpEn Glossaries[3] are lexica specific to the biomedical domain. A total of 46 bilingual medical glossaries for various language pairs are available. The lexica were generated based on hand-crafted glossaries made by professional translators [24].

4.2. Cross-lingual Lexicon Induction

In some cases, bilingual lexica of interest for a given task or domain may not be available for a language pair of interest. In this case, translation pairs can be inferred via triangulation [19]. This approach consists of leveraging available lexical resources in the source language and a pivot language, i.e., a language which has correspondences to the source and target languages, as a means to create a mapping between both. More specifically, we generated a bilingual dictionary for the language pair English-French based on Apertium RDF using Spanish as pivot language as follows: For each entry that links a source language term t_S to its translation t_P in the pivot language, if there is an entry linking t_P to a target language term t_T, a translation from t_S to t_T can be inferred and stored in a newly created source-target lexicon. Subsequently, (i) all duplicate entries and (ii) entries with divergent part-of-speech categories[4] in t_S and t_T are removed from the resulting lexicon. This induction procedure yields an induced open-domain EN–FR lexicon comprising 15,703 entries; for comparison, the existing MeSpEn Glossary resource comprises 6,571 domain-specific EN–FR entries.

4.3. Monolingual Word Embeddings

In addition to the bilingual lexical resources described above, LTTL also requires monolingual word embeddings. In our experiments, we use publicly available word embed-

---

[2]https://github.com/acoli-repo/acoli-dicts/tree/master/stable/apertium/ apertium-rdf-2020-03-18
[3]https://doi.org/10.5281/zenodo.2205690
[4]This procedure relies on the PoS information that is integrated into Apertium 2.0 via mapping lexical entries to the LexInfo ontology [8].

Embeddings	Language	Type	Vocabulary Size	Vector Dimensions
google-news	English	open-domain	55,627	300
fr-wiki	French	open-domain	2,500,733	300

Table 1. Overview of monolingual embeddings used in our current experiments with the LTTL framework.

dings[5] pre-trained on different corpora. Table 1 describes the language, domain, vocabulary size and dimensionality of the used embeddings.

5. Data Sets

We use an English–French comparable corpus made up of anonymized posts from several openly accessible medical and health-related online fora to generate and/or annotate training and evaluation data sets for different HRQoL facets. The corpus contains extremely varied, uncontrolled language as the texts are mostly authored by patients and their relatives. This can be observed below for three representative examples from diverse QoL facets, with (a) denoting the original French texts and (b) their English machine-generated translations.

(1) **Sleep and rest** (SR)

> (a) *Cetrizirine c'est quoi les filles ? Depuis un certain temps je suis insomniaque ...tisane...chronodorm... mélisse...rien n'y fait*
>
> (b) What's Cetrizirine girls? I've been having insomnia for some time... herbal tea... chronodorm... lemon balm... nothing helps...

(2) **Activities of daily living** (DL)

> (a) *Actuellement en arrêt maladie du a mon cancer j'ai de la chimiothérapie a l'hôpital. Les écoles de ma commune ferme je suis incapable de m'occuper de mes enfants.*
>
> (b) Currently on hold disease from my cancer I have chemotherapy in the hospital. The schools in my commune are closed I am unable to take care of my children.

(3) **Body image and appearance** (BA)

> (a) *je ne veux pas forcément que ça se sache que je suis malade et avec perruque et maquillage je veux passer incognito lol ... car je suis qlq un qui manque bcp de confiance en soi.*
>
> (b) But I don't want him to shout it from the roof-tops at school or anything else because I don't necessarily want it to be known that I'm sick and with wigs and make-up I want to go incognito lol ... because I'm one who lacks a lot of self-confidence.

---

[5]Available from `https://drive.google.com/open?id=1GpyF2h0j8K5TKT7y7Aj00yPgpFc8pMNS` and `https://wikipedia2vec.github.io/wikipedia2vec/pretrained/`, respectively.

Quality of life dimensions	Facets within dimensions	Size of training set	
		positive	negative
Physical health	Energy and Fatigue (EF)	3000	3000
	Pain and discomfort (PD)	3000	3000
	Sleep and rest (SR)	707	689
Psychological health	Body image and appearance (BA)	1164	1139
	Negative feelings (NF)	1464	1428
	Positive feelings (PF)	3000	3000
	Thinking, learning, memory and concentration (TM)	380	379
Level of independence	Mobility (MB)	2112	2006
	Activities of daily living (DA)	842	830
	Work capacity (WO)	606	590
Social relations	Personal relationships (PR)	3000	3000
	Sexual activity (SA)	44	44
	Social support (SO)	834	813
Environment	Financial resources (FR	1488	1446
	Health and social care (HC)	1625	1577
	Home environment (HE)	751	745
	Participation in and opportunities for recreation and leisure (RL)	3000	3000
	Physical environment (PE)	3000	3000
	Transport (TR)	1567	1518

Table 2. Overview of QoL dimensions and contained facets with their training data size in terms of number of posts (facets in boldface are part of the manually annotated gold standard)

5.1. English training data

We generate annotation labels for the English data using a rule-based pattern matching engine from the in-house Semalytix technology stack. These rules, in addition to plain text matching, include regular expressions to capture morphological variation, part-of-speech tagging, dependency syntax or knowledge graph type constraints. This rule-based system allows for rapid generation of labeled training data for 19 HRQoL concepts that are in scope in this paper. Data set sizes vary per HRQoL concept depending on the available number of matches produced by the monolingual rules and are capped at 3,000 positive and negative examples per concept (6,000 in total). The resulting English data sets are randomly split into a training and development set (80/20). Table 2 provides an overview of all concepts and their respective data volume.

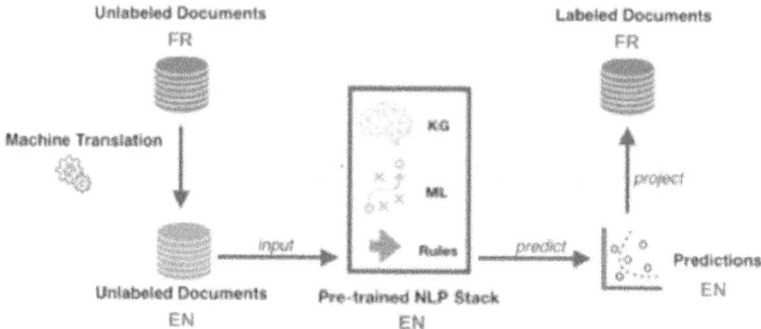

Figure 3. Label propagation from labeled source language (EN) to unlabeled target language (FR) documents.

5.2. French evaluation data (Silver Standard)

In light of the multitude of HRQoL concepts under investigation in this study, we rely on a heuristic label propagation procedure in order to create a large-scale evaluation corpus for validation purposes in the target language. To make use of the described monolingual rule system for texts that are not written in English, the target language texts are algorithmically translated into English via DeepL[6]. Thus, the rule engine can be run on the translated texts in the same way as on originally English ones. The resulting concept labels are then propagated back to the target-language documents. An illustration of this process is depicted in Figure 3.

However, it needs to be emphasized that the resulting target language labels were not manually checked for correctness. Hence, even though the underlying rule-based classifiers available for English are optimized for precision, the test collection resulting from this procedure must be considered a silver standard. Again, data set sizes vary depending on the available number of matches. They are capped at 100 positive and 100 negative examples per facet. The French target data sets are used for evaluation exclusively and thus are divided into a development and test set (50/50).

5.3. French evaluation data (Gold Standard)

In the interest of a thorough evaluation of concept detection performance in the target language for at least a subset of concepts, we selected one concept from each QoL domain (highlighted in bold face in Table 2) to create a hand-curated gold standard. These gold standard data sets consist of 100 positive and 100 negative texts samples per HRQoL facet which each were verified to be correct by manual annotation. As the French silver standard data, these data sets are also exclusively used for evaluation and evenly divided into a development and test set (50/50).

---

[6]https://www.deepl.com/pro?cta=header-pro/

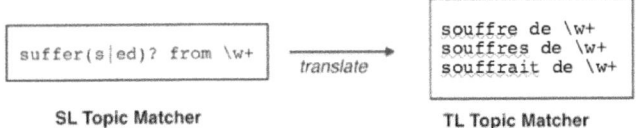

Figure 4. Illustration of translation procedure for Baseline 1.

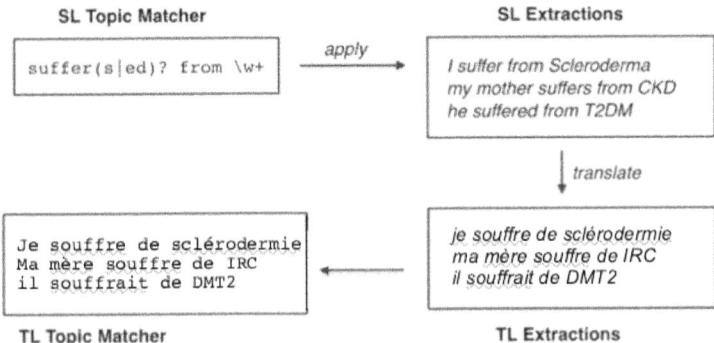

Figure 5. Illustration of translation procedure for Baseline 2.

6. Baseline Models based on Machine Translation and Rules

As comparison to our LTTL model, we generate two baseline models based on machine translation in combination with the previously described rule engine (cf. Section 5.1). As illustrated in Figure 4, our approach for Baseline 1 (BL1) is to first extract all rules used in the monolingual rule engine for English for each required concept in the source language (SL). These are then directly translated into the target language (TL) using the DeepL translation API[7]. The resulting TL rule sets can subsequently be used as rule-based extractors on the TL test set such that matching documents are classified as positive instances of the respective concept, others as negative ones.

Baseline 2 (BL2) is following a slightly different approach (cf. Figure 5). First the original monolingual rules for each concept are applied to the English training data. Then, all English phrases that match those patterns are extracted and translated into the target language. Subsequently, those extractions (which in comparison to Baseline 1 do not usually contain any regular expressions or other formal constraints) are then used as target language extraction rules and run on the TL test set, analogously to Baseline 1.

7. Evaluation

The experiments reported in this section address the problem of HRQoL concept detection from French online health communities. We simulate a real-world setting in which

---

[7]This includes a shallow post-processing step to remove broken rule syntax.

no labeled training examples are available in the target language. Therefore, we approach the task in a cross-lingual manner, transferring knowledge that is available in existing models or resources for English to French as target language. Our primary interest is in answering the following research questions:

1. How does cross-lingual concept detection performance via LTTL compare to state-of-the-art cross-lingual transformer architectures?
2. Focusing on the specific lexical resource needs of LTTL, what is the impact of a large, open-domain lexicon induced from Apertium RDF [25] via a pivot language vs. a smaller, biomedical, directly applicable lexicon [26]?
3. How does LTTL concept detection performance differ across HRQoL concepts, i.e., can our approach effectively be applied to a large number of different concepts?

7.1. Experiment 1: Gold Standard Evaluation

7.1.1. Settings.

In a first experiment, we evaluate LTTL against the gold standard described in Section 5.3. For comparison, we obtained results for both baselines BL1 and BL2 introduced in Section 6. Additionally, we explore the setting of combining the LTTL model with each baseline in a sequential way. This was done by first executing LTTL and subsequently feeding all data points (from both the positive and the negative samples) that had been classified as negative by the model into the respective baseline.

Furthermore, we challenge LTTL in another comparison against the state-of-the art cross-lingual XLM-R model [17]. It is a transformer-based multilingual masked neural language model that is pre-trained for cross-lingual NLP tasks. In our use case, the model is fine-tuned on the English task-specific data and then tested on French evaluation data where it performs zero-shot cross-lingual classification.

7.1.2. Results and Discussion.

Results for this experiment are shown in Table 3 in terms of precision, recall and F1 measure for the positive class. We observe that, for four among the five concepts under investigation, LTTL outperforms both baselines based on machine translation (BL1 and BL2). While both baselines show divergent patterns across concepts (favoring precision on some concepts, recall on others), they are largely complementary with LTTL: With *Positive Feelings* as an exception, the sequential combinations of LTTL with one of BL1 or BL2 yield a boost in classification performance over LTTL in isolation. Apparently, this blend of cross-lingual word embeddings with cross-lingual rule engineering constitutes an effective approach to the HRQoL concept detection problem. To some extent, this still holds in view of the performance of the neural state-of-the-art XLM-R model, which outperforms LTTL+BL1/2 in three out of five cases, but obtains lower results for *Recreation and Leisure* and *Positive Feelings*.

The excellent generalization properties of XLM-R notwithstanding, these results suggest that cross-lingual HRQoL concept detection does not necessarily require the heavy machinery of cross-lingual transformer models in all facets of interest. We argue that, given the much higher model complexity of cross-lingual transformers, architectures based on bilingual word embeddings such as LTTL may pose a practical compro-

Model	Lexicon	WO			SA			SR			RL			PF		
		Pre	Rec	F1	Pre	Rec	F1	Pre	Rec	F1	Pre	Rec	F1	Pre	Rec	F1
LTTL	ES PoS	0.60	0.74	0.66	0.53	0.92	0.67	0.63	0.92	0.75	0.71	0.78	0.74	0.65	0.74	**0.69**
	MedGl	0.59	0.78	0.67	0.49	0.81	0.61	0.70	0.84	0.76	0.73	0.44	0.55	0.75	0.12	0.21
LTTL +BL1	ES PoS	0.64	0.82	0.72	0.56	0.99	0.71	0.64	0.94	0.76	0.50	1.00	0.67	0.51	0.81	0.63
	MedGl	0.59	0.81	0.68	0.53	0.95	0.68	0.69	0.90	0.78	0.50	1.00	0.67	0.50	0.79	0.62
LTTL +BL2	ES PoS	0.65	0.84	0.73	0.56	0.99	0.71	0.64	0.95	0.76	0.71	0.87	0.78	0.68	0.23	0.34
	MedGl	0.60	0.83	0.70	0.53	0.93	0.67	0.69	0.91	0.78	0.73	0.69	0.71	0.69	0.20	0.31
Baseline 1		1.00	0.08	0.15	1.00	0.84	**0.92**	0.97	0.37	0.54	0.50	0.98	0.66	0.50	0.79	0.62
Baseline 2		1.00	0.15	0.26	1.00	0.82	0.90	0.96	0.63	0.76	0.89	0.41	0.56	0.69	0.20	0.31
XLM-R		0.97	0.68	**0.80**	0.76	0.92	0.83	0.98	0.80	**0.88**	0.80	0.74	**0.77**	0.74	0.58	0.65

Table 3. Results for EN-FR concept transfer via both baseline models and LTTL, separately and in sequential combination for all 5 gold standard data sets. Lexicons refer to the ES single pivot version including PoS information (ES PoS) and the MeSpEn medical glossary (MedGl). Results are reported in terms of precision, recall and F1 measure for the positive class. Best F1 performance per concept is highlighted in bold. Concept abbreviations are in line with Table 2.

mise in many application scenarios. Moreover, we noted in additional experiments not reported here that when using smaller data sets (comparable to the one available for *Sexual Activity*), the margin between LTTL and XLM-R results becomes much narrower, which might suggest that LLOD-based bilingual word embeddings can cope better with smaller sets of training data. This conjecture requires deeper investigation in future work.

7.2. Experiment 2: Evaluation against Large-scale Silver Standard

7.2.1. Settings.

In a second experiment, we investigate cross-lingual classification performance for all 19 HRQoL concepts summarized in Table 2. We run individual text classification models that are instantiated from LTTL on each of these concepts and evaluate them against the silver standard presented in Section 5.3. Besides enabling a large-scale comparison across this multitude of concepts, this experiment is mainly designed to explore the resource requirements of LLOD-based cross-lingual transfer learning: Given that Apertium RDF does not include English–French translations, we induced a bilingual lexicon via the pivot language Spanish. Here, we want to assess the prospects of LLOD-based lexicon induction relative to a readily existing English-French bilingual medical lexicon MeSpEn Glossaries.

7.2.2. Results and Discussion.

Table 4 shows the results of this experiment in terms of F1 measure for the positive class. While LTTL surpasses both baselines for a substantially large number of concepts, only in a minority of cases (4 out of 19) it is conversely outperformed by one of them, with BL1 and BL2 not showing a clear trend to one outperforming the other in the majority of cases. Being designed as precision-oriented extraction rules for English documents,

Facet	BL 1	BL 2	LTTL	LTTL+BL1	LTTL+BL2	LTTL	LTTL+BL1	LTTL+BL2
				ES PoS			MedGl	
DA	0.56	0.56	0.69	**0.75**	0.73	0.62	0.73	0.72
BA	0.67	0.58	0.68	0.68	0.68	**0.70**	**0.70**	**0.70**
EF	0.65	**0.83**	0.35	0.68	*0.83*	0.60	0.68	0.77
FR	0.56	0.67	0.67	0.67	0.66	0.73	**0.75**	0.67
HC	0.55	0.23	0.67	0.67	0.67	**0.71**	0.70	0.70
HE	0.52	0.34	0.71	**0.74**	0.71	0.20	0.55	0.43
MB	0.55	0.49	0.66	**0.74**	0.71	0.67	0.67	0.67
NF	0.20	0.29	0.52	0.56	0.60	0.67	0.66	**0.68**
PD	0.49	0.49	0.57	**0.74**	**0.74**	0.65	0.66	0.66
PR	0.24	**0.82**	0.67	0.67	0.67	0.63	0.67	0.77
PE	0.50	0.52	0.71	**0.73**	**0.73**	0.43	0.71	0.72
PF	0.65	0.43	0.49	**0.67**	**0.67**	0.00	0.65	0.43
RL	0.66	0.56	0.73	0.67	**0.74**	0.67	0.66	0.69
SA	**0.86**	0.83	0.45	0.83	0.81	0.62	0.77	0.76
SR	0.43	0.71	0.72	0.72	**0.79**	0.63	0.69	0.75
SO	0.04	0.67	**0.78**	0.77	0.67	0.58	0.52	0.67
TM	0.41	0.36	0.58	0.65	0.63	**0.69**	0.68	0.68
TR	0.52	0.48	**0.73**	0.71	0.71	0.36	0.57	0.54
WO	0.17	0.31	0.67	0.69	0.70	**0.77**	0.76	0.76

Table 4. Results for EN–FR concept transfer evaluated on 19 silver standard QoL facets for both baseline models and LTTL separately and in sequential combination, denoted by F1-measure for the positive class. Abbreviations stem from Table 2. Lexicons refer to the ES single pivot version including PoS information (ES PoS) and the MeSpEn medical glossary (MedGl). Bold results highlight best performance for a given concept.

most of the baselines still favour precision after being transferred to French: For roughly 90% of the concepts at least one of the baselines shows a noticeably better precision than LTTL. However, apart from a small number of cases, LTTL benefits from a much higher recall, which results in a better overall performance in terms of F1.

Therefore, the strong degree of complementarity between LTTL and BL1/2 observed in Experiment 1 is confirmed in this large-scale setting as well: For the majority of concepts the performance of the LTTL+Baselines combination exceeds LTTL and is among the best configurations. This is the case for about 70% of the tasks, while in 90-95% of them LTTL+BL1/2 performs better or at least equally well as LTTL. Winning results are obtained by the combined models by a sometimes considerable margin compared to LTTL.

Regarding the different lexicon configurations employed, it becomes evident that the automatically created open-domain lexicon which was induced leveraging LLOD information from Apertium RDF (denoted as ES-PoS in the table) performs better than the directly available medical domain-specific lexicon (denoted as MedGl in the table) in 12 out of 19 concepts. This shows that LLOD-based lexicon induction is a useful flexible process that could potentially be refined further in future work in order to boost performance even more.

8. Summary and Conclusions

We presented LTTL as a language- and task-informed framework for cross-lingual transfer learning. LTTL can be flexibly used in order to induce bilingual task-specific word embeddings as lexical representations for NLP models that are needed for multilingual text classification tasks. Being embedded into an LLOD exploitation pipeline, LTTL is flexibly applicable to different languages and for various tasks, which we demonstrated in this paper for the task of detecting HRQoL concepts from French online health communities.

In the experiments reported, we showed that it can be employed even when a bilingual lexicon for a particular language pair is not readily available, thanks to LLOD-driven lexicon induction via one or more pivot languages. Furthermore, the LTTL model can effectively be combined sequentially with rule-based concepts detectors, resulting in a noticeable increase of classification performance, all while making use of openly available LLOD resources. Comparing LTTL against the state-of-the-art cross-lingual neural language model XLM-R, we find that the HRQoL concept detection task does not necessarily lean itself against the high complexity of transformer-based architectures. In fact, our results suggest that architectures based on bilingual word embeddings such as LTTL may pose a practical compromise for the task at hand in many real-world application contexts. In future work, we plan to exploit the richness of Apertium RDF and other existing LLOD lexical resources in large-scale experiments on lexicon induction. Our goal is to further enhance bilingual dictionaries via multiple pivot languages, with the potential goal of bringing the performance of LTTL even closer to cross-lingual transformers.

Acknowledgments

This work was funded by the Prêt-à-LLOD project within the European Union's Horizon 2020 research and innovation programme under grant agreement no. 825182.

References

[1] Declerck T, McCrae JP, Hartung M, Gracia J, Chiarcos C, Montiel-Ponsoda E, et al. Recent Developments for the Linguistic Linked Open Data Infrastructure. In: Proc. of LREC; 2020. p. 5660-7.
[2] McDonald L, Malcolm B, Ramagopalan S, Syrad H. Real-world Data and the Patient Perspective: the PROmise of Social Media? BMC Medicine. 2019;17.

[3]   Bullinger M, Quitmann J. Quality of life as patient-reported outcomes: principles of assessment. Dialogues in Clinical Neuroscience. 2014 Jun;16(2):137-45.

[4]   World Health Organization. WHOQOL: Measuring Quality of Life; 1997. Available from: `https://apps.who.int/iris/handle/10665/63482`.

[5]   Søgaard A, Vulić I, Ruder S, Faruqui M. Cross-Lingual Word Embeddings. Morgan & Claypool; 2019.

[6]   Yarowsky D, Ngai G, Wicentowski R. Inducing Multilingual Text Analysis Tools via Robust Projection across Aligned Corpora. In: Proc. of HLT; 2001. .

[7]   Barnes J, Klinger R, Schulte im Walde S. Bilingual Sentiment Embeddings: Joint Projection of Sentiment Across Languages. In: Proc. of ACL; 2018. p. 2483-93.

[8]   Gracia J, Fäth C, Hartung M, Ionov M, Bosque-Gil J, Veríssimo S, et al. Leveraging Linguistic Linked Data for Cross-Lingual Model Transfer in the Pharmaceutical Domain. In: The Semantic Web – ISWC 2020. Cham: Springer; 2020. .

[9]   Conneau A, Lample G, Ranzato M, Denoyer L, Jégou H. Word Translation Without Parallel Data. arXiv:171004087 [cs]. 2017. Available from: `http://arxiv.org/abs/1710.04087`.

[10] Chen X, Cardie C. Unsupervised Multilingual Word Embeddings. In: Proc. of EMNLP; 2018. p. 261-70.

[11] Ruder S, Søgaard A, Vulić I. Unsupervised Cross-Lingual Representation Learning. In: Proc. of ACL; 2019. p. 31-8.

[12] Feng Y, Wan X. Learning Bilingual Sentiment-Specific Word Embeddings without Cross-lingual Supervision. In: Proc. of NAACL:HLT; 2019. p. 420-9.

[13] Vulić I, Glavaš G, Reichart R, Korhonen A. Do We Really Need Fully Unsupervised Cross-Lingual Embeddings? In: Proc. of EMNLP-IJCNLP; 2019. p. 4407-18.

[14] Artetxe M, Ruder S, Yogatama D, Labaka G, Agirre E. A Call for More Rigor in Unsupervised Cross-lingual Learning. In: Proc. of ACL; 2020. p. 7375-88.

[15] Glavaš G, Litschko R, Ruder S, Vulić I. How to (Properly) Evaluate Cross-Lingual Word Embeddings: On Strong Baselines, Comparative Analyses, and Some Misconceptions. In: Proc. of ACL; 2019. p. 710-21.

[16] Karthikeyan K, Wang Z, Mayhew S, Roth D. Cross-Lingual Ability of Multilingual BERT: An Empirical Study; 2020. Available from: `https://arxiv.org/abs/1912.07840`.

[17] Conneau A, Khandelwal K, Goyal N, Chaudhary V, Wenzek G, Guzmán F, et al. Unsupervised Cross-lingual Representation Learning at Scale. In: Proc. of ACL; 2020. p. 8440-51.

[18] Strubell E, Ganesh A, McCallum A. Energy and Policy Considerations for Deep Learning in NLP. In: Proceedings of the 57th Annual Meeting of the Association for Computational Linguistics. Florence, Italy: Association for Computational Linguistics; 2019. p. 3645-50.

[19] Tanaka K, Umemura K. Construction of a bilingual dictionary intermediated by a third language. In: Proc. of COLING; 1994. p. 297-303.

[20] Villegas M, Melero M, Bel N, Gracia J. Leveraging RDF Graphs for Crossing Multiple Bilingual Dictionaries. In: Proc. of LREC; 2016. p. 868-76.

[21] Gracia J, Kabashi B, Kernerman I, editors. Proceedings of TIAD-2019 Shared Task – Translation Inference Across Dictionaries. vol. 2493. CEUR-WS.org; 2019.

[22] Forcada ML, Ginestí-Rosell M, Nordfalk J, O'Regan J, Ortiz-Rojas S, Pérez-Ortiz JA, et al. Apertium: a free/open-source platform for rule-based machine translation. Machine Translation. 2011;25(2):127-44.

[23] Fäth C, Chiarcos C, Ebbrecht B, Ionov M. Fintan - Flexible, Integrated Transformation and Annotation eNgineering. In: Proc. of LREC; 2020. p. 7212-21.

[24] Marimon M, Krallinger M. MeSpEn_Glossaries. Zenodo; 2018.

[25] Gracia J, Villegas M, Gómez-Pérez A, Bel N. The Apertium Bilingual Dictionaries on the Web of Data. Semantic Web. 2018;9(2):231-40.

[26] Villegas M, Intxaurrondo A, Gonzalez-Agirre A, Marimón M, Krallinger M. The MeSpEN Resource for English-Spanish Medical Machine Translation and Terminologies: Census of Parallel Corpora, Glossaries and Term Translations. In: Workshop on Multilingual Biomedical Text Processing; 2018. .

Further with Knowledge Graphs. M. Alam et al. (Eds.)
AKA Verlag and IOS Press, 2021
© *2021 Akademische Verlagsgesellschaft AKA GmbH, Berlin*

doi:10.3233/SSW210038

Knowledge Graph Question Answering Using Graph-Pattern Isomorphism

Daniel VOLLMERS [a] Rricha JALOTA [a] Diego MOUSSALLEM [a,d]
Hardik TOPIWALA [a] Axel-Cyrille NGONGA NGOMO [a] and Ricardo USBECK [b,c]

[a] *Data Science Group, Paderborn University, Germany*
[b] *Fraunhofer IAIS, Dresden, Germany*
[c] *Universität Hamburg, Germany*
[d] *Globo, Rio de Janeiro, Brazil*

Abstract. Knowledge Graph Question Answering (KGQA) systems are often based on machine learning algorithms, requiring thousands of question-answer pairs as training examples or natural language processing pipelines that need module fine-tuning. In this paper, we present a novel QA approach, dubbed TeBaQA. Our approach learns to answer questions based on graph isomorphisms from basic graph patterns of SPARQL queries. Learning basic graph patterns is efficient due to the small number of possible patterns. This novel paradigm reduces the amount of training data necessary to achieve state-of-the-art performance. TeBaQA also speeds up the domain adaption process by transforming the QA system development task into a much smaller and easier data compilation task. In our evaluation, TeBaQA achieves state-of-the-art performance on QALD-8 and delivers comparable results on QALD-9 and LC-QuAD v1. Additionally, we performed a fine-grained evaluation on complex queries that deal with aggregation and superlative questions as well as an ablation study, highlighting future research challenges.

Keywords. Question Answering, Basic Graph Pattern, Isomorphism, QALD

1. Introduction

The goal of most Knowledge Graph (KG) Question Answering (QA) systems is to map natural language questions to corresponding SPARQL queries. This process is known as semantic parsing [5] and can be implemented in various ways. A common approach is to utilize query templates (alias graph patterns) with placeholders for relations and entities. The placeholders are then filled with entities and relations extracted from a given natural language question [1,16,26] to generate a SPARQL query, which is finally executed. Semantic parsing assumes that a template can be constructed or chosen to represent a natural language question's internal structure. Thus, the KGQA task can be reduced to finding a matching template and filling it with entities and relations extracted from the question.

The performance of KGQA systems based on this approach depends heavily on the implemented query templates, which depend on the question's complexity and the KG's topology. Consequently, costly hand-crafted templates designed for a particular KG cannot be easily adapted to a new domain.

In this work, we present a novel KGQA engine, dubbed TeBaQA. TeBaQA alleviates manual template generation's effort by implementing an approach that learns templates from existing KGQA benchmarks. We rely on learning of templates based on isomorphic basic graph patterns.

The goal of TeBaQA is to employ machine learning and feature engineering to learn to classify natural language questions into isomorphic basic graph pattern classes. At execution time, TeBaQA uses this classification to map a question to a basic graph pattern, i.e., a template, which it can fill and augment with semantic information to create the correct SPARQL query.

TeBaQA achieves state-of-the-art performance partially without any manual effort. In contrast to existing solutions, TeBaQA can be easily ported to a new domain using only benchmark datasets, partially proven by our evaluation over different KGs and train-test-sets. We use a best-effort to work with the data at hand instead of either (i) requiring a resource-intensive dataset creation and annotation process to train deep neural networks or (ii) to hand-craft mapping rules for a particular domain. Our contributions can be summarized as follows:

- We present TeBaQA, a QA engine that learns templates from benchmarks based on isomorphic basic graph patterns.
- We describe a greedy yet effective ranking approach for query templates, aiming to detect the best matching template for a given input query.
- We evaluate TeBaQA on several standard KGQA benchmark datasets and unveil choke points and future research directions.

The code is available at `https://github.com/dice-group/TeBaQA` and a demo of TeBaQA over encyclopedic data can be found at `https://tebaqa.demos.dice-research.org/`. We also provide an online appendix which contains more details about our algorithms and their evaluations at `https://github.com/dice-group/TeBaQA/blob/master/TeBaQA_appendix.pdf`.

2. Related Work

The domain of Knowledge Graph Question Answering has gained traction over the last few years. There has been a shift from simple rule-based systems to systems with more complex architectures that can answer questions with varying degrees of complexity. In this section, we provide an overview of the recent work. We begin with approaches that took part in QALD challenge series [29,28,27].

gAnswer2 [35] addresses the translation of natural language to SPARQL as a sub-graph matching problem. Following the rule-based paradigm, QAnswer [9] utilizes the semantics embedded in the underlying KG (DBpedia and Wikidata) and employs a combinatorial approach to create SPARQL queries from natural language questions. QAnswer overgenerates possible SPARQL queries and has to learn the correct SPARQL query ranking from large training datasets.

Second, we introduce approaches that rely on templates to answer natural questions over knowledge bases. Hao et al. [15] introduced a pattern-revising QA system for answering simple questions. It relies on pattern extraction and joint fact selection, enhanced by relation detection, for ranking the candidate subject-relation pairs. NEQA [1] is a template-based KBQA system like TeBaQA, which uses a continuous learning paradigm to answer questions from unseen domains. Apart from using a similarity-based approach for template-matching, it relies on user feedback to improve over time. QUINT [2] also suggests a template learning system that can perform on compositional questions by learning sub-templates. KBQA [7] extracted 27 million templates for 2782 intents and their mappings to KG relations from a QA corpora (Yahoo! Answers). The way these templates are generated and employed differs from that of TeBaQA. NEQA relies on active learning on sub-parts and thereby, possibly misses the semantic connection between question parts. KBQA learns many templates and can hence fail to generalize well to other domains or KB structures.

In 2019, Zheng et al. [34] use structural query pattern, a coarse granular version of SPARQL basic graph patterns which they later augment with different query forms and thus can generate also SPARQL query modifiers. The closest work to ours is by Athreya et al. [3] based on a tree-based RNN to learn different templates on LC-QuAD v1 which the authors directly derive from the LC-QuAD v1 inherent SPARQL templates and thus cannot generalize to other KGs or datasets. CONQUEST [4] is an enterprise KGQA system which also assumes the SPARQL templates are given. It then matches the questions and templates by vectorizing both and training one classifier, namely Gaussian Naïve Bayes.

QAMP [31] is an unsupervised message passing system using a similarly simple approach to information extraction as TeBaQA. QAMP outperforms QAnswer on LC-QuAD v1. Recently, Kapanipathi et al. [17] present a system, dubbed NSQA, which is in pre-print. NSQA is based on a combination of semantic parsing and reasoning. Their modular approach outperforms gAnswer and QAnswer on QALD-9 as well as QAnswer and QAMP on LC-QuAD V1. In contrast to seminal semantic parsing work, e.g., by Berant et al. [5], we assume relatively small training data; thus, learning a generalization via semantic building blocks will not work and consequently learn the whole template on purpose.

Third, there are also other QA approaches which work with neural networks relying on large, templated datasets such as sequence-to-sequence models [24,33]. However, we do not focus on this research direction in this work. We refer the interested reader to extensive surveys and overview papers such as [6,10,16].

3. Approach

TeBaQA is based on isomorphic graph patterns, which can be extracted across different SPARQL queries and hence be used as templates for our KGQA approach. Figure 1 provides an overview of TeBaQA's architecture and its five main stages:

First, all questions run through a **Preprocessing** stage to remove semantically irrelevant words and create a set of meaningful n-grams. The **Graph-Isomorphism Detection and Template Classification** phase uses the training sets to train a classifier based on a natural language question and a SPARQL query by analyzing the basic graph pattern for graph isomorphisms. The main idea is that structurally identical SPARQL queries represent syntactically similar questions. At runtime, a question is classified into a ranked list of SPARQL templates. While **Information Extraction**, TeBaQA extracts all critical information such as entities, relations and classes from the question and determines the answer type based on a KG-agnostic set of indexes. In the **Query Building** phase, the extracted information are inserted into the top templats, the SPARQL query type is determined, and query modifiers are added. The resulting SPARQL queries are executed, and their answers are compared with the expected answer type. The subsequent **Ranking** is based on a combination of all information, the natural language question and the returned answers.

In the following, we present each of these steps in more detail. We use DBpedia [18] as reference KG for the sake of simplicity in our description.

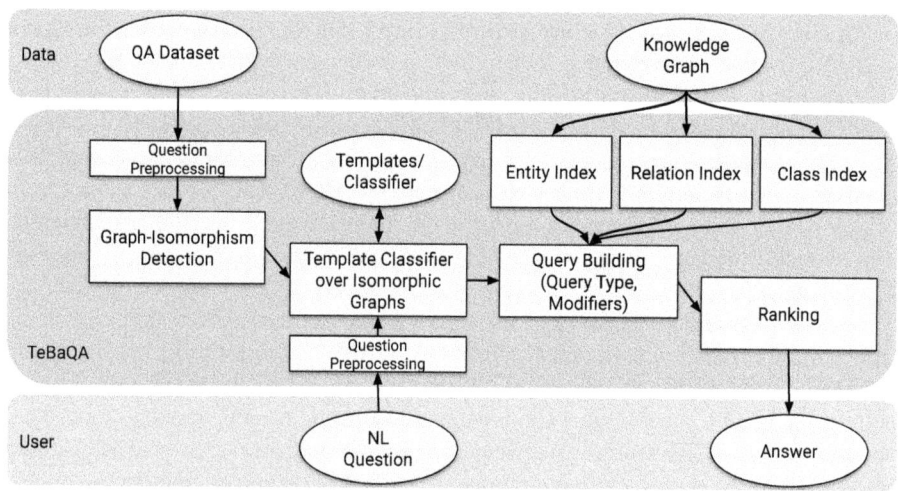

Figure 1. TeBaQA architecture on the running example.

3.1. Question Preprocessing

There are often words that do not contribute any information to the answer to natural language questions. Thus, we distinguish semantically relevant and irrelevant n-grams. Irrelevant n-grams can lead to errors that could propagate through the architecture. An example of this is the entity `dbr:The_The`[1]. If the word *The* were to be wrongly associated with this entity every time *the* occurs in a question, the system's performance would decrease severely. However, irrelevant words are sometimes part of entities, e.g., `dbr:The_Two_Towers`, so we cannot always filter these words. For this reason, we combine up to six neighboring words from the question to n-grams and remove all n-grams that contain stop words only. To identify irrelevant words, we provide a stop word list that contains the most common words of a particular language that are highly unlikely to add semantic value to the sentence. Additionally, TeBaQA distinguishes relevant and irrelevant n-grams using part-of-speech (POS) tags. Only n-grams beginning with JJ, NN or VB POS-tags are considered as relevant. After this preprocessing step, TeBaQA maps the remaining n-grams to entities from DBpedia in the information extraction step.

---

[1]`dbr:` is a prefix which stands for `http://dbpedia.org/resource/`

3.2. Graph-Isomorphism Detection and Template Classification

TeBaQA classifies a question to determine each isomorphic basic graph pattern (BGP). Since SPARQL is a graph-based query language [21], the structural equality of two SPARQL queries can be determined using an isomorphism. At runtime, TeBaQA can classify incoming questions to find the correct query templates, in which later semantic information can be inserted at runtime.

3.2.1. SPARQL BGP Isomorphism to Create Template Classes:

Using the training datasets, TeBaQA generates one basic graph pattern for each given question and its corresponding SPARQL query, see Figure 2. Subsequently, all *isomorphic* SPARQL queries are grouped into the same class. Now, each class contains semantically different natural language questions but structurally similar SPARQL queries.

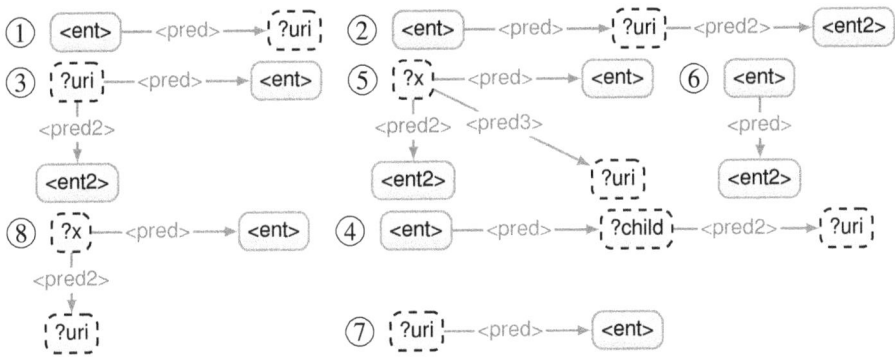

Figure 2. All basic graph patterns used as classes for QALD-8 and QALD-9 which later become templates. Note, the depicted templates contain more than five examples in the training dataset. Our running example, "Who was the doctoral advisor of Albert Einstein?" belongs to template (1).

Theorem 1 (Isomorphism of labeled graphs) *Two labeled graphs are isomorphic when a 1:1 relationship and surjective function is present between the nodes of the graphs, wherein the node labels, edge labels, and neighborhood relationships are preserved by the mapping [13].*

3.2.2. Question Features and Classification

Next, TeBaQA trains a classifier that uses all questions of an isomorphism class as input to calculate features for this class. A feature vector holds all the information required to make a reliable statement about which question belongs to which class. The features can be seen in Table 1.

The features can be divided into semantic and syntactic features. *QuestionWord, EntityPerson* and *QueryResourceType* form the group of semantic features and represent particular content aspects of the question, e.g., persons or specific topics that are mentioned in the question. All other features describe the structure of the question.

Note, other features were investigated, which did not improve the model's recognition rate. We report these features to aid future research in this area: 1) Cultural Categories: Mainly included music and movies, e.g., *Who is the singer on the album The*

Table 1. Features to map a question to an isomorphic basic graph pattern.

Feature	Type	Description
QuestionWord	Nominal	Adds the question word (e.g. Who, What, Give) as a feature.
EntityPerson	Boolean	Checks the named entity tags of the sentence to see if any persons are mentioned in it.
NumberOfToken	Numeric	Stores the number of tokens separated by spaces excluding punctuation.
QueryResourceType	Nominal	Categorizes the question based on a list of subject areas, e.g., film, music, book or city.
Noun	Numeric	Aggregates the number of nouns.
Number	Numeric	Indicates how often numbers occur in the question.
Verb	Numeric	Aggregates the number of verbs.
Adjective	Numeric	Aggregates the number of adjectives.
Comperative	Boolean	Indicates whether comparative adjectives or adverbs are included in the sentence.
TripleCandidates	Numerical	Estimates how many SPARQL triples are needed to answer the question based on the number of verbs, adjectives, and related nouns.

Dark Side of the Moon? and 2) Geographical entities: Questions in which countries or cities occur, as well as where questions, e.g., *In which country is Mecca located?*

Using features above, it is possible to represent the question *Who was the doctoral advisor of Albert Einstein?* with the following vector:

```
<Who, Person ,8 , dbo : Person ,1 ,0 ,1 ,0 , NoComperative ,1 >
```

TeBaQA trains a statistical classifier using the described features extracted from the input question and the isomorphic basic graph patterns as class labels. A feature vector's target class can be determined by generating the basic graph pattern for the corresponding SPARQL query and assigning the class, which represents this pattern. An evaluation can be found in Section 4.2.

3.3. Information Extraction

TeBaQA identifies entities, classes, and relations to fill the placeholders of a particular SPARQL template. Since questions are shorter than usual texts, semantic entity linking tools such as DBpedia Spotlight [8] or MAG [20,19] do not perform correctly due to the lack of semantic context information. For example, in *Who was the doctoral advisor of Albert Einstein?*, the word *Einstein* has to be linked to `dbr:Albert_Einstein` and not to any other person with that name. For this reason, we apply a KB-agnostic search index-based approach to identify entity, relation and class candidates. TeBaQA uses three indexes, which are created before runtime.

3.3.1. Entity Index

The entity index contains all entities from the target knowledge graph. To map an n-gram from the preprocessing step to an entity, TeBaQA queries against the index's label field. The index contains information about entities, relations and classes connected to the entity at hand.

3.3.2. Relation Index and Class Index

These two indexes contain all OWL classes and relations from a KG. The indexes are used to map n-grams to relations and classes of the ontologies of the KB.TeBaQA additionally indexes hypernyms and synonyms for all relations and classes.[2]

Consider the question *Who was the doctoral mentor of Einstein?*. DBpedia contains only the relation `dbo:doctoralAdvisor`[3] and not `dbp:mentor`[4]. Through the synonym *advisor* of *mentor*, the relation `dbo:doctoralAdvisor` can be determined. This example highlights the lexical and semantic gap between natural language and knowledge graphs.

3.3.3. Disambiguation

By querying the indexes for an n-gram, we get candidates for entities, relations and classes, whose labels contain all tokens of the n-gram. Since a candidate's label may contain more tokens than the n-gram, we apply a Levenshtein-distance filter of 0.8 on the candidates. All remaining candidates are used to fill a given template.

3.4. Query Building

3.4.1. Template Filling

For filling the templates, we facilitate the information about connected entities and connected relations for the found entities from the entity-index. For the triples in a template, there are two cases:

1.) The triple contains one placeholder for an entity and one placeholder for a relation. In this case, we resort to only the connected relation information from the entity index. An entity candidate e and a relation candidate p are combined to a triple $< e, p, ?v >$ or $< ?v, p, e >$ if the set of connected relations $S(e)$ of the entity e contains p and if the connected n-grams do not contain each other.

2.) The triple contains only one placeholder for a relation p'. This case only occurs when at least one triple in the template matches case 1. We can utilize these triples to generate matching triples for the given triple. Thus, we query the entity index and search for a set of entities $S(e')$ connected with the entity e by the relation p. All connected relations from the entities in $S(e')$ in the set of relation candidates and whose n-grams do not cover the n-grams of e and p are candidates for p'.

Each candidate SPARQL query is checked for consistency with the ontology. In general, there are query patterns that do not contain variables. This case only occurs in ask queries like *Did Socrates influence Aristotle?*. We ignore this case to keep simplicity and aware of the performance impact. To summarize, TeBaQA creates several candidate SPARQL queries per template and thus per question.

---

[2]The dictionary can be found at `https://github.com/dice-group/NLIWOD/tree/master/qa.annotation/src/main/resources` which was previously used by [23]
[3]`dbo:` stands for `http://dbpedia.org/ontology/`
[4]`dbp:` stands for `http://dbpedia.org/property/`

3.4.2. Query Modifiers and Query Types

To translate a question into a semantically equivalent SPARQL query, it is often not enough to recognize the entities, relations or classes in the question and insert them into a SPARQL query. For example, the question *How many children did Benjamin Franklin have?* asks for the number of children and not the concrete list. Thus, we apply a rule-based look-up to add query modifiers and choose a query type. The supported modifiers are $COUNT$, if the question contains keywords like *How many or How much*, $Filter(?x < ?y)$, if we identify comparatives and $ORDER BY [ASC(?x) | DESC(?x)] LIMIT 1$, if the question contains superlatives. Additionally, we support ASK-type questions, if keywords like *Is* or *Are* are identified.

Note, the templates and their respective basic graph pattern neither contain information about the query type nor information about query modifiers. Thus, TeBaQA generates one SPARQL query per candidate SPARQL query for each cross-product of query type and modifier that is recognized. The outcome is a list of executable queries for each input question.

3.5. Ranking

Since the *conciseness* of an answer plays a decisive role in QA in contrast to full-text search engines, only the answer that corresponds best to the user's intention should be returned. Thus, all generated SPARQL queries and their corresponding answers are ranked. This ranking is carried out in two steps. First, we filter by 1) the expected answer type of the question in comparison to the actual answer type of the query and by 2) the cardinality of the result set. Second, TeBaQA ranks the quality of the remaining SPARQL queries.

3.5.1. Answer Type and Cardinality Check:

For certain types of answer sets, only those that match the question's expected answer type are considered for the next ranking step. We empirically analyzed the benchmark datasets and derived a rule-based system for the most common expected answer type and their distinguishing features.

- Temporal questions usually begin with the question word *When*, e.g., *When was the Battle of Gettysburg?*. TeBaQA expects a date as the answer type.
- Decision questions mostly start with a form of *Be, Do* or *Have*. The possible answer type is boolean.
- Questions that begin with *How much* or *How many* can be answered with numbers. This also includes questions that begin with a combination of the question word *How* and a subsequent adjective such as *How large is the Empire State Building?*

If none of the above rules apply to a question, the result set's cardinality is checked. There are two cases: First, when several answers are needed to answer a question fully. Consider *Which ingredients do I need for carrot cake?*, if only one answer is found for this question, it can be assumed that it is either wrong or incomplete. Second, when there is only one answer to a question, e.g., *In which UK city are the headquarters of the MI6?*, an answer consisting of several entities would not be correct.

To recognize to which query type (ASK or SELECT) a question belongs, the first noun or the first compound noun after the question word is checked. If they occur in the singular form, a single answer is needed to answer the question. For the above question *In which UK city are the headquarters of the MI6?*, the compound noun would be *UK city*. Since both words occur in the singular, it is assumed that only a single answer is required. If the first noun or group of nouns occurs in the plural, this indicates that the question requires multiple answers. In the question *Which ingredients do I need for carrot cake?* the decisive word *ingredients* is in the plural.

However, the answer type of question may not be recognized correctly. For instance, if the question is grammatically correct but words whose singular form is identical to the plural form exist, such as *news*, we cannot determine the correct answer type. These issues will be tackled in future research.

Once the type of question and answer has been determined, all the answers whose type or cardinality does not match the question will be discarded.

3.5.2. Quality Ranking:

For the remaining SPARQL queries, TeBaQA calculates a *rating* based on the sum of the individual scores of the bindings *B* and the input question *phrase*. A binding *B* is the mapping of entities, relations and classes to placeholders contained in one SPARQL query *q*. To compute the relatedness factor *r*, the following factors are taken into account:

- **Annotation Density**: The annotation density measures that the more words from the sentence are linked to an entity, class or relation, the more likely it is that it corresponds to the intention of the user. For the question *What is the alma mater of the chancellor of Germany Angela Merkel?* one candidate query may apply the binding `dbr:Angela`, while another query applies the binding `dbr:Angela_Merkel`. The former refers only to the word *Angela*. The latter refers to two words of the sentence: *Angela Merkel* and covers longer parts of the *phrase*.
- **Syntactic Similarity**: The syntactic similarity is an indicator of how similar a n-gram of the sentence and the associated binding are. For example, in the question *Who is the author of the interpretation of dreams?* the n-gram *the interpretation of dreams* can be linked with `dbr:The_Interpretation_of_Dreams` or `dbr:Great_Book_of_Interpretation_of_Dreams` among others. The former has a smaller Levenshtein distance and a greater syntactic similarity with the selected n-gram.

We cover both aspects with the following formulas:

$$rating = \sum_{B \in q} r(B, phrase)$$

$$r(entity, phrase) = |words(phrase)| - levenshtein\_ratio(label(B), phrase)$$

After all entities, classes, and relations used in a query have been evaluated and summed up, the rating is corrected down by 30% if more than 50 results are returned by the query, based on empirical observations in the datasets.

4. Evaluation

4.1. Datasets

We performed the evaluation on the 8th and 9th Question Answering over Linked Data challenge training datasets (QALD-8 train [28] and QALD-9 train [27]), which contain 220 (QALD-8) and 408 (QALD-9) heterogeneous training questions. Additionally, we evaluated on the two LC-QuAD [25,11] datasets with 4000 train and 1000 test questions and 24.000 train and 6.000 test questions, respectively. Across datasets, the questions vary in complexity since they also include comparatives, superlatives, and temporal aggregations. An example of a simple question is *How tall is Amazon Eve?*. A more complex example is *How many companies were founded in the same year as Google?* since it contains a temporal aggregation (*the same year*). We created separate instances of TeBaQA for each of the training datasets and evaluated each instance on the corresponding test dataset.

4.2. Classification Evaluation

For the QALD-8 and QALD-9 datasets, eight classes were identified for each dataset, compare Figure 2. For LC-QuAD v1 and LC-QuAD v2, TeBaQA identified 17 classes for both datasets. Since the two LC-QuAD datasets were constructed for more diversity, the classification is more challenging. Note, we omitted classes with less than five examples in the training dataset. We are aware that we are trading our overall performance for classification accuracy.

To this end, we evaluated a variety of machine learning methods, which required questions to be converted into feature vectors. In particular, we used the QALD-8 and QALD-9 training datasets as our training data and used 10-fold cross-validation to evaluate the computed models. All duplicate questions and questions without SPARQL queries were removed from the training datasets. We tested multiple machine learning algorithms with the WEKA framework[5] [12] on our training data using 10-fold cross-validation. To achieve comparable results, TeBaQA uses only the standard configuration of the algorithms. The macro-weighted F-Measure for one fold in cross-validation is calculated from the classes' F-Measures, weighted according to the size of the class. After that, we calculated the average macro-weighted F-Measure across all folds. On the QALD datasets, the algorithm *RandomizableFilteredClassifier* achieves the highest F-Measures of 0.523964 (QALD-8) and 0.528875 (QALD-9), respectively. On LC-QuAD v1, we achieve a template classification f-measure of 0.400464 and 0.425953 on LC-QuAD v2 using a MultilayerPerceptron. Consequently, we use the best performing classifiers for the end-to-end evaluation.

Similar experiments can be found in Athreya et al.'s work [3]. The authors use a recurrent neural network, i.e., a tree-LSTM, to identify templates in LC-QuAD and achieve an accuracy of 0.828 after merging several template classes manually.

---

[5]https://www.cs.waikato.ac.nz/ml/weka/

4.3. GERBIL QA Benchmark

For evaluation, we used the FAIR benchmarking platform GERBIL QA [30] to ensure future reproducibility of the experiments.

Table 2 contains the results of selected Question Answering systems, measured against the QALD-8 and the QALD-9 test benchmarks[6]. We focused on English questions only, as English is supported by all available QA systems at the time of these experiments. The macro value for Precision, Recall and F-Measure was selected. The evaluation was performed with GERBIL version 0.2.3 if possible. We report always the highest numbers if several papers reported numbers and evaluation with GERBIL was not possible.

Table 2. Results of TeBaQA and other state-of-the-art QA systems for multiple datasets. * indicates F-1 measure instead of QALD F-Measure [30]. ** Numbers taken from the corresponding paper.

System	KB	Dataset	Precision	Recall	QALD F-Measure	Avg. Time in s
gAnswer2 [35]	DBpedia	QALD-8	0.337	0.354	0.440	4.548
QAnswer [9]	DBpedia	QALD-8	0.452	0.480	0.512	0.446
Zheng et al. [34]**	DBpedia	QALD-8	0.459	0.463	* 0.461	-
TeBaQA	DBpedia	QALD-8	0.476	0.488	**0.556**	28.990
Elon [27]	DBpedia	QALD-9	0.049	0.053	0.100	0.219
gAnswer [35]	DBpedia	QALD-9	0.293	0.327	0.430	3.076
NSQA [17]**	DBpedia	QALD-9	0.314	0.322	*0.453	-
QAnswer [9]	DBpedia	QALD-9	0.261	0.267	0.289	0.661
QASystem [27]	DBpedia	QALD-9	0.097	0.116	0.200	1.014
Zheng et al. [34]**	DBpedia	QALD-9	0.458	0.471	*0.463	-
TeBaQA	DBpedia	QALD-9	0.241	0.245	0.374	5.049
NSQA [17]**	DBpedia	LC-QuAD v1	0.382	0.404	*0.383	-
QAMP [31]**	DBpedia	LC-QuAD v1	0.250	0.500	*0.330	0.720
QAnswer [9] **	DBpedia	LC-QuAD v1	0.590	0.380	*0.460	1.500
TeBaQA	DBpedia	LC-QuAD v1	0.230	0.229	0.300	36.000
TeBaQA	Wikidata	LC-QuAD v2	0.140	0.136	0.227	–

On the QALD-8 benchmark, TeBaQA achieved the best results in terms of F-Measure by 5% QALD F-measure. Our average time is significantly larger than the other reported systems since the ranking mechanism gets activated and then fires several SPARQL queries after the initial null-retrieving SPARQL query.

On QALD-9, TeBaQA is in fourth place with a QALD F-Measure of 0.37. This implies that TeBaQA achieves comparable or partially better results than other semantic QA systems with a wide margin of possible improvements, as shown in the ablation study. QALD-9 is a more challenging benchmark than QALD-8 since it contains many questions that require complex queries with more than two triples. A more in-depth analysis shows that questions from QALD-9 often require complex templates that are not contained in the training queries or have only low support in the training set [14]. This mismatch leads to a high number of misclassifications and explains the limited perfor-

---

[6]The links to our GERBIL-experiments can be found on our Github page: `https://github.com/dice-group/TeBaQA/blob/master/README.md`

mance on QALD-9 compared to QALD-8 and, thus, its limited generalization abilities to unseen templates. Although we are not outperforming the state-of-the-art systems on QALD-9, TeBaQA a novel research avenue w.r.t. learning from data.

On the LC-QuAD dataset, which contains the most complex questions, TeBaQA achieves an F-Measure of 0.30. We ran this benchmark only once in our system and had some errors during runtime. We will further investigate the performance on LC-QuAD in our future research. Note, we ran LC-QuAD only once through the system to test our independence of the dataset similar to the methodology of Berant et al. [32].

To the best of our knowledge and after reaching out to the authors of LC-QuAD, we are the first system to evaluate on LC-QuAD v2. Since LC-Quad v2 uses Wikidata instead of DBpedia, we generated separate indexes for the Wikdata KG. The rest of the system remained unchanged. This shows, that TeBaQA can be easily adapted to other Knowledge Graphs.

4.4. SPARQL operation modifiers

The Achilles heel of most QA systems is their inability to deal with SPARQL operation modifiers, e.g., questions involving aggregations or superlatives [22]. In contrast to those other systems, TeBaQA contains functionalities to identify the query type and other modifiers. We analyzed the results of TeBaQA on these benchmark questions and found that TeBaQA was able to answer many of those questions, while other systems like QAswer and gAnswer fail on this; see supplementary material.

4.5. Ablation Study

Table 3. Ablation study for TeBaQA on the QALD-9 test benchmark.

QA System	Precision	Recall	Avg. Time	QALD F-Measure
Perfect classification	0.205	0.210	4.618	0.337
Perfect classification + EL	0.407	0.407	0.355	0.578
Perfect classification + ranking	0.245	0.257	4.029	0.399
Perfect EL	0.301	0.317	0.713	0.473
Perfect EL + ranking	0.302	0.320	0.653	0.477
Perfect ranking	0.258	0.270	6.281	0.405
Perfect classification + EL + ranking	0.407	0.407	0.251	0.578

We performed an ablation study to find the modules of TeBaQA's pipeline, which influence the end-to-end performance the most. Since the number of possible entities is roughly a magnitude larger than the number of relations and for the sake of experiment time, we omitted to test for perfect relation and class linking.

For the perfect classification experiment, the QALD F-Measure is lower than for the overall system, see Table 2. Investigating the detailed outputs, TeBaQA selects the simple templates containing only one triple more often than the more complex templates because they have more instances, i.e., support, on the QALD-9 train dataset. In many cases, a simple query generates a result set that is a superset of the target result set and, in consequence, decreases the precision.

When TeBaQA fails to fill the correct complex template with the correct entities, the query result set is often disjoint from the target result set. It is also reasonable that TeBaQA fails to fill the more complex templates due to missing or incorrect entity links.

Still, there is a gap in the system, which becomes evident when looking at the perfect classification plus ranking. Ranking gets only activated if the perfect template filled with semantic information does not retrieve any answer. That is, TeBaQA fails to find the correct modifiers or needs to circle through other semantic information candidates.

When the perfect classification is combined with perfect entity linking, the results reach a QALD F-measure of 0.58, which clearly would outperform any other system. The same happens if we add the perfect ranking. The results are the same in both cases because the ranking is most often not triggered since the perfect template is already filled correctly.

The strongest, single influence is the entity linking part, enabling TeBaQA to jump to 0.47 F-measure. We will tackle this challenging module in future work.

Regarding runtime, failing to find the perfect template and then iterating through the ranking, i.e., querying the SPARQL endpoint often, increases the average time needed significantly.

5. Summary and Future Work

We presented TeBaQA, a QA system which learns to map question to SPARQL template mappings using basic graph pattern isomorphisms. TeBaQA significantly eases the domain/KB adoption process as it relies only on a benchmark dataset at its core.

In the future, we will evaluate TeBaQA on more heterogeneous KG benchmarks to identify further choke points. We will also improve the question classification and information extraction by using novel deep learning mechanism.

Acknowledgements We acknowledge the support of the Federal Ministry for Economic Affairs and Energy (BMWi) project SPEAKER (FKZ 01MK20011A), ScaDS.AI (01/S18026A) as well as the Fraunhofer Zukunftsstiftung project JOSEPH and the Eurostars Project PORQUE (FKZ 01QE2056C). This work was partially supported by the German Federal Ministry of Transport and Digital Infrastructure (BMVI) in the project LIMBO (no. 19F2029I) and by the German Federal Ministry of Education and Research (BMBF) in the project SOLIDE (no. 13N14456) within 'KMU-innovativ: Forschung für die zivile Sicherheit' in particular 'Forschung für die zivile Sicherheit'.

References

[1] A. Abujabal, R. S. Roy, M. Yahya, and G. Weikum. Never-ending learning for open-domain question answering over knowledge bases. In Proceedings of the 2018 World Wide Web Conference on World Wide Web, WWW, pages 1053–1062, 2018.

[2] A. Abujabal, M. Yahya, M. Riedewald, and G. Weikum. Automated template generation for question answering over knowledge graphs. In Proceedings of the 26th International Conference on World Wide Web, WWW '17, pages 1191–1200, 2017.

[3] R. G. Athreya, S. Bansal, A. N. Ngomo, and R. Usbeck. Template-based question answering using recursive neural networks. CoRR, abs/2004.13843, 2020.

[4] C. V. S. Avila, W. Franco, J. G. R. Maia, and V. M. P. Vidal. CONQUEST: A framework for building template-based IQA chatbots for enterprise knowledge graphs. In NLDB, volume 12089, pages 60–72. Springer, 2020.

[5]   J. Berant, A. Chou, R. Frostig, and P. Liang. Semantic parsing on freebase from question-answer pairs. In Proceedings of the 2013 Conference on Empirical Methods in Natural Language Processing, pages 1533–1544, 2013.

[6]   N. Chakraborty, D. Lukovnikov, G. Maheshwari, P. Trivedi, J. Lehmann, and A. Fischer. Introduction to neural network based approaches for question answering over knowledge graphs. CoRR, abs/1907.09361, 2019.

[7]   W. Cui, Y. Xiao, H. Wang, Y. Song, S. Hwang, and W. Wang. KBQA: learning question answering over QA corpora and knowledge bases. PVLDB, 10(5):565–576, 2017.

[8]   J. Daiber, M. Jakob, C. Hokamp, and P. N. Mendes. Improving efficiency and accuracy in multilingual entity extraction. In Proceedings of the 9th International Conference on Semantic Systems (I-Semantics), 2013.

[9]   D. Diefenbach, A. Both, K. Singh, and P. Maret. Towards a question answering system over the semantic web. Semantic Web, 11(3):421–439, 2020.

[10] D. Diefenbach, V. López, K. D. Singh, and P. Maret. Core techniques of question answering systems over knowledge bases: a survey. Knowl. Inf. Syst., 55(3):529–569, 2018.

[11] M. Dubey, D. Banerjee, A. Abdelkawi, and J. Lehmann. Lc-quad 2.0: A large dataset for complex question answering over wikidata and dbpedia. In Proceedings of the 18th International Semantic Web Conference (ISWC). Springer, 2019.

[12] F. Eibe, M. Hall, I. Witten, and J. Pal. The weka workbench. Online Appendix for "Data Mining: Practical Machine Learning Tools and Techniques", 4, 2016.

[13] O. Gervasi and V. Kumar. Computational Science and Its Applications - ICCSA 2006: International Conference, Glasgow, UK, May 8-11, 2006, Proceedings. Computational Science and Its Applications: ICCSA 2006. Springer, 2006.

[14] Y. Gu, S. Kase, M. Vanni, B. M. Sadler, P. Liang, X. Yan, and Y. Su. Beyond I.I.D.: three levels of generalization for question answering on knowledge bases. CoRR, abs/2011.07743, 2020.

[15] Y. Hao, H. Liu, S. He, K. Liu, and J. Zhao. Pattern-revising enhanced simple question answering over knowledge bases. In Proceedings of the 27th International Conference on Computational Linguistics, COLING, pages 3272–3282, 2018.

[16] K. Höffner, S. Walter, E. Marx, R. Usbeck, J. Lehmann, and A. N. Ngomo. Survey on challenges of question answering in the semantic web. Semantic Web, 8(6):895–920, 2017.

[17] P. Kapanipathi, I. Abdelaziz, S. Ravishankar, S. Roukos, A. G. Gray, R. F. Astudillo, M. Chang, C. Cornelio, S. Dana, A. Fokoue, D. Garg, A. Gliozzo, S. Gurajada, H. Karanam, N. Khan, D. Khandelwal, Y. Lee, Y. Li, F. P. S. Luus, N. Makondo, N. Mihindukulasooriya, T. Naseem, S. Neelam, L. Popa, R. G. Reddy, R. Riegel, G. Rossiello, U. Sharma, G. P. S. Bhargav, and M. Yu. Question answering over knowledge bases by leveraging semantic parsing and neuro-symbolic reasoning. CoRR, abs/2012.01707, 2020.

[18] J. Lehmann, R. Isele, M. Jakob, A. Jentzsch, D. Kontokostas, P. N. Mendes, S. Hellmann, M. Morsey, P. van Kleef, S. Auer, and C. Bizer. Dbpedia - A large-scale, multilingual knowledge base extracted from wikipedia. Semantic Web, 6(2):167–195, 2015.

[19] D. Moussallem, R. Usbeck, M. Röder, and A. N. Ngomo. Entity linking in 40 languages using MAG. In ESWC, pages 176–181, 2018.

[20] D. Moussallem, R. Usbeck, M. Röeder, and A.-C. N. Ngomo. Mag: A multilingual, knowledge-base agnostic and deterministic entity linking approach. In Proceedings of the Knowledge Capture Conference, pages 1–8, 2017.

[21] J. Pérez, M. Arenas, and C. Gutierrez. Semantics and complexity of sparql. ACM Trans. Database Syst., 34(3):16:1–16:45, Sept. 2009.

[22] M. Saleem, S. N. Dastjerdi, R. Usbeck, and A. N. Ngomo. Question answering over linked data: What is difficult to answer? what affects the F scores? In 2nd International Workshop on Benchmarking Linked Data and NLIWoD3. CEUR-WS.org, 2017.

[23] K. Singh, A. Both, A. S. Radhakrishna, and S. Shekarpour. Frankenstein: A platform enabling reuse of question answering components. In ESWC, volume 10843 of Lecture Notes in Computer Science, pages 624–638. Springer, 2018.

[24] T. Soru, E. Marx, A. Valdestilhas, D. Esteves, D. Moussallem, and G. Publio. Neural machine translation for query construction and composition. CoRR, abs/1806.10478, 2018.

[25] P. Trivedi, G. Maheshwari, M. Dubey, and J. Lehmann. Lc-quad: A corpus for complex question answering over knowledge graphs. In International Semantic Web Conference, pages 210–218. Springer,

2017.

[26]   C. Unger, L. Bühmann, J. Lehmann, A. N. Ngomo, D. Gerber, and P. Cimiano. Template-based question answering over RDF data. In Proceedings of the 21st World Wide Web Conference 2012, WWW, pages 639–648, 2012.

[27]   R. Usbeck, R. H. Gusmita, A. N. Ngomo, and M. Saleem. 9th challenge on question answering over linked data (QALD-9). In Joint proceedings of (SemDeep-4) and (NLIWOD-4), volume 2241 of CEUR Workshop Proceedings, pages 58–64, 2018.

[28]   R. Usbeck, A. N. Ngomo, F. Conrads, M. Röder, and G. Napolitano. 8th challenge on question answering over linked data (QALD-8). In Joint proceedings of (SemDeep-4) and (NLIWOD-4), volume 2241 of CEUR Workshop Proceedings, pages 51–57, 2018.

[29]   R. Usbeck, A. N. Ngomo, B. Haarmann, A. Krithara, M. Röder, and G. Napolitano. 7th open challenge on question answering over linked data (QALD-7). In ESWC, pages 59–69, 2017.

[30]   R. Usbeck, M. Röder, M. Hoffmann, F. Conrads, J. Huthmann, A. N. Ngomo, C. Demmler, and C. Unger. Benchmarking Question Answering Systems. Semantic Web, 10(2):293–304, 2019.

[31]   S. Vakulenko, J. D. F. Garcia, A. Polleres, M. de Rijke, and M. Cochez. Message passing for complex question answering over knowledge graphs. In W. Zhu, D. Tao, X. Cheng, P. Cui, E. A. Rundensteiner, D. Carmel, Q. He, and J. X. Yu, editors, CIKM, pages 1431–1440. ACM, 2019.

[32]   Y. Wang, J. Berant, and P. Liang. Building a semantic parser overnight. In ACL, pages 1332–1342, 2015.

[33]   X. Yin, D. Gromann, and S. Rudolph. Neural machine translating from natural language to SPARQL. CoRR, abs/1906.09302, 2019.

[34]   W. Zheng and M. Zhang. Question answering over knowledge graphs via structural query patterns. CoRR, abs/1910.09760, 2019.

[35]   L. Zou, R. Huang, H. Wang, J. X. Yu, W. He, and D. Zhao. Natural language question answering over RDF: a graph data driven approach. In International Conference on Management of Data, SIGMOD 2014, Snowbird, UT, USA, June 22-27, 2014, pages 313–324, 2014.

Further with Knowledge Graphs. M. Alam et al. (Eds.)
AKA Verlag and IOS Press, 2021
© 2021 Akademische Verlagsgesellschaft AKA GmbH, Berlin
doi:10.3233/SSW210039

Optimizing RDF Stream Processing for Uncertainty Management

Robin Keskisärkkä, Eva Blomqvist and Olaf Hartig

Linköping University, Linköping, Sweden

Abstract. RDF Stream Processing (RSP) has been proposed as a way of bridging the gap between the Complex Event Processing (CEP) paradigm and the Semantic Web standards. Uncertainty has been recognized as a critical aspect in CEP, but it has received little attention within the context of RSP. In this paper, we investigate the impact of different RSP optimization strategies for uncertainty management. The paper describes (1) an extension of the RSP-QL* data model to capture bind expressions, filter expressions, and uncertainty functions; (2) optimization techniques related to lazy variables and caching of uncertainty functions, and a heuristic for reordering uncertainty filters in query plans; and (3) an evaluation of these strategies in a prototype implementation. The results show that using a lazy variable mechanism for uncertainty functions can improve query execution performance by orders of magnitude while introducing negligible overhead. The results also show that caching uncertainty function results can improve performance under most conditions, but that maintaining this cache can potentially add overhead to the overall query execution process. Finally, the effect of the proposed heuristic on query execution performance was shown to depend on multiple factors, including the selectivity of uncertainty filters, the size of intermediate results, and the cost associated with the evaluation of the uncertainty functions.

Keywords. RSP, CEP, Uncertainty, RSP-QL

1. Introduction

RDF Stream Processing (RSP) is based on existing Semantic Web standards but extends traditional approaches to support continuous processing of streaming RDF data. While several RSP systems have been inspired by data stream management systems [1,2,3], RSP has also been proposed as a candidate for bringing together the Complex Event Processing (CEP) paradigm and the Semantic Web standards [4,5,6,7] in order to target information integration and stream reasoning. CEP focuses on detecting events from streaming sources, where a high-level event may be viewed as an abstraction of a set of low-level events.

Within the CEP domain, representing and reasoning with uncertainty has been recognized as a critical aspect for dealing with real-world data, which can be imprecise, incomplete, and noisy [8,9,10]. However, within the RSP domain uncertainty has received little attention. In previous work, we evaluated the impact of explicitly managing different uncertainty types in RSP, which showed a need for research on query optimization strategies to improve uncertainty management efficiency [11].

The main contributions of this paper are (1) an extension of the RSP-QL* data model we proposed in [11], to capture the syntax and semantics of uncertainty functions along with filter and bind expressions, (2) two technical optimization strategies for increasing query execution performance, and a heuristic to support reordering of uncertainty filters, and (3) an evaluation of these strategies in a prototype implementation.

The outline of the paper is as follows. Section 2 briefly introduces some basic concepts, and Section 3 extends the syntax and semantics of RSP-QL*. Section 4 provides query re-write rules, describes optimization strategies, and provides a heuristic for reordering uncertainty filters. Section 5 presents an evaluation of the proposed strategies in a prototype implementation. Finally, Section 6 summarizes the findings and outlines future work.

2. Preliminaries

Uncertainty in CEP can broadly be viewed as belonging to three main types: *occurrence uncertainty*, *attribute uncertainty*, and *pattern uncertainty* [8,9,12]. Variations of these uncertainty types have been modeled and implemented in existing CEP systems to deal with data that may be, e.g., incomplete, imprecise, vague, contradictory, or noisy [8,10]. In this paper, we explicitly focus on issues related to attribute uncertainty.

Attribute uncertainty generally refers to uncertainty about the content of event objects [8,12]. For example, when a sensor reports a value, the *true* value is usually assumed to be near the reported value but limited by the precision of the sensor and additional factors of the environment. While such uncertainty is often ignored for simplicity it can have important consequences. For example, consider a case where the task is to generate an alert whenever the oxygen concentration in a room falls below 19.5%. Should an alert be generated if the oxygen concentration is reported to be 19.7%? When also considering that the sensor is only accurate to within 1%, or biased towards higher values?

Attribute uncertainty is often expressed as a distribution around a value, typically described as a probability distribution. While there are no standardized formats for representing probability distributions in RDF, in this paper we will use a literal datatype, defined for this purpose in our previous work [11]. The literal datatype is denoted by the URI *rspu:distribution*, and is of the form $f(p_1, p_2, ..., p_n)$, where f is a string identifier for a probability distribution type, and every p_i is a floating-point number. For example, a normal distribution with a mean μ of 19.7 and variance σ^2 of 1 could be represented using the literal `"N(19.7,1)"`. Similarly, a uniform distribution between 18.7 and 20.7 could be represented as `"U(18.7,20.7)"`.

In order to deal with streaming RDF data, several RSP models and implementations have been proposed over the past decade, and Dell'Aglio et al. defined RSP-QL as a way of unifying the syntax and semantics of these initial proposals [13,14]. The RSP-QL language extends SPARQL 1.1 to enable querying of streaming data by allowing discrete portions of RDF streams to be defined and queried. In earlier work we proposed RSP-QL*, which extends RSP-QL to support statement-level annotations as an alternative to RDF reification [15]. Listing 1 provides an example query demonstrating the main features of the RSP-QL* language, leveraging two uncertainty functions described later in Section 3.1. For an in-depth description of the RSP-QL* data model and syntax, the reader is referred to the original paper [15].

```
REGISTER STREAM <warning/oxygen> COMPUTED EVERY PT10S AS
SELECT ?value
FROM NAMED WINDOW <w> ON <http://stream/oxygen> [RANGE PT10S STEP PT10S]
WHERE {
    WINDOW <w> {
        GRAPH ?g {
            ?o sosa:hasSimpleResult ?value .
            << ?o sosa:hasSimpleResult ?value >> rspu:uncertainty ?unc .
            BIND(rspu:add(?unc, ?value) AS ?d)
            FILTER(rspu:greaterThan(?d, 0.195) > 0.90)
        }
    }
}
```

Listing 1: An RSP-QL* query that passes events to the output stream when the reported oxygen concentration is greater than 19.5% with a probability greater than 0.90. The measurement error is combined with the reported value before being compared with the threshold value.

3. Syntax and Semantics of RSP-QL*

RSP extends traditional RDF/SPARQL by introducing a time dimension to process-ing [13]. In RSP-QL, the time dimension is managed via windows that define dis-crete subsets over RDF streams that can then be queried as regular RDF datasets. RSP-QL* [15] extends RSP-QL by extending it along the lines of RDF*/SPARQL* [16, 17]. Essentially, RDF* allows RDF triples to be used as subjects and objects in triples, while SPARQL* supports the querying of such triples. We use RSP-QL* as the start-ing point for this work. For the SPARQL-specific constructs, we adopt the algebraic SPARQL syntax introduced by Pérez et al. [18]. Due to space constraints, we here limit ourselves to presenting only the core concepts of the language and an extension to a subset of the SPARQL algebra.

The basic building block of SPARQL [19] is a *basic graph pattern* (BGP), that is, a finite set of *triple patterns*. A triple pattern is a tuple $(s, p, o) \in (\mathcal{V} \cup \mathcal{B} \cup \mathcal{I}) \times (\mathcal{V} \cup \mathcal{I}) \times (\mathcal{V} \cup \mathcal{B} \cup \mathcal{I} \cup \mathcal{L})$, where $\mathcal{V}$ is the set of query variables disjoint from $\mathcal{I}$ (all IRIs), $\mathcal{B}$ (all blank nodes) and $\mathcal{L}$ (all literals), respectively. A *solution mapping* is a partial function that maps query variables to blank nodes, IRIs, or literals $\eta : \mathcal{V} \to (\mathcal{I} \cup \mathcal{B} \cup \mathcal{L})$.

RSP-QL* extends triple patterns to support the concept of *triple* patterns* [17,16], which allow triple patterns to be nested (arbitrarily deep). A triple* pattern is defined recursively as follows: i) any triple pattern is a triple* pattern, and ii) given two triple* patterns tp and tp', and $s \in (\mathcal{I} \cup \mathcal{V})$, $p \in (\mathcal{I} \cup \mathcal{V})$, and $o \in (\mathcal{I} \cup \mathcal{L} \cup \mathcal{V})$, then (tp, p, o), (s, p, tp), and (tp, p, tp') are triple* patterns. A finite set of triple* patterns is referred to as a *BGP**.

Similarly, the notion of solution mappings is extended to *solution* mappings* that allow both RDF terms and RDF* triples to be bound to query variables. A solution* mapping is defined as a partial mapping $\eta : \mathcal{V} \to (\mathcal{T} \cup \mathcal{I} \cup \mathcal{L})$, where $\mathcal{T}$ is an RDF* triple.

We use the notion of *comparison terms* to denote the terms that can be used in SPARQL *built-in conditions*. For a complete list of the built-in predicates, we refer the reader to the SPARQL specification [19].

Definition 1. Comparison terms are defined recursively as follows:

- a variable is a comparison term,
- a URI is a comparison term,
- a literal is a comparison term,
- if f denotes a SPARQL built-in predicate [19] and $x_1, ..., x_n$ are comparison terms, then $f(x_1, ..., x_n)$ is a comparison term, and
- if f is a URI that denotes an uncertainty function defined in Section 3.1 and $x_1, ..., x_n$ are comparison terms, then $f(x_1, ..., x_n)$ is a comparison term.

Definition 2. Built-in conditions are defined recursively as follows:

- if x and y are comparison terms, then $x = true$, $x = y$, $x < y$, $x \leq y$, $x > y$, $x \geq y$, $x \neq y$ are built-in conditions, and
- if c_1 and c_2 are built-in conditions, then $c_1 \wedge c_2$, $c_1 \vee c_2$ and $\neg c_1$ are built-in conditions.

3.1. Syntax of Uncertainty Functions

We here leverage the set of extension functions for managing probability distributions introduced in our previous work [11]. The functions support some useful operations on probability distributions. For these definitions, let $\mathcal{L}_d$ be the set of all *rspu:distribution* literals and $\mathcal{L}_n$ be the set of all literals with numeric data types. For every literal $l \in \mathcal{L}_d$, we write $val(l)$ to denote the probability distribution that l represents, and for every $l \in \mathcal{L}_n$, $val(l)$ denotes the numeric value represented by l.

Definition 3. The URI **rspu:add** denotes a function f_{add} that, for every $c_1 \in \mathcal{L}_d$ and $c_2 \in \mathcal{L}_d \cup \mathcal{L}_n$, returns a literal $c_3 \in \mathcal{L}_d$ such that $val(c_3)$ is the probability distribution obtained by adding $val(c_1)$ to $val(c_2)$.

Definition 4. The URI **rspu:subtract** denotes a function $f_{subtract}$ that, for every $c_1 \in \mathcal{L}_d$ and $c_2 \in \mathcal{L}_d \cup \mathcal{L}_n$, returns a literal $c_3 \in \mathcal{L}_d$ such that $val(c_3)$ is the probability distribution obtained by subtracting $val(c_2)$ from $val(c_1)$.

Definition 5. The URI **rspu:greaterThan** denotes a function $f_{greaterThan}$ that, for every $c_1 \in \mathcal{L}_d$ and $c_2 \in \mathcal{L}_d \cup \mathcal{L}_n$, returns a literal $c_3 \in \mathcal{L}_n$ such that $val(c_3)$ is the probability that $val(c_1)$ is greater than $val(c_2)$.

Definition 6. The URI **rspu:lessThan** denotes a function $f_{lessThan}$ that, for every $c_1 \in \mathcal{L}_d$ and $c_2 \in \mathcal{L}_d \cup \mathcal{L}_n$, returns a literal $c_3 \in \mathcal{L}_n$ such that $val(c_3)$ is the probability that $val(c_1)$ is less than $val(c_2)$.

Definition 7. The URI **rspu:between** denotes a function $f_{between}$ that, for every $c_1 \in \mathcal{L}_d$ and $c_2, c_3 \in \mathcal{L}_d \cup \mathcal{L}_n$, returns a literal $c_4 \in \mathcal{L}_n$ such that $val(c_4)$ is the probability that $val(c_1)$ is greater than $val(c_2)$ and less than $val(c_3)$.

3.2. Syntax of RSP-QL*

RSP-QL* extends RSP-QL to support all the forms of graph patterns that have been introduced for SPARQL and SPARQL* [15]. For brevity, we here cover only the core constructs of the language. An RSP-QL* query consists of two parts: an RSP-QL* pattern, and a set of *window declarations* associated with IRIs that serve as names for the corresponding windows in the query.

Definition 8. An **RSP-QL* pattern** is defined recursively as follows:

- Any BGP* is an RSP-QL* pattern.
- If $n \in (\mathcal{V} \cup \mathcal{I})$ and P is an RSP-QL* pattern, then (WINDOW n P) and (GRAPH n P) are RSP-QL* patterns.
- If P_1 and P_2 are RSP-QL* patterns, then (P_1 AND P_2), (P_1 OPT P_2), and (P_1 UNION P_2) are RSP-QL* patterns.
- If P is an RSP-QL* pattern and R is a built-in condition, then the expression (P FILTER R) is an RSP-QL* pattern.
- If P is an RSP-QL* pattern, C is a comparison term and $?v$ is a variable that neither occurs in P nor in C, then (P BIND$_{?v}$ C) is an RSP-QL* pattern.

Definition 9. A **window declaration** is a tuple $(u_S, \alpha, \beta, \tau_0)$ where $u_S \in \mathcal{I}$ is an IRI (representing the name of a named RDF* stream), α is a time duration (representing a window width), β is a time duration (representing a slide parameter), and τ_0 is a timestamp (representing a start time).

Definition 10. An **RSP-QL* query** is a pair (ω, P) where ω is a partial function that maps some IRIs in $\mathcal{I}$ to window declarations, and P is an RSP-QL* pattern such that for every sub-pattern (WINDOW n P') in P it holds that if $n \in \mathcal{I}$, then ω is defined for n, i.e., $n \in \text{dom}(\omega)$.

3.3. Semantics of RSP-QL*

The semantics of RSP-QL* has been described in previous work [15], but is here extended to cover the notions of comparison terms (cf. Definition 1), bind expressions, and filter expressions. The standard notions of *compatibility*, *merging*, and *application* of solution mappings in SPARQL are adapted for solution* mappings as follows.

Definition 11. Two solution* mappings η, η' are **compatible**, denoted $\eta \sim \eta'$, if $\eta(?v) = \eta'(?v)$ for every variable $?v \in \text{dom}(\eta) \cap \text{dom}(\eta')$.

Definition 12. The **merge** of two compatible solution* mappings η and η', denoted by $\eta \cup \eta'$, is a solution* mapping η'' with the following three properties:

- $\text{dom}(\eta'') = \text{dom}(\eta) \cup \text{dom}(\eta')$,
- $\eta''(?v) = \eta(?v)$ for all $?v \in \text{dom}(\eta)$, and
- $\eta''(?v) = \eta'(?v)$ for all $?v \in \text{dom}(\eta') \setminus \text{dom}(\eta)$.

Definition 13. The **application** of a solution* mapping η to an RSP-QL* pattern P, denoted by $\eta[P]$, is the RSP-QL* pattern obtained by replacing all variables in P according to η.

Next, we define the evaluation function for comparison terms, with respect to a given solution* mapping. This can be regarded as a *lifting* of the definitions of comparison terms and uncertainty functions into the SPARQL context.

Definition 14. Let $eval(c, \eta)$ denote the evaluation function of a comparison term c given a solution* mapping η:

- if c is a variable and $c \in dom(\eta)$, then $eval(c, \eta)$ is $\eta(c)$;
- if c is a URI or a literal, then $eval(c, \eta)$ is c;
- if c is of the form $f(c_1, ..., c_n)$ where f denotes a SPARQL built-in predicate and c_i are comparison terms, then $eval(c, \eta)$ is $f(eval(c_1, \eta), ..., eval(c_n, \eta))$, where f is evaluated according to the SPARQL specification [19];
- if c is of the form rspu:add(c_1, c_2) such that $eval(c_1, \eta) \in \mathcal{L}_d$ and $eval(c_2, \eta) \in \mathcal{L}_d \cup \mathcal{L}_n$ then return $f_{\mathsf{add}}(eval(c_1, \eta), eval(c_2, \eta))$;
- if c is of the form rspu:subtract(c_1, c_2) such that $eval(c_1, \eta) \in \mathcal{L}_d$ and $eval(c_2, \eta) \in \mathcal{L}_d \cup \mathcal{L}_n$ then return $f_{\mathsf{subtract}}(eval(c_1, \eta), eval(c_2, \eta))$;
- if c is of the form rspu:greaterThan(c_1, c_2) such that $eval(c_1, \eta) \in \mathcal{L}_d$ and $eval(c_2, \eta) \in \mathcal{L}_d \cup \mathcal{L}_n$ then return $f_{\mathsf{greaterThan}}(eval(c_1, \eta), eval(c_2, \eta))$;
- if c is of the form rspu:lessThan(c_1, c_2) such that $eval(c_1, \eta) \in \mathcal{L}_d$ and $eval(c_2, \eta) \in \mathcal{L}_d \cup \mathcal{L}_n$ then return $f_{\mathsf{lessThan}}(eval(c_1, \eta), eval(c_2, \eta))$;
- if c is of the form rspu:between(c_1, c_2, c_3) such that $eval(c_1, \eta) \in \mathcal{L}_d$, $eval(c_2, \eta) \in \mathcal{L}_d \cup \mathcal{L}_n$ and $eval(c_3, \eta) \in \mathcal{L}_d \cup \mathcal{L}_n$ then return $f_{\mathsf{between}}(eval(c_1, \eta), eval(c_2, \eta), eval(c_3, \eta))$;
- else return an error.

Finally, let $filter(R, \eta)$ be the evaluation function for the built-in condition R w.r.t. to the solution* mapping η that returns a literal, IRI, or an error. We say that a *filter condition* R *satisfies* some solution* mapping η if the evaluation of the constraint is true. That is, a filter condition eliminates any solutions that, when substituted into the expression, either result in an effective boolean value of false or produce an error. For a complete definition of the evaluation of SPARQL built-in conditions we refer the reader to the work of Pérez et al. [18] and the SPARQL specification [19]. The corresponding algebraic operations join ($\bowtie$), union ($\cup$), difference ($\setminus$), left join ($⧑$), projection (π), selection (σ), and bind (ρ) are then defined as follows.

Definition 15. Let Ω, Ω_1, and Ω_2 be sets of solution* mappings, $S \subset \mathcal{V}$ be a finite set of variables, R denote a built-in condition, and η_0 be the empty solution* mapping (i.e., $dom(\eta_0) = \emptyset$).

$$\Omega_1 \bowtie \Omega_2 = \{\eta_1 \cup \eta_2 \mid \eta_1 \in \Omega_1, \eta_2 \in \Omega_2, \eta_1 \sim \eta_2\}$$
$$\Omega_1 \cup \Omega_2 = \{\eta \mid \eta \in \Omega_1 \text{ or } \eta \in \Omega_2\}$$
$$\Omega_1 \setminus \Omega_2 = \{\eta \in \Omega_1 \mid \text{ for all } \eta' \in \Omega_2, \eta \not\sim \eta'\}$$
$$\Omega_1 ⧑ \Omega_2 = (\Omega_1 \bowtie \Omega_2) \cup (\Omega_1 \setminus \Omega_2)$$
$$\pi_S(\Omega) = \{\eta \mid \exists \eta' \in \Omega : \eta \text{ is a restriction of } \eta' \text{ to the variables in } S\}$$
$$\sigma_R(\Omega) = \{\eta \in \Omega \mid \eta \text{ satisfies } R\}$$
$$\rho_{?v \leftarrow C}(\Omega) = \{\eta \cup \eta' \mid \eta \in \Omega, ?v \notin dom(\eta), \text{ and } \eta' = \eta_0 \text{ if } eval(C, \eta) \text{ returns an error, otherwise } dom(\eta') = \{?v\} \text{ and } \eta'(?v) = eval(C, \eta)\}$$

Based on the definitions of the algebra operators above, RSP-QL* patterns are evaluated over a background dataset and a set of named windows at a given timestamp.

Definition 16. Let W be a partial function that maps some IRIs in $\mathcal{I}$ to a window over some RDF* stream, respectively, and P be an RSP-QL* pattern such that for every sub-pattern (WINDOW n P') in P with $n \in \mathcal{I}$, it holds that W is defined for n, i.e., $n \in dom(W)$. Furthermore, let D be an RDF* dataset, G be an RDF* graph, and τ be a timestamp. Then, the **evaluation of P** over D and W at τ with G, denoted by $[\![P]\!]_G^{D,W,\tau}$, is defined recursively as follows:

1. If P is the empty BGP*, then $[\![P]\!]_G^{D,W,\tau} = \{\eta_0\}$ where η_0 is the empty solution* mapping (i.e., $dom(\eta_0) = \emptyset$).
2. If P is a non-empty BGP*, then $[\![P]\!]_G^{D,W,\tau} = \{\eta \mid dom(\eta) = var(P) \text{ and } \eta[P] \in G\}$ where $var(P)$ denotes the set of variables occurring in P.
3. If P is (GRAPH u P'), then $[\![P]\!]_G^{D,W,\tau} = [\![P']\!]_{G'}^{D,W,\tau}$ where $(u, G') \in D$.
4. If P is (GRAPH $?x$ P'), then $[\![P]\!]_G^{D,W,\tau} = \bigcup_{(u,G') \in D} [\![(\text{GRAPH } u\ P')]\!]_G^{D,W,\tau}$.
5. If P is (WINDOW u P'), then $[\![P]\!]_G^{D,W,\tau} = [\![P']\!]_{G'}^{DS(\mathcal{W}),\emptyset,\tau}$ where $\mathcal{W} = W(u)$ and G' is the default graph of the window dataset denoted by $DS(\mathcal{W})$.
6. If P is (WINDOW $?x$ P'), then $[\![P]\!]_G^{D,W,\tau} = \bigcup_{u \in dom(W)} [\![(\text{WINDOW } u\ P')]\!]_G^{D,W,\tau}$
7. If P is (P_1 AND P_2), then $[\![P]\!]_G^{D,W,\tau} = [\![P_1]\!]_G^{D,W,\tau} \bowtie [\![P_2]\!]_G^{D,W,\tau}$.
8. If P is (P_1 UNION P_2), then $[\![P]\!]_G^{D,W,\tau} = [\![P_1]\!]_G^{D,W,\tau} \cup [\![P_2]\!]_G^{D,W,\tau}$.
9. If P is (P_1 OPT P_2), then $[\![P]\!]_G^{D,W,\tau} = [\![P_1]\!]_G^{D,W,\tau} \bowtie\!\!\!\!\!\!\shortmid\ [\![P_2]\!]_G^{D,W,\tau}$.
10. If P is (P' FILTER R), then $[\![P]\!]_G^{D,W,\tau} = \sigma_R([\![P']\!]_G^{D,W,\tau})$.
11. If P is (P' BIND$_{?v}$ C), then $[\![P]\!]_G^{D,W,\tau} = \rho_{?v \leftarrow C}([\![P']\!]_G^{D,W,\tau})$.

It remains to define the semantics of RSP-QL* queries, which contain window declarations in addition to an RSP-QL* pattern (cf. Definition 10).

Definition 17. Let $\mathcal{S}$ be a finite set of named RDF* streams and $q = (\omega, P)$ be an RSP-QL* query such that for every IRI $u_S \in dom(\omega)$ there exists a named RDF* stream $(u_S, S) \in \mathcal{S}$. Furthermore, let D be an RDF* dataset and τ be a timestamp. The **evaluation of q** over D and $\mathcal{S}$ at τ, denoted by $[\![q]\!]^{D,\mathcal{S},\tau}$, is defined as $[\![q]\!]^{D,\mathcal{S},\tau} = [\![P]\!]_G^{D,W,\tau}$ where G is the default graph of D and W is a partial function such that $dom(W) = dom(\omega)$ and for every IRI $u \in dom(W)$ it holds that $W(u)$ is the time-based window $\mathcal{W}(S, x - \alpha, x)$ with $(u_S, S) \in \mathcal{S}$, $(u_S, \alpha, \beta, \tau_0) = \omega(u)$ and $x = \tau_0 + \alpha + \beta \times i$ for the greatest possible value of $i \in \mathbb{N}$ for which $x < \tau$.

4. RSP-QL* Query Optimization

Following the definitions of the syntax and semantics of RSP-QL*, we now define a set of RSP-QL* algebra equivalences. These equivalences can be applied to arbitrary RSP-QL* patterns to support query rewriting. We say that two patterns P_1 and P_2 are equivalent, denoted by $P_1 \equiv P_2$, if $[\![P_1]\!]_G^{D,W,\tau} = [\![P_2]\!]_G^{D,W,\tau}$ for every RDF* dataset D, RDF* graph G, timestamp τ, and set of named windows W.

Table 1 includes a subset of the equivalence rules that have previously been described for the SPARQL algebra [18,20]. These rewrite rules also apply to RSP-QL* patterns. For proofs of these equivalences, the reader is referred to Peréz et al. [18] and Schmidt et al. [20]. Group I describes the common algebraic laws for query expressions. For example, *JAss* and *JComm* show the commutativity and associativity of join expres-

Table 1. Algebraic equivalence rules or RSP-QL*. P, P_1 and P_2 are RSP-QL* patterns, R, R_1 and R_2 are built-in conditions, n is a URI or variable, and C is a comparison term.

I. Associativity, Commutativity, Distributivity

$((P_1 \text{ UNION } P_2) \text{ UNION } P_3) \equiv (P_1 \text{ UNION } (P_2 \text{ UNION } P_3))$	(UAss)
$((P_1 \text{ AND } P_2) \text{ AND } P_3) \equiv (P_1 \text{ AND } (P_2 \text{ AND } P_3))$	(JAss)
$(P_1 \text{ UNION } P_2) \equiv (P_2 \text{ UNION } P_1)$	(UComm)
$(P_1 \text{ AND } P_2) \equiv (P_2 \text{ AND } P_1)$	(JComm)
$((P_1 \text{ UNION } P_2) \text{ AND } P_3) \equiv ((P_1 \text{ AND } P_3) \text{ UNION } (P_2 \text{ AND } P_3))$	(JUDistR)
$((P_1 \text{ UNION } P_2) \text{ OPT } P_3) \equiv ((P_1 \text{ OPT } P_3) \text{ UNION } (P_2 \text{ OPT } P_3))$	(LUDistR)

II. Filter decomposition

$(P \text{ FILTER } R_1 \wedge R_2) \equiv ((P \text{ FILTER } R_1) \text{ FILTER } R_2)$	(FDecompI)
$(P \text{ FILTER } R_1 \vee R_2) \equiv ((P \text{ FILTER } R_1) \text{ UNION } (P \text{ FILTER } R_2))$	(FDecompII)
$(P \text{ FILTER } R_1 \wedge R_2) \equiv (P \text{ FILTER } R_2 \wedge R_1)$	(FReordI)
$(P \text{ FILTER } R_1 \vee R_2) \equiv (P \text{ FILTER } R_2 \vee R_1)$	(FReordII)

III. Filter pushing

$((P_1 \text{ UNION } P_2) \text{ FILTER } R) \equiv ((P_1 \text{ FILTER } R) \text{ UNION } (P_2 \text{ FILTER } R))$	(FUPush)
If $\forall\, ?v \in vars(R) \,:\, ?v \in cVars(P_1) \wedge ?v \notin pVars(P_2)$	
$((P_1 \text{ AND } P_2) \text{ FILTER } R) \equiv ((P_1 \text{ FILTER } R) \text{ AND } P_2)$	(FJPush)
$((P_1 \text{ OPT } P_2) \text{ FILTER } R) \equiv ((P_1 \text{ FILTER } R) \text{ OPT } P_2)$	(FLPush)
If $\forall\, ?v \in vars(R) \,:\, ?v \in cVars(P)$	
$((\text{WINDOW } n\ P) \text{ FILTER } R) \equiv ((\text{WINDOW } n\ (P \text{ FILTER } R))$	(FWPush)

IV. Bind pushing

$((\text{GRAPH } n\ (P \text{ BIND}_{?v}\ C)) \equiv ((\text{GRAPH } n\ P) \text{ BIND}_{?v}\ C)$	(BGPush)
$((\text{WINDOW } n\ (P \text{ BIND}_{?v}\ C)) \equiv ((\text{WINDOW } n\ P) \text{ BIND}_{?v}\ C)$	(BWPush)
If $\forall\, ?v \in vars(C) \,:\, ?v \in cVars(P_1) \wedge ?v \notin pVars(P_2)$	
$((P_1 \text{ AND } P_2) \text{ BIND}_{?v}\ C) \equiv ((P_1 \text{ BIND}_{?v}\ C) \text{ AND } P_2)$	(BJPush)
$((P_1 \text{ OPT } P_2) \text{ BIND}_{?v}\ C) \equiv ((P_1 \text{ BIND}_{?v}\ C) \text{ OPT } P_2)$	(BLPush)

sions. Group II and III contain rules for the manipulation of filters, including filter decomposition, filter reordering, and filter pushing. The final rule in group III has been defined as part of this work and shows how filter pushing may be applied for window patterns. Group IV includes additional equivalence rules for pushing bind expressions, where *BGPush* and *BWPush* have been defined as part of this work.

Following the notation used by Schmidt et al. [20], we write $cVars(P)$ to denote the subset of variables that are *certain* to be bound when evaluating the pattern P, and use $pVars(P)$ to represent the set of variables that are *possibly* bound when evaluating the pattern P. By $vars(x)$ we denote the set of variables occurring in x, where x is either a built-in condition, a comparison term, or an RSP-QL* pattern.

4.1. Query Optimization

SPARQL queries are built up around triple patterns, which result in a large number of join operations. In SPARQL, these joins generally dominate the query execution time, and optimizing queries with respect to these joins has received considerable attention in literature [21,22]. Many of the heuristics that have been proposed for SPARQL can also be applied for RSP-QL* queries, such as triple pattern reordering based on *variable counting*. We use the most common heuristics proposed for SPARQL to provide a baseline in this work, and we assume that data is stored in triple tables (or some similar structure) that provide fast index-based access to stored RDF* data for each possible order of subject, predicate, and object (i.e., spo, sop, pso, pos, osp, and ops). Below, we describe the heuristics considered in this work.

H1: Triple patterns should be ordered based on their *selectivity*, i.e., based on how likely they are to produce smaller intermediate results [21,22]. Given the position and the number of variables in a triple* pattern, we use the following order starting from the most selective: $(s, p, o) \prec (s, ?, o) \prec (?, p, o) \prec (s, p, ?) \prec (?, ?, o) \prec (s, ?, ?) \prec (?, p, ?) \prec (?, ?, ?)$. We consider a nested triple* pattern to be a variable if it contains at least one variable.

H2: Graph patterns should be ordered based on their selectivity. A triple pattern evaluated over a specific named graph has higher selectivity than one executed over all graphs: $(\text{GRAPH } u\ P) \prec (\text{GRAPH } ?x\ P)$. A triple pattern that does not appear in a graph pattern is evaluated over the default graph.

H3: Filters should be broken up into their constituent pieces and applied as *early* as possible. The idea of pushing filters is one of the most commonly applied optimization strategies in database systems since filters reduce size of intermediate results.

H4: Filters containing references to uncertainty functions (cf. Definition 3.1) should be applied as *late* as possible. The intuition is that there exists some trade-off between evaluating a computationally expensive filter condition early and the degree to which the size of the incoming results is reduced. If a filter condition only marginally decreases the size of the intermediate results, it may be more efficient to apply the filter later in the query evaluation when additional query constraints have been applied. Conversely, if the number of join partners increases, the number of times the filter condition needs to be evaluated increases. However, by employing caching, as we shall see later, the cost of these additional filter evaluations is expected to be comparably small. When applied, the heuristic supersedes H3 with respect to filters that reference uncertainty functions.

Further, we provide two technical optimization techniques related to uncertainty functions. *Lazy variables* provide a mechanism for just-in-time evaluation of values calculated using uncertainty functions. A lazy variable is resolved only when the variable value is requested, and if the value is never used the evaluation can be skipped. The hypothesis is that it will have a positive impact on query execution performance when uncertainty functions are used in bind expressions, since unnecessary evaluations may be avoided.

The second optimization involves the use of a *cache* to store calls to uncertainty functions within a single query execution (i.e., the cache is cleared between query evaluations). Rather than evaluating a given uncertainty function multiple times for the same input, the results can then be looked up in the cache. The cache in the implementation is a basic in-memory hash table, where a serialization of the function calls and referenced nodes are used as keys. If the query plan results in multiple calls to uncertainty functions with the same inputs, e.g., if a filter is preceded by an increase in the number of join partners, the hypothesis is that the cost of these additional filter evaluations will be small.

H1–H3 help minimize the impact of the order of operations in the original queries, and provide the baseline for the evaluation presented in the next section.

5. Evaluation

In this section, we present an evaluation of the proposed heuristic (H4) and the two optimization techniques. The experiments were performed on a MacBook Pro 2015, with a quad-core 2.8 GHz Intel Core i7 processor, 16 GB of 1600MHz DDR3, and 8 GB of memory allocated to the JVM. The prototype, along with the experiment files and queries, is available under the MIT License[1]. The implementation of the engine has been described in previous work [15,11] but has been extended to support the technical optimizations and heuristics described in the previous section.

5.1. Experiment Setup

While a number of benchmarks have been proposed for evaluating RSP systems, such as LSBench [23], SRBench [24], and CityBench [25], adopting these for the evaluation of performance under uncertainty is out-of-scope for this work. Instead, we provide a concrete scenario for the evaluation based on a variation of the Tunnel Ventilation System (TVS) scenario from Cagula et al. [10]. A TVS uses several types of sensors to detect possible failures in tunnels, such as TVS malfunctioning. For the evaluation, we consider two cases: 1) detect when the oxygen concentration is less than 18% while the temperature is above 30 degrees within the same tunnel sector, and 2) detect when two oxygen sensors in a location report conflicting values, while the temperature is above 30.

We assume that sensors for measuring temperature and oxygen concentration are evenly distributed along the length of a tunnel. A total of 1000 tunnel sectors are equipped with four different sensor types each: two sensors measuring oxygen concentration, and two measuring temperature. Each sensor type generates data into a separate stream at a rate of 1 observation/second. The static dataset, consisting of around 23k triples, provides descriptions of tunnel sectors, observable properties, and sensors. Measurement uncertainty is modeled as part of this static data for two of the sensor types (i.e., similar to how accuracy is often represented in sensor data sheets). For the other two sensor types, uncertainty is instead modeled as annotations on the streamed values. The generated data streams were randomly sampled, such that 95% of the reported values were within the scenario thresholds.

We define a total of 6 queries that are executed under different conditions. Queries 1–3 focus on filters containing calls to uncertainty functions. Query 1 is evaluated over two sensor streams and generates a notification if the oxygen concentration threshold is violated above some probability threshold and the reported temperature value is above 30. Query 2 is evaluated over all four streams and requires all values to simultaneously violate the scenario thresholds with a probability greater than some threshold. Query 3 is evaluated over three of the sensor streams and generates a notification if two reported oxygen concentrations differ with a probability greater than some threshold and the reported temperature is above 30 degrees.

Queries 4–6 are similar to queries 1–3, but rather than filtering on probability thresholds they bind the uncertainty function results to variables and report these as part of the query result.

The query heuristics do not perform any reordering of window patterns, and to reduce ordering bias, we execute two versions of each query (a and b) with reversed window orders. Due to space constraints, we include here only the query shown in Listing 2[2].

---

[1]`https://github.com/keski/RSPUEngine`
[2]The full list of queries are available at `https://github.com/keski/RSPUEngine`

```
REGISTER STREAM <warning/tvs> COMPUTED EVERY PT4S AS
SELECT ?location ?oxValue ?tempValue
FROM NAMED WINDOW <w1> ON <http://stream/oxygen> [RANGE PT10S STEP PT1S]
FROM NAMED WINDOW <w2> ON <http://stream/temperature> [RANGE PT10S STEP PT1S]
WHERE {
    WINDOW <w1> {
        GRAPH ?g1 {
            ?o1 sosa:hasSimpleResult ?oxValue ;
                sosa:hasFeatureOfInterest ?location .
            << ?o1 sosa:hasSimpleResult ?oxValue >> rspu:uncertainty ?unc .
            # The oxygen is below 0.18 with a probability of at least 80%
            FILTER(rspu:lessThan(rspu:add(?unc, ?oxValue), 0.18) >= 0.80)
        }
    }
    WINDOW <w2> {
        GRAPH ?g2 {
            ?o2 sosa:hasSimpleResult ?tempValue ;
                sosa:hasFeatureOfInterest ?location .
            # The reported temperature is greater than 30
            FILTER(?tempValue > 30)
        }
    }
}
```

Listing 2: The query passes the location, oxygen concentration, and temperature to the output stream when the reported oxygen concentration is less than 18% with a probability of at least 0.80, and the reported temperature at the same location is above 30 degrees. Prefixes left out for brevity.

5.2. Results

Query 1–3 are used to evaluate the impact of the H4 heuristic for different probability thresholds. An increase in probability threshold value corresponds to an increase in *filter selectivity*. The term *selectivity* is used to refer to the degree to which the result size is reduced when applying the filter. A small selectivity value is thus *highly* selective (i.e., it greatly reduces the size of the result). The caching optimization is applied both for the baseline and the H4 heuristic, while the lazy variable mechanism has no impact for these queries.

The results of executing queries 1–3 for varying thresholds are presented in Figure 1. The impact of applying the H4 heuristic differs between queries, and with respect to the selectivity of the uncertainty filters. For example, in query 2b applying the H4 heuristic leads to an increase in query execution times for all probability thresholds. On the other hand, in queries 1a and 3a, the H4 heuristic reduces query execution time by up to an order of magnitude across all probability thresholds.

Queries 4–6 focus instead on the impact of the lazy variable mechanism and caching. These queries include no uncertainty filters, and the application of the H4 heuristic has no impact on these queries. The results of executing the queries are shown in Figure 2. The lazy variable mechanism reduces query execution time across all test queries, from a few percents up to an order of magnitude in query 6a. The lazy variable mechanism improves query execution performance whenever unresolved variable bindings are trimmed from

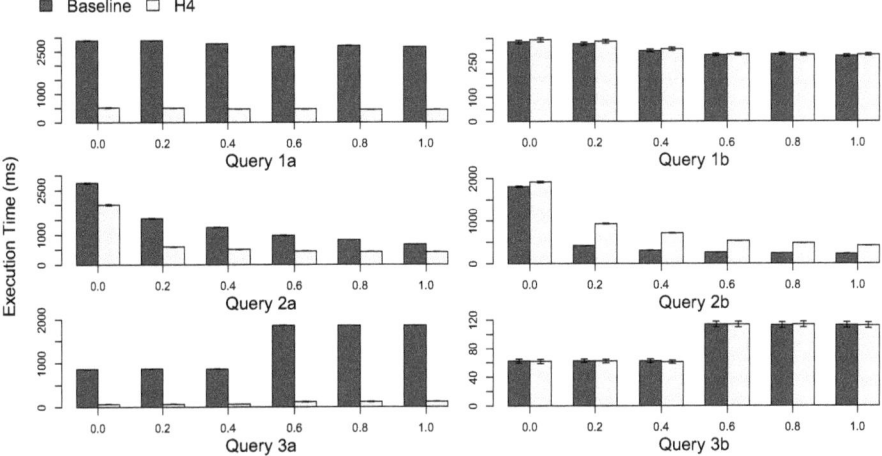

Figure 1. Average query execution times over 20 query executions for queries 1–3. Letters a and b indicate semantically equivalent queries but with reversed window ordering.

the result, and that the overhead of using lazy variables is negligible. The results also show that caching of uncertainty functions generally has a positive impact on query execution performance. However, in query 4a we see that the cache increases overall query execution, showing that the cost of maintaining the cache can add overhead to overall execution if the number of cache hits is low.

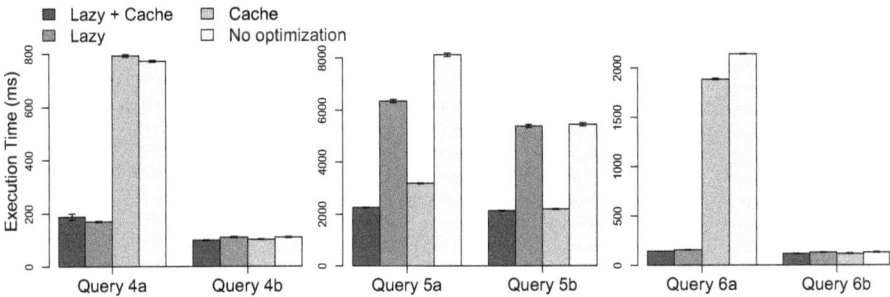

Figure 2. Average query execution times over 20 query executions for queries 4–6, where a and b represent queries with reversed window ordering.

5.3. Follow-up Experiment

To further study how the H4 heuristic impacts performance under different conditions, we generate an independent dataset to support a more precise measure of filter selectivity, and as well as control of the join cardinality between streams (i.e., the factor by which the results will increase when the two windows are joined). We produce two event streams that report randomly sampled values annotated with measurement uncertainty. Each event in the first stream contains four *cardinality properties* that link it to events in

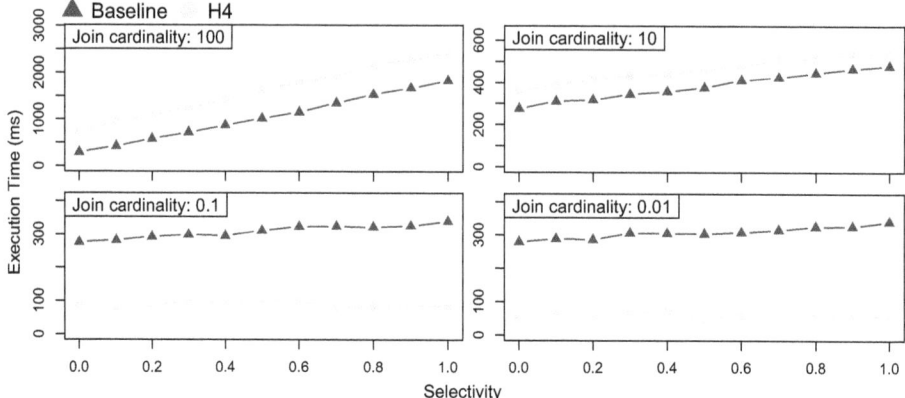

Figure 3. Query execution time for different join cardinalities with varying filter selectivity.

the second stream occurring at the same timestamp. For example, the cardinality property representing a 1-to-100 cardinality maps every event in stream 1 to exactly 100 events in stream 2. An uncertainty filter is applied to the contents of the first stream window. The results of the experiments are presented in Figure 3. The caching optimization is applied both for the baseline and the H4 heuristic.

The results show that when the join cardinality between the windows is high (i.e., the join increases the intermediate result size), the cost of performing the join operation dominates the query execution time, and the baseline outperforms the use of H4, regardless of filter selectivity. However, as the join cardinality decreases, the cost of applying the uncertainty filter becomes the dominating factor and the H4 heuristic then outperforms the baseline across all selectivity thresholds. Generally, applying the H4 heuristic will reduce the number of uncertainty functions that need to be resolved whenever there is a reduction in the number of join partners in the rest of the query pattern. Caching ensures that no uncertainty function will have to be evaluated more than once for the same input, but an increase in the number of join partners can still lead to a high number of cache look-ups that can be detrimental to query execution performance.

6. Conclusions and Future Work

The time required for performing joins between basic graph patterns is generally the dominating factor of execution times in SPARQL processing [21,22]. Pushing filters in order to apply them as early as possible to reduce intermediate results is therefore a common optimization technique. This is true also in the RSP context, but when filters contain calls to uncertainty functions that may be associated with relatively high costs, filter pushing can have the opposite effect. In this paper, we have evaluated a heuristic that instead pulls filters containing references to uncertainty functions, and thereby executes these filters late. The impact of the heuristic depends on both the selectivity of the uncertainty filters, the join cardinalities of subsequent query patterns, and the cost of evaluating the uncertainty filters. Generally, query execution times are reduced when uncertainty filters are pulled if the number of join partners are reduced by subsequent query patterns, since some filter executions can then be avoided.

The two technical optimization techniques proposed to improve query execution performance, have a positive impact on query execution times under most conditions. Caching avoids repeated evaluation of uncertainty functions for the same input, but maintaining the cache and performing cache look-ups also adds to overall execution time. The use of lazy variables reduces the cost of query execution for all affected queries, with performance gains ranging from a few percent to an order of magnitude since no uncertainty function will be executed unless its results are actually used.

In order to effectively combine these findings with other query optimization techniques, such as reordering of operators during query execution, the order of window operations should also be taken into consideration, since it could significantly improve query execution performance. Methods for estimating filter selectivity, improving join cardinality estimation, and switching between query execution strategies to adapt to changing data characteristics also remain important areas for future research.

Acknowledgments

Olaf Hartigs's contributions to this work has been funded in equal parts by the Swedish Research Council (Vetenskapsrådet, project reg. no. 2019-05655) and the CENIIT program at Linköping University (project no. 17.05).

References

[1] Danh Le-Phuoc, Minh Dao-Tran, Josiane Xavier Parreira, and Manfred Hauswirth. A Native and Adaptive Approach for Unified Processing of Linked Streams and Linked Data. In *The Semantic Web – ISWC 2011*, pages 370–388, Berlin, Heidelberg, 2011. Springer Berlin Heidelberg.

[2] Calbimonte, Jean-Paul and Corcho, Oscar and Gray, Alasdair J. G. Enabling Ontology-Based Access to Streaming Data Sources. In *The Semantic Web – ISWC 2010*, pages 96–111, Berlin, Heidelberg, 2010. Springer Berlin Heidelberg.

[3] Davide Francesco Barbieri, Daniele Braga, Stefano Ceri, Emanuele Della Valle, and Michael Grossniklaus. Querying RDF Streams with C-SPARQL. *ACM SIGMOD Record*, 39(1):20–26, 9 2010.

[4] Darko Anicic, Sebastian Rudolph, Paul Fodor, and Nenad Stojanovic. Stream Reasoning and Complex Event Processing in ETALIS. *Semant. Web*, 3(4):397–407, 2012.

[5] Minh Dao-Tran and Danh Le-Phuoc. Towards Enriching CQELS with Complex Event Processing and Path Navigation. In *HiDeSt 2015*, pages 2–14, 2015.

[6] Daniele Dell'Aglio, Minh Dao-Tran, Jean-Paul Calbimonte, Danh Le Phuoc, and Emanuele Della Valle. A Query Model to Capture Event Pattern Matching in RDF Stream Processing Query Languages. In *EKAW 2016*, pages 145–162, 2016.

[7] Syed Gillani, Antoine Zimmermann, Gauthier Picard, and Frédérique Laforest. A Query Language for Semantic Complex Event Processing: Syntax, Semantics and Implementation. *Semant. Web*, 10:53–93, 2019.

[8] Elias Alevizos, Anastasios Skarlatidis, Alexander Artikis, and George Paliouras. Probabilistic Complex Event Recognition: A Survey. *ACM Comput. Surv.*, 50(5), 2017.

[9] Alexander Artikis, Opher Etzion, Zohar Feldman, and Fabiana Fournier. Event Processing Under Uncertainty. In *DEBS'12*, pages 32–43, 2012.

[10] Gianpaolo Cugola, Alessandro Margara, Matteo Matteucci, and Giordano Tamburrelli. Introducing Uncertainty in Complex Event Processing: Model, Implementation, and Validation. *Computing*, 97(2):103–144, 2015.

[11] Robin Keskisärkkä, Eva Blomqvist, Leili Lind, and Olaf Hartig. Capturing and Querying Uncertainty in RDF Stream Processing. In *EKAW 2020*, pages 37–53, 2020.

[12] Alessandro Margara, Jacopo Urbani, Frank van Harmelen, and Henri Bal. Streaming the Web: Reasoning over Dynamic Data. *J. Web Semant.*, 25:24–44, 2014.

[13] Daniele Dell'Aglio, Jean-Paul Calbimonte, Emanuele Della Valle, and Oscar Corcho. Towards a Unified Language for RDF Stream Query Processing. In *Revised Selected Papers of the ESWC 2015 Satellite Events on The Semantic Web*, pages 353–363, 2015.

[14] Daniele Dell'Aglio, Emanuele Della Valle, Jean-Paul Calbimonte, and Oscar Corcho. RSP-QL Semantics: A Unifying Query Model to Explain Heterogeneity of RDF Stream Processing Systems. *Int. J. Semant. Web Inf. Syst.*, 10(4):17–44, 2014.

[15] Robin Keskisärkkä, Eva Blomqvist, Leili Lind, and Olaf Hartig. RSP-QL*: Enabling Statement-Level Annotations in RDF Streams. In *SEMANTiCS 2019*, 2019.

[16] Olaf Hartig and Bryan Thompson. Foundations of an Alternative Approach to Reification in RDF. *CoRR*, abs/1406.3399, 2014.

[17] Olaf Hartig. Foundations of RDF* and SPARQL* – An Alternative Approach to Statement-Level Metadata in RDF. In *Proc. of the 11th AMW Workshop*, 2017.

[18] Jorge Pérez, Marcelo Arenas, and Claudio Gutierrez. Semantics and Complexity of SPARQL. *ACM Trans. Database Syst.*, 34(3), 2009.

[19] Eric Prud'hommeaux, Steve Harris, and Andy Seaborne. SPARQL 1.1 Query Language. Technical report, W3C, 2013.

[20] Michael Schmidt, Michael Meier, and Georg Lausen. Foundations of SPARQL Query Optimization. In *Proc. of the 13th Int. Conf. on Database Theory*, pages 4–33, 2010.

[21] Markus Stocker, Andy Seaborne, Abraham Bernstein, Christoph Kiefer, and Dave Reynolds. SPARQL Basic Graph Pattern Optimization Using Selectivity Estimation. In *WWW '08*, 2008.

[22] Petros Tsialiamanis, Lefteris Sidirourgos, Irini Fundulaki, Vassilis Christophides, and Peter Boncz. Heuristics-Based Query Optimisation for SPARQL. In *Proc. of EDBT*, 2012.

[23] Danh Le-Phuoc, Minh Dao-Tran, Minh-Duc Pham, Peter Boncz, Thomas Eiter, and Michael Fink. Linked Stream Data Processing Engines: Facts and Figures. In *The Semantic Web – ISWC 2012*, volume 7650, pages 300–312. Springer, Berlin, Heidelberg, 2012.

[24] Haopeng Zhang, Yanlei Diao, and Neil Immerman. Recognizing Patterns in Streams with Imprecise Timestamps. *Proc. VLDB Endow.*, 3(1-2):244–255, 2010.

[25] Muhammad Intizar Ali, Feng Gao, and Alessandra Mileo. CityBench: A Configurable Benchmark to Evaluate RSP Engines Using Smart City Datasets. In *The Semantic Web - ISWC 2015*, pages 374–389, Cham, 2015. Springer.

Further with Knowledge Graphs. M. Alam et al. (Eds.)
AKA Verlag and IOS Press, 2021
133

doi:10.3233/SSW210040

Personalizing Type-Based Facet Ranking Using BERT Embeddings

Esraa ALI [a,1], Annalina CAPUTO [b,2], Séamus LAWLESS [a] and Owen CONLAN [a]

[a] *ADAPT Centre, School of Computer Science and Statistics, Trinity College Dublin*
[b] *ADAPT Centre, School of Computing, Dublin City University*

Abstract.

In Faceted Search Systems (FSS), users navigate the information space through facets, which are attributes or meta-data that describe the underlying content of the collection. Type-based facets (aka t-facets) help explore the categories associated with the searched objects in structured information space. This work investigates how personalizing t-facet ranking can minimize user effort to reach the intended search target. We propose a lightweight personalisation method based on Vector Space Model (VSM) for ranking the t-facet hierarchy in two steps. The first step scores each individual leaf-node t-facet by computing the similarity between the t-facet BERT embedding and the user profile vector. In this model, the user's profile is expressed in a category space through vectors that capture the users' past preferences. In the second step, this score is used to re-order and select the sub-tree to present to the user. The final ranked tree reflects the t-facet relevance both to the query and the user profile. Through the use of embeddings, the proposed method effectively handles unseen facets without adding extra processing to the FSS. The effectiveness of the proposed approach is measured by the user effort required to retrieve the sought item when using the ranked facets. The approach outperformed existing personalization baselines.

Keywords. Type-based Facets, Faceted Search, Personalization.

1. Introduction

Faceted Search Systems (FSS) have become one of the main search interfaces used in vertical search systems, offering users meaningful facets to refine their search query and narrow down the results. As the magnitude of data in a collection increases, the number of facets becomes impractical to display on a single page. Ranking the top facets is required as it assists the searcher in locating the target document with minimum effort.

When the information space is structured, type-based facets (t-facets) are extracted from the types of objects (e.g. values of isA or rdfs:type relationships) [1]. Hierarchical taxonomies of types are derived from ontologies by exploiting the subClassOf relationships. When the t-facets belong to a large multilevel hierarchy of categories, it is particularly important to prioritize the most relevant t-facets that can help the user filtering the results by type.

---

[1]Corresponding Author: E-mail: esraa.ali@adaptcentre.ie
[2]Corresponding Author: E-mail: annalina.caputo@adaptcentre.ie

In this work, we analyse the role of personalization in t-facet ranking in isolation from other FSS aspects. Existing facet ranking methods rely on attribute frequencies, navigation cost models, textual queries or click logs to order the facets [1]. This study contributes to the research in this area by introducing a light and effective ranking algorithm for type-based facets.

The algorithm exploits the user's past preferences to build a vector which represents the user profile. T-facets are scored according to their similarity with user profile by exploiting their BERT embeddings. The proposed approach works in two steps. First, it generates personalized relevance scores for each t-facet in the last level of the taxonomy. Then, the second stage aggregates these scores to re-arrange the ancestor t-facets and re-build the final t-facet tree to be rendered to the user. Our experiment aims at answering the following research question: *RQ: Does personalizing the t-facet ranking using BERT embeddings minimize users effort to fulfil their search needs?*

The implemented approach is evaluated using the TREC Contextual Suggestion (TREC-CS) track dataset [2]. TREC-CS is a personalized Point-Of-Interest (POI) recommendation task. We solve the POI suggestion problem by ranking the types of venues as t-facets. In our evaluation, we measure the extent to which this ranked tree minimizes the user effort to reach the first relevant POI.

2. Personalized Facet Ranking Related Research

Several approaches have been proposed in the literature to solve the problem of personalized facet ranking that make use of individual user models, collaborative filtering (CF), or a mixture between the two. Factic [3] is a FSS that personalizes by building models from semantic usage logs. Several layers of user adaption are implemented and integrated with different weights to enhance the facet relevance model . Koren et al. [4] suggested a CF approach by leveraging explicit user feedback about the facets, which is used to build a facet relevance model for individuals. They also use the aggregated facet ratings to build a collaborative model for the new users in order to provide initial good facets in absence of a user profile. The Adaptive Twitter search system generates user models from Twitter to personalize facet ordering [5]. The user model contains entities extracted from the user's tweets. The facets are weighted higher if they exist in the user profile. Le et al. [6] also collects user profile from social networks. The profile is learned from user activities and preferences using a tf-idf feature vector model. Important facets are then highlighted through a matching with the model. A personalized ranking based on CF features was suggested by Chantamunee et. al [7, 8].They used user ratings and Matrix Factorization via SVM and Autoencoders to learn facet ranks.

All the aforementioned approaches do not address the special case of t-facets. Sah and Wade [9] employ session-based user interaction to personalize t-facets. When the searcher selects a t-facet, the system re-organizes the other t-facets according to their similarity to the selected one. Neither the user interests nor the hierarchical nature of the t-facets are considered by this method. Our approach exploits VSM to build user profile, which employs users' historical ratings to infer their preferred t-facets, an unexplored area in literature.

3. Proposed Approach

Our method works in the context of personalized venue search. When a user submits a query, the underlying search engine retrieves a relevant set of venues for it[3]. In order to achieve query relevance, our method works on this set by collecting the t-facets associated with the retrieved venues. The proposed t-facet ranking approach consists of two steps. The first step assigns a relevance score to each t-facet leaf node. The input to this step are the retrieved venues with their relevancy score, the t-facets to which they belong, and the user profile. The second step constructs the final t-facet tree to be displayed to the user. The input to this step are both the score for each t-facet (from the first step) and the original hierarchical taxonomy from which the t-facets are derived. The output of the t-facet ranking is a sub-tree, which contains the ordered set of relevant t-facets.

Step 1: T-Facet Scoring using BERT vectors.   At this step, we establish relevance between the t-facet and the user profile through their vector representation. Each t-facet f_i is represented by a BERT embedding $\overrightarrow{f_i}$. We employ the t-facet's label to generate its corresponding BERT embedding using pre-trained BERT model[4]. BERT provides a meaningful vector representation of text and has been proven effective in many IR tasks. It is particularly useful in this task as it semantically embeds the meaning of the type in the vector. This is important in handling new and unseen t-facet which did not exist in the user profile before. In this case the model will handle them based on their similarity with existing t-facets. In our early experiments we also experimented word2vec models but BERT-based models gave better results. However we acknowledge that other semantic-based embedding can be used in this approach and improve the results.

The vector representing the user profile is obtained using the Rocchio formula, which is a classical approach to relevance feedback in IR. Since in our case we only have the user feedback (i.e. ratings) at POI level, we assume that the rating can also be transferred to the types associated with the POI. Based on this assumption, we represent the user profile through a vector combining positive, negative and neutral preferences (i.e. rated POI types). We define the positive (pos.) user vector $\overrightarrow{u_i}^{pos}$ as the average of t-facet vectors rated positively by the user u_i:

$$\overrightarrow{u_i}^{pos} = \frac{\sum_{j=1}^{|F_u^{pos}|} \overrightarrow{f_j} \times w_{f_i^{pos}}}{|F_u^{pos}|} \tag{1}$$

Where F_u^{pos} is the set of t-facets rated positively by the user. Each vector is weighted by $w_{f_j^{pos}}$ (see eq 2). The weight averages the probability that this specific user will rate the t-facet as positive $Pr(f_j^{pos}|u_i)$ and the probability that any user in the system will rate the t-facet as positive $Pr(f_j^{pos}|U)$. In absence of any personal preference only the general probability will be used. The value $w_{f_j^{pos}}$ affects how each t-facet contributes to the final positive profile vector.

---

[3]How the venue ranking is performed is outside scope of this research.

[4]https://spacy.io/universe/project/spacy-transformers, model used: en_trf_bertbaseuncased_lg

$$w_{f_j^{pos}} = \begin{cases} \gamma \times Pr(f_j^{pos}|U) + (1-\gamma) \times Pr(f_j^{pos}|u) & \text{, if } Pr(f_j^{pos}|u) > 0 \\ \\ Pr(f_j^{pos}|U) & \text{, otherwise} \end{cases} \tag{2}$$

The parameter $\gamma \in [0,1]$, is used to balance between individual user feedback versus general population feedback. In a similar manner, the negative (neg.) and the neutral (neu.) user vectors are computed. In order to model the final vector representation of the user's interest, we experimented with two versions of the Rocchio formula. The first (*Rocchio-BERT*) is the traditional version computed according to equation 3.

$$\vec{u_i} = \alpha \times \vec{u_i}^{neu} + \beta \times \vec{u_i}^{pos} - \lambda \times \vec{u_i}^{neg} \tag{3}$$

The contribution of each user vector is regulated through the weights $\alpha, \beta, \lambda \in [0,1]$. The second (*Ortho-BERT*) is a modified version of Rocchio formula proposed by [10], in which instead of subtracting the negative vector they add the user negative vector's orthogonal complement ($\vec{u_i}^{neg\perp}$). Equation 4 illustrates the computation.

$$\vec{u_i} = \alpha \times \vec{u_i}^{neu} + \beta \times \vec{u_i}^{pos} + \lambda \times \vec{u_i}^{neg\perp} \tag{4}$$

The orthogonal complement is obtained using Gram–Schmidt process. The weights are the same as equation 3. Finally, the query t-facets are ranked according to the cosine similarity score between the user profile vector $\vec{u_i}$ and the the t-facet vector $\vec{f_j}$.

Step 2: T-Facet Tree Building   The tree construction algorithm re-orders the original taxonomy tree by using the generated scores from the previous step. It follows a bottom-up approach where the t-facets at the lower level in the taxonomy are sorted first, then it proceeds by sorting all the ancestors of those t-facets, and so on up to the root of the hierarchy. To build a final t-facet tree with v levels, we adopted a *fixed level* strategy [11]. The strategy respects the original taxonomy hierarchy and uses a predefined fixed page size for each t-facet level. It starts by grouping t-facets at level-v by their parent. Then, it sorts the parent nodes at level-$(v-1)$ by aggregating the scores of their top k children, the children are ordered by their relevance score generated in step 1, and so on up to level-1. We use *Max.* aggregation function to keep the top ranked t-facet at the top of the final tree.

4. Experimental Results

Experimental setup.   Our approach is evaluated on TREC-CS 2016 dataset [2]. The t-facet taxonomy is derived from the Foursquare venue category hierarchy [5]. To link as much Foursquare venues to TREC-CS POIs as possible, we complement the original data with three Foursquare supplementary datasets from [12, 13] and our own crawled POIs. The final dataset has 58 requests and an average of 208 t-facets per request to be ranked. Only the first two levels of the taxonomy are included. The document search engine implements BM25 with NDCG value of 0.4023, the query is formed by combining user tags weighed by their most common rating. The existence of relevance judgments makes

---

[5]https://developer.foursquare.com/docs/resources/categories, version: 20180323

it possible to evaluate our approach against a well established ground-truth. We follow the strategy used in Faceted Search task of INEX 2011 Data-Centric Track [14]. We report two metrics suggested by the organizers. The number of actions (#Actions) counts how many clicks the user has to perform on the ranked facets in order to reach the first relevant document in the top 5 results. The faceted scan (F-Scan) measures the user's effort to scan facets and documents until user reach the same document. It is calculated as the sum of the t-facet rank in the tree plus the document position in the list after being filtered using this t-facet. We focus on these metrics as a proxy for user's effort, which will help in answering our research question. To chose the optimal weights for equations 4 and 3, we used hyper-parameter tuning with range from 0 to 1 and step of 0.25. We report results for the Rocchio-BERT and Ortho-BERT methods in addition to KNN-BERT, which uses a trained KNN model for each user to predict the user's preference to a given t-facet, with $k = 1$. All scoring results are reported by adopting the Fixed Level-Max strategy, with level-1 and level-2 page size set to three.

Results. Table 1 summarizes our results; the first 3 rows shows our BERT based scoring methods. The Rocchio-BERT method outperformed both Ortho-BERT and KNN-BERT methods. The normalization step by Gram-Schmidt process used in Ortho-BERT neutralises the personalized negative profile weight, which negatively affects the results. Rocchio-BERT achieved best results with $\alpha = 0$,

Table 1.: **Results for our scoring models using Fixed-level(Max) strategy.**

Scoring Method	F-Scan	#Actions
KNN-BERT	4.825	1.667
Ortho-BERT	3.754	1.421
Rochio-BERT	**3.281**	**1.281**
Prob. Scoring [11]	3.456	1.333
MF-SVM [7]	3.912	1.491
Most Prob. (Person) [4]	3.737	1.6142
Most Prob. (Collab) [4]	3.351	1.333

$\beta \in \{0.25, 0.5, 0.75, 1\}$, and $\lambda = 0$, which means that the positive vector profile is the key component in the formula. $\gamma = 0$, which means that the person probability is favoured over the global probability in the t-facets weighting(2.

The second part of Table 1 reports the results of other existing personalization methods. As these methods do not handle the hierarchical nature of the t-facets, we use them as scoring methods with the Fixed Level-Max strategy. Rocchio-BERT still results in the minimum #Actions and F-scan when compared with these models. In addition, the proposed VSM approach has other advantages. It provides a light yet effective personalized ranking. The user profile vectors can be pre-computed and stored offline, reducing the computation at retrieval time of the cosine distance between the query t-facets and the user profile. This can be further optimized by pre-computing a distance matrix for the user and all t-facets in the FSS. User profiles on the other hand, can be updated offline as the user rates new venues. Optimizing this step will reduce the total time needed by FSS to populate its final results page.

5. Conclusions

This work presented a two-step t-facet ranking approach employing BERT embeddings to personalize the t-facet ranking. The first step assigns score to t-facets. The second step uses the score to re-arrange and build the final t-facet tree. To personalize the scores, we explored several methods based on vector space model. They showed promising results when combined with the personal preferences of the users. We plan to experiment with additional POI suggestion datasets and explore learning to rank methods for the t-facet scoring step.

Acknowledgements

This work was supported by the ADAPT Centre, funded by Science Foundation Ireland Research Centres Programme (Grant 13/RC/2106; 13/RC/2106_P2) and co-funded by the European Regional Development Fund.

References

[1] Yannis Tzitzikas, Nikos Manolis, and Panagiotis Papadakos. Faceted exploration of rdf/s datasets: a survey. *Journal of Intelligent Information Systems*, 2017.

[2] Seyyed Hadi Hashemi, Charles LA Clarke, Jaap Kamps, Julia Kiseleva, and Ellen M Voorhees. Overview of the trec 2016 contextual suggestion track. In *TREC*, 2016.

[3] Michal Tvarožek and Mária Bieliková. Factic: personalized exploratory search in the semantic web. In *ICWE*. Springer, 2010.

[4] Jonathan Koren, Yi Zhang, and Xue Liu. Personalized interactive faceted search. In *WWW*. ACM, 2008.

[5] Fabian Abel, Ilknur Celik, Geert-Jan Houben, and Patrick Siehndel. Leveraging the semantics of tweets for adaptive faceted search on twitter. *The Semantic Web*, 2011.

[6] T. Le, B. Vo, and T. H. Duong. Personalized facets for semantic search using linked open data with social networks. In *IBICA*, 2012.

[7] Siripinyo Chantamunee, Kok Wai Wong, and Chun Che Fung. Collaborative filtering for personalised facet selection. In *IAIT*. ACM, 2018.

[8] Siripinyo Chantamunee, Kok Wai Wong, and Chun Che Fung. An exploration of user–facet interaction in collaborative-based personalized multiple facet selection. *Knowledge-Based Systems*, 209:106444, 2020. ISSN 0950-7051. doi: https://doi.org/10.1016/j.knosys.2020.106444. URL http://www.sciencedirect.com/science/article/pii/S0950705120305736.

[9] Melike Sah and Vincent Wade. Personalized concept-based search and exploration on the web of data using results categorization. In *The Semantic Web:2013*.

[10] Pierpaolo Basile, Annalina Caputo, and Giovanni Semeraro. Negation for document re-ranking in ad-hoc retrieval. In *ICTIR 2011*.

[11] Séamus Lawless Esraa Ali, Annalina Caputo and Owen Conlan. A probabilistic approach to personalize type-based facet ranking for poi suggestion. In *ICWE 2021*.

[12] Mohammad Aliannejadi, Ida Mele, and Fabio Crestani. A cross-platform collection for contextual suggestion. In *SIGIR*. ACM, 2017.

[13] Mostafa Bayomi and Séamus Lawless. Adapt_tcd: An ontology-based context aware approach for contextual suggestion. In *TREC*, 2016.

[14] Qiuyue Wang, Georgina Ramírez, Maarten Marx, Martin Theobald, and Jaap Kamps. Overview of the INEX 2011 Data-Centric Track. In *Focused Retrieval of Content and Structure*. Springer, 2012.

Further with Knowledge Graphs. M. Alam et al. (Eds.)
AKA Verlag and IOS Press, 2021
© 2021 Akademische Verlagsgesellschaft AKA GmbH, Berlin
This article is published online with Open Access by IOS Press and distributed under the terms
of the Creative Commons Attribution License 4.0 (CC BY 4.0).
doi:10.3233/SSW210041

Annotating Entities with Fine-Grained Types in Austrian Court Decisions

Artem Revenko[1][0000−0001−6681−3328], Anna Breit[1][0000−0001−6553−4175], Victor Mireles[1][0000−0003−3264−3687], Julian Moreno-Schneider[2][0000−0003−1418−9935], Christian Sageder[3], and Sotirios Karampatakis[1][0000−0001−7436−7620]

[1] Semantic Web Company GmbH, Austria
{firstname.secondname}@semantic-web.com
[2] DFKI GmbH, Germany
julian.moreno_schneider@dfki.de
[3] Cybly GmbH, Austria
christian.sageder@cybly.tech

Abstract. The usage of Named Entity Recognition tools on domain-specific corpora is often hampered by insufficient training data. We investigate an approach to produce fine-grained named entity annotations of a large corpus of Austrian court decisions from a small manually annotated training data set. We apply a general purpose Named Entity Recognition model to produce annotations of common coarse-grained types. Next, a small sample of these annotations are manually inspected by domain experts to produce an initial fine-grained training data set. To efficiently use the small manually annotated data set we formulate the task of named entity typing as a binary classification task – for each originally annotated occurrence of an entity, and for each fine-grained type we verify if the entity belongs to it. For this purpose we train a transformer-based classifier. We randomly sample 547 predictions and evaluate them manually. The incorrect predictions are used to improve the performance of the classifier – the corrected annotations are added to the training set. The experiments show that re-training with even a very small number (5 or 10) of originally incorrect predictions can significantly improve the classifier performance. We finally train the classifier on all available data and re-annotate the whole data set.

Keywords: Named Entity Recognition · Entity Typing · Legal Corpus · Natural Language Processing

1 Introduction

The ever-increasing amount of unstructured data available in digital form results in a need for technologies that support users in the task of structuring, interpreting or, on a general level, making sense of these data, ideally in an automated way [6, 3]. This is basically the core business of semantic processing, and one of the tasks that has traditionally been very central is Named Entity Recognition (NER). NER is usually an upstream task to concrete use cases such as text knowledge graph population, information extraction or question answering. Such downstream applications benefit from high-quality NER output, which is why the task of NER is an important and often critical one. At the same time, many NER tools are limited to distinguishing only a relatively small set of entity types, because most of the popular corpora and data sets that are used for training these tools [24, 16] are annotated for the entity types person, location and organisation only. It is especially difficult to find annotated corpora in languages other than English. Producing such a data set is a very expensive task and is completely infeasible in practical applications. In domain-specific corpora it might be even difficult to produce the annotations of the coarse-grained types mentioned above, because the domain-specific use of language and the special terms can easily confuse the general-purpose NER tools resulting in noisy annotations.

In this paper, we tackle the task of classifying the entities recognized by a general-purpose NER tool into fine-grained entity types chosen by a domain expert. We conduct a case study on the corpus of Austrian court decisions collected from The Legal Information System of the Republic of Austria[4] in German language. We consider real industry settings, therefore, we rely on a very small amount of annotated training data that is produced by a domain expert in frames of this work, and we additionally aim at recovering from noisy annotations produced by the general purpose NER tool on the domain-specific corpus.

The task is motivated by the commercial tool `LawThek`[5] that offers its customer a way to access the Austrian legislation and related legal documents. The customers benefit from additional enrichments produced by the system and a domain-specific NER model would provide a further extension that would help the user to better retrieve the relevant documents and identify useful information in those documents.

Open Data All the data, including the original corpus and the manual annotations is publicly available[6]. The code to repeat the experiments is also publicly available[7].

2   Related Work

The most popular NER tools, e. g., SpaCy[8], Stanford CRF-NER[9], and the Open-NLP NameFinder[10], require large amounts of training data and typically distinguish only a small set of entity types. A significant effort has been undertaken

---

[4] https://www.ris.bka.gv.at
[5] https://lawthek.eu/home
[6] https://doi.org/10.5281/zenodo.4625767
[7] https://github.com/semantic-web-company/austrian_court_decisions
[8] https://spacy.io
[9] https://nlp.stanford.edu/software/CRF-NER.shtml
[10] https://opennlp.apache.org/docs/1.8.3/apidocs/opennlp-
    uima/opennlp/uima/namefind/NameFinder.html

to create training data sets with more fine-grained entity types, for example two benchmarks: FIGER [1] and OntoNotes [19]. In the work presented here, we investigate a method that significantly reduces the required amount of training data.

Fine-grained NER Several systems addressing the fine-grained NER task have been successfully applied on those data sets. In [28] and [27] authors exploit modern transformer-based language models to learn joint embeddings of words and entities from large entity-annotated corpora. These models allow one to effectively combine the semantic signals retrieved from both words and entities. The authors of K-Adapter [26] also build on top of modern transformer language models adding special adapters that inject multiple kinds of diverse knowledge. These adapters are task-specific and are, therefore, able continuously infuse knowledge, without forgetting.

The mentioned models reach state of the art performance on the mentioned fine-grained data sets. However, these and other similar models (e.g. [23, 15]) rely on significant amounts of data, incorporating external knowledge bases to learn each type of entities. On the contrast, we are interested in learning the basic "concept" of type verification from very small data and seek to find a model that is able to benefit from cross-type interactions.

Entity Linking and Distant Supervision Solving the problem of typing entities can also be addressed by the methods of Entity Linking (EL), in which a diversity of string-matching techniques are employed to relate found mentions of NEs with known entities. Common tools for entity linking include DBPedia Spotlight[4], Entity Fishing[13] or Babelfly[14]; and the number of approaches to EL continues to increase (see [18] for a recent overview). EL, however, assumes the existence of a catalog of entities (preferably containing additional knowledge). In domain-specific settings, such as the one treated here, this is an unreasonable assumption that limit the potential range of use cases. One reason is that no entity catalog is complete and the entities specific to a domain are unlikely to be found in general domain ones. Another reason is that, for some purposes, entities of interest in the text do not correspond to any particular real world entity. For example, *the complainant* or *the buyer* are specific entities within a document, but are not a surface form of any particular real world entity.

The idea of Distant Supervision [7, 21] is to employ EL to create an (entity) annotated corpora. The drawbacks are the inevitable errors produced by the EL tools, especially false negatives. To mitigate this problem, researchers design neural models that are able to cope with such noisy data and/or help to recover from noisy [22, 12]. Yet, the Distant Supervision approach and its extension suffer from the same shortcomings as EL, because these techniques rely on EL and external data sources, whereas our approach is bound only to the domain-specific corpus and domain experts.

3   Data

The current paper presents a use case study of re-tagging entities with fine-grained types selected by the domain expert in a legal corpus in German language. The corpus is downloaded from Legal Information System of the Republic of Austria (RIS) – a computer-assisted information system on Austrian law[11]. The corpus for the current experiments consists of 2500 randomly selected court decisions taken from the category "Judikatur" (= Judicature of the courts), section "Bundesverwaltungsgericht" (= Federal Administrative Court). These documents are not older than 2014 and provided in the original German language. A large part of the decisions concern decisions on asylum procedures. The personal information is anonymised in the documents, see Example 1.

Example 1. The following quote is taken from the document with European Case Law Identifier `ECLI:AT:BVWG:2021:W109.2195466.1.00`. The replacement token *XXXX* mask the real name and the birth date of an individual.

> Gemäß § 8 Abs. 1 Asylgesetz 2005 wird *XXXX* , geb. *XXXX* , StA. AFGHANISTAN, der Status der subsidiär Schutzberechtigten in Bezug auf den Herkunftsstaat Afghanistan zuerkannt.

3.1   Original Named Entity Annotations

The corpus is initially annotated with a NER tool, based on BERT neural networks, which is developed following the work of Kamal Raj.[12] The original approach is adapted to allow for training of a new model on the WikiNer data set [17] – a general purpose data set containing four coarse-grained types. In the initial annotation process the tool annotated 39,324 Persons (`PER`), 215,699 Locations (`LOC`), 183,045 Organizations (`ORG`) and 324,926 Miscellanea (`MISC`). As expected, given the type of documents, court decisions, the `PER` type is the least abundant, while the other three types are present one order of magnitude as many times.

The model is quite confused by the domain-specific usage of language and also special symbols such as anonymization masks and frequent abbreviations. Therefore, we identified many noisy annotations in the original coarse-grained annotations.

3.2   Selection of Named Entity Types of Interest

The original annotations are collected and analysed to group the entities and produce new entity types[13]. These new types are reviewed by the domain expert from the point of view of the targeted functionality of the final application and

---

[11] https://www.ris.bka.gv.at/UI/Erv/Info.aspx accessed on March 26
[12] https://github.com/kamalkraj/BERT-NER
[13] For the purpose of the current work we omit the details of type induction as the presented classification approach does not depend on the type selection procedure.

9 fine-grained entity types are selected for further analysis, see also Table 1 for the definitions of types.

Gericht to recognize the different courts, therefore, identify the level at which a certain decision was taken. This could be potentially accomplished with the usage of a gazetteer for Austrian courts, however, colloquial usages and international courts would be missed.

Behörde, Administration to be able to see the involvement of different government offices into processes, therefore identifying in the stakeholders from the government.

Verwandtschaft to group physical persons into clusters. Could be further used for information extraction or grouping by kinship.

Land, Staat to identify potential international involvement.

Information, Quelle, Daten to find external information sources that could potentially be interlinked.

Zocken, Spielhallen to group documents w.r.t exact type of criminal activity. This activity was particularly prominent.

Rolle, Gruppe von Personen to identify roles, persons can be assigned too used to for further grouping / information retrieval. E. g. person is a complainant, a buyer, a seller, etc.

Kriegshandlung, Konflikt to group documents w.r.t. exact type of non-criminal activity that could be triggers. In this case, many armed conflicts lead to asylum procedures.

Strasse, Addresse to get more detailed GEO locations down to an exact address which can be checked against an address database.

The new types are chosen from the analysed data and with the idea to provide some additional value for the end user. However, the types appear to have overlaps and do not necessarily cover all the data. For example, the types "Gericht" and "Behörde" are much closer to each other than to "Strasse, Addresse", for example. On the other hand, the type "Rolle, Gruppe" comprises entities of quite different semantics and could be potentially split into two types; the choice is done in favor of this joint type because in the random sample we find many borderline entities such as "complainants" or 'legal representatives". We note that this choice of types makes the classification task more challenging, often an entity might belong to more than one type. We see it necessary to cope with this choice as it was provided by the expert from the point of view of the domain of application itself.

In the following we add an artificial type "Other" that is reserved for 1) original noisy annotations and 2) entities that do not belong to any of the described types.

3.3   Manual Annotations

We annotate a small sample of data manually. For this purpose we choose a few seed entities that unambiguously belong to the chosen fine-grained types and

Table 1. Fine-grained types with definitions and synonyms.

Type	Definition
	Synonyms
Gericht	Ort zur gesetzlichen Entscheidung von Rechtsstreitigkeiten
	Place where legal disputes are decided
	Gericht, Gerichtshof, Tribunal
	Court, tribunal, court of law
Behörde, Administration	eine öffentliche Stelle, die die Aufgaben der öffentlichen Verwaltung wahrnimmt
	A public body that is involved in public administration
	Behörde, Administration, Amt
	government office
Verwandtschaft	Zugehörigkeit zur gleichen Familie, gleiche Abstammung
	Family or ancestry relations
	Verwandtschaft, Angehörige, Familie
	Relatives, family, kinship
Land, Staat	unabhängiges politisches Gebilde
	Independent political entity
	Land, Staat
	Country, State
Information, Quelle, Daten	wissenschaftlich auswertbares Primärmaterial
	Primary material for scientific research
	Information, Quelle, Daten
	Information, source, data
Zocken, Spielhallen	Spiel um Geld, bei dem Gewinn und Verlust vom Zufall abhängen
	A game where money is waged and whose outcome depends on change
	Glücksspiel, Zocken
	Games of chance
Rolle, Gruppe von Personen	eine Gruppe, deren Mitglieder sich in Kontakt miteinander befinden, gemeinsame Ziele verfolgen und sich als zusammengehörig empfinden
	A group whose members are in contact with each other, pursue common goals and feel that they belong together
	Rolle, Gruppe
	Role, group
Kriegshandlung, Konflikt	Vorgehen gegen einen Gegner oder Feind
	Violent actions against an enemy
	Kriegshandlung, Konflikt, Anschlag, Angriff
	War waging, conflict, attack, aggression
Strasse, Addresse	die genaue örtliche Bezeichnung
	An exact description of a location
	Straße, Addresse, Anschrift
	Street, Address

identify their occurrences in the documents, see Example 2. We then manually verify the correctness. This original manually annotated data set is publicly available, the number of entities is presented in Table 2. There are in total 109 annotated instances for 9 types resulting in ≈12 instances per type on average.

We choose clean, unambiguous entities as the seed entities. This process is tedious for the expert, as it requires to skim through the documents to identify those entities, therefore it is not feasible to produce a large initial data set. Yet, these initial manual annotations are not expected to represent the whole data set, but rather produce a good seed data set for the chosen fine-grained types.

Example 2. The following quote is taken from the document with European Case Law Identifier ECLI:AT:BVWG:2015:W162.1418315.1.00. The entity "**Tschetschenien**" is an example of type "Land, Staat".

> Seit 2002 sind in **Tschetschenien** über 2.000 Personen entführt worden, von denen über die Hälfte bis zum heutigen Tage verschwunden bleibt.

Table 2. Statistics of manually annotated and manually verified data sets.

Type	Annotated	Verified
Gericht	9	47
Behörde, Administration	12	36
Verwandtschaft	12	1
Land, Staat	12	60
Information, Quelle, Daten	12	44
Zocken, Spielhallen	20	15
Rolle, Gruppe von Personen	11	67
Kriegshandlung, Konflikt	15	3
Strasse, Addresse	6	19
Other	-	255
Total	109	547

4 Classifier

We design a classifier that is capable of verifying the type of a given entity. We take into account the lack of training data and, therefore, aim at a robust solution that would be capable to efficiently use some preliminary training to solve the task. Therefore, we focus our attention on the Target Sense Verification (TSV) task [2]. The core task is a binary classification task – given an entity of interest in a context and definitions / hypernyms of an entity's sense decide if the entity is mentioned in the given sense or not. The main challenge of the task is to generalize the ability of verifying the sense of an entity to unseen domains and senses.

Our task setting can be formulated in a similar way, with the difference of verifying the type of an entity instead of its sense – target type verification. Yet the inputs – the target in context, the definition and the synonyms of the target type – are very similar to TSV. Therefore, we reuse the results of the challenge and employ the model from [25][14] that showed the best results in Task 3 of the challenge. The model is based on a transformer model (we use Bert [5][15]), and it marks the input to let the encoder focus on the target and sense/type identifiers.

4.1 General Purpose Fine-tuning

For fine-tuning our model on the proposed task, we chose a learning setup similar to [2]: we created a training set where each instance consists of a target word in a context (e.g. *the **spring** was broken*), and a target sense, indicated by the definition and hypernyms of the target word (e.g., *the season of growth* and *season*) as well as a label indicating if the target word was used in the target sense (in this case, *F*). As it has been shown, that the proposed classifier is to some extent able to transfer intrinsic classification capabilities gained on a general purpose data set into specific domains [25], we generated this training set from German Wiktionary. Herefore, we scraped the entries of nouns for which multiple meanings, definitions, hypernyms and examples were available. We removed senses that were too close (i.e., those that were listed as *[1a]* and *[1b]* instead of *[1]* and *[2]*) and manually cleaned the data set to reduce noise. The final training set consists of 3,564 instances, with 55% positive examples and 45% negative ones.

4.2 Training

We always start from a model tuned on TSV data set. We remind that the classification task is binary and the input is encoded as:

```
[CLS] T₁ T₂ ... $ TARGET_T₁ TARGET_T₂ ... $ Tₙ ...
[SEP] DEF_T₁ DEF_T₂ ... $ SYN₁_T₁ SYN₁_T₂ ... $ SYN₂_T₁ ... [SEP],
```

where T_i stands for ith token of the context, TARGET_T_i stands for ith token of the target entity, DEF_T_i – ith token of the definition of the target type, SYN$_j$_T_i – ith token of the jth synonym of the target type, and [CLS], [SEP] are the special tokens used by the model, "..." denotes a continuation of an enumeration, i.e. T_i or DEF_T_i. It is straightforward to generate negative training examples – it is enough to substitute the definition and the synonyms of the correct type with some other type's definition and synonyms. In the preliminary experiments on a

---

[14] We note that a very similar model is introduced in [8]. However, the former is an extension and is better suited for the task at hand.

[15] It has been demonstrated that domain-specific pre-trained language models such as BioBert [10] or PatentBert [9] can improve the performance on various NLP tasks, however, to our best knowledge no publicly available legal German language model exists at the moment.

different similar data set reported in [11] we identified that the optimal number of negative examples is ≈70% of the available other types, therefore, in our experiments for each positive example we generate 6 negative examples.

In the first experiment with only manually annotated data we use all the data for continuing fine tuning, because the size of the data set is small, see Section 3.3 and in particular Table 2. We train the model for 3 epochs. For the consecutive experiments experiments with manually verified data we use up to 15 instances per type from the verified data with 2 negative examples per positive as the development data set. The model is trained for 7 epochs in each run and the best scoring model (in terms of F_1 score on the development data set) is chosen for further evaluation. The training batch size is set to 8, for the rest the parameters are set either as reported by authors or as the defaults by the training framework PyTorch [20].

5 Experiment

We recap that the goal of the experiment is to annotate the originally recognized entities of coarse types with new fine-grained types as defined in Table 1. For this purpose we first fine-tune the model (Section 4) on the German TSV data set (Section 4.1). Then we manually annotate a small sample of data with target fine-grained types (Section 3.3). Further we fine-tune the model on this small manually annotated data set and generate predictions of new entities. We randomly take 547 predictions and manually evaluate the correctness of predictions (Section 5.1). Finally, we combine all the manually annotated entities – the initial manually annotated data set and the verified sample – and fine tune our model on the whole data set. We use this latter model to generate predictions for the complete corpus.

As described in Section 3.1 the original coarse annotations contain many noisy annotations that actually do not belong to any type. Another goal of the experiment is to evaluate how efficiently we can recover from these noisy annotations and correctly reject them.

5.1 Manual Verification

After fine-tuning on the manually annotated data set, we manually verify the results. The trained model is used to automatically generate predictions on the original corpus. Then, a sample of those predictions is taken to manually verify their correctness. We take ≈55 randomly sampled predictions per **predicted** fine-grained type.

For each of the fine-grained type, we create a separate spreadsheet, containing one prediction per row. In detail, on each row, the surface form of the entity, the predicted type, the position of the entity in the context and the full context are given. Six independent reviewers were tasked to examine the correctness of these samples. The review is performed as a binary classification task, by determining if the prediction is correct or not. Additionally, in case of a false prediction, the reviewers are required to provide a proper classification for the entity according to 9 types described in Table 1. The reviewers are instructed to be tolerant only in the case of incomplete boundaries of the annotations.

Example 3. In the following sample, Eurostat is tagged as of type "Information, Quelle, Daten". Even that the annotation is incomplete, i. e. it does not contain the date reference, this prediction is considered correct.

> (...)4. Qu. 2015 655 35 35 15 565 GESAMT 3.510 345 170 120 2.870 Die Daten werden auf die Endziffern 5 oder 0 auf- bzw. abgerundet. (Eurostat 18.9.2015a; Eurostat 18.9.2015b; Eurostat 10.12.2015; **Eurostat** 3.3.2016b) In erster Instanz für das Asylverfahren in Polen zuständig ist das Office for Foreigners(...)

As the predictions are often incorrect, the resulting verified data set is quite unbalanced, with many wrongly annotated entities that end up in the type "Other". The actual frequencies of the verified fine-grained types are presented in 2.

5.2   Results

In the first run the model is trained on manually annotated data for 3 epochs, the results are presented in Table 3[16]. We note that only one type "Gericht" reaches F_1 score above 0.5. It is remarkable that the performance does not always correlate with the size of the training set for a given types; for example, "Strasse, Addresse" with only 6 training samples reaches F_1 of 0.35 that is significantly higher than F_1 score of "Kriegshandlung, Konflikt" with 15 training samples.

Overall accuracy and F_1 are below 0.3. These low scores can be explained by a significantly different real verified data as compared to the clean seed instances used for the manual annotations. Therefore, we do further runs of the experiment taking a few samples of the manually verified types. In these runs we extend the training set by 5 and 10 instances, respectively, of the *incorrectly labelled* manually verified data set. We add those instances with the corrected tag and, in the preparation of the training set, we generate negative examples for them as described in Section 4.2. We only do it for those types that have at least 20 incorrectly labelled instances, namely for "Information, Quelle, Daten", "Rolle, Gruppe von Personen", "Behörde, Administration", "Gericht", "Land, Staat". We also add 5 and 10 instances from the type "Other" to generate negative examples for training. Therefore, we use roughly 5% and 10% of the manually verified data set, respectively, to extend the training set. For both settings 3 runs were performed with randomly chosen 5 and 10 instances, average results are reported.

The results of training on the data set extend by 5 additional instances are presented in Table 4. We note that now for 5 types the F_1 scores are 0.5 and

---

[16] We used the functionality of `scikit-learn` (https://scikit-learn.org/stable/modules/model_evaluation.html#classification-report visited on 02.04.2021) to produce the classification report.

Table 3. Results of the evaluation of the model trained on manually annotated data set. Overall accuracy is .27. The values above 0.5 are in **bold**, the maximum value per column is in *italics*.

	precision	recall	F_1 score	support
Gericht	**.51**	**.55**	**.53**	47
Behörde, Administration	.06	.08	.07	36
Verwandtschaft	0	0	0	1
Land, Staat	.43	.43	.43	60
Information, Quelle, Daten	.25	.30	.27	44
Zocken, Spielhallen	.28	*1.0*	.44	15
Rolle, Gruppe von Personen	.17	.13	.15	67
Kriegshandlung, Konflikt	.05	*1.0*	.09	3
Strasse, Addresse	.24	**.63**	.35	19
Other	*.66*	.16	.26	255
macro avg	.27	.43	.26	547
micro avg	.46	.27	.28	547

above. Remarkably, for the type "Zocken, Spielhallen" the results have grown significantly, though no additional training instances were added. On the other hand, the type "Strasse, Addresse" is now much more often misclassified as false negative, therefore recall and F_1 are much lower. This demonstrates the cross-type interactions in our model, i. e. the model seems to be able to learn the idea of type verification in general and not fit to the specific training data at hand.

Overall accuracy and F_1 scores grow by ≈0.2, which can be considered a very significant growth. This demonstrates that with the current model and training routine even a very small amount of real annotated data can have a significant impact on classification results.

We are further interested if adding more data can still have a significant impact and proceed with 10 additional instances per type for the populated types (with support more than 20), the results are presented in Table 5. We observe further grows of scores, now 6 types have F_1 scores of 0.5 and above. Though the absolute values now demonstrate a more moderate growth of not more than 0.1 for accuracy and average F_1, the variance has significantly decreased for most scores. This might due to the fact that the verified data set is very challenging for classification, including noisy and arguable entities. Therefore, we slowly see the "saturation" of scores, i. e. some entities are outliers in its types and can either not be classified well or corrupt the model if added as training instances. However, as the variance decreases, with 10 added instances we observe less impact from those noisy instances. We also note further cross-type learning as, for example, for "Strasse, Addresse" and "Zocken, Spielhallen" the scores keep growing without any further training instances of this type.

We see that using the extended data set we also manage to train the model to recover from noise to a certain extent. In the latter experiment the F_1 score for the type "Other" is above 0.5. Yet, in both extended experiments we observe that often the precision for this type is higher than recall.

Table 4. Averaged results of the evaluation of the model trained on manually annotated with 5 additional instances for each type with support higher than 20. Best models after epochs 4, 3, 3. Overall accuracy is **.50** ± .04. The values above 0.5 are in **bold**, the maximum value per column is in *italics*.

	precision	recall	F_1 score	support
Gericht	**.69** ± .09	*.91* ± .04	*.77* ± .04	47
Behörde, Administration	.25 ± .04	**.67** ± .03	.36 ± .04	36
Verwandtschaft	0	0	0	1
Land, Staat	**.70** ± .08	**.85** ± .03	**.76** ± .05	60
Information, Quelle, Daten	.28 ± .05	**.75** ± .10	.40 ± .03	44
Zocken, Spielhallen	*.83* ± .17	.45 ± .10	**.54** ± .06	15
Rolle, Gruppe von Personen	**.74** ± .05	**.64** ± .07	**.68** ± .02	67
Kriegshandlung, Konflikt	**.80** ± .20	**.56** ± .10	**.60** ± .10	3
Strasse, Addresse	.42 ± .20	.09 ± .05	.14 ± .07	19
Other	**.66** ± .01	.26 ± .10	.35 ± .10	255
macro avg	**.55** ± .03	**.55** ± .03	.47 ± .03	547
micro avg	**.62** ± .01	**.50** ± .04	.48 ± .06	547

Table 5. Averaged results of the evaluation of the model trained on manually annotated with 10 additional instances for each type with support higher than 20. Best models after epochs 6, 5, 7. Overall accuracy is **.59** ± .02. The values above 0.5 are in **bold**, the maximum value per column is in *italics*.

	precision	recall	F_1 score	support
Gericht	**.63** ± .08	*.96* ± .01	**.75** ± .05	47
Behörde, Administration	.40 ± .04	**.60** ± .04	.47 ± .03	36
Verwandtschaft	0	0	0	1
Land, Staat	**.69** ± .05	**.88** ± .01	**.77** ± .02	60
Information, Quelle, Daten	.34 ± .02	**.71** ± .07	.46 ± .01	44
Zocken, Spielhallen	**.82** ± .13	.49 ± .06	**.61** ± .08	15
Rolle, Gruppe von Personen	**.62** ± .06	**.84** ± .01	**.71** ± .04	67
Kriegshandlung, Konflikt	*.83* ± .16	**.67** ± .00	**.72** ± .08	3
Strasse, Addresse	**.64** ± .05	.35 ± .06	.44 ± .03	19
Other	**.76** ± .02	.39 ± .06	**.51** ± .06	255
macro avg	**.57** ± .03	**.59** ± .01	**.54** ± .02	547
micro avg	**.66** ± .02	**.59** ± .02	**.58** ± .03	547

Analysis of errors Some errors are listed in Table 6. For the first row the entity **Art** (stands for "article") is annotated as "Other" because the phrase is incomplete. However, the model still classifies it as "Information, Quelle, Daten". In the second row we see the inverse error. These errors are due to incomplete original annotations, therefore we think some heuristics to extend the annotations to complete entities could be useful. In the third and fourth rows we see examples of entities that could be classified into more than one type, however, the manual annotators had to choose only one type for their input.

Table 6. Table of some prediction errors by a model trained on manually annotated with 10 additional instances for each type with support higher than 20.

Context with **target**	True type	Predicted type
ihrer Religion, ihrer Nationalität, ihrer Zugehörigkeit zu einer bestimmten sozialen Gruppe oder ihrer politischen Ansichten bedroht wäre (**Art**. 33 Z 1 GFK), es sei denn, es bestehe eine innerstaatliche Fluchtalternative (§ 11 AsylG 2005).	Other	Information, Quelle, Daten
Gemäß § 9 Abs. 2 BFA-VG sind bei der Beurteilung des Privat- und Familienlebens im Sinne des Art. **8 EMRK** insbesondere folgende Punkte zu berücksichtigen	Information, Quelle, Daten	Other
Zwar hat auch die **somalische Polizei** eine eigene Anti-Terror-Einheit gegründet, trotzdem ist die NISA bei der Reaktion auf Terrorangriffe in Mogadischu hauptverantwortlich (EASO 2.2016).	Rolle, Gruppe von Personen	Behörde, Administration
Quellen: - **AA** - Auswärtiges Amt (1.4.2015b): Russische Föderation - Reise- und Sicherheitshinweise	Behörde, Administration	Information, Quelle, Daten

6 Conclusion

We aim at producing an annotated fine-grained domain-specific data set for training an NER tool, while attempting to reduce the high cost of manual annotations produced by domain experts. In particular, we address a realistic case of 1) having to cope with the choice of fine-grained types produced by domain experts and 2) small golden training data set. Therefore, we formulate the (named) entity typing task as a binary classification task and explore the cross-type learning of the model. We exploit a binary classifier that has shown good results on a similar binary task of sense verification.

The experiments demonstrate that the initial clean and manually annotated data set might not be enough to achieve good classification results. However, adding even a small amount of randomly sampled incorrectly classified entities to the training set might significantly improve the performance. Moreover, we observe that the performance of the model increases even for those types where no additional instances are added, therefore exploiting cross-type learning effect. We also observe the models increasing ability to recover from original incorrect (noisy) annotations produced by the general purpose NER model.

Finally, we train the model on all the available manual data and (re-)annotate the whole original corpus.

Acknowledgments

This work has been partially funded by the project LYNX, which has received funding from the EU's Horizon 2020 research and innovation programme under grant agreement no. 780602, see http://www.lynx-project.eu.

References

1. Abhishek, A., Taneja, S.B., Malik, G., Anand, A., Awekar, A.: Fine-grained entity recognition with reduced false negatives and large type coverage (2019)
2. Breit, A., Revenko, A., Rezaee, K., Pilehvar, M.T., Camacho-Collados, J.: WiC-TSV: An evaluation benchmark for target sense verification of words in context. In: Proceedings of the 16th Conference of the European Chapter of the Association for Computational Linguistics: Main Volume. pp. 1635–1645. Association for Computational Linguistics, Online (Apr 2021)
3. Castleberry, A., Nolen, A.: Thematic analysis of qualitative research data: Is it as easy as it sounds? Curr Pharm Teach Learn **10**(6), 807–815 (2018)
4. Daiber, J., Jakob, M., Hokamp, C., Mendes, P.N.: Improving efficiency and accuracy in multilingual entity extraction. In: Proceedings of the 9th I-Semantics (2013)
5. Devlin, J., Chang, M.W., Lee, K., Toutanova, K.: BERT: Pre-training of Deep Bidirectional Transformers for Language Understanding arXiv:1810.04805 (Oct 2018)
6. Fernández-Macías, E.: Automation, digitalisation and platforms: Implications for work and employment (2018)
7. Fries, J., Wu, S., Ratner, A., Ré, C.: SwellShark: A Generative Model for Biomedical Named Entity Recognition without Labeled Data arXiv:1704.06360 (Apr 2017)
8. Huang, L., Sun, C., Huang, X.: GlossBERT: BERT for word sense disambiguation with gloss knowledge. In: Proceedings of EMNLP-IJCNLP 2019. pp. 3507–3512. Association for Computational Linguistics, Hong Kong, China (Nov 2019)
9. Lee, J.S., Hsiang, J.: PatentBERT: Patent Classification with Fine-Tuning a pre-trained BERT Model arXiv:1906.02124 (May 2019)
10. Lee, J., Yoon, W., Kim, S., Kim, D., Kim, S., So, C.H., Kang, J.: BioBERT: a pre-trained biomedical language representation model for biomedical text mining. Bioinformatics **36**(4), 1234–1240 (09 2019)
11. Leitner, E., Rehm, G., Moreno-Schneider, J.: Fine-grained Named Entity Recognition in Legal Documents. In: Acosta, M., Cudré-Mauroux, P., Maleshkova, M., Pellegrini, T., Sack, H., Sure-Vetter, Y. (eds.) Proceedings of SEMANTiCS 2019. pp. 272–287. No. 11702 in LNCS, Springer, Karlsruhe, Germany (9 2019)
12. Liang, C., Yu, Y., Jiang, H., Er, S., Wang, R., Zhao, T., Zhang, C.: BOND: BERT-Assisted Open-Domain Named Entity Recognition with Distant Supervision arXiv:2006.15509 (Jun 2020)

13. Lopez, P.: entity-fishing. https://github.com/kermitt2/entity-fishing (2016–2020)
14. Moro, A., Raganato, A., Navigli, R.: Entity Linking meets Word Sense Disambiguation: a Unified Approach. Transactions of the Association for Computational Linguistics (TACL) **2**, 231–244 (2014)
15. Murty, S., Verga, P., Vilnis, L., Radovanovic, I., McCallum, A.: Hierarchical losses and new resources for fine-grained entity typing and linking. In: Proceedings of the 56th ACL: Volume 1. pp. 97–109. Association for Computational Linguistics, Melbourne, Australia (Jul 2018)
16. Nothman, J., Ringland, N., Radford, W., Murphy, T., Curran, J.R.: Learning multilingual named entity recognition from wikipedia. Artif. Intell. **194**, 151–175 (Jan 2013)
17. Nothman, J., Ringland, N., Radford, W., Murphy, T., Curran, J.R.: Learning Multilingual Named Entity Recognition from Wikipedia. Artif. Intell. **194**, 151–175 (Jan 2013)
18. Oliveira, I.L., Fileto, R., Speck, R., Garcia, L.P., Moussallem, D., Lehmann, J.: Towards holistic entity linking: Survey and directions. Information Systems **95**, 101624 (2021)
19. Ontonotes release 5.0. https://catalog.ldc.upenn.edu/LDC2013T19, accessed: 2021-03-21
20. Paszke, A., Gross, S., Massa, F., Lerer, A., Bradbury, J., Chanan, G., Killeen, T., Lin, Z., Gimelshein, N., Antiga, L., Desmaison, A., Kopf, A., Yang, E., DeVito, Z., Raison, M., Tejani, A., Chilamkurthy, S., Steiner, B., Fang, L., Bai, J., Chintala, S.: Pytorch: An imperative style, high-performance deep learning library. In: Wallach, H., Larochelle, H., Beygelzimer, A., d'Alché-Buc, F., Fox, E., Garnett, R. (eds.) Advances in Neural Information Processing Systems 32, pp. 8024–8035. Curran Associates, Inc. (2019)
21. Ren, X., El-Kishky, A., Wang, C., Tao, F., Voss, C.R., Han, J.: Clustype: Effective entity recognition and typing by relation phrase-based clustering. In: Proceedings of the 21th ACM SIGKDD. p. 995–1004. KDD '15, Association for Computing Machinery, New York, NY, USA (2015)
22. Shang, J., Liu, L., Ren, X., Gu, X., Ren, T., Han, J.: Learning Named Entity Tagger using Domain-Specific Dictionary arXiv:1809.03599 (Sep 2018)
23. Shimaoka, S., Stenetorp, P., Inui, K., Riedel, S.: Neural architectures for fine-grained entity type classification. In: Proceedings of the 15th ACL: Volume 1. pp. 1271–1280. Association for Computational Linguistics, Valencia, Spain (Apr 2017)
24. Tjong Kim Sang, E.F., De Meulder, F.: Introduction to the conll-2003 shared task: Language-independent named entity recognition. In: Proceedings of HLT-NAACL 2003: Volume 4. p. 142–147. CONLL '03, Association for Computational Linguistics, USA (2003)
25. Vandenbussche, P.Y., Scerri, A., Daniel, Ron, J.: Word sense disambiguation with transformer models. In: Proceedings of SemDeep-6. Association for Computational Linguistics (to appear)
26. Wang, R., Tang, D., Duan, N., Wei, Z., Huang, X., Cao, C., Jiang, D., Zhou, M., et al.: K-adapter: Infusing knowledge into pre-trained models with adapters. arXiv:2002.01808 (2020)
27. Yamada, I., Asai, A., Shindo, H., Takeda, H., Matsumoto, Y.: Luke: Deep contextualized entity representations with entity-aware self-attention. In: EMNLP (2020)
28. Yamada, I., Shindo, H., Takefuji, Y.: Representation learning of entities and documents from knowledge base descriptions. arXiv:1806.02960 (2018)

154

Further with Knowledge Graphs. M. Alam et al. (Eds.)
AKA Verlag and IOS Press, 2021
© 2021 Akademische Verlagsgesellschaft AKA GmbH, Berlin
This article is published online with Open Access by IOS Press and distributed under the terms
of the Creative Commons Attribution License 4.0 (CC BY 4.0).
doi:10.3233/SSW210042

When is the Peak Performance Reached? An Analysis of RDF Triple Stores

Hashim Khan[1], Manzoor Ali[1], Axel-Cyrille Ngonga Ngomo[1], and Muhammad Saleem[1,2]

[1] DICE, Paderborn University, Germany
hashim.khan@uni-paderborn.de
manzoor@campus.uni-paderborn.de
axel.ngonga@upb.de
[2] AKSW, University of Leipzig, Germany
saleem@informatik.uni-leipzig.de

Abstract. With significant growth in RDF datasets, application developers demand online availability of these datasets to meet the end users' expectations. Various interfaces are available for querying RDF data using SPARQL query language. Studies show that SPARQL endpoints may provide high query runtime performance at the cost of low availability. For example, it has been observed that only 32.2% of public endpoints have a monthly uptime of 99–100%. One possible reason for this low availability is the high workload experienced by these SPARQL endpoints. As complete query execution is performed at server side (i.e., SPARQL endpoint), this high query processing workload may result in performance degradation or even a service shutdown. We performed extensive experiments to show the query processing capabilities of well-known triple stores by using their SPARQL endpoints. In particular, we stressed these triple stores with multiple parallel requests from different querying agents. Our experiments revealed the maximum query processing capabilities of these triple stores after which point they lead to service shutdowns. We hope this analysis will help triple store developers to design workload-aware RDF engines to improve the availability of their public endpoints with high throughput.

Keywords: triple store, Throughput, Queries-per-Second, Availability

1 Introduction

One of the basic requirements of many semantic web applications is the ability to access and query live linked data. The term "live queryable" linked data demands that the data should be queryable via online SPARQL interfaces (without first downloading the entire knowledge graph) and processed locally to retrieve the desired information [27]. It is one of the most important demands for the successful deployment of many linked data-based applications. Various interfaces such as SPARQL endpoints and Triple Pattern Fragments (TPF) provide live SPARQL querying [27].

SPARQL endpoints offer a public interface to execute SPARQL queries over the underlying RDF datasets. In this interface, the client sends a complete SPARQL query to the server (i.e., SPARQL endpoint). The server executes the query and returns the final results. The server is responsible for the execution of a complete query while the client is idle most of the time [15]. This model of query processing generally leads to better runtime performance due to the optimization techniques used in the server. Furthermore, the network overhead is low, as the complete query processing task is performed at one end. However, many of the SPARQL endpoints suffer from low availability rates [27,7]. According to the SPARQLES [26][3] current statistics[4], only 176 (i.e. 20.71%) were found available out of a total 557 public endpoints. One potential reason for this low availability could be service shutdowns due to the high workload experienced by these SPARQL endpoints and the complex and expressive nature of SPARQL queries, which may require large processing time and resources. For example, the well-known public endpoints such as DBpedia[5] and Wikidata[6] receive more than 100K queries per day [19]. The RDF data storage and SPARQL query execution is performed by the backend triple store. For example, the DBpedia SPARQL endpoint is powered by the Virtuoso [11] triple store. The Wikidata endpoint works on top of the BlazeGraph[7] triple store. Every RDF query processing engine has a certain peak performance point when exposed to multiple parallel querying users. Exceeding the user workload beyond the maximum query processing capability of an engine would generally lead to performance degradation or even a service shutdown. The peak performance points of RDF triple stores depend upon multiple factors, including parallel query processing capabilities, the type of hardware resources being allocated, the efficiency of the underlying query planner, and the type of workload experienced. Multiple studies [20,2,12,22,6,30] have compared the performance of different triple stores; however, little attention has been paid to assessing parallel query processing capabilities of these triple stores [8]. To the best of our knowledge, no studies have reported the peak performance points under parallel loads of the state-of-the-art triple stores. We fill this gap by conducting extensive experiments and report the peak performance points of the triple stores with varying multiple parallel querying clients.

Our contributions are as follows:

- We performed experiments to show the maximum query processing capabilities of some well-known triple stores, with respect to the number of querying agents they can support, by using their SPARQL endpoints. In particular, we stressed these triple stores with multiple parallel requests from different numbers of querying agents.
- Beyond their peak performance points, We further stressed the selected triple stores towards launching a DoS attack.

---

[3] SPARQLES Monitoring: https://sparqles.ai.wu.ac.at/availability
[4] Data taken on 31st of March, 2021 at 11:30 (CET)
[5] http://dbpedia.org/sparql
[6] https://query.wikidata.org/
[7] https://blazegraph.com/

The rest of the paper is organised as follows: In section 2, we provide a summary of the different evaluations related to RDF triple stores. Section 3 explains the evaluation setup and the evaluation results are presented in Section 4. Section 5 explains the availability of resources and their reusability and section 6 concludes this work. The complete data to reproduce the presented results is available from https://github.com/dice-group/RDF-Triplestores-Evaluation.

2   Related Work

The focus of this section is to show the details of the experiments performed to evaluate the state-of-the-art triple stores. The main aim is to highlight the lack of research into the stress tolerance of different triple stores for their peak performance capabilities.

The importance of linked data and knowledge graphs has motivated the development of several RDF triple stores. Ali et al. [1] categorized a total of 116 triple stores: each employs different data storage and querying processing mechanisms. Consequently, various triple store benchmarks also have been developed. Saleem et al. [21] provide an analysis of 10 triple store benchmarks, each employing a different evaluation setup and experiments. Table 1 shows the list of the triple stores evaluated and details of the experiments conducted in these state-of-the-art triple stores benchmarks.

The performance metrics used by state-of-the-art triple store benchmarks to compare triple stores can be divided into four main categories.

- **Processing Related Metrics.** The metrics included in this category are related to the query processing capabilities of the triple stores. In this category, the Queries per Second (QpS), Queries Mix per Hour (QMpH), and Processing Overhead (PO) are the key metrics used in the state-of-the-art benchmarks.
- **Storage Related Metrics.** The metrics included in this category are related to the data storage and indexing techniques used in the triple stores. In this category, the data Loading Time (LT), the Storage Space (SS) required, and the Size of generated Indexes (IS) are the key metrics used in the state-of-the-art benchmarks.
- **Result Set Related Metrics.** The metrics included in this category are related to the result sets of the query execution over underlying triple stores. In this category, Result Set Completeness (RCm) and Correctness (RCr) are the key metrics used in the state-of-the-art benchmarks.
- **Additional Metrics.** This category includes additional metrics pertaining to the use of Multiple parallel Clients (MC) to assess the parallel querying capabilities of the triple store, and the Dataset Updates (DU).

The MC is the central metric related to our study, which is clearly missing in the majority of benchmark evaluations. Some basic evaluation is shown in BSBM and BioBench by multiple parallel querying clients. However, they did not report the peak performance points of tested triple stores.

Table 1: Details of Benchmarks and type of experiments performed

Benchmarks	Triple Stores	Experimental Details
DBPSB[18]	Virtuoso Sesame Jena-TDB BigOWLIM	QpS and QMpH of all mentioned triple stores were evaluated. These triple stores were loaded with real-world DBpedia dataset and one querying agent (user) at a time was used.
FEASIBLE[20]	Virtuoso OWLIM-SE Jena-TDB (Fuseki) Sesame	QpS, QmpH and performance metrics relating to result set correctness and completeness were evaluated. Two datasets, i.e., real-world DBpedia and synthetic WatDiv, were used. Only one querying agent was used at a time.
WatDiv[2]	4Store RDF-3X MonetDB Virtuoso	Query execution time for synthetic datasets of different sizes was measured for only one querying user at a time. The experiments aim to compare triple stores by using synthetically generated data.
FishMark[5]	Virtuoso Quest	QpS for all the selected triple stores was evaluated against one querying user at a time. A synthetic dataset was used in this benchmark.
Bowlogna[10]	RDF-3X 4Store Virtuoso Diplodocus	Performance metrics relating to storage, i.e., RDF data loading time and the index size of all triple stores were evaluated. A synthetic dataset relating to the university data was used.
TrainBench[24]	RDF4J Jena-TDB	All mentioned triple stores were loaded with synthetic datasets of different sizes. After that, they were evaluated for result size completeness and correctness.
BioBench [30]	OWLIM-SE Virtuoso Bigdata Mulgara 4Store	Performance metrics relating to load time, storage space, and result sets were evaluated for single and multi users. However, the triple stores were not evaluated for query processing.
BSBM [6]	Sesame Jena-TDB Jena-SDB Virtuoso	The mentioned triple stores were loaded with synthetic datasets of different sizes and were evaluated for QpS, QMpH, and some other metrics related to data storage and result sets.
SP2Bench[22]	Sesame Virtuoso ARQ Redland	The selected triple stores were evaluated for processing overhead, storage and result set related performance metrics. Synthetic datasets were used and only one querying user was used.

Apart from the evaluations conducted in triple store benchmarks, additional performance evaluations can be found in the literature as well. Voigt et al. [29] evaluated triple stores for data loading time, query runtimes, and result set completeness. They aimed to test the systems for some specific type of queries like `SELECT` (with or without `UNION`, `REGEX`, `FILTER` or `sub-queries`). For the multi-client scenario, they measured the avg. query performance, as well as how many queries could be executed within a 10-minute time slot. In addition, some experiments related to memory requirements were conducted. Conrads et al. [8] presented a generic framework for benchmarking the read/write performance of triple stores in the presence of multiple querying agents. They evaluated three triple stores (Virtuoso, Fuseki and Blazegraph) for QpH and QMpH for different dataset sizes (DBpedia and SWDF[8]). Rohloff et al. [23] evaluated some triple store technologies, such as MySQL[9], DAML DB[10] and BigOWLIM[11] (currently called GraphDB), in combination with RDF4J[12] and Jena[13], as query frameworks for data loading time and query response time, by changing the dataset sizes. Stegmaier et al. [23] performed an evaluation on some of the RDF database technologies, including RDF4J[14], AllegroGraph [25], and Jena-SDB[15] for their query execution time by using the SP2 [22] benchmark. Cudré-Mauroux et al. [9] empirically evaluated the NoSQL databases for RDF. Their evaluation is based on a comparison of several NoSQL stores, along with a native triple store, i.e., 4Store [13] for RDF processing. Furthermore, Verborgh et al. [28] evaluate their query engine named `Triple Pattern Fragments (TPF)` based on performance metrics *Number of Timeouts*, *Query Execution Time*, and *Network Usage*. Similarly, Minier et al. in $S_A G_E$ [17] perform evaluations based on avg. workload completion time for 50 clients and compare their system with brTPF [14], TPF [28] and Virtuoso [11]. Finally, Azzam et al. [4] compare `SMART-KG` with TPF, Virtuoso and $S_A G_E$ by using performance metrics *Number of Timeouts*, *Execution Time* and *Resource Consumption*.

However, to the best of our knowledge, none of these additional evaluations tested the performance of triple stores for their maximum throughput during parallel querying workload.

3   Evaluation Setup

In this section, we explain the evaluation setup used in the experiments. In general, any evaluation related to RDF systems comprises an RDF dataset, a collection of SPARQL queries, and a set of performance metrics. Here, we present

---

[8] Semantic Web Dog Food
[9] http://www.mysql.com/
[10] http://www.daml.org/2001/09/damldb/
[11] https://www.ontotext.com/products/graphdb/
[12] http://www.openrdf.org/
[13] https://jena.apache.org/
[14] http://www.openrdf.org/
[15] https://jena.apache.org/documentation/sdb/

key features of each of these components that are important to consider for fair evaluation. Many of these features come from state-of-the-art research contributions mentioned in [20,21,2].

Benchmarks. Benchmarks for the evaluation of triple stores can either be synthetic or real-data [21]. The synthetic-data benchmarks make use of a data generator to generate synthetic data. Queries can be generated by using query templates on the underlying data. Synthetic-data benchmarks are useful in testing the scalability of triple stores with varying dataset sizes. However, they often fail to reflect characteristics of the real-world queries posted by users of the datasets in practice [21,19,3]. On the other hand, real-data benchmarks contain both data and queries, selected from real-world RDF datasets and their corresponding query logs. Such benchmarks more closely reflect the real-world deployment of triple stores. However, analysis of real-world queries [19,3] show that they are quite simple in terms of the structural features (number of triple patterns, types of joins, projections, etc.) and data-driven features (result sizes, selectivity, etc.) of SPARQL queries [21,2]. Keeping in mind the pros and cons of both types of benchmarks, we consider both real-world as well as synthetic benchmarks in our evaluation:

- **FEASIBLE[20]**: is a real-data benchmark generator, which generates benchmarks by using the real-world query logs of RDF datasets. We used the same benchmark (analyzed in [21]) that was generated by the FEASIBLE framework. This benchmark is based on the DBpedia3.5.1 dataset.[16] The dataset contains a total of 232M (English version) triples, 18,425k distinct subjects, 39,672 predicates, and 65,184k objects. The benchmark includes a total of 50 real queries selected from the DBpedia3.5.1 SPARQL endpoint log. These queries cover most of the required structural and data-driven features of the SPARQL queries [21]. Furthermore, it is the most diverse benchmark in comparison to other triple store benchmarks included in [21].
- **WatDiv[2]**: is a synthetic benchmark generator. Again, we used the same benchmark analyzed in [21] that was generated by WatDiv generators having 108M triples, usually called 100M WatDiv dataset. Similarly, for more diverse evaluation and to test the scalability of the triple stores w.r.t. varying dataset sizes, we considered two more datasets generated by the same benchmark having 10M and one billion triples. The total number of query templates used in benchmarks is 50, including 20 basic testing query templates and 30 extensions to basic testing. The basic testing consists of queries in four categories, namely, linear queries (L), star queries (S), snowflake-shaped queries (F) and complex queries (C) [2].

The coefficient of variation, which shows diversity scores [21] across different SPARQL query features, is shown in Fig. 1. The coverage of different SPARQL clauses and join vertex types is shown in Table 2. Further detailed analysis of the datasets as well as queries about the selected benchmarks can be found in [21].

---

[16] DBpedia3.5.1: dbpedia.org

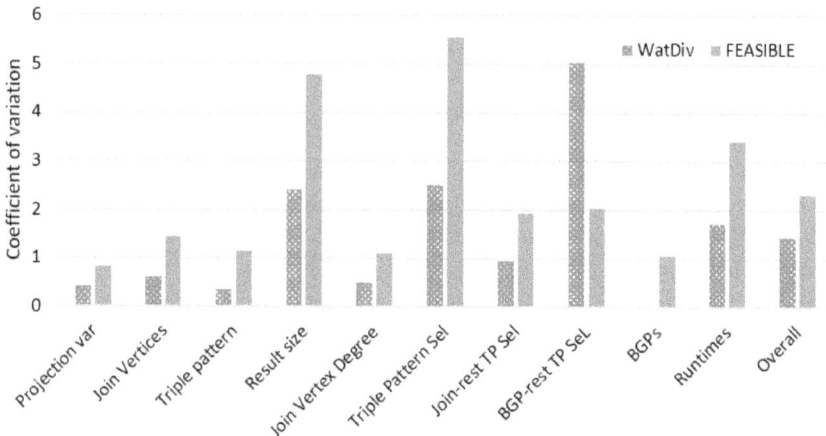

Fig. 1: Diversity scores across different SPARQL query features of the benchmarks.

	Distributions of SPARQL Clauses							Distr. of Join Vertex Type				
Benchmark	DIST	FILT	REG	OPT	UN	LIM	ORD	Star	Path	Sink	Hyb.	N.J.
Watdiv	0.0	0.0	0.0	0.0	0.0	0.0	0.0	28.0	64.0	26.0	20.0	0.0
FEASIBLE	56.0	58.0	22.0	28.0	40.0	42.0	32.0	58.0	18.0	36.0	16.0	30.0

Table 2: Coverage of SPARQL clauses and join vertex types used in the benchmarks in percentages. SPARQL clauses: DIST[INCT], FILT[ER], REG[EX], OPT[IONAL], UN[ION], LIM[IT], ORD[ER BY]. Join vertex types: Star, Path, Sink, Hyb[rid], N[o] J[oin].

Please note that these are the two most diverse benchmarks according to the benchmarks analysis conducted in [21].

Performance Metric. Since we are measuring the throughput of triple stores, we use Queries per Second (QpS) as the main performance indicator.

Triple Stores. We selected triple stores to be included in the evaluation based on the following criteria: (1) the triple stores should be available for free, therefore we excluded commercial triple stores, (2) they should be able to load and process both the selected datasets and the corresponding queries, (3) they should offer SPARQL HTTP endpoints, (4) they should support the SPARQL features included in the FEASIBLE benchmark, therefore triple stores which only support BGP[17] queries are excluded, and (5) they should have no benchmarking restrictions, e.g., the maintainers had to approve the inclusion of their system results in the publication to the public.

---

[17] https://www.w3.org/TR/rdf-sparql-query/#BasicGraphPatterns

Based on the above criteria we have considered the following triple stores in our evaluation[18]:

1. **Virtuoso**[19] is flexible enough to configure most of its parameters through config file. We used Virtuoso version 7.2.6 with `NumberOfBuffers=680000` and `MaxDirtyBufferes=500000`, which is recommended settings for 8 GB of free system memory. The parameter `MaxClientConnections` in the HTTP Server section, is set according to the number of querying users (i.e., one connection per querying user) for all the individual experiments. The `ThreadsPerQuery=32` is set according to the number of CPU cores.

2. **Jena TDB**[20] Version 3.13.1 with **Fuseki** as HTTP interface with Java heap size set to 8g. The documentation[21] about parallelism shows that Jena's query mechanism is itself multi-threaded, and it supports parallel querying by default.

3. **Blazegraph**[22] Version 2.1.4, with Jetty as HTTP interface and Java heap size set to 8g. Through its configuration file, we changed the `QueryThreadPoolSize=32` and `ReadOnly=True`. All other parameters were kept default.

4. **Ontotext GraphDB**[23] with `Java heap=8g`.

5. **Parliament** [16] with `MIN_MEM=1g` and `MAX_MEM=8g` of Java heap and jetty as HTTP interface.

In some cases, we also contacted the maintainers of the systems to get the recommended and comparable settings.

Benchmark Execution. All the experiments were performed using the benchmark execution framework Iguana V2.1.2 [8], which is particularly developed to measure the read/write performance of RDF triple stores in the presence of multiple querying agents. As recommended by the maintainer, we set the query time-out to 10 minutes per query, and each experiment was performed in a stress test with 60 minutes run time. All the experiments were performed for 1, 2, 4, 8, 16, 32, 64 and 128 concurrently executing clients. Before starting the evaluation, we bulk loaded each of the datasets into the triple stores. During each run of the experiment, the triple stores contained only the dataset upon which the benchmarking was being carried out. Moreover, we tested the selected triple stores up to 128 concurrent clients to ensure the service unavailability.

Hardware. All experiments were performed on a machine with two Intel Xeon E5-2620 v4 CPUs having each 8 physical cores and 16 logical cores, 256GB RAM, 11 TB HDD and running Ubuntu 20.04.2 LTS.

---

[18] We tried our best to test the selected triple stores with matching configuration settings.

[19] Virtuoso:https://virtuoso.openlinksw.com/

[20] Jena TDB: https://jena.apache.org/documentation/tdb/

[21] https://jena.apache.org/documentation/notes/concurrency-howto.html

[22] Blazegraph: https://blazegraph.com/

[23] GraphDB: http://graphdb.ontotext.com/

4   Results and Discussion

Fig. 2d shows the results when all the triple stores are loaded with the DB-pedia3.5.1 dataset and FEASIBLE [20] benchmark queries were executed on them. Similarly, Fig. 2a, 2b, and 2c show the WatDiv benchmarking results when the triple stores are tested with 10 million, 100 million and one billion triples datasets, respectively. From these graphs, we want to look for the key findings pertaining to the following research questions: (1) Which triple store achieved the highest throughput in terms of QpS? (2) On avg., which triple store is performing the best? (3) What is the peak performance point of each of the selected triple stores and when is it achieved? (4) How do the triple stores scale to the increasing number of parallel querying agents? (5) At which point does the DoS occur? and (6) How do systems scale with the increasing dataset sizes? In the following, we discuss each of these key questions[24].

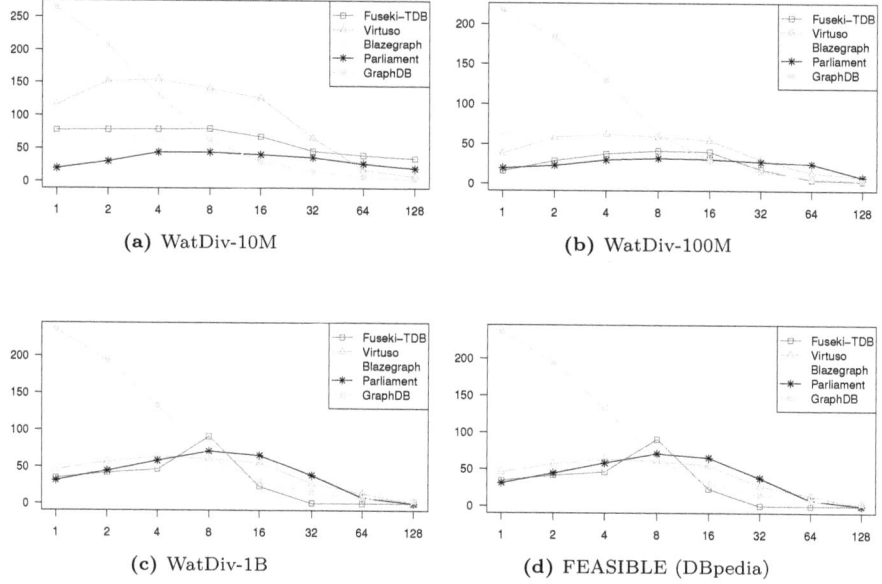

Fig. 2: Benchmark results on (a), (b), (c) and (d) for all the triple stores - For each benchmark, the x-axis shows the No. of querying users while y-axis shows the avg. QpS per user.

---

[24] Please note that the aim of this paper is to report the triple stores performances with different stress testing. The reason why one triple store performs better than others is out of the scope of this paper.

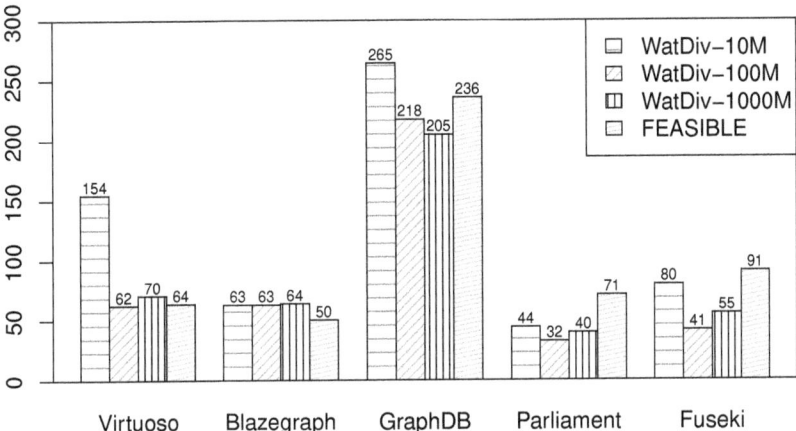

Fig. 3: Peak throughput in terms of avg. QpS per client of all given triple stores with different benchmarks.

Highest Throughput: Fig. 4a shows that GraphDB achieves the highest peak performance point, i.e., 231 on avg., as well as in the case of all the individual benchmarks (ref. Figure 2). Followed by GraphDB, Virtuoso achieves the second position by achieving maximum avg. throughput of 88 QpS, and in the case of WatDiv-10-Million benchmark, it has the highest individual QpS value as shown in Fig. 3. Then Fuseki-TDB, Blazegraph and Parliament achieve the 3rd, 4th and 5th position, respectively. Finally, Blazegraph achieves almost the same maximum QpS in all WatDiv benchmarks.

Average Throughput: The avg. throughput of the selected triple stores can be measured by calculating the area under the curve in the corresponding through-put graphs. The higher the area covered, the higher the avg. throughput. Fig. 4b shows that Virtuoso achieves the maximum avg. throughput of 3621. It is followed by Parliament having 3101, then Fuseki-TDB having 2727, followed by GraphDB with 2364 and then Blazegraph with 1775. From the Fig. 3 and 4b, it can be observed that the maximum peak performance in terms of QpS, does not necessarily mean that the same system will perform well in terms of avg. throughput.

Peak Performance Points: The results in Fig. 2 show that there is a peak performance point for each triple store. This peak point of any triple store differs for all the benchmarks, but is reached during the same number of querying agents. Once that point is reached, further increase in the querying workload leads to gradual decrease in performance.

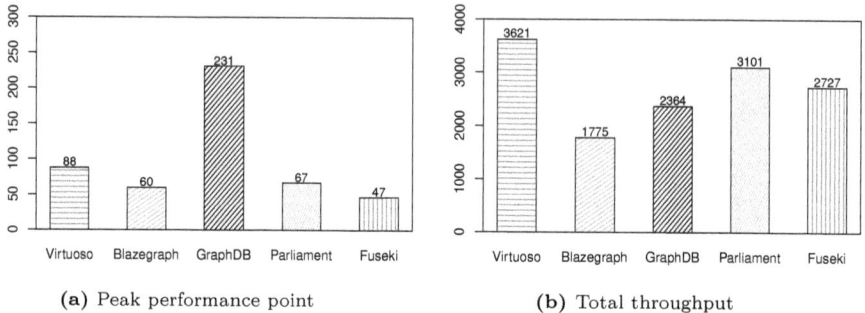

(a) Peak performance point   (b) Total throughput

Fig. 4: (*a*) shows the peak performance point in terms of the avg. maximum QpS per user, while (*b*) shows the total throughput of the systems (triple stores) in terms of the area covered under the curve of avg. QpS of all benchmarks.

Parallel Scalability: It refers to how triple stores react to the increasing querying agents. A highly parallel scalable triple store's throughput would gradually increase with the increasing number of multiple querying agents. We can see from Fig. 5f, that this is not the case for the majority of selected triple stores, i.e., the peak performance point of these triple stores is reached quite early. In this regard, the parallel scalable triple store ranking is: Fuseki-TDB and Parliament are scalable up to 8 querying agents, followed by Virtuoso with 4, Blazegraph with 2, and GraphDB with only one. It is worth mentioning here that Parliament achieve the least avg. peak performance but is scalable in terms of the maximum number of querying agents it supports.

Denial of Service (DoS): Our results show that the throughput of the selected triple stores almost reaches zero when exposed to 128 querying agents. This is the point at which triple stores almost stop responding.

Scalability with Increasing Dataset: Finally, we want to measure the scalability of the selected triple stores in terms of varying datasets sizes as well as increasing querying agents. Fig. 5a, 5b, 5c, 5d and 5e show the corresponding results for each of the selected triple stores. We can clearly see that, in general, performance is decreased with the increase in the number of agents as well as the size of dataset. These results are as expected because increasing the workload or the dataset size will lead to more processing work to be performed by the triple stores to get the desired query results. However, a sub question to be investigated is that which triple store scale better with increasing dataset size? Fig 5b shows that the throughput of Blazegraph is not much affected by increasing the size of the dataset. It is followed by GraphDB (ref. Figure 5e) with little effect on the varying dataset sizes. On the other hand, we can clearly see a short performance drop on the other three selected triple stores. In particular, the performance of Virtuoso is greatly affected by the dataset sizes. In conclusion, the results sug-

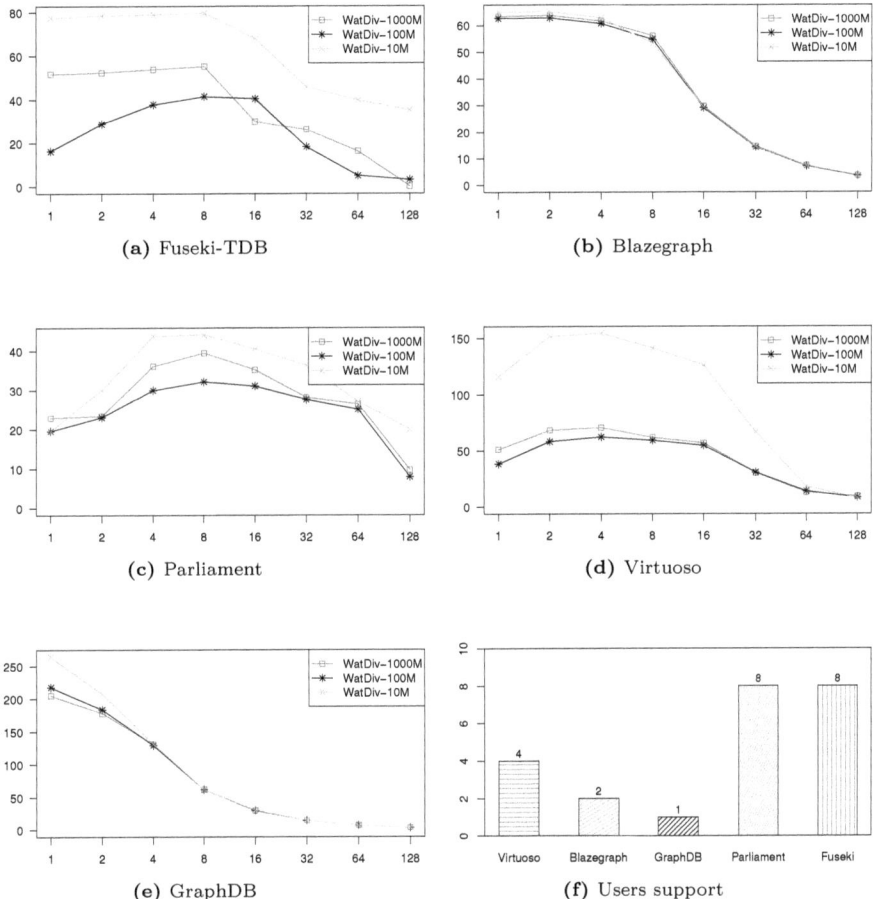

Fig. 5: Benchmark results on WatDiv-10-Million (a), WatDiv-100-Million (b), WatDiv-One-Billion (c) and DBpedia (d); For each benchmark, x-axis shows the No. of querying users while y-axis shows the avg. QpS per user. (f) shows the No. of users that triple stores support concurrently with highest throughput.

gest that Blazegraph is the most scalable triple store to handle big data with smaller effect on the throughput.

In summary, our results reveal the parallel query processing capabilities of selected triple stores. In particular, there exists a peak performance point for each of these triple stores which is generally reached with only a small number of multiple querying agents, as shown in Fig. 5f. Hence, these triple stores can easily lead to performance degradation or even a service shutdown when they are exposed to multiple querying users.

5   Resource Availability and Reusability

The datasets and queries used in this work are based on state-of-the-art benchmarks [20,2]. The query execution was performed by using the IGUANA [8] benchmark execution framework. All data required to reproduce these experiments or conduct a new set of experiments are available from the aforementioned repository homepage. Since we used standard state-of-the-art benchmarks and a standard benchmark execution framework, new triple store developers can use the same setup to test their own triple stores and compare with the state of the art. Finally, we also provide the complete evaluation results to enable a more fine-grained analysis. The current queries used in the FEASIBLE-DBpedia benchmark were selected from the query log of the DBpedia version 3.5.1. However, new queries for other versions of DBpedia are now available from the LSQ [19] dataset, which can be directly consumed by the FEASIBLE benchmark generation framework. In the future, we will provide more FEASIBLE-DBpedia benchmarks for the newer versions of DBpedia from the same resource home page. This will ensure triple store testing for their scalability with respect to varying sizes of DBpedia.

6   Conclusion

State-of-the-art linked data querying interfaces face the problem of finding a reasonable solution for the trade-off between performance and availability of RDF triple stores. Serving requests with high efficiency, and at the same time ensuring high availability of the endpoints, is crucial for the success of the Semantic Web. We conducted experiments with the aim of facilitating the design of smart query processing interfaces that ensure both high performance and availability. In particular, we showed the peak performance points and the parallel query processing capabilities of selected triple stores. Furthermore, we showed the extreme workloads that lead to potential service shutdowns on these triple stores. Finally, we measured the effect of varying dataset sizes on the query runtime performances of the selected triple stores. In the future, we want to include more triple stores and measure the effect of the resources (allocated RAM memory in particular) on the performance.

Acknowledgments

This work has been supported by the project LIMBO (Grant no. 19F2029I), OPAL (no. 19F2028A), KnowGraphs (no. 860801), and SOLIDE (no. 13N14456). In addition, the higher education commission of Pakistan.

References

1. Ali, W., Saleem, M., Yao, B., Hogan, A., Ngomo, A.C.N.: A survey of rdf stores & sparql engines for querying knowledge graphs (2021)
2. Aluç, G., Hartig, O., Özsu, M.T., Daudjee, K.: Diversified stress testing of rdf data management systems. In: Mika, P., Tudorache, T., Bernstein, A., Welty, C., Knoblock, C., Vrandečić, D., Groth, P., Noy, N., Janowicz, K., Goble, C. (eds.) The Semantic Web – ISWC 2014. pp. 197–212 (2014)
3. Arias, M., Fernández, J.D., Martínez-Prieto, M.A., de la Fuente, P.: An empirical study of real-world SPARQL queries. CoRR **abs/1103.5043** (2011), http://arxiv.org/abs/1103.5043
4. Azzam, A., Fernandez, J.D., Acosta, M., Beno, M., Polleres, A.: Smart-kg: Hybrid shipping for sparql querying on the web. In: Proceedings of The 2020 World Wide Web Conference, WWW 2020. (To appear) (2020)
5. Bail, S., Alkiviadous, S., Parsia, B., Workman, D., van Harmelen, M., Gonçalves, R.S., Garilao, C.: FishMark: A linked data application benchmark. In: Proceedings of the Joint Workshop on Scalable and High-Performance Semantic Web Systems. pp. 1–15 (2012), http://ceur-ws.org/Vol-943/SSWS_HPCSW2012_paper1.pdf
6. Bizer, C., Schultz, A.: The Berlin SPARQL benchmark. Int. J. Semantic Web Inf. Syst. **5**(2), 1–24 (2009). https://doi.org/10.4018/jswis.2009040101, https://doi.org/10.4018/jswis.2009040101
7. Buil-Aranda, C., Hogan, A., Umbrich, J., Vandenbussche, P.Y.: Sparql web-querying infrastructure: Ready for action? In: The Semantic Web – ISWC 2013. pp. 277–293. Springer Berlin Heidelberg, Berlin, Heidelberg (2013)
8. Conrads, F., Lehmann, J., Saleem, M., Morsey, M., Ngomo, A.N.: IGUANA: A generic framework for benchmarking the read-write performance of triple stores. In: ISWC. pp. 48–65. Springer (2017)
9. Cudré-Mauroux, P., Enchev, I., Fundatureanu, S., Groth, P., Haque, A., Harth, A., Keppmann, F.L., Miranker, D., Sequeda, J.F., Wylot, M.: Nosql databases for rdf: An empirical evaluation. In: The Semantic Web – ISWC 2013. pp. 310–325. Springer Berlin Heidelberg, Berlin, Heidelberg (2013)
10. Demartini, G., Enchev, I., Wylot, M., Gapany, J., Cudré-Mauroux, P.: BowlognaBench - benchmarking RDF analytics. In: Data-Driven Process Discovery and Analysis SIMPDA. pp. 82–102. Springer (2011)
11. Erling, O., Mikhailov, I.: Virtuoso: RDF Support in a Native RDBMS, pp. 501–519. Springer Berlin Heidelberg, Berlin, Heidelberg (2010)
12. Guo, Y., Pan, Z., Heflin, J.: LUBM: a benchmark for OWL knowledge base systems. J. Web Sem. **3**(2-3), 158–182 (2005). https://doi.org/10.1016/j.websem.2005.06.005, https://doi.org/10.1016/j.websem.2005.06.005
13. Harris, S., Lamb, N., Shadbolt, N., Ltd, G.: 4store: The design and implementation of a clustered rdf store. Proc. SSWS (01 2009)

14. Hartig, O., Aranda, C.B.: brtpf: Bindings-restricted triple pattern fragments (extended preprint). CoRR (2016), http://arxiv.org/abs/1608.08148
15. Khan, H.: Towards more intelligent sparql querying interfaces. In: International Semantic Web Conference (2019), http://ceur-ws.org/Vol-2548/paper-12.pdf
16. Kolas, D., Emmons, I., Dean, M.: Efficient linked-list rdf indexing in parliament
17. Minier, T., Skaf-Molli, H., Molli, P.: Sage: Web preemption for public sparql query services. In: The World Wide Web Conference. pp. 1268–1278. WWW '19, ACM, New York, NY, USA (2019). https://doi.org/10.1145/3308558.3313652, http://doi.acm.org/10.1145/3308558.3313652
18. Morsey, M., Lehmann, J., Auer, S., Ngomo, A.N.: DBpedia SPARQL benchmark - performance assessment with real queries on real data. In: ISWC. pp. 454–469 (2011)
19. Saleem, M., Ali, M.I., Hogan, A., Mehmood, Q., Ngomo, A.N.: LSQ: the linked SPARQL queries dataset. In: ISWC. pp. 261–269. Springer (2015)
20. Saleem, M., Mehmood, Q., Ngomo, A.N.: FEASIBLE: a feature-based SPARQL benchmark generation framework. In: ISWC. pp. 52–69. Springer (2015)
21. Saleem, M., Szárnyas, G., Conrads, F., Bukhari, S.A.C., Mehmood, Q., Ngonga Ngomo, A.C.: How representative is a sparql benchmark? an analysis of rdf triplestore benchmarks. In: The World Wide Web Conference. pp. 1623–1633. WWW '19, ACM, New York, NY, USA (2019). https://doi.org/10.1145/3308558.3313556, http://doi.acm.org/10.1145/3308558.3313556
22. Schmidt, M., Hornung, T., Meier, M., Pinkel, C., Lausen, G.: SP2Bench: A SPARQL Performance Benchmark, pp. 371–393. Springer Berlin Heidelberg, Berlin, Heidelberg (2010)
23. Stegmaier, F., Gröbner, U., Döller, M., Kosch, H.: Evaluation of current rdf database solutions
24. Szárnyas, G., Izsó, B., Ráth, I., Varró, D.: The train benchmark: cross-technology performance evaluation of continuous model queries. Software and systems modeling **17**(4), 1365—1393 (2018). https://doi.org/10.1007/s10270-016-0571-8, https://europepmc.org/articles/PMC6132656
25. Tajabor, P., Raafat, T.: Challenges over two semantic repositories - owlim and allegrograph. Indonesian Journal of Electrical Engineering and Computer Science **2**, 194 (04 2016). https://doi.org/10.11591/ijeecs.v2.i1.pp194-204
26. Vandenbussche, P.Y., Umbrich, J., Matteis, L., Hogan, A., Buil-Aranda, C.: Sparqles: Monitoring public sparql endpoints. Semantic Web **8**, 1–17 (01 2017). https://doi.org/10.3233/SW-170254
27. Verborgh, R., Vander Sande, M., Hartig, O., Van Herwegen, J., De Vocht, L., De Meester, B., Haesendonck, G., Colpaert, P.: Triple pattern fragments: a low-cost knowledge graph interface for the web. JOURNAL OF WEB SEMANTICS **37-38**, 184–206 (2016), http://dx.doi.org/10.1016/j.websem.2016.03.003
28. Verborgh, R., Vander Sande, M., Hartig, O., Van Herwegen, J., De Vocht, L., De Meester, B., Haesendonck, G., Colpaert, P.: Triple pattern fragments: A low-cost knowledge graph interface for the web. Journal of Web Semantics **37-38**, 184–206 (2016). https://doi.org/https://doi.org/10.1016/j.websem.2016.03.003, https://www.sciencedirect.com/science/article/pii/S1570826816000214
29. Voigt, M., Mitschick, A., Schulz, J.: Yet another triple store benchmark? practical experiences with real-world data. In: SDA (2012)
30. Wu, H., et al.: BioBenchmark Toyama 2012: An evaluation of the performance of triple stores on biological data. J. Biomedical Semantics **5**, 32 (2014). https://doi.org/10.1186/2041-1480-5-32, https://doi.org/10.1186/2041-1480-5-32

Further with Knowledge Graphs. M. Alam et al. (Eds.)
AKA Verlag and IOS Press, 2021
© 2021 Akademische Verlagsgesellschaft AKA GmbH, Berlin
This article is published online with Open Access by IOS Press and distributed under the terms
of the Creative Commons Attribution License 4.0 (CC BY 4.0).
doi:10.3233/SSW210043

Building a Data Processing Activities Catalog: Representing Heterogeneous Compliance-Related Information for GDPR Using DCAT-AP and DPV

Paul RYAN[ab,1] and Harshvardhan PANDIT[c] and Rob BRENNAN[a]

[a] *ADAPT Centre, School of Computing, Dublin City University, Dublin 9, Ireland*
[b] *Uniphar PLC, Dublin 24, Ireland*
[c] *ADAPT Centre, Trinity College Dublin, Dublin 2, Ireland*

Abstract. This paper describes a new semantic metadata-based approach to describing and integrating diverse data processing activity descriptions gathered from heterogeneous organisational sources such as departments, divisions, and external processors. This information must be collated to assess and document GDPR legal compliance, such as creating a Register of Processing Activities (ROPA). Most GDPR knowledge graph research to date has focused on developing detailed compliance graphs. However, many organisations already have diverse data collection tools for documenting data processing activities, and this heterogeneity is likely to grow in the future. We provide a new approach extending the well-known DCAT-AP standard utilising the data privacy vocabulary (DPV) to express the concepts necessary to complete a ROPA. This approach enables data catalog implementations to merge and federate the metadata for a ROPA without requiring full alignment or merging all the underlying data sources. To show our approach's feasibility, we demonstrate a deployment use case and develop a prototype system based on diverse data processing records and a standard set of SPARQL queries for a Data Protection Officer preparing a ROPA to monitor compliance. Our catalog's key benefits are that it is a lightweight, metadata-level integration point with a low cost of compliance information integration, capable of representing processing activities from heterogeneous sources.

Keywords. Legal Compliance, Data Governance

1. Introduction

Organisations can be large and complex entities that perform heterogeneous processing on large volumes of diverse personal data. In practice, organisations often consist of (semi-)autonomous data processing units such as divisions, departments, or subsidiaries to achieve organisational goals. Organisations may also employ external parties like contractors, processors, or operational partners. This heterogeneity contrasts with existing LegalTech solutions for GDPR compliance that require the organisation to adhere to whatever data model is required by the solution [1].

From a legal perspective, administrative fines and actions are imposed on organisations as singular entities instead of individual units (GDPR Rec.150). Hence, the organisation is responsible for creating, maintaining, and demonstrating legal

---

[1] Corresponding Author, Paul Ryan, ADAPT Centre, School of Computing, Dublin City University, Dublin 9, Ireland; E-mail: paul.ryan76@mail.dcu.ie.

compliance information in its entirety. GDPR requires organisations to appoint a Data Protection Officer (DPO) to advise and assist them with compliance-related tasks. The DPO's challenge is to document all personal processing activities, which multiple parties carry out across the extended organisation. In practice, the DPO is the early warning indicator of adverse data processing activities within the organisation [2]. This challenging role requires the DPO to arduously document processing activities carried out by internal (e.g. departments) and external (e.g. contractors) units; and thereby establish, monitor, and advise the organisation on its compliance accordingly.

Processes can be intra-organisational involving internal departments or business functions, or inter-organisational where external parties are involved in the process. This information must be fed into the legal compliance 'graph' or 'product'. In practical terms, these 'sources' of data processing activities may evolve independently and have requirements and management methods that do not necessarily match the organisation's compliance processes.

As an example of the challenge, consider an organisation creating its Register of Processing Activities (ROPA), which is the first item requested by a regulator to investigate and must be produced on request (GDPR Art.30.4). The organisation must collect the information required for inclusion in the ROPA from potentially diverse sources such as business functions, departments, and affiliates. In practice, organisations rely on manual and informal methods such as spreadsheets, customised software, or internally developed systems to catalog their processing activities [1], which are then presented to the DPO in multiple heterogeneous forms by the various sources responsible for processing personal data. These practices result in organisations struggling to meet their ROPA obligations [1] and is an ongoing issue as inter and intra-organisational processes and their relevance in crafting the legal compliance documentation such as ROPA are yet to be resolved [3].

Our solution to this challenge is the development of DPCat. This is a profile of the well-established DCAT W3C standard for data catalog [4][5]. Our technical approach analyses the legal requirements to establish the data required to complete a ROPA. We develop DPCat, a profile of DCAT-AP [6], by supplementing it with terms from the Data Privacy Vocabulary (DPV) [7]. This solution will enable organisations to collect information under a standard form and offer a consolidated view of their processing activities. We will conduct a use case to evaluate our research goal to establish the extent that a Data Processing Activities Catalog based on DCAT-AP and Data Privacy Vocabulary (DPV)can overcome the heterogeneity of sources to facilitate a ROPA.

The structure of our paper describes the use case based on real-world examples in section 2. We describe our deployment scenario where an organisation that consists of multiple business functions and an outsourced processor holding data in many diverse heterogeneous sources is required to identify and record all personal data processing activities to meet its GDPR compliance obligations. In section 3, we evaluate the related work of the cataloguing of Data Processing activities. We identify that the development of vocabularies and ontologies in this domain, whilst prolific, would benefit from deploying a data processing catalog to collect unified metadata to be utilised for ROPA creation, particularly the ability to span graph-based and non-graph data sources. Section 4 proposes a data processing activities catalog for representing heterogeneous compliance-related Information for GDPR and identifying the key benefits of a data catalog. Section 5 presents the design of our proto-type Data Processing Activities Catalog system based upon DCAT-AP. We present the regulatory requirements of a ROPA and express these in RDF form based upon the Data Privacy Vocabulary (DPV).

We identify the key features that the Data Processing Catalog must contain to enable automatic ROPA generation. In the remainder of the paper, we implement our DCAT-AP-based catalog and evaluate our research goal to establish the extent that a Data Processing Activities Catalog based on DCAT-AP and DPV can overcome the heterogeneity of sources to facilitate the preparation of a ROPA. For the remainder of the paper, we evaluate how effective the data catalog performed to meet the research goal.

2. Use Case

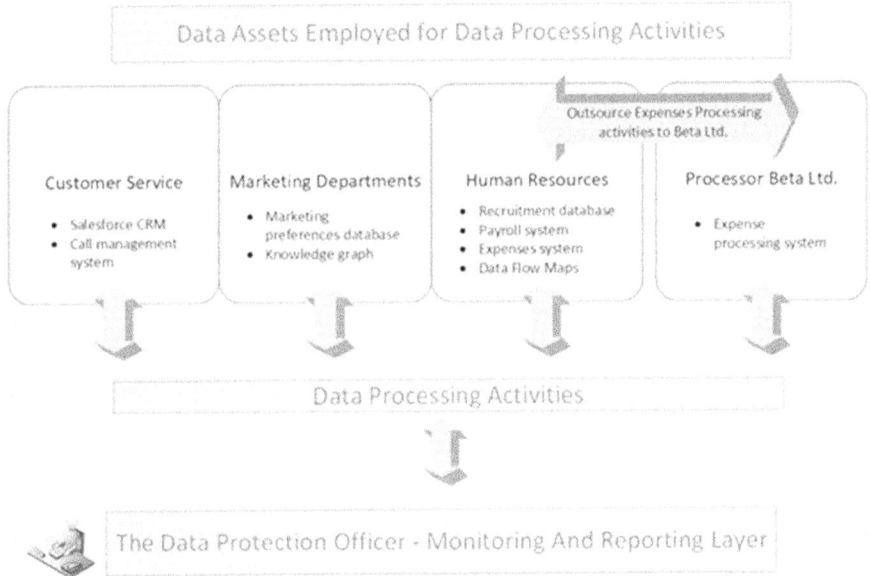

Fig. 1. Diverse Sources and Formats for Data Processing Activities in Organisations

Our use case scenario involves an organisation known as Alpha Ltd. The organisation comprises three distinct departments: Customer service, Human Resources and Marketing (see Fig.1). The departments are part of the same legal entity but carry out a variety of data processing activities. These departments collect and process different personal data according to their purposes. The tools and systems they use to manage information and processing can be distinct (see Fig.1), such as CRM systems, ERP systems, data flow models, semantic models, spreadsheets, etc. The distribution of platforms tends to reflect historical acquisitions by Alpha Ltd and local deployments by market segment leaders rather than homogeneous development of corporate IT systems, including data management or governance platforms.

Alpha Ltd has engaged the Data Processor Beta Ltd. to assist the HR department in processing employee expense claims. Beta Ltd carries out this processing activity in Canada, outside the European Union and is designated as providing appropriate safeguards for personal data transfers (GDPR Art.46.1). As a Data Controller, Alpha Ltd must ensure that all personal data processing activities are collected and recorded in its ROPA. To do this, the DPO, as a 'compliance officer' for Alpha, needs to liaise with each of the individual departments and request required information from them. In turn, the responsible departments must identify and extract this information from the information management systems used to track activities. As a result, the information about data processing activities within the organisation is presented to the DPO in heterogeneous forms. Further, the DPO must engage with relevant people or 'contacts' within each department in case of further information, clarity, or communication needs.

Hence, the requirements that a tool for creating a ROPA must deliver are:

1. Supports the heterogeneity of data sources describing data processing activities within an organisation
2. Enables standards-based collation of the data required for completion of a ROPA
3. Recording temporal validity of processing activities, e.g. active period
4. Supports periodic or continuous changes to data processing activity descriptions to reflect the dynamic lifecycle of data processing activities in an organisation
5. Records identity of activity host and organisational unit and relevant contact, e.g. to assist the DPO to collect additional information
6. Facilitate searching records, e.g. identify activities active on a specific date
7. Enable the creation of ROPA and other compliance-related documentation using information collected in the records
8. Minimises the data to be collected and integrated
9. Easy to deploy, e.g. based on established or commonly used software platforms

Next, we examine current systems' abilities to deliver these functionalities to DPO.

3. Related Work

We have established that organisations need to capture and express data processing activities carried out by their affiliates/ business functions and associated entities irrespective of the source data's heterogeneity. These processing activity descriptions need to be recorded and maintained in a ROPA. This section will review the extent to which the existing related work can meet the requirements set out in our use case. We will discuss the ability to exist commercial solutions [8], enterprise architecture and semantic-based solutions to meet the use case requirements.

Firstly, if we examine existing commercial solutions, we find a fragmented approach to recording processing activities to prepare ROPAs [1]. Organisations most commonly create and maintain ROPAs through informal tools, such as visual data flow mapping, customised in house software, and spreadsheets [1]. Data Protection Regulators encourage this practice by providing spreadsheet-based templates to help organisations prepare and maintain ROPAs [3]. A spreadsheet, while being a simple and commonly utilised versatile medium, requires effort to enter information and keep it updated. As a human-oriented application, spreadsheets often lack the rich data structures and semantics suitable for building automated toolchains, especially when modelling complex legal concepts beyond numerical or financial models. Furthermore, these approaches present challenges in that they are stand-alone and lack interoperability [3]. The maintained ROPA fails to meet the minimum threshold in many circumstances as they fail to be "sufficiently detailed for purpose" [9].

Enterprise Architecture (EA) models have offered the potential to generate a ROPA by augmenting existing EA models with the necessary information to maintain and generate a ROPA [10]. Huth et al. propose an approach where all required ROPA information is queried and presented in a structured format. The data in this structured form can be displayed in a custom-built application or exported to a ROPA presentation spreadsheet. However, the heterogeneity of data processing activities from diverse sources, both Inter and Intra organisational, creates challenges as the EA architecture may not extend to all the business units or domains required. In addition, specialised knowledge and tools are often not in-house, are required to build and extend EA models.

Many Semantic-based projects provide vocabularies, ontologies, and policy languages that can be used to represent GDPR concepts. These solutions mainly focus on providing informational items referenced in GDPR rights and obligations. They tend to focus on modelling/advanced use cases rather than deployment and interoperability. These projects focus on legal compliance evaluation. They do not consider the critical aspect of how the information required for (a) evaluating legal obligations and (b) demonstrating legal compliance - is maintained or generated within/by organisations and the entities involved in this process. The ability to demonstrate compliance is integral to the principle of accountability (GDPR Art.5.2). In many cases, many of the open-source ontologies and vocabularies are obsolete or without new developments in recent years, except for a small number of open vocabularies such as **BPR4GDPR's IMO** [11], **GDPRov** [12], **GConsent** [13], **DPV** [7], **GDPRtEXT** [14] and **PrOnto** [15] being the only ones that continue.

BPR4GDPR (Business Process Re-engineering and functional toolkit for GDPR compliance) [11] is a compliance ontology used to dictate and evaluate processes by considering them as workflows where actions or operations are connected dependencies and data flows performed by actors who can include assets or artefacts. Process mining is performed on the knowledge extracted from event logs of information systems to discover, monitor, and improve processes not assumed or modelled before evaluation. BPR4GDPR is utilised to create a process monitoring architecture. These rules are intended to act as constraints in conformance checking and repair the processes by identifying components that need to be changed to satisfy rules. GDPRov, [12] is a linked data ontology for expressing consent and data lifecycles' provenance to document user compliance. GConsent [13] is an OWL2-DL ontology representing consent and associated information, such as provenance. It uses R2RML to produce mappings for generating RDF metadata and focuses on using a standard model for each consent instance. This would also facilitate using data validation of information regarding consent. GDPRtEXT [14] is a linked data resource using the European Legislation Identifier (ELI) ontology for exposing the GDPR as linked data and is published using DCAT. The dataset contains a SPARQL endpoint.

GDPRtEXT also provides a SKOS vocabulary for defining terms and concepts in GDPR. The PrOnto [15] ontology provides concepts regarding GDPR associated with data types and documents, agents and roles, processing purposes, legal bases, processing operations, and deontic operations for modelling rights and duties. It has been applied for legal compliance checking over Business Process Model and Notation (BPMN). Though several vocabularies feature concepts for GDPR compliance, none of these has been utilised in modelling ROPA (through GDPR). We identify that the development of vocabularies and ontologies in this domain is certainly prolific but would benefit from deploying a data processing catalog to collect unified metadata to be utilised for ROPA creation, particularly the ability to span graph-based and non-graph data sources.

Currently, there are no vocabularies explicitly addressing or supporting ROPAs. Of the specified existing works, the DPV is the only one deployed to represent ROPAs [3]; however, this is a conceptual initiative with no deployment to date.

4. A Data Processing Activities Catalog

Alpha Ltd. can create a ROPA using existing solutions; however, the challenge for Alpha ltd. is to do this accurately and maintain an up to date ROPA [9]. Therefore, we propose a data processing activities catalog for representing heterogeneous compliance-related data for GDPR. The key benefits of a data catalog for this task are as follows:

- The design of data catalogs span heterogeneity based on common metadata and thus only require the collection of a small amount of data to describe the processing activities
- Data catalogs are widely used by industry, with many increasing numbers of organisations having expertise in their area
- Data catalogs such as CKAN [16] offer user interfaces that facilitate use by non-technical personnel
- Data catalogs support federated and distributed systems of data processing knowledge collection
- Data catalogs have specified standards for interoperability that we show below that can align with the data required for a ROPA
- Data catalog models and tools can be extended easily to gather additional data required for the completion of a specialised dataset such as a ROPA

We will base our data processing activities catalog on DCAT-AP. This profile specification is based on W3C's Data Catalog vocabulary (DCAT) for describing public sector datasets in the EU's Open Data portals. DCAT-AP enables cross-data portal search by harmonising the metadata collected and enables common metadata collection and search about diverse datasets. This is achieved by the exchange of standard descriptions of datasets among data portals. In addition, DCAT-AP proposes mandatory, recommended, or optional classes and properties to be used for a particular application; It identifies requirements to control vocabularies for this particular application; It gathers other elements to be considered as priorities or requirements for an application such as conformance statement, agent roles or cardinalities.

Our catalog will be known as DPCat. It will be a profile of DCAT-AP and will be focused on representing data processing activities for the generation of a ROPA. DPCat will build on the specifications of DCAT-AP to represent the processing activities required for ROPA. DPCat will also utilise the DPV as the controlled vocabulary used for the catalog. The terms required for ROPA are aligned to the DPV namespace and are a controlled vocabulary for the fields in the profile. The DPV is taxonomical modelling of concepts associated with personal data processing based on the GDPR. It is an outcome of the W3C Data Privacy Vocabularies and Controls Community Group (DPVCG), representing a community agreement between different stakeholders. The creation of the DPV ontology follows guidelines and methodologies deemed 'best practice' by the semantic web community [17]. The DPV is helpful as a machine-readable representation of personal data processing and can be adopted in relevant use-cases such as legal compliance documentation and evaluation, policy specification, consent representation and requests, a taxonomy of legal terms, and annotation of text and data. The use of DPV as part of DPCat will provide an extensive personal data processing vocabulary that will sufficiently expressively represent the terms required in ROPA.

5. DPCat Specifications

Our system requires the representation of the legal data required to complete the ROPA and operational information to maintain the ROPA on an ongoing basis. Article 30 of the GDPR sets out the legal information required to prepare the ROPA. In addition, the regulation states that each controller and, where applicable, the controller's representative, shall maintain a record of processing activities under its responsibility. That record shall contain all the following information:

(a) the name and contact details of the controller and, where applicable, the joint controller, the controller's representative, and the data protection officer

(b) the purposes of the processing

(c) description of the categories of data subjects and the categories of personal data

(d) the categories of recipients to whom the personal data have been or will be disclosed include recipients in third countries or international organisations.

(e) where applicable, transfers of personal data to a third country or an international organisation, including the identification of that third country or international organisation and, in the case of transfers referred to in the second subparagraph of Article 49(1), the documentation of suitable safeguards

(f) where possible, the envisaged time limits for erasure of the different categories of data

(g) A general description of the technical and organisational security measures referred to in Article 32(1) is possible.

In practice, many regulators provide ROPA templates that prescribe a format for the presentation of ROPA [3]. Whilst these templates are not mandatory; they are a minimum expectation of what is required by the regulator to demonstrate the organisation's accountability. For our use case, we will create a ROPA based upon the fields specified by regulation in Article 30 of the GDPR.

In section 4, we present DPCat as a solution to represent data processing activities. We have identified the data required for representation in the ROPA from Article 30 of the GDPR. To achieve this representation in DPCat, we identify the mandatory, recommended, and optional fields already specified in DCAT-AP and build on this, as DPCat is a profile of DCAT-AP. We find that we can utilise several DCAT properties to meet our requirement list's needs for a Processing Activities catalog as set out in section 2. We utilise the DPV to specify all additional properties that we require to populate ROPA. We document this specification for representing data processing activities using DPCat in table 1 with the following notation: M for Mandatory fields, C for Conditionally applicable, R for Recommended, and O for Optional. We provide a specification overview for the DPCat catalog in Figure 2.

Table 1. Specification for Representing the Data Processing Activities in DPCat

ROPA Requirement	Obligation	DPCat Property	DPCat Property Range
Controller	M	dct:publisher	foaf:Agent, dpv:Controller, adms:PublisherType
Purpose	M	dpv:hasPurpose	dpv:Purpose
Categories of Data Subjects	M	dpv:hasDataSubject	subclass of dpv:DataSubject
Categories of Personal Data	M	dpv:hasPersonalDataCategory	subclass of dpv:PersonalDataCategory
Categories of Recipients	C	dpv:hasRecipient	subclass of foaf:Agent, adms:PublisherType, dpv:LegalEntity
Data Transfer	C	dpv:hasProcessing	dpv:Transfer
Data Transfer Location	M	dpv:hasLocation	dpv:Location
Data Transfer Recipient	M	dpv:hasRecipient	foaf:Agent, adms:PublisherType, dpv:LegalEntity
Data Transfer Safeguards (see note below)	C	dpv:hasSafeguard	dpv:Safeguard
Time limits for erasure of different categories of data	R	dpv:hasDuration	dpv:StorageDuration
Technical and Organisational Measures	R	dpv:hasTechnicalOrganisationalMeasure	dpv:TechnicalOrganisationalMeasure
Processors responsible for processing	R	dpv:hasRecipient	dpv:Processor

Note: The Property dpv:hasSafeguard and the property range dpv:Safeguard have been submitted to the Data Privacy Community Controls Group for inclusion in the DPV vocabulary.

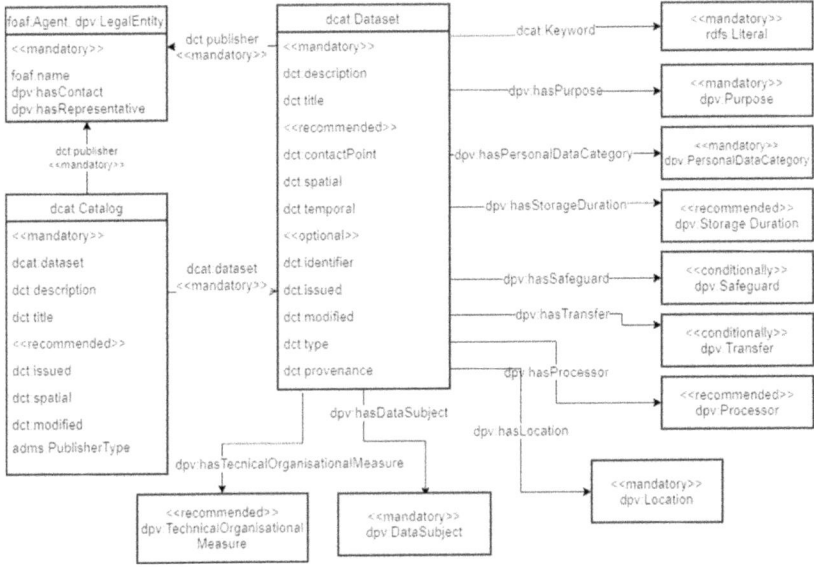

Fig. 2. DPCat specification for ROPA datasets

In section 2, we set out the requirements that a data processing catalog for ROPA must provide. We have proposed that our specialised data catalog DPCat can provide the DPO with a solution for representing a ROPA where data must be gathered from heterogeneous sources. In Table 2, we set out how DPCat can meet these requirements, and we support this with a demonstration of DPCat in section 6.

Table 2. How DPCat Meets our Requirements for a Data Processing

Req. no	Data Processing Catalog Requirement	DPCat Property
1.	Heterogeneity of data	dct:publisher ;dcat:dataset
2.	Enables standards-based collation of the data for ROPA	Refer to section 6 (Demonstration)
3.	Temporal information	dct:issued ; dct:temporal ; dct:modified
4.	Changes to the records	dct:modified ; dct:issued
5.	Identity of organisational unit	dct:publisher ; dct:contactPoint ; dpv:LegalEntity
6.	Facilitate searching records	dct:issued ; dct:temporal ; dct:identifier ; dct:modified
7.	Facilitate the creation of ROPA	Refer to section 6 (Demonstration)
8.	Minimises the data to be collected and integrated	
9.	Easy to deploy	

6. Demonstration and Discussion

To demonstrate the application of the catalog and evaluate its feasibility in addressing the requirements identified in Section 2, we created sample data reflecting the structure and operation of departments within the organisation Alpha Inc. and used queries to extract information to create ROPA. In our use-case scenario, the DPO must collect and inspect information from multiple departments for Marketing, Human Resources (HR) and Customer Services - each of which has its record-keeping practices. Also, the HR department employs the processor Beta Ltd. - which must also maintain its ROPA as a processor. The catalog, datasets, queries, and outputs for this use case are available here: https://github.com/coolharsh55/DPCat.

Each department maintains its records in our use case and has a separate catalog, while the organisation's catalog references these as datasets. The information maintained in a department's catalog and records fields are produced based on how they conduct their activities. The outcome is an RDF graph used in the catalog records. SPARQL queries were then used to create 'views' for presenting a summary and overview of activities—for example, and Table 3 specifies a snippet of processing activities in terms of information required for ROPA, their temporal periods, and the contact point for further communication with the complete ROPA available in the DPCat repository mentioned above.

Table 3. Sample Extract of Controller ROPA

Department	Customer Service Dept.	HR Dept.	Marketing Dept.
Title	Record001	Record004	Record001
Period Start	2019-01-01	2019-01-01	2019-01-01
Period End	2022-12-13	2022-12-13	2022-12-13
Contact Name	Alice	Bob	Emily
Contact e-mail	alice@example.com	bob@example.com	emily@example.com
Purpose Category	Customer care	Service Provision	Direct Marketing
Purpose	Recording of customer calls	Expenses activities	Direct marketing via e-mail
Data Subject	Customers	Employees	Customers
Personal Data Category	Voice recordings	Financial	E-mail addresses
Recipient	Null	Beta Ltd.	Null
Recipient Category	Null	Data Processor	Null
Recipient Location	Null	Canada	Null
Storage years	2.0	7.0	1.0
Measures	Standard	Standard	Standard

We used GraphDB Free [18] [2] as a triple-store to store and query the information. In the queries, we relied on utilising reasoning and inferences capabilities in GraphDB (RDFS and OWL2) to retrieve results where triples were not explicitly specified correctly. We initially opted to utilise separate named graphs for each department's information to represent independent maintenance with SPARQL CONSTRUCT queries to ingest them into a global organisation-level graph. However, we discovered that this approach creates SPARQL queries due to the requirements that each named graph be explicitly specified in the query. Therefore, we decided to use a single organisation-level graph where each department maintains its catalog for demonstration purposes. We comment on this in our discussion on practicality later in the paper.

Our approach also strived to create each dataset record as a self-contained graph since the information maintained represents a 'snapshot' of activities for that organisation or its unit in a specific temporal period. This process involved using blank nodes and owl:sameAs to related entities within the organisation's global graph. This also helped validate the dataset on its own by using SHACL to check that mandatory fields are present and the correctness of the information. This approach has further benefits by making documentation and validation possible at any arbitrary stage - from individual records and organisational units to the entire organisation without conflicts or dependencies. Thus, the ROPA queries could target a specific catalog, department, or the entire organisation.

In addressing the requirements specified in section 2, the use-case sufficiently demonstrates that catalogs are a good design paradigm for record-keeping connected with GDPR compliance and ROPA documentation. The approach enables documenting data processing activities in terms of their temporal period, limiting the scope to organisational units, and assigning contact points within the organisation for further information. The inherent design of catalogs as a 'collection of records' permits the responsible unit to continue updating and maintaining records while reducing the burden on DPOs by utilising the catalog itself as a single point of reference for all related information. The use of SPARQL facilitates information searching, filtering, and exporting for ROPA creation. The paper's contribution is that the organisation can span heterogeneity based on common metadata requiring the collection of only a small amount of data to describe the processing activities. The organisation can thus generate, maintain and query a ROPA efficiently by relying on the common metadata-based records provided by DPCat to aggregate and homogenise access within the diverse sources of information required for compliance.

6.1. Discussion on Practicality and Avenues for future research

Automation. In terms of functioning and integration with existing organisational tools, the creation of datasets and records in RDF can be automated using approaches such as R2RML - which is a standardised specification for mappings from relational/SQL databases to RDF, or using data cataloging tools such as CKAN provides tools for catalog creation and maintenance. More importantly, the catalog is a DCAT-AP profile based on the standardised DCAT vocabulary and is itself a standard maintained by the EU to provide interoperability for sharing data between its data portals.

---

[2] https://www.ontotext.com/products/graphdb/graphdb-free/

Data sources. As we mentioned earlier in this section, we discovered the complexity of querying information when departments utilised individual named graphs for housing catalog records. In practical terms, whether each department should independently maintain compliance-related information or only submit it to a single monolithic repository is based on the organisation's practices. However, for interoperability, this information needs to be present somewhere in the catalog. We, therefore, intend on further exploring the suitability of existing fields within DCAT-AP and the more recent developments in DCAT v2 to represent information regarding sources, data formats, access controls, and SPARQL endpoints. This can also allow the specification to facilitate appropriate tooling and programmatic interfaces that can actively search and accommodate other heterogeneous tools and data sources.

Controlled Vocabularies. Currently, the specification uses DPV as a pseudo-controlled vocabulary to ensure information is expressed using the same concepts as those required for a ROPA (or broadly for GDPR compliance). Utilising a different vocabulary to specify the fields (such as purpose or recipient) is possible but requires changing the catalog specification in its entirety. Furthermore, any vocabulary chosen cannot foresee all possible concepts owing to the reality of how purposes and personal data categories can be defined. However, DPV, by being a 'community-driven standard', provides stability and interoperability in addition to expressing taxonomies from a top-down approach which makes it possible to extend and customise to situations. Therefore, it is recommended that other controlled vocabularies, where they are needed and used, be aligned to DPV concepts to ensure continued interoperability of the catalog information.

Representing complexity, e.g. Catalog of Catalogs. The use-case demonstrates functionality for a dataset catalog, which is more straightforward to understand due to its smaller scope and size. However, practical requirements may dictate many records and organisational units represented within the catalog's catalog. For the specification and tooling to function correctly in such situations, it is essential to formalise how such catalogs should be defined and the resulting interpretation.

Shared Information. The use-case considers complete dissociation between organisational departments, which may not be the case in practice. For example, the IT department may be responsible for ensuring appropriate technical and organisational measures are implemented, or a Controller may wish to record what measures a Processor has in place. In this case, organisations may want to delegate or import some catalog information from specific units. It is not currently possible to denote this with the outlined specification. We, therefore, specify this as an open research question regarding how to represent and maintain heterogeneous information within a catalog.

Common registries. The specification for a catalog of data processing activities provides an exciting possibility where a data portal can be set up for representing associated information. This can have several use-cases ranging from an open-source catalog of an organisation's practices and policies to enabling communication between controllers and/or processors. Another practical application of the specification is that it enables authorities to request and manage information about data processing activities through a dedicated data portal. This is promising given the drive for digital services and inter-jurisdictional information sharing for compliance within the EU.

Conclusions

The heterogeneity of data sources representing the organisation's data processing activities presents significant challenges when completing a ROPA. Our research sought to establish the extent to which implementing a Data Processing Activities Catalog based on DCAT-AP and DPV can overcome the heterogeneity of sources to facilitate the preparation of a ROPA. For this, we presented a use case and developed a prototype system to catalog the organisation's diverse data processing activities using SPARQL queries to output a ROPA document. Its key benefits are providing a lightweight, low cost, and metadata-level integration for compliance information regarding processing activities from heterogeneous sources. In addition, our DPCat solution advances alignments between disciplinary and domain-specific metadata standards. Finally, it enables data catalog implementations by providing a common interoperable base for ROPA without requiring full alignment or merging all the underlying data sources.

Acknowledgements

The ADAPT Centre supports this work for Digital Content Technology, funded under the SFI Research Centres Programme (Grant 13/RC/2106_P2) and co-funded under the European Regional Development Fund. Uniphar PLC supports Paul Ryan. Harshvardhan J. Pandit is funded under the Irish Research Council Government of Ireland Postdoctoral Fellowship Grant#GOIPD/2020/790 and the European Union's Horizon 2020 research and innovation programme under NGI TRUST Grant#825618 for Project#3.40 Privacy-as-Expected: Consent Gateway. For the purpose of Open Access, the author has applied a CC BY public copyright licence to any Author Accepted Manuscript version arising from this submission

References

[1] International Association of Privacy Professionals (IAPP), Trust Arc.: Measuring Privacy Operations. (2019).
[2] Drewer, D., Miladinova, V.: The Canary in the Data Mine. Computer Law and Security Review 34, 806-815 (2018).
[3] Ryan, P., Pandit, H., Brennan, R.: A Common Semantic Model of the GDPR Register of Processing Activities (2020), doi:10.3233/FAIA200876.
[4] Profiles Ontology Homepage, http://www.w3.org/TR/dx-prof/ , last accessed 2021/04/11.
[5] DCAT Homepage, http://www.w3.org/TR/vocab-dcat-2/ , last accessed 2021/04/11.
[6] DCAT-AP Homepage, https://data.gov.ie/dataset/dcat-ap , last accessed 2021/04/11.
[7] DPV Homepage,https://w3.org/ns/dpv, last accessed 2021/04/11
[8] International Association of Privacy Professionals (IAPP),: 2020 Privacy Tech Vendor Report. (2020).
[9] Castlebridge Report (2020), https://castlebridge.ie/research/2020/ropa-report/ , last accessed 2021/04/11.
[10] Huth, D., Tanakol, A., Matthes, F.: Using Enterprise Architecture Models for Creating the Record of Processing Activities. IEEE 23rd International Enterprise Distributed Object Computing Conference (EDOC), 98-104 (2019) DOI: 10.1109/EDOC.2019.00021.
[11] BPR4GDPR Homepage, http://www.bpr4gdpr.eu/ , last accessed 2021/04/11.
[12] Pandit, H.J., Lewis, D.: Modelling provenance for gdpr compliance using linked open data vocabularies. (2017).

[13] Pandit, H.J., et al.: GConsent - A Consent Ontology based on the GDPR, Lecture Notes in Computer Science, Vol. 11530, 270-282, (2019)

[14] Pandit, H.J., et al.: GDPRtEXT - GDPR as a Linked Data Resource, The semantic web— 15th international conference, ESWC (2018), Notes in Computer Science, vol 10843, 481– 495, (2018) https://doi.org/10.1007/978-3-319-93417-4_31

[15] Palmirani, M., Martoni, M., Rossi, A., Bartolini, C., Robaldo. L.: PrOnto: Privacy Ontology for Legal Compliance. In Proceedings of the 18th European Conference on Digital Government ECDG (2018)

[16] CKAN Homepage, https://ckan.org/ , last accessed 2021/04/11.

[17] Pandit, H.J., et al.: Creating a Vocabulary for Data Privacy. In: Panetto H., Debruyne C., Hepp M., Lewis D., Ardagna C., Meersman R. (eds) On the Move to Meaningful Internet Systems: OTM, (2019).

[18] GraphDB Homepage, https://www.ontotext.com/products/graphdb/graphdb-free/ , last accessed 2021/04/11.

Further with Knowledge Graphs. M. Alam et al. (Eds.)
AKA Verlag and IOS Press, 2021
© *2021 Akademische Verlagsgesellschaft AKA GmbH, Berlin*
This article is published online with Open Access by IOS Press and distributed under the terms
of the Creative Commons Attribution License 4.0 (CC BY 4.0).
doi:10.3233/SSW210044

A Fully Decentralized Triplestore Managed via the Ethereum Blockchain

Damien GRAUX ⊚ ᵃ and Sina MAHMOODI ᵇ

ᵃ *Inria, Université Côte d'Azur, CNRS, I3S, France* - `damien.graux@inria.fr`
ᵇ *Ethereum Foundation* - `sina.mahmoodi@ethereum.org`

Abstract. The growing web of data warrants better data management strategies. Data silos are single points of failure and they face availability problems which lead to broken links. Furthermore the dynamic nature of some datasets increases the need for a versioning scheme. In this work, we propose a novel architecture for a linked open data infrastructure, built on open decentralized technologies. IPFS is used for storage and retrieval of data, and the public Ethereum blockchain is used for naming, versioning and storing metadata of datasets. We furthermore exploit two mechanisms for maintaining a collection of relevant, high-quality datasets in a distributed manner in which participants are incentivized. The platform is shown to have a low barrier to entry and censorship-resistance. It benefits from the fault-tolerance of its underlying technologies. Furthermore, we validate the approach by implementing our solution.

Keywords. RDF store, Decentralized solution, Versioning management, Smart contracts

1. Introduction

Over the last decade, as more and more linked data in the form of RDF [7] triples were published, a set of data management practices [18] were proposed and adopted which aimed to improve integration and reuse among datasets, forming the web of data, which can be seen as a global namespace connecting individual graphs and statements. From a logical point of view, linked data is inherently decentralized. However, from a practical point of view, the actual data reside on data silos which suffer from low availability [10], leading to broken links. Furthermore, when considering dynamic datasets [19], a lack of robust versioning scheme can lead to inconsistencies when an external linked dataset is modified. But versioning datasets using HTTP has so far proven difficult [27]. Another implication of the unprecedented volume of data being published in web of data is the varying quality of datasets. Expert quality assessment [33] and curation produces the best result, but in large scale incurs high costs in terms of expert time and labor.

The contributions of this work include a novel architecture for a decentralized linked open data infrastructure, based on IPFS [4] and the public Ethereum blockchain [32]. The design includes an indexing scheme suitable for linked data, and a mechanism for retrieval of data by performing triple pattern or SPARQL queries. It further outlines how smart contracts can be employed to provide a persistent identifier for data objects stored on IPFS, to describe and version datasets, to control write access and to ensure source of provenance. A prototype of the aforementioned architecture has been implemented, and is available under an open license[1]. Moreover, on this foundation, and to further explore crowdsourcing data curation in scale, we exploit two mechanisms, first proposed by Ethereum community members [5,14], which facilitate distributed, truthful, incentivized consensus on a curated list of datasets. The mechanisms are agnostic to the domain and the actual quality metrics.

The rest of this article is divided as follows. First we provide some necessary presentation about the considered technologies in Section 2. In Section 3, we present the decentralized architecture we propose to store data; and the Ethereum smart contract solutions we set up to manage the knowledge graphs (KG) in Section 4; before presenting data curation strategies in Section 5. Then we show how data can be retrieved and report on experimental validations in Section 6. Finally we review related work and conclude in Sections 7 and 8.

2. Background

IPFS [4] is a peer-to-peer protocol for content-addressable storage and retrieval of data. It is a peer-to-peer network, with no difference between the participating nodes. It utilizes routing mechanisms to keep track of data storage, and block exchange mechanisms to facilitate the transfer of data. Every node stores IPFS objects in their local storage. These objects could be published by the node, or retrieved from other nodes and replicated locally. Objects in IPFS are comprised of immutable content-addressed data structures (such as files), that are connected with links, forming a Merkle DAG (directed acyclic graph). Addressing is done using cryptographic hashes. Content can be identified uniquely by its hash, and after retrieval, the integrity of it can be verified against the hash that was used to address it. IPFS, however, does not guarantee persistence, only permanence. A piece of content can always be referred by its hash, but it doesn't necessarily exist in the nodes of the network at all times.

IPLD[2] is a data model that aims to provide a unified address space for hash-linked data structures, such as IPFS objects, git objects, Ethereum transaction data, etc., which would allow traversing data regardless of the exact underlying protocol. The benefits of such a data model include protocol-independent resolution and cross-protocol integration, upgradability, self-descriptive data models that map to a deterministic wire encoding, backward-compatibility and format-independence. A key aspect of IPLD, is a self-describing content-addressed identifier format, called CID[3] which describes an address along with its base, version of the CID format, format of the data being addressed, hash function, hash size and finally the hash (address). This allows CID to address objects from various

---

[1]Our implementation is provided on Github: https://github.com/dgraux/open-knowledge ⬈
[2]https://github.com/ipld/specs
[3]https://github.com/ipld/cid

protocols. IPLD, inter alia, defines merkle-dag, merkle-links and merkle-paths. Merkle-dag is a graph, the edges of which are merkle-links. A merkle-path, is a unix-like path, that traverses within objects, and across objects by dereferencing merkle-links.

Ethereum [32] For the purposes of this study, Ethereum smart contracts can be seen as state machines, that are deployed to the network along with an initial state, and the code necessary for future state transitions, by way of invoking public functions. Upon deployment, they will be assigned an address, which can hence be used to interact with them. This interaction takes place, by crafting a transaction containing the target address, the sender, value of ether to be transferred, and if target is a contract, the input data passed to the contract.

Transactions are broadcast to the network, and so-called miners propose blocks which contain a list of the previously broadcast transactions. Every other node, upon receiving a block, runs all transactions inside, and validates the computed state, against the state put forth by the miner. Miners receive a reward in ether, the native currency of the network, for helping secure the network, and to protect against Sybil attacks [8], miners compete for proposing blocks by solving a Proof of Work [22].

As mentioned, every node in the network verifies every block, which imposes a limit on the size and frequency of blocks, which results in a limited number of slots for transactions. Users, compete for the limited slots, by sending gas (in ether) along with their transactions, which the miner earns for including the transaction in a block. Gas also acts as a deterrent for spamming the network. Miners, often employ the simple strategy of including transactions which have the most payoff.

3. A fully decentralized storage system

Our proposed architecture relies on two open technologies. First, IPFS for the actual storage and retrieval of raw data (see Section 6), and Ethereum, for tracking ownership, versioning and other metadata belonging to the KG (more details in Section 4), and later on, as will be discussed, for decentralized curation of datasets (cf. Section 5).

Permissioned, centralized triplestores often store all inserted triples in a single index. However, this is not desirable in a permissionless setting where any entity has write access to the same store, meaning, entities can even publish triples that are in conflict with others already in the triplestore. Hence, in our effort, KGs are not only conceptual, but they are actually stored in separate indices, that are managed by their corresponding publishing entity. The KGs are still connected by the URI scheme, and it is possible to do federated queries across multiple KGs. One can imagine KGs to be the counterpart of servers which contain a single dataset as opposed to multi-dataset repositories. The access control mechanism is controlled on the blockchain level (Section 4), and the P2P storage layer is agnostic to access. Due to the immutable nature of IPFS, this introduces no conflict, as each modification to an existing object results in a totally new object with a new address, regardless of who has published the modified dataset.

Each KG is indexed as a Hexastore [31] on IPFS. However, the Hexastore is not stored as a single data object, but is rather broken into smaller data nodes,

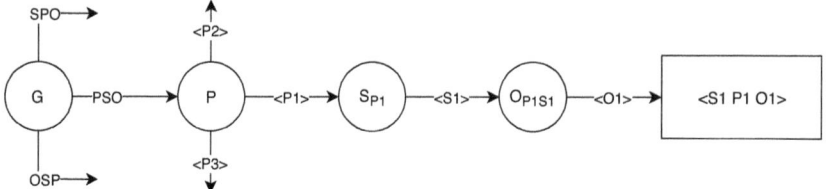

Figure 1. Example Hexastore Merkle-DAG for graph G.

which are connected via links, forming an IPLD merkle-dag. Practically, each KG has a root object, with 6 keys, namely `spo`, `sop`, `pso`, `pos`, `osp`, `ops` where the value of each key is a link to another object containing the triples for that subindex. Each subindex is itself a merkle-dag of depth 3. It contains the first part of the triple, with links to objects containing the second part, which in turn have links to objects containing the third part. The leaves are a simple boolean, indicating that the triple with part 1, 2 and 3 exists in the index.

As an example, consider graph G, as shown in Figure 1. The figure only displays the merkle-path to the triple `<S1 P1 O1>`, via the subindex `pso`. P is the set of all predicates in G. If `<P1>` is one of those predicates, by traversing the link for `<P1>`, we arrive at the object S_P1, which is the set of all subjects in G for which at least one triple exists with predicate `<P1>`. In a similar manner, if `<S1>` is a subject in S_P1, by traversing the link, we arrive at the object O_P1S1, which is the set of all objects in G for which triples exist with the triple pattern `<S1 P1 ?O>`. Traversing the link for `<O1>` we arrive at the leaf object { `"exists": true` }. In Figure 1, only the path for subindex `pso` is shown. However, the same triple is indexed under the other subindices. Therefore, if G has the root hash `QmAA...AA`, the merkle-paths `QmAA...AA/pso/P1/S1/O1`, `QmAA...AA/sop/S1/O1/P1`, etc. would all be `true`.

4. A smart-contract based management system

So far we've seen the structure of indices, how KGs are stored. Each graph G is identified by the multihash of the root of its index, and updating the graph results in a completely new and unpredictable root hash. As a result, data consumers need a means for tracking the history of changes to G and consequently its root hashes, in order to be able to perform queries. In this section, two **smart contracts,** namely `Graph` and `SimpleRegistry`, will be introduced, which facilitate tracking the history of graphs and their metadata, and improving findability by naming them.

4.0.1. Graph

The `Graph` smart contract is meant to represent a single dataset, maintained by a single entity. It tracks the history of the graph, stores relevant information such as version, and points to additional metadata that the author wishes to attach to their dataset.

When creating a new KG, the publisher must publish the RDF triples on IPFS, as outlined in the previous section, and deploy an instance of the `Graph` contract, providing the root hash of the index as input. The deployed instance has a permanent address, which they can distribute to data consumers. Consumers can then query the Ethereum blockchain to fetch the state of the aforementioned contract instance, find the current root hash which they can use to perform queries. To update the KG, they update the index on IPFS, and make a transaction to the contract, providing the new hash as input. Consumers who are subscribing to events emitted by Ethereum, will be informed of the new root hash. The smart contract holds the following state fields:

Listing 1: State of the Graph contract in Solidity. For brevity, the rest of the contract has been omitted.

```
1   contract Graph { address public owner; uint public version;
2       bytes32 public id; bytes32 public root;
3       bytes32 public metadata; bytes32 public license; }
```

Ownership – In listing 1, `owner` refers to the Ethereum account who deployed the smart contract. From then on, only `owner` is able to modify the state of *c*, but ownership can easily be transferred to other accounts by submitting a transaction, invoking the specific `setOwner` method.

History – The field `root` is an IPFS hash which points to the root of the knowledge graph's hexastore index in IPFS. When *G* is updated, `owner` sends a transaction to *c*, updating `root`. This removes the need for a side-channel to announce new versions of *g*, and the need for maintaining a list of previous `root`s, as Ethereum full-archive nodes store all of the previous states by default. Furthermore, versions of *G* are automatically tagged by an auto-increment `version` field, which can be used to query specific versions of *G* without referring to the full IPFS hash in SPARQL, as will be discussed in the next section.

Metadata & Attribution – The smart contract also keeps an optional `metadata` field, which is an IPFS hash. The IPFS object identified by `metadata` could contain additional information about the knowledge graph such as details about the authors, citations to other graphs or a website link.

4.0.2. Simple Registry

The `SimpleRegistry` contract (*R*) acts as a KG name registry, and a list for data consumers to find KGs. Without it, data consumers would have to know the address for every KG, and would have to specify that address in their queries. *R* allows registering graphs under a unique name, and later on request the contract address for a certain graph with its name. It's important to note that, this contract is also openly available, and an instance of it can be deployed by any party. Data producers can decide which registry they want to be a part of. `SimpleRegistry` also allows a convenience method `newGraph(bytes32 _name)` for deploying an empty `Graph` contract and thus registering a name for it in one transaction.

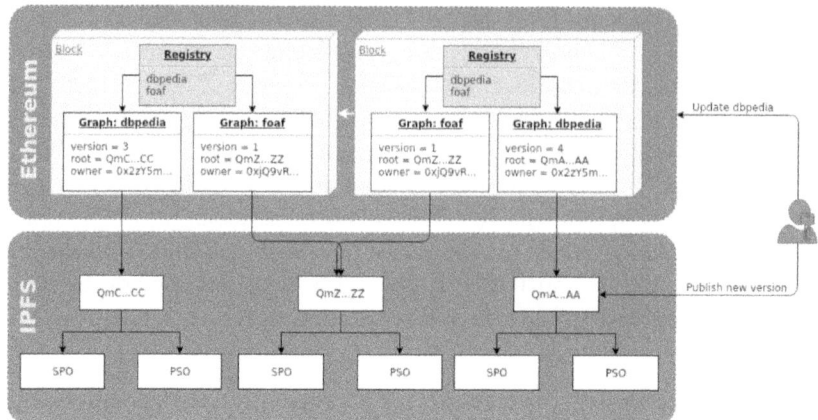

Figure 2. General Architecture.

4.0.3. The General Architecture

As presented in Figure 2, the general architecture of our solution is twofold. The bottom layer is made of the IPFS and the upper one is in the Ethereum blockchain. The various structural levels of the managing issues represented in the Ethereum are displayed in Figure 2: inside a specific block, the registry points of the associated graphs it includes and thereby could provide us with the version number and all the necessary piece of information. For example, when users want to update data, they have to publish a new version in IPFS and then update the Ethereum via the smart contracts accordingly.

5. Scalable Curation

With a growing number of datasets, it becomes increasingly costlier for consumers to find knowledge graphs suitable for their purposes, and upon finding graphs, for them to gauge their quality. This highlights the need for scalable curation mechanisms, which we will try to address in the following chapter. Free participation and censorship-resistance in our architecture has two sides. On the one hand, these characteristics ease the publication of useful and high-quality data for everyone. On the other hand, they make the infrastructure prone to being flooded with low-quality and less relevant data.

Any entity can easily create as many KGs as desired. The gas costs act as a deterrent for spamming the network. Even so, the number of legitimate graphs could potentially increase to be high enough, as to make the cost of finding suitable graphs among them non-trivial, assuming there exists a channel from which consumers can find the address of all graphs. Moreover, because `Graph` contracts have a unique and persistent identifier, namely the address of the contract, it's possible to create public lists (or collections) of graphs that are relevant for a given purpose or satisfying certain quality requirements, which consumers can refer to.

The goal is therefore to consider curation mechanisms, the output of which is a list of valid and relevant KGs for data consumers. In the following, two mechanisms will be discussed.

5.1. Adjudication via Prediction Markets

As seen previously, our architecture only stores the root hash of the index stored on IPFS, and not the index itself in the Ethereum smart contract. The main reason behind that, is transaction costs that are incurred due to storage.

As a consequence, the smart contract has no way of verifying whether the hash h actually points to a valid knowledge graph stored on IPFS. However, using Merkle proofs, or a zk-SNARK[25] proof, it is possible to prove to the smart contract, that a valid graph index would result in h as root of the index. Although verifying this proof is much cheaper than sending or storing the whole graph index, the transaction cost is still high enough to make it infeasible to do for every graph update. Nevertheless, if we have the expensive method M for verifying the validity of a graph on-chain (e.g. a zk-SNARK verifier), by utilizing prediction markets, we can still check a larger number of graphs for validity, with only a smaller subset of them needing to revert to M for verification [5].

Any entity e_1 could claim that a given graph g is invalid by creating a bet of size x in the prediction market. If e_2 doesn't agree with g being invalid, they would put a bet of size y on the opposite side. If, after a pre-specified period has passed, no other entity has challenged the bet, g would hence be considered as invalid. Otherwise, verifying via M the winning side is determined. Each entity in the winning side is rewarded proportional to their bet, a part of the bets of the losing side. The process can be further optimized to deter incorrect betting and volume manipulation, by having the amount won to be only 75% of the amount lost. The other 25%, could for example be distributed to producers of valid graphs.

The rationale here is that, verifying the validity of a graph is much cheaper done off-chain, than on-chain. Therefore, users would be incentivized to "fish" invalid graphs. They are disincentivized to bet against a valid graph, because others can challenge the bet in the market, and an on-chain verification would result in the loss of their bet.

5.2. Token-Curated Registry

Token-curated registry (TCR) [14] is a mechanism, in which rational actors are incentivized to maintain a decentrally-curated list. As the name suggests, TCRs rely on a native token, which has a value relative to another base currency (fiat currencies, such as EUR). Apart from consumers of the curated list, which desire a high-quality list of KGs, other actors require tokens to interact with the TCR. **Actors** – Actors of a TCR include candidates, voters and challengers. A candidate, is an actor, who wishes to add a graph to the list, and stakes N tokens along with the application. A challenger, is an actor, who believes the item that a candidate proposed, does not belong in the list, and is willing to stake N tokens to challenge the application. When a challenge occurs, a voting period starts, during which, token holders can cast a vote, either for or against the item in question.

Votes are weighted proportional to the number of tokens the token holder speci-fies. The tokens would not be spent during a vote. After the voting period comes to an end, the side with most token-weighted votes wins, and depending on the outcome, either the candidate or the challenger loses a portion of their stake, and this portion is split among the winners, in proportion to the number of tokens they participated with.

Rewarding honest behaviour – The rationale behind TCRs is that, rational voters seeking to increase their long-term profit, would vote to accept items that have a higher quality, which increases usefulness among consumers, resulting in more demand among candidates to be listed, increasing the value of the native to-ken with respect to the base currency. This complements their short-term benefit of being rewarded with more tokens, if they vote for high-quality items.

Disincentives – The risk associated with losing the stake disincentivizes candi-dates to apply for a graph, they consider either of low quality or invalid. At the same time, challenging a high quality graph also comes with the risk of losing a portion of challenger's stake. If this was not the case, participants would have been incentivized to challenge every application, effectively requiring a vote on every application, and thereby reducing the efficiency of the mechanism.

Vote-splitting – The aforementioned specification failed to address the "nothing at-stake" problem for voters, or in particular, the "vote-splitting" issue, in which, a rational strategy for voters could be to split their tokens in half, and vote for both side, thereby earning revenue regardless of the outcome of the vote, and without putting in any effort. TCR v1.1[4] addresses this issue, by slashing a portion of the minority bloc's tokens, and adding it to the rewards of the majority's bloc.

Commit-reveal voting – Due to Ethereum transactions being public, during a voting period, voters can see the current tally, and vote with the majority, without inspecting the item in question. This can be prevented, by splitting the voting period into two phases: first, all voters make a cryptographic commitment to a vote, after the commit period has come to an end, everyone must reveal their vote, by submitting the secret used to make the commitment. Consequentially, the tally of the votes is unknown by everyone other than the voter until the end of the commit period. This effectively prevents voters from basing their decisions on how others are voting.

Listing item status – Graphs are added to the list, either if they face no chal-lenge after application, or if they are challenged, and voters vote for inclusion of the graph. The stake, which is a requirement of applying to the TCR, remains locked while the item is in the list. The candidate, can, at any moment withdraw the stake, and thereby removing the item from the list. Furthermore, even after a graph has been listed, it can be challenged and therefore removed from the list. This is inevitable, because an append-only list, could grow large enough to lose its usefulness, and as such, when higher quality graphs are added to the list, lower quality graphs can be challenged and removed, in order to maintain a limited number of slots in the list.

---

[4] https://medium.com/@ilovebagels/token-curated-registries-1-1-2-0-tcrs-new-theory-and-dev-updates-34c9f079f33d

6. Retrieval

As seen in the previous sections, triples of a knowledge graph are stored in the form of a merkle-dag on IPFS. Merkle-paths allow querying triple patterns, but not other features of an advanced query language such as SPARQL [16]. It is however possible to perform a subset of all SPARQL constructs, by combining the results of several triple pattern searches. First, we will demonstrate how a simple triple pattern search can be performed, and then discuss how full SPARQL queries, either on single graphs or a federation thereof, can be executed by using triple patterns as building blocks.

6.1. Triple Patterns

A triple pattern, is a triple where any of the parts can be a variable instead of a concrete value. In the simplest case, it is possible to query the existence of a triple, that has no variable, in the KG. In this case, the merkle-path for the triple `<a b c>` would look like `QmAA...AA/spo/a/b/c` which returns `true` if the triple exists, and throws an error otherwise.

Given a graph G which has root hash G_h and a triple pattern T, the algorithm for constructing the corresponding merkle-path P and retrieving the values at this path is given below:

1. Initialize P to G_h
2. Parse T to get list of fixed and variable parts
3. Compute best subindex: bring fixed parts first, then append variable ones
4. Add subindex to P
5. Append values for fixed parts to merkle-path, separated by a "/"
6. Fetch result (R) of P from IPFS
7. If result is nonempty, construct triples by adding the values for fixed parts to the results which were returned for the variable parts, and return them.

As an example, running the algorithm over a KG which contains [`<a b c>`, `<f b c>`], with T = `<?s b c>`, implies to use a *pos* index and will result in P = `QmAA...AA/pos/b/c` and R = `[a,f]`, and the algorithm will return [`<a b c>`, `<f b c>`].

6.2. SPARQL Queries

Although querying triple patterns and compositions thereof would suffice for some applications, it falls short for others. In order to allow SPARQL queries, we build on the Linked Data Fragments framework[29] by implementing the Triple Patterns Fragments interface. By doing so, the TPF client decomposes a SPARQL query into triple patterns, retrieves the corresponding responses, and computes the final SPARQL response therefrom.

In implementing the TPF interface, some specific points had to be taken into account. TPF has been design with REST APIs in mind. In our architecture, the client and the implementation of the TPF interface reside on the same node, and they communicate via faster intra-process means. In addition, the original TPF interface implementation runs on a server and fetches data from a local database, whereas with our solution, triples are stored across peers, and in case the required triples are not replicated locally, each triple pattern query is automatically translated into requests to fetch triples from other peers. Finally, pagination and control functions such as `nextPage`, are a requirement of the TPF interface; currently pagination is done after fetching all of the triples matching a pattern.

Federated SPARQL queries –i.e. queries requesting several graphs at once– are performed in a similar manner, by utilizing the TPF interface. In a nutshell, the query is first split according to the various implied graphs to obtain distinct Linked Data Fragments; then we process as described above; before joining together the results. However, whereas TPF originally requests the result of triple patterns from servers via HTTP, in our architecture, all triple pattern queries are done simply over different graphs which exist on the same P2P filesystem following the concerned hash addresses.

6.3. Complete Evaluation Process

More generally, as already presented in Figure 2, the solution has two layers: one on top based in Ethereum which offers managing features and the bottom one on IPFS where data is actually stored.

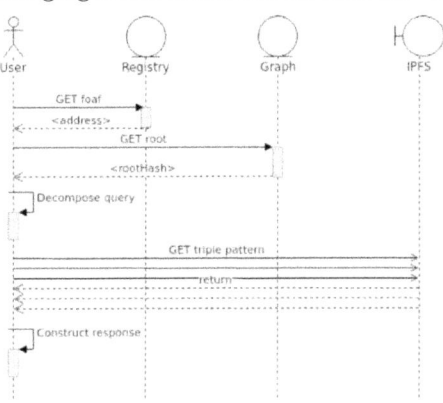

As a consequence, during the query phase, the system takes into account this specificity. We present in Figure 3 the details of the query process around the information retrieval. Indeed, the first step requires to look for graph addresses in the Registry, then to obtain the correct root hashes from each Graph (taking e.g. into account the version number). Once these information are obtained, we are done with the

Figure 3.: Evaluation Process.

Ethereum side and can decompose the query in order to get the triple pattern from the IPFS. Once they are retrieved, the answer can be constructed and the complete process to evaluate a SPARQL query is done.

6.4. Experimental Validation

In this section, the results of a benchmark performed on the prototype implementation is presented. To verify the correct functionality of the architecture and its implementation, the source code also includes a test suite. Moreover, we generated a WatDiv [2] dataset with scale 1 which contains 107 665 triples, stored the dataset on our system and performed the 20 queries provided in the WatDiv (v0.6) packaging, comprising of linear queries (L), star queries (S), snowflake-shaped queries (F) and complex queries (C). The benchmark was executed on a computer with Intel(R) Core(TM) i7-2640M CPU @ 2.80GHz, SSDSA2BW16 disk and 8

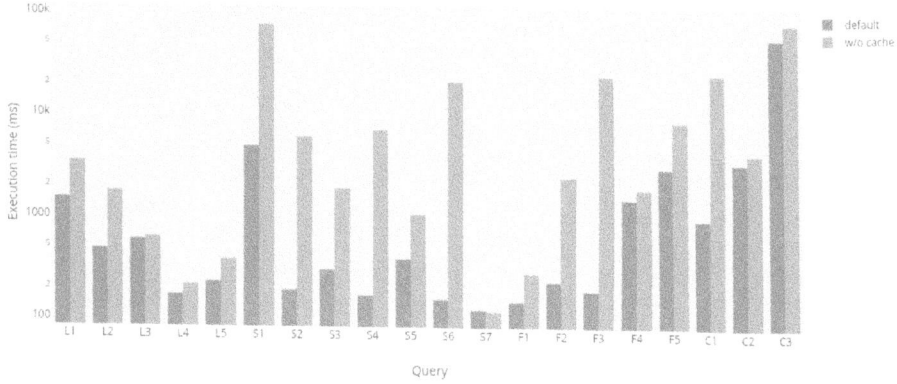

Figure 4. Query execution times.

GB of memory, running a Linux kernel (v4.19.1). We set up virtual nodes for IPFS to test our architecture. The goal was more to validate the feasability of the approach rather than benchmarking it. By default the SDK maintains a cache of results fetched from IPFS. To measure query execution times, each query has been executed 5 times with a warm cache, and 5 times with a cold cache. Results of the queries have been compared for correctness against the ARQ engine[5].

Loading Phase – Storing the dataset comprises of two main phases, constructing the index tree locally and storing the tree on IPFS from leaves to the root. Constructing the tree locally took 1 503 ms, and storing it on IPFS took 18.52 minutes and translated into 318 972 IPFS PUT requests.

Query Execution – Figure 4 displays execution times measured for the aforementioned queries using a logarithmic scale. The difference between *default* and *w/o cache* traces is in caching the results of IPFS get requests in the engine. Table 1 outlines measurements of metrics during each query, providing additional insight into factors potentially influencing the execution times. *Triple patterns* denotes the number of triple patterns each SPARQL query is decomposed into by Triple Pattern Fragments client, *IPFS gets* is the number of GET requests to IPFS, *Repeated paths* is the number of paths that had been requested from IPFS during the same query and *returned triples* denotes the total number of triples that have been returned from IPFS to construct the final SPARQL result.

Our implementation can be seen as a global linked open data repository which facilitates storing KGs and retrieving triples from either single graphs or a multitude of them. In particular, the metrics shown in Table 1 point to the number of decomposed triple patterns and IPFS requests as a potential factor that correlates with execution time. The *repeated paths* metric reemphasizes the benefits of a cache for intermediate results retrieved from IPFS.

---

[5]https://jena.apache.org/documentation/query/index.html

Query	Triple patterns	IPFS gets	Repeated paths	Returned triples
L1	131	403	79	1897
L2	26	225	3	387
L3	27	253	1	1107
L4	11	34	1	39
L5	13	296	45	297
S1	375	6849	152	8357
S2	13	990	1	1205
S3	14	305	10	664
S4	9	725	1	752
S5	16	220	1	242
S6	6	1405	3	1510
S7	3	1424	13	1499
F1	11	1743	10	2201
F2	27	2135	104	2235
F3	9	2212	1	3552
F4	271	5269	3748	6565
F5	363	68196	62629	72297
C1	51	8343	6057	10120
C2	183	17895	14906	36216
C3	3672	6851	3148	53821

Table 1. Performance metrics for WatDiv queries.

7. Related Work

There has been extensive research on centralized RDF data storage and retrieval. A survey of such storage and query processing schemes has been done by Faye et al. [11], in which triplestores are categorized based on multiple factors. These factors include native vs non-native and in-memory vs disk-based storage solutions. Non-native solutions for example are triplestores that use an existing data store, such as relational databases. Hexastore [31] stores six indices, enabling efficient lookup of triple patterns for each parts of the triple, including subject, predicate and object. This gain in performance comes at a cost in storage. When it comes to querying data from remote servers, Verborgh et al. argue that there's a spectrum between data dumps and SPARQL endpoints, and that there's a trade-off along the spectrum between factors including performance, cost, cache reuse, bandwidth, etc. for servers and clients. They propose Linked Data Fragments [29] which lies somewhere in the middle of the spectrum. In this design, clients turn a SPARQL query into a series of triple pattern requests that servers respond to, lowering load servers, decreasing bandwidth,... Centralized data repositories can process queries efficiently, but they are single points of failure and they have limited scalability and availability. In this study we adopt core ideas from Hexastore and LDF and apply them to the P2P network setting.

Content distribution over P2P networks has been an area of active research during the last two decades. Motivations over the client-server architecture include scalability, fault-tolerance, availability, self-organization and symmetry of nodes [17]. Androutsellis-Theotokis et al. classify P2P technologies [3] in the context of content distribution into applications and infrastructure. P2P applications themselves are classified into file exchange applications, such as Napster [23], which facilitate one-off file exchange between peers, and content publishing and storage applications, such as Publius [30], which are distributed storage schemes in which users can store, publish and distribute content securely and persistently. Technologies targeted for routing between peers and locating content have been classified under P2P infrastructure, and include inter alia Chord [28] or CAN [24]. P2P networks also differ in their degree of centralization. Some, like Napster, rely on a central server which holds metadata crucial for routing and locating content, limiting scalability, fault-tolerance and censorship-resistance, but offering efficient lookups. Lua et al. review overlay network structures, comparing *structured* and *unstructured* networks [21].

Unstructured P2P networks have been employed in protocols such as Bibster [15] and [34] to store RDF data and process queries. They use semantic similarity measures to form semi-localized clusters and to propagate queries to peers who are most likely to contain relevant data for. These protocols offer higher fault tolerance, but limited guarantees for retrieving query results even the underlying data exists in the network due to their propagation mechanisms.

Filiali et al. has performed a comprehensive survey [12] of RDF storage and retrieval over structured P2P networks. To index the triples, most protocols rely on variants of hash-indexing, e.g. RDFPeers [6], or semantic indexing, e.g. GridVine [1]. Two general strategies have been observed by Filiali et al., either retrieving all relevant triples from other peers and evaluating the result of the query locally, or propagating the query and partial results through the network, as in QC and SBV [20]. Unlike the aforementioned protocols, in this study we don't design a custom P2P network specifically built for RDF data storage, but use the live global IPFS filesystem [4], which is simultaneously being used for other purposes. Triples are indexed as a Hexastore. To process queries, all relevant triples are fetched, and result is evaluated using the Triple Pattern Fragments [29] framework.

Sicilia et al. [26] explore publishing datasets on IPFS, either by storing the whole graph as a single object or by storing each dereferenceable entity as an object. Furthermore they propose using IPNS to refer to the most recent dataset version. In this study, versioning is handled by a smart contract on Ethereum.

English et al. [9] explore both utilizing public blockchains for the semantic web, improving on the current URI schemes, storing values on the Bitcoin network, and creating ontologies for representing blockchain concepts. We share the idea that blockchains and web of data are complementary, and use the Ethereum blockchain to store metadata, and perform curation for KGs.

8. Conclusion & Future Work

In this article, we proposed a novel architecture for a fully decentralized linked data infrastructure, which has a very low barrier to entry, is censorship-resistant and benefits from fault-tolerance properties of its underlying open technologies. Due to immutability of each version of a dataset, consumers can cache the data objects they interact with, and perform queries even while offline. By replicating these data objects, they are at the same time contributing to the availability of those datasets. In addition, we explored two mechanisms which allow a community to come to consensus over a collection of datasets which they find relevant or high-quality in a distributed manner, by utilizing smart contracts to align the incentives of participants. IPFS replicates a document on every node that interacts with it. Therefore, more popular KGs are expected to be highly replicated. However, IPFS doesn't guarantee persistence. If the node that published a document goes offline, and there's no other replica, that document won't be accessible until the node comes back online. This might lower accessibility for KGs that have less demand. Future works can improve on this by incentivizing nodes to replicate pieces of data and asking them to provide *proof-of-replication* [13].

References

[1] Aberer, K., Cudré-Mauroux, P., Hauswirth, M., Van Pelt, T.: Gridvine: Building internet-scale semantic overlay networks. In: ISWC. pp. 107–121. Springer (2004)

[2] Aluç, G., Hartig, O., Özsu, M.T., Daudjee, K.: Diversified stress testing of RDF data management systems. In: ISWC. pp. 197–212. Springer (2014)

[3] Androutsellis-Theotokis, S., Spinellis, D.: A survey of peer-to-peer content distribution technologies. ACM computing surveys (CSUR) **36**(4), 335–371 (2004)

[4] Benet, J.: Ipfs-content addressed, versioned, p2p file system. arXiv preprint arXiv:1407.3561 (2014)

[5] Buterin, V.: Scaling adjudication with prediction markets. https://ethresear.ch/t/list-of-primitives-useful-for-using-cryptoeconomics-driven-internet-social-media-applications/3198 (2018), accessed: April 2021

[6] Cai, M., Frank, M.: Rdfpeers: a scalable distributed rdf repository based on a structured peer-to-peer network. In: Proceedings of the 13th international conference on World Wide Web. pp. 650–657. ACM (2004)

[7] Consortium, W.W.W., et al.: Rdf 1.1 concepts and abstract syntax (2014)

[8] Douceur, J.R.: The sybil attack. In: International workshop on peer-to-peer systems. pp. 251–260. Springer (2002)

[9] English, M., Auer, S., Domingue, J.: Blockchain technologies & the semantic web: a framework for symbiotic development. In: Computer Science Conference for University of Bonn Students. pp. 47–61 (2016)

[10] Ermilov, I., Martin, M., Lehmann, J., Auer, S.: Linked open data statistics: Collection and exploitation. In: International Conference on Knowledge Engineering and the Semantic Web. pp. 242–249. Springer (2013)

[11] Faye, D.C., Curé, O., Blin, G.: A survey of rdf storage approaches. Revue Africaine de la Recherche en Informatique et Mathématiques Appliquées **15**, 11–35 (2012)

[12] Filali, I., Bongiovanni, F., Huet, F., Baude, F.: A survey of structured p2p systems for rdf data storage and retrieval. In: Transactions on large-scale data-and knowledge-centered systems III, pp. 20–55. Springer (2011)

[13] Fisch, B.: Poreps: Proofs of space on useful data. Cryptology ePrint Archive, Report 2018/678 (2018), https://eprint.iacr.org/2018/678

[14] Goldin, M.: Token-curated registries 1.0. https://docs.google.com/document/d/1BWWC__-Kmso9b7yCI_R7ysoGFIT9D_sfjH3axQsmB6E (2018), accessed: April 2021

[15] Haase, P., Broekstra, J., Ehrig, M., Menken, M., Mika, P., Olko, M., Plechawski, M., Pyszlak, P., Schnizler, B., Siebes, R., et al.: Bibster–a semantics-based bibliographic peer-to-peer system. In: ISWC. pp. 122–136. Springer (2004)

[16] Harris, S., Seaborne, A., Prud'hommeaux, E.: Sparql 1.1 query language. W3C recommendation **21**(10) (2013)

[17] Hasan, R., Anwar, Z., Yurcik, W., Brumbaugh, L., Campbell, R.: A survey of peer-to-peer storage techniques for distributed file systems. In: ITCC. vol. 2, pp. 205–213. IEEE (2005)

[18] Heath, T., Bizer, C.: Linked data: Evolving the web into a global data space. Synthesis lectures on the semantic web: theory and technology **1**(1), 1–136 (2011)

[19] Käfer, T., Abdelrahman, A., Umbrich, J., O'Byrne, P., Hogan, A.: Observing linked data dynamics. In: ESWC. pp. 213–227. Springer (2013)

[20] Liarou, E., Idreos, S., Koubarakis, M.: Evaluating conjunctive triple pattern queries over large structured overlay networks. In: International Semantic Web Conference. pp. 399–413. Springer (2006)

[21] Lua, E.K., Crowcroft, J., Pias, M., Sharma, R., Lim, S.: A survey and comparison of peer-to-peer overlay network schemes. Surveys & Tutorials **7**(2), 72–93 (2005)

[22] Nakamoto, S.: Bitcoin: A peer-to-peer electronic cash system (2008)

[23] Napster, L.: Napster. http://www.napster.com (2001), accessed: April 2021

[24] Ratnasamy, S., Francis, P., Handley, M., Karp, R., Shenker, S.: A scalable content-addressable network, vol. 31. ACM (2001)

[25] Sasson, E.B., Chiesa, A., Garman, C., Green, M., Miers, I., Tromer, E., Virza, M.: Zerocash: Decentralized anonymous payments from bitcoin. In: 2014 IEEE Symposium on Security and Privacy (SP). pp. 459–474. IEEE (2014)

[26] Sicilia, M.A., Sánchez-Alonso, S., García-Barriocanal, E.: Sharing linked open data over peer-to-peer distributed file systems: the case of ipfs. In: Research Conference on Metadata and Semantics Research. pp. 3–14. Springer (2016)

[27] Van de Sompel, H., Sanderson, R., Nelson, M.L., Balakireva, L.L., Shankar, H., Ainsworth, S.: An http-based versioning mechanism for linked data. arXiv preprint arXiv:1003.3661 (2010)

[28] Stoica, I., Morris, R., Karger, D., Kaashoek, M.F., Balakrishnan, H.: Chord: A scalable peer-to-peer lookup service for internet applications. ACM SIGCOMM Computer Communication Review **31**(4), 149–160 (2001)

[29] Verborgh, R., Vander Sande, M., Hartig, O., Van Herwegen, J., De Vocht, L., De Meester, B., Haesendonck, G., Colpaert, P.: Triple pattern fragments: a low-cost knowledge graph interface for the web. Web Semantics: Science, Services and Agents on the World Wide Web **37**, 184–206 (2016)

[30] Waldman, M., Rubin, A.D., Cranor, L.F.: Publius: A robust, tamper-evident censorship-resistant web publishing system. In: USENIX Security Symp. (2000)

[31] Weiss, C., Karras, P., Bernstein, A.: Hexastore: sextuple indexing for semantic web data management. Proceedings of the VLDB Endowment **1**(1), 1008–1019 (2008)

[32] Wood, G.: Ethereum: A secure decentralised generalised transaction ledger. Ethereum project yellow paper **151**, 1–32 (2014)

[33] Zaveri, A., Rula, A., Maurino, A., Pietrobon, R., Lehmann, J., Auer, S.: Quality assessment for linked data: A survey. Semantic Web **7**(1), 63–93 (2016)

[34] Zhou, J., Hall, W., De Roure, D.: Building a distributed infrastructure for scalable triple stores. Journal of Computer Science and Technology **24**(3), 447–462 (2009)

Further with Knowledge Graphs. M. Alam et al. (Eds.)
AKA Verlag and IOS Press, 2021
© 2021 Akademische Verlagsgesellschaft AKA GmbH, Berlin

doi:10.3233/SSW210045

BESOCIAL: A Sustainable Knowledge Graph-Based Workflow for Social Media Archiving

Sven LIEBER [a,1], Dylan VAN ASSCHE [a], Sally CHAMBERS [b,c], Fien MESSENS [c],
Friedel GEERAERT [c], Julie M. BIRKHOLZ [b,c] and Anastasia DIMOU [a]

[a] *Ghent University – imec – IDLab, Department of Electronics and Information Systems,*
Technologiepark-Zwijnaarde 122, 9052 Ghent, Belgium
[b] *Ghent Centre for Digital Humanities, Ghent University, Ghent, Belgium*
[c] *KBR Royal Library of Belgium, Brussels, Belgium*

Abstract. Social media as infrastructure for public discourse provide valuable information that needs to be preserved. Several tools for social media harvesting exist, but still only fragmented workflows may be formed with different combinations of such tools. On top of that, social media data but also preservation-related metadata standards are heterogeneous, resulting in a costly manual process. In the framework of BESOCIAL at the Royal Library of Belgium (KBR), we develop a sustainable social media archiving workflow that integrates heterogeneous data sources in a Europeana and PREMIS-based data model to describe data preserved by open source tools. This allows data stewardship on a uniform representation and we generate metadata records automatically via queries. In this paper, we present a comparison of social media harvesting tools and our Knowledge Graph-based solution which reuses off-the-shelf open source tools to harvest social media and automatically generate preservation-related metadata records. We validate our solution by generating Encoded Archival Description (EAD) and bibliographic MARC records for preservation of harvested social media collections from Twitter collected at KBR. Other archiving institutions can build upon our solution and customize it to their own social media archiving policies.

Keywords. Social Media, GLAM, Knowledge Graph, RML

1. Introduction

The web, and in particular social platforms, have become social infrastructures for public discourse [1,12] which serve as records of the past. However, these records are usually centrally maintained by profit-based social media providers and, thus, preservation by third parties is necessary.

Data preservation is a resource expensive task which requires long term commitment involving software, data and human resources [3]. Social media poses preservation

---

[1] Corresponding Author: Sven Lieber, Ghent University – imec – IDLab, Department of Electronics and Information Systems, Technologiepark-Zwijnaarde 122, 9052 Ghent, Belgium; E-mail: Sven.Lieber@ugent.be

challenges: non-technical experts of the GLAM domain[2] have to select harvesting tools, and social media consists of dynamic content[28] and heterogeneous data formats which have to be adequately processed and described.

Furthermore, preservation-related metadata for social media is also heterogeneous, aggravating interoperability and data stewardship. Usually metadata documents which describe collections allow efficiently identifying sources [3]. Yet, different preservation systems may require metadata in different syntax which also represent different perspectives. For example, MARCXML[3] records from the library domain may be used to describe a social media collection from a bibliographic point of view, whereas Encoded Archival Description (EAD) [4] XML records from the archive domain may be used to describe the collection's content hierarchically in more detail. This hampers data stewardship because there is no uniform and interoperable description of the preserved social media collections, let alone provenance of the collection process itself which is crucial[21,28].

Semantic Web and Knowledge Graphs are promising solutions in the GLAM domain [2] as they enable applications across heterogeneous data and address the mentioned issues. However, existing approaches [7,18] assume already curated metadata records as inputs for Knowledge Graphs. Thus, they do not solve the initial issue of a costly manual curation of metadata records. Instead, a Knowledge Graph-based solution can be applied earlier in the workflow to support data stewardship by a uniform description of both social media collections and provenance information about the collection process.

We reuse existing open-source tools – and metadata they produce – to generate a Knowledge Graph, addressing interoperability issues and enabling data stewardship. Therefore we support users in the GLAM domain with basic IT understanding but limited technical skills [24]. Because we provide a workflow based on open source software and data models, independent of particular archiving use cases, we consider our solution sustainable. We analyzed existing social media harvesting tools to identify promising reuse candidates. Then we complemented selected tools with open source components to design a sustainable workflow driven by a Knowledge Graph: heterogeneous data are mapped to RDF, from which domain-specific metadata records are generated via queries. We validate our workflow by applying it on a social media archiving use case at Royal Library of Belgium (KBR). in which we created a Knowledge Graph based on harvested Twitter content, and generate MARC and EAD records.

Our contributions are (i) a comparative analysis of existing social media archiving tools, and (ii) a sustainable social media archiving workflow based on declarative RML mapping rules to generate Europeana Data Model and PREMIS-based [8] RDF from heterogeneous data sources, and metadata record generation based on reusable templates and Knowledge Graph queries. These open source resources as well as a full version of the comparison are available at `https://github.com/RMLio/social-media-archiving`.

In Section 2 we present related work. In Section 3 we provide a comparative analysis of social media harvesting tools. In Section 4 we present our Knowledge Graph-based

---

[2]Galleries, Libraries, Archives, and Museums.
[3]`https://www.loc.gov/marc/bibliographic/`
[4]`https://www.loc.gov/ead/`

solution which we validate in an archiving use case in Section 5. Finally, in Section 6 we discuss and conclude.

2. Related Work

To the best of our knowledge, there are no openly available workflows for social media archiving which cover both harvesting and cataloguing in an automated fashion. We discuss (i) tools and frameworks related to web archiving and social media harvesting in Section 2.1, to reflect on existing efforts to archive social media, (ii) metadata standards of the GLAM domain related to archiving in Section 2.2, to elaborate on domain-specific practices, and (iii) how our solutions compares to existing Knowledge Graph-based solutions in Section 2.3.

2.1. Social Media Archiving

We discuss web archiving, tools to harvest social media, as well as methodologies and tools used in the GLAM domain to analyze social media.

Commonly-used workflows for web archiving involve (i) describing collections, i.e. which website domains should be harvested and how often, (ii) fetching content using web harvesters, e.g., Heritrix [22] to preserve websites in Web ARChive (WARC) files [20], a format to preserve both content and HTTP requests, and (iii) accessing archived collections using replay software, e.g., WaybackMachine [27] or pyweb[5] as in the internet archive[6]. Software like Web Curator Tool [23] or Annotation and Curation Tool (w3act)[7] can be used as management interface to describe collections and schedule harvests. Websites for preservation are usually selected based on their top-level domain for which archival institutions may have a legal obligation to preserve its content. However, such workflows keep harvested information and metadata locked up in several data formats. Social media poses different challenges compared to web archiving due to its dynamic content [28] and different data formats used by different providers. Thus, web archiving workflows cannot be adjusted to sustainable social media harvesting workflows out of the box.

Similar tooling exists for social media archiving, but is limited to collection creation and harvesting. The modular frameworks Social Feed Manager (SFM) [15,21] and STACKS [17] create collections and schedule harvests. SFM reuses existing social media harvesters and wraps collections in WARC files, preserving harvested metadata while providing a uniform file format across harvested social media data. However, the replay of WARC files harvested in this way is difficult, because the content of the WARC files varies in format, i.e. harvested from different social media providers using different harvesting methods.

Social media can be harvested either by fetching data from Application Programming Interfaces (APIs) or via simulating a web browser. API-based tools, e.g., Twarc[8]

---

[5]https://github.com/webrecorder/pywb
[6]https://archive.org/
[7]https://github.com/ukwa/w3act
[8]https://github.com/DocNow/twarc

for Twitter or Instaloader[9] for Instagram, provide command line interfaces abstracting concrete API requests. They usually provide rich metadata represented as structured data. Tools like Brozzler[10] or Webrecorder/Conifer[11] harvest less metadata but preserve the look and feel. They simulate a browser or provide live recording functionality to harvest the HTML-based web version of social media content using the WARC format [20]. The aforementioned frameworks and tools create, describe and harvest social media collections. Technical details of API access are wrapped into user interfaces or command line tools, suitable for GLAM institutions with limited technical skills [24].

Several GLAM-related frameworks concern social media analysis related to social media harvesting, but not necessarily to social media archiving. In the case of ArchivesUnleashed[24], a project aiming to improve scholarly access to web archives, the collection development and harvests are explicitly excluded. Similarly, the GLAM workbench[12] aims for scholarly access by providing Jupyter notebooks[13], a combination of narrative text and live code. Candela et al. [4] investigated a methodology to create reproducible notebooks for the GLAM domain. Such frameworks are more concerned with analysis of already collected/described data and thus are complementary to our solution, i.e. they can be applied on archived data described with our Knowledge Graph.

2.2. Metadata Standards and Cataloguing

We discuss existing metadata standards and tools to create records adhering to those standards. The Online Computer Library Center (OCLC)[14], a global library cooperative, released recommendations for web archiving metadata fields [9]. They distilled 14 elements from the general vocabularies Dublin Core[15] and Schema.org[16], the XML-based standards Encoded Archival Description (EAD)[4], MARC21[3], and the Metadata Object Description Schema (MODS)[17].

However, the structure in which such elements are used is equally important, several subtly different standards exist. The General International Standard Archival Description (ISAD(G))[18] provides general guidance for the preparation of archival descriptions. EAD is a document-based hierarchical standard used to describe archival records. Although EAD is criticized to be document-centered rather than data-centered[13], hierarchical EAD records can be used to describe social media collections[19]. Compared to archival standards, MARC21 and MODS are bibliographic standards more focused on the library domain. The Metadata Encoding & Transmission Standard (METS)[20] encodes

---

[9]https://github.com/instaloader/instaloader
[10]https://github.com/internetarchive/brozzler
[11]https://github.com/Rhizome-Conifer/conifer
[12]https://glam-workbench.github.io/web-archives/
[13]https://jupyter.org/
[14]https://www.oclc.org/en/home.html
[15]https://dublincore.org/
[16]https://schema.org/
[17]http://www.loc.gov/standards/mods/
[18]https://www.ica.org/en/isadg-general-international-standard-archival-description-second-edition
[19]Collection of social media posts from Facebook and Twitter: https://tiaki.natlib.govt.nz/#details=ecatalogue.1016365   https://tiaki.natlib.govt.nz/#details=ecatalogue.1016484
[20]https://www.loc.gov/standards/mets/

descriptive, administrative, and structural metadata regarding objects within a digital library, popular to describe elements on an item level[7,10]. Incorporating all standards in a single model is difficult, as they take different perspectives [14]. Thus, we designed a Knowledge Graph in RDF, generated from heterogeneous born-digital data sources and described using domain-specific vocabularies. This allows generating records of different metadata standards.

Existing tools to generate archival metadata records are usually manual or semi-automatic cataloguing tools, closed source or commercial. According to embedded technical metadata, available EAD records for social media collections[19] are generated from the tool KE EMu[25]. Similarly, the ArchivesHub[21], a portal to integrate collections of several UK archives, uses the commercial software CIIM[22]. Such cataloguing tools are commercial software relying on existing archival records, either created manually or integrated from existing collections, and do not solve the problem of a costly manual creation. In our case, collection information is integrated via open source software from heterogeneous data sources and metadata records are generated automatically. Thus, web archivists are supported by initially generated metadata records to refine if necessary.

2.3. Knowledge Graph-based solutions

The GLAM domain already recognized Knowledge Graphs as promising future direction [2]. Dedicated ontologies and RDF representations for data models were developed, such as the official RDF ontology for MODS[23] and XSL Stylesheets to transform EAD documents to some RDF representation[24]. However, those RDF representations and ontologies do not describe data and their provenance, but metadata records summarizing data from a specific perspective.

The Europeana Data Model (EDM) [8], developed with technical experts from the GLAM domain, was designed to accommodate different standards. It represents a cultural heritage object together with different representations of it and contextual metadata. ArDO [30] is an ontology for hierarchical multimedia archival records based on specific application requirements and thus not extending EDM, but reusing it as guidance. Hierarchical archival data are also possible metadata records in our case. We use EDM and enrich our data with other more domain-specific vocabularies, e.g., TweetsKB [11] for social media content, and Dublin Core Collection Description[25] to describe social media collections. The PREMIS Data Dictionary for Preservation Metadata is a standard for which an ontology was developed [5], in version 2.2, meanwhile succeeded by a new ontology version to reflect PREMIS changes of version 3[26]. PREMIS was built on the Open Archival Information System (OAIS) reference model, an ISO standard [19] which among others describes different information packages. We reuse the PREMIS ontology to describe harvested data and its provenance. Similarly to EDM, PREMIS distinguishes between an actual object and its different representations, easing the integration with EDM and the rest of our model.

---

[21]https://archiveshub.jisc.ac.uk/

[22]https://www.k-int.com/products/ciim/

[23]https://www.loc.gov/standards/mods/modsrdf/

[24] http://data.archiveshub.ac.uk/ead2rdf/

[25]https://www.dublincore.org/specifications/dublin-core/collection-description/collection-application-profile/

[26]https://www.loc.gov/standards/premis/ontology/owl-version3.html

Tool	Approach	Output format	Social Media providers			Setup	Config	PROV
			T	F	I			
4CAT	Framework	JSON	+	-	+	advanced	UI	+
APIBlender	Framework	JSON	+	+	-	n/a	file	n/a
Brozzler	Browser	WARC/ HTML	+	+	+	advanced	file	+
Instaloader	API	JSON	-	-	+	beginner	file	+
DMI-TCAT	API	SQL	+	-	-	advanced	file	+
STACKS	Framework	JSON	+	-	-	advanced	file	+
SFM	Framework	WARC/ JSON	+	-	-	advanced	UI	++
Twarc	API	JSON	+	-	-	beginner	file	+
WebRecorder/ Conifer	Browser	WARC/ HTML	+	+	+	advanced	UI	+

Table 1. A comparison of features of different social media harvesting tools, T=Twitter, F=Facebook, I=Instagram. Full version available online `https://github.com/RMLio/social-media-archiving`

Regarding archival records, Knowledge Graph solutions are mostly applied on top of existing archival descriptions. Dobreski et al. [7] generate Linked Data for non-textual item-level data, e.g., images, sound, and videos, from XML-based archival records. Hennicke et al. [18] described how existing Bibliopolis and EAD records can be converted to EDM. Although only few Linked Data principles are followed, Gartner [13] devised a solution to represent archival description in a more constrained version of EAD as XML Schema from which regular EAD records can be generated. In contrast to these solutions, we do not generate a Knowledge Graph from existing metadata records and taking their perspective, but integrate raw data into a Knowledge Graph and generate different domain and perspective-specific metadata records in a following step. This way, we avoid the costly manual creation of archival records in the first place, while still providing means to curate data and metadata records.

3. Comparative Analysis of Social Media Harvesting Tools

Several social media archiving tools exist, varying in supported social media providers, usability and functionality. We compare available open source tools based on features relevant to social media archiving (Table 1).

We adapt a framework of the Data Together Initiative[27] originally used to compare generic web harvester tools. We reuse existing columns and add specific columns related to social media archiving in the GLAM domain. We compare the tested tools based on their approach, output format, setup, supported social media providers, configuration, and provenance. All tools but *APIBlender* are still maintained, i.e. commits or pull requests which indicate maintenance.

---

[27]`https://github.com/datatogether/research/tree/master/web_archiving`

Approach and output format   The approach followed by the tool to harvest social media data and influences the output format: querying data from a single API, simulating a browser, or providing a whole framework. Despite their different approaches, all tools provide interfaces to abstract from the technical aspects of harvesting, and therefore have the potential to suit users in the GLAM-domain.

Different use cases demand different approaches. API-based tools provide machine-readable JSON data and can be used to harvest large amounts of data facilitating further analyses. Even though most JSON harvesting tools store data as files, STACKS stores JSON in a MongoDB and DMI-TCAT in a relational MySQL database. This may increase performance when interacting with the data, but in the case of MySQL also involves yet another data format negatively influencing interoperability. On the other hand, tools simulating a browser store HTML content in WARC containers and thus preserve the look and feel and performed HTTP requests, but usually are slower and may pose more technical challenges compared to API-harvesters as social media content is dynamic [28].

Frameworks provide harvesting functionality for several social media providers and graphical user interfaces, and a promising code base for GLAM institutions. They are usually extensible with own modules or use existing harvesters, e.g. SFM uses Twarc for Twitter harvests. The output format for such frameworks usually depends on the harvesters used, but interestingly, SFM harvests data in JSON format, but preserves it in WARC files [21]. Thus, it provides a uniform interface of harvested social media data across providers while preserving technical metadata which positively influences downstream tasks requiring provenance.

Supported social media providers   From which social media providers the tool can harvest data. For this analysis we consider Twitter, Instagram and Facebook as they are part of the long-term goals for our BeSocial use case. Most tools support Twitter, some Instagram and only a few Facebook. Tools harvesting Facebook are simulated browsers, technological challenges for Facebook might be a reason [29] why no tool uses other harvesting means for Facebook. API-based tools are focused on a single provider, frameworks usually support several providers, and tools simulating a browser are technically not limited to any provider as they aim to harvest web content in general. Therefore, either frameworks or simulated browser tools are promising candidates if several social media providers should be supported by the use case.

Setup of the tool   We distinguish two levels of difficulty for setting up tools for harvesting: *beginner*, where only a script needs to be installed using a package manager; *advanced*, where several components need to be installed. Most tools can be set up with minimum programming experience, e.g., only by installing one command line tool. The majority of tools requires more steps as they consist of several components. However, such tools usually provide means to compensate, e.g. by providing docker images which, can be started and stopped as containers with minor configuration and a single command, or by providing the harvester as a service. Yet, debugging of such a docker setup, if needed, requires a deeper technical understanding, possibly challenging for users in the GLAM domain.

Tool's configuration   How the tools can be used to create social media collections: the more technical abstractions, the better considering less-technical users. All tools are configured via config files or web interfaces, lowering the reuse barrier.

Provenance information   Technical metadata captured via the harvesting process and/or descriptive metadata from the harvested content, considering archiving: usually the more the better. In terms of harvested content, tools harvesting data from APIs usually provide rich descriptive metadata facilitating analyses and data stewardship tasks, whereas tools harvesting HTML content in WARC files only provide technical metadata within the WARC HTTP headers. From a collection-level point of view, descriptive metadata in form of collection description needs to be added manually via the configuration of the tools. Regarding provenance information, SFM provides the best trade-off as it preserves technical metadata from harvests within WARC files, descriptive metadata of harvested content as part of the API responses, and descriptive metadata of collections – entered by users via a UI – within a relational database.

Discussion   Since frameworks may reuse existing harvesters, they are promising reuse candidates for use cases where several social media providers are considered for archiving. Compared to other frameworks, SFM has the advantage of storing harvested data within WARC files which provides additional provenance information. Additionally, collections in SFM are configured via an user interface which addresses users of the GLAM domain and thus our use case.

4. Sustainable Workflow

Our workflow reused open-source components to (i) describe social media collections, (ii) harvest social media content, and generate (iii) Knowledge Graphs and (iv) domain-specific metadata records. We present our modular architecture (Fig. 1) based on open source frameworks in Section 4.1 and discuss design decisions regarding regarding RDF representations in Section 4.2.

4.1. Architecture and Components

Our modular solution integrates into an existing framework and provides three declarative ways to control the social media archiving workflow. We describe the components of our architecture with the following contributions: (i) integration of automatic Knowledge Graph generation into the existing social media harvesting framework SFM, (ii) reusable declarative Knowledge Graph generation rules to describe social media archives, and (iii) reusable declarative queries and templates to generate domain-specific metadata records.

Social media harvesting   We reuse the Social Feed Manager (SFM) where a central RabbitMQ message queue is used for communication among components. Archivists create social media collections via a UI where they specify the seeds to harvest, a harvesting schedule, and provenance information regarding the collection (Fig. 1, ❶), i.e. title and description. At specified intervals a harvesting message is sent to the message queue which triggers existing social media harvesters, e.g., Twarc for Twitter, to fetch data.

SFM supports several API-based harvesters and uses a WARC proxy to preserve technical provenance information by recording performed HTTP requests and store them together with the received HTTP response in WARC files (Fig. 1, ❷). Thus, SFM offers a uniform file format with technical provenance information for differently described so-

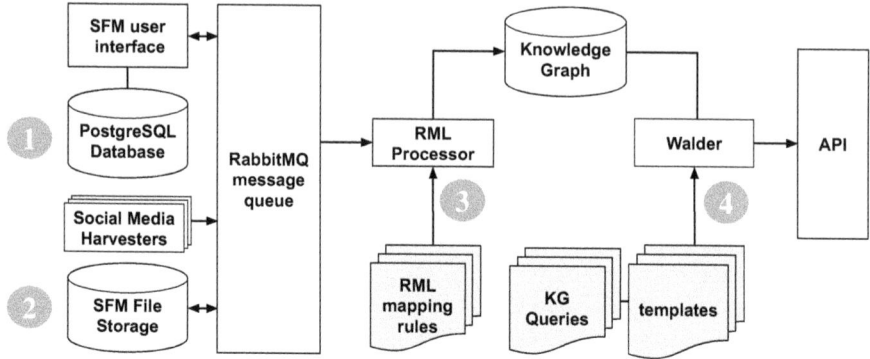

Figure 1. Our sustainable social media archiving workflow's architecture is based on open source components and is controlled with only three lightweight and declarative components (orange): RML mapping rules to create Knowledge Graphs, templates to specify metadata records, and queries to populate the templates.

cial media content from different social media providers. We utilize this uniform format to generate interoperable provenance across social media content. Harvesters indicate the status to the message queue, e.g., a successful harvest with listed information such as the location of newly created WARC files, which we use as input for our Knowledge Graph generation.

Knowledge Graph generation SFM provides a rich source of heterogeneous (meta) data which we lift to a Knowledge Graph to get a uniform and interoperable description of captured and preserved social media. We integrate descriptive collection metadata from SFM and the content harvested, as well as technical metadata produced by SFM and enclosed in preserved WARC files.

We use the RML.io framework[28] (Fig. 1, ③) to generate the BESOCIAL Knowledge Graph. RML.io generalizes the W3C recommended R2RML specification [6] to integrate heterogeneous data based on declarative mapping rules which is needed for our use case. We use the RMLMapper[29] to generate the Knowledge Graph based on declarative mapping rules following the RML specification.

Metadata records generation Although a Knowledge Graph-based data model enables semantic interoperability of data, concrete preservation systems or other stakeholders in the GLAM domain demand metadata records summarizing certain data in a domain-specific syntax, e.g. MARC21 for libraries, EAD for archives. We provide a component to automatically generate such metadata records from our Knowledge Graph avoiding a costly manual curation. We use Walder[30] which allows setting up a website or API over decentralized knowledge graphs. Using existing template libraries from web development, e.g., Handlebars[31], templates for metadata records are created. The query language GraphQL-LD [26] is used to query the Knowledge Graph and populate declarative templates with content, generating metadata records published via an API using Walder (Fig. 1, ④), while avoiding needing in-depth programming experience.

---

[28]https://rml.io
[29]https://github.com/RMLio/rmlmapper-java
[30]https://github.com/KNowledgeOnWebScale/walder
[31]https://handlebarsjs.com/

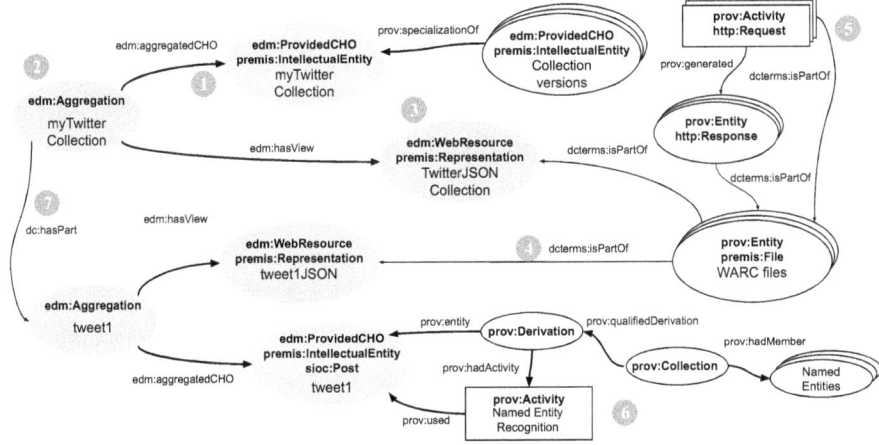

Figure 2. The Europeana Data Model (EDM) is used to represent social media collections and posts as cultural heritage objects (green) and their different representations (violet), aligned with PREMIS and PROV to represent provenance.

4.2. Data-driven Workflow

We describe how the Europeana Data Model (EDM), the de-facto standard for cultural heritage data, and other common W3C recommended vocabularies can be used to represent social media collections in an interoperable way.

We followed a Competency Question (CQ)-based approach, commonly used to express requirements in ontology engineering [16]. We defined more than 20 CQs for our archival use case based on user-stories to determine which data needs to be integrated. A full list is openly available at our online resource.

We reuse the EDM to describe harvested social media content because it enables us to represent not only the object itself, e.g. a Tweet via its ID, but also differently harvested representations, e.g. captured JSON or HTML representations of a Tweet stored in WARC files. A whole collection, created by users via SFM and stored in a relational database, and social media posts (items of the collection) are represented as cultural heritage objects using the class edm:ProvidedCHO and premis:IntellectualEntity (Fig. 2, ❶). Such a collection or item may have different representations linked by an instance of edm:Aggregation (Fig. 2, ❷), in our case the harvesters used by SFM fetch information in JSON from APIs, and thus we use edm:WebResource and premis:Representation to represent a JSON representation (Fig. 2, ❸); someone may harvest social media posts (additionally) in their HTML representation which would then be another edm:WebResource, linked to the associated aggregation (Fig. 2, ❷). To increase interoperability we represent social media posts also using sioc:Post from TweetsKB [11].

Harvested social media data is enclosed in WARC files by SFM (Fig. 2, ❹) preserving harvest metadata of HTTP requests. We represent such harvest metadata using PROV activities, listing when and how WARC files were created (Fig. 2, ❺), WARC files are represented using premis:File. On item level, we perform Named Entity Recognition

(NER) during mapping via the DBpedia spotlight API[32] to enrich our Knowledge Graph (Fig. 2, ⑥). This information is useful later when generating archival records. PROV is used to preserve information of the NER process. Hierarchical information, such as which item belongs to which collection, is explicitly represented using Dublin Core and following EDM guidelines[33] (Fig. 2, ⑦).

5. Social Media Archiving at KBR

BESOCIAL is a cross-institutional research project, aiming to develop a sustainable strategy for archiving and preserving social media in Belgium. The solution supports this goal by offering a sustainable social media archiving workflow. We outline the use case and describe how we applied our workflow within a pilot.

BESOCIAL use case   KBR, as the federal scientific library of Belgium, is legally mandated to collect and preserve all Belgian publications. To tackle challenges of the digital-era, KBR invests in the digital preservation of online content. In the past KBR worked on a federal strategy for the preservation of the Belgian Web [28]. Due to the uniqueness and ephemeral nature of social media, BESOCIAL brings together interdisciplinary partners to consider conservation, preservation and accessibility of developing a social media archive.[34] Twitter was selected as promising social media platform, but Instagram and Facebook are considered in the long-term. Recent outcomes of BESOCIAL are the analysis of an online survey in which 15 international archiving institutions participated, and which showed that many institutions are engaged in social media archiving, but also that the stage and efforts vary in size and scope [29].

Content selection   Web archivists define so-called seed lists with content that should be archived. For BESOCIAL, a seed list with 86 relevant Belgian entities of 14 categories, such as governmental institutions and online news, was curated by KBR for a test pilot. From these 86 entities, 79 had accounts on Twitter. We used the user interface of SFM to create a collection for these accounts.

Content collection   Collections created with the user interface of SFM were scheduled to harvest social media data daily. This, so far, resulted in 50 compressed WARC files of 88 MB enclosing around 200,000 Tweets in JSON format. The first harvest resulted in roughly 150,000 tweets as the used Twarc harvester of SFM fetches the most recent 3,200 tweets per account. Subsequent daily harvests resulted in less content of up to 2,000 tweets. These are heterogeneous data which we need to lift to a Knowledge Graph to facilitate data stewardship tasks.

Knowledge Graph generation   We used the data model and its requirements expressed as Competency Questions (CQs) described in Section 4.2 to systematically guide the integration process, i.e. one RML mapping contributes data to answer at least one CQ. Applying these mappings resulted in one RDF file per WARC file and one RDF file for collection-level metadata extracted from the SFM PostgreSQL database. We generated

---

[32]https://www.dbpedia-spotlight.org/api
[33]https://pro.europeana.eu/files/Europeana_Professional/Share_your_data/
Technical_requirements/EDM_Documentation/EDM_Mapping_Guidelines_v2.4_102017.pdf
[34]https://kbr.be/en/projects/besocial

RDF triples consisting among others of 213,000 EDM cultural heritage object resources representing collections and social media posts, and 222,000 W3C PROV activities reflecting provenance.

Metadata records generation   Different domain-specific data formats exist. Already available social media collections are described using EAD records[19], thus we consider this a baseline, and KBR as a library works with bibliographic MARC-based records to describe collections. Additionally, human users may want to browse collections. Thus, we created two XML-based and one HTML-based template and related GraphQL queries for Walder to populate these templates from our Knowledge Graph to accommodate these use cases; available at our online resource[35]. We can query heterogeneous data, to among others, get aggregated information about named entities, enabling users to assess the content i.e. which locations or events are mentioned within a whole social media collection. Hierarchical information is present in our Knowledge Graph as we reused terms like dc:hasPart (Fig. 2, ⑦).

Discussion   We discuss the added value of the Knowledge Graph in our use case and findings related to the Knowledge Graph's use with respect to collection-level and item-level (social media post) data.

Instead of many-to-many mappings from heterogeneous data sources to heterogeneous metadata records, our solution results in a semantically described RDF Knowledge Graph which facilitates data stewardship as it describes all preserved data including provenance information. The generation of metadata records and HTML views are thus not limited to harvested data, but also profit from contextual information of the Knowledge Graph, because item-level data (social media posts) are put in relationship to collections and provenance information. This information can be queried using SPARQL or GraphQL, therefore we are able to identify e.g. social media posts belonging to different collections or collections/posts mentioning similar named entities. Similarly, more fine-grained queries are possible with more integrated linked data in the future, i.e. archivists may rather spend manual curation efforts in enriching the Knowledge Graph instead of domain-specific metadata records.

Use cases related to the collection-level may not need the full graph. Whereas harvested data preserved and compressed in WARC files are relatively small, the Knowledge Graph is considerably larger. This may present a performance bottleneck for smaller setups without adequate RDF database or hardware. However, HTML views providing an overview of collections, or MARC records describing bibliographic information of collections do not need all item-level details such as detailed post provenance. We used decentralized Knowledge Graphs partitioned between collection and item level data to improve performance of collection-level tasks.

If certain use cases demand some item-level information we declaratively create aggregations. Based on the data model and extracted information, we used SPARQL-CONSTRUCT queries to enrich collection-level information with aggregated information from item-level, such as most often used named entities and their type; vocabularies such as the W3C recommended WebAnnotations[36] or DataCube[37] may be used to semantically describe aggregates, further research is required.

---

[35]https://github.com/RMLio/social-media-archiving
[36]https://www.w3.org/TR/annotation-model/
[37]https://www.w3.org/TR/vocab-data-cube/

Libraries usually provide full access to collections only via reading rooms or after login, and from a legal perspective it is also problematic to provide public access to harvested social media data. However, collection-level related parts of the Knowledge Graph including aggregations present a smaller sub-graph which may be made publicly available, directly as API or via HTML views. Therefore, end users may assess more detailed information about collections using contextual-rich collection information before requesting access to the full collection on-premise or online which could positively influence the user experience. However, more research towards the needs of different types of users is needed.

6. Conclusion

Social media is already a paramount part of our society and, thus, its content needs to be preserved. However, archiving is an expensive long-term commitment and currently only fragmented workflows for social media archiving exists. We developed an open source Knowledge Graph-based solution using the Europeana Data Model and PREMIS to describe WARC-preserved social media as cultural heritage objects with different representations. Now we can support automatic generation of GLAM-related metadata records, e.g., MARC and EAD, or provide collection overviews via HTML for users to assess the collections' content.

Human-in-the-loop provenance   Social media harvesting tools play a crucial role regarding provenance information, as they cover initial phases of selection and collection where human users define what to harvest and when. Currently SFM provides a detailed change history of collections, but descriptive information is limited to titles and descriptions. Similar to how some web archiving tools require the upload of legal deposit documents before harvests are initiated [23], SFM could be extended with UI fields to collect specific information from users in a uniform fashion. Our Knowledge Graph-based solution allows a data-centric perspective driven by downstream tasks which can inform improvements of SFM's UI and database, to include more, and more-specific metadata fields which would positively influence the quality of generated metadata records.

Data stewardship of digital collections   Social media archives are not static and pose new challenges for which data stewardship is needed: some content may have to be removed from public access due to intellectual property or privacy-related take-down requests, and on top of that several terms of services from different social media providers need to be taken into account. Such stewardship tasks are supported by our solution. For example, our Knowledge Graph already encodes provenance information of harvesting, and as it is based on PREMIS and W3C PROV, existing data can be annotated or additional provenance information regarding take-down requests can be included in the same fashion. Therefore, consuming applications can perform policy-compliant operations with the harvested data.

Future Work   Future work will investigate the quality of generated metadata records and extend the metadata record queries if necessary. The modular tool SFM can be extended with new functionality or other social media harvesters. Based on our Knowledge Graph, operational and legal challenges of social media archiving can be reconsidered and addressed.

Acknowledgements   The research activities were supported by the Belgian Federal Science Policy Office (BELSPO) BRAIN 2.0 Research Project BESOCIAL, Ghent University, imec, and Flanders Innovation & Entrepreneurship (VLAIO).

References

[1]   Acker, A., Kreisberg, A.: Social Media Data Archives in an API-driven World. Archival Science **20**(2), 105–123 (2020)

[2]   Bahnemann, G., Carroll, M., Clough, P., Einaudi, M., Ewing, C., Mixter, J., Roy, J., Tomren, H., Washburn, B., Williams, E.: Transforming metadata into linked data to improve digital collection discoverability (2021)

[3]   Borgman, C.L.: Scholarship in the digital age: Information, infrastructure, and the Internet. MIT press (2010)

[4]   Candela, G., Sáez, M.D., Escobar Esteban, M., Marco-Such, M.: Reusing digital collections from GLAM institutions. Journal of Information Science (2020)

[5]   Coppens, S., Verborgh, R., Peyrard, S., Ford, K., Creighton, T., Guenther, R., Mannens, E., Van de Walle, R.: PREMIS OWL. International Journal on Digital Libraries **15**(2), 87–101 (2015)

[6]   Das, S., Sundara, S., Cyganiak, R.: R2RML: RDB to RDF Mapping Language. Working group recommendation, World Wide Web Consortium (W3C) (Sep 2012), `http://www.w3.org/TR/r2rml/`

[7]   Dobreski, B., Park, J., Leathers, A., Qin, J.: Remodeling archival metadata descriptions for linked archives. In: International Conference on Dublin Core and Metadata Applications. pp. 1–11 (2020)

[8]   Doerr, M., Gradmann, S., Hennicke, S., Isaac, A., Meghini, C., Van de Sompel, H.: The Europeana Data Model (EDM). In: World Library and Information Congress: 76th IFLA general conference and assembly. vol. 10, p. 15 (2010)

[9]   Dooley, J.M., Bowers, K.: Descriptive Metadata for Web Archiving: Recommendations of the OCLC Research Library Partnership Web Archiving Metadata Working Group. OCLC Research (2018)

[10] Elings, M.W., Waibel, G.: Metadata for all: Descriptive standards and metadata sharing across libraries, archives and museums. First Monday (2007)

[11] Fafalios, P., Iosifidis, V., Ntoutsi, E., Dietze, S.: TweetsKB: A Public and Large-Scale RDF Corpus of Annotated Tweets. In: European Semantic Web Conference. pp. 177–190 (2018)

[12] Fondren, E., McCune, M.M.: Archiving and Preserving Social Media at the Library of Congress: Institutional and Cultural Challenges to Build a Twitter Archive. Preservation, Digital Technology & Culture **47**(2), 33–44 (2018)

[13] Gartner, R.: An XML schema for enhancing the semantic interoperability of archival description. Archival Science **15**(3), 295–313 (2015)

[14] Gartner, R., Mouren, R.: Archives, museums and libraries: breaking the metadata silos. In: Paper presented at IFLA WLIC 2019. Athens, Greece (2019)

[15] George Washington University Libraries: Social feed manager. version 2.3.0 (May 2020). https://doi.org/10.5281/zenodo.3784836

[16] Grüninger, M., Fox, M.S.: The Role of Competency Questions in Enterprise Engineering. In: BenchmarkingTheory and practice, pp. 22–31. Springer (1995)

[17] Hemsley, J., Jackson, S., Tanupabrungsun, S., Ceskavich, B.: STACKS - Social Media Tracker, Analyzer, & Collector Toolkit at Syracuse (Apr 2019). https://doi.org/10.5281/zenodo.2638848

[18] Hennicke, S., Olensky, M., de Boer, V., Isaac, A., Wielemaker, J.: A data model for cross-domain data representation. In: Proceedings of the 12th International Symposium on Information Science. pp. 136–147 (2011)

[19] ISO Central Secretary: ISO 14721:2012 Space data and information transfer systems. Standard ISO 14721:2012, International Organization for Standardization, Geneva, CH (2012)

[20] ISO Central Secretary: ISO 28500:2017 Information and documentation WARC file format. Standard ISO 28500:2017, International Organization for Standardization, Geneva, CH (2017)

[21] Littman, J., Chudnov, D., Kerchner, D., Peterson, C., Tan, Y., Trent, R., Vij, R., Wrubel, L.: API-based social media collecting as a form of web archiving. International Journal on Digital Libraries **19**(1), 21–38 (2018)

[22] Mohr, G., Stack, M., Rnitovic, I., Avery, D., Kimpton, M.: Introduction to Heritrix. In: 4th International Web Archiving Workshop. pp. 109–115 (2004)

[23] Paynter, G., Joe, S., Lala, V., Lee, G.: A year of Selective Web Archiving with the Web Curator at the National Library of New Zealand. D-Lib Magazine **14**(5/6), 1082–9873 (2008)

[24] Ruest, N., Lin, J., Milligan, I., Fritz, S.: The Archives Unleashed Project: Technology, Process, and Community to Improve Scholarly Access to Web Archives. In: Proceedings of the ACM/IEEE Joint Conference on Digital Libraries in 2020. pp. 157–166 (2020)

[25] Sendino, M.C.: KE EMu and the future for natural history collections. Collections **5**(2), 149–158 (2009)

[26] Taelman, R., Vander Sande, M., Verborgh, R.: GraphQL-LD: Linked Data Querying with GraphQL (2018)

[27] Tofel, B.: 'Wayback' for Accessing Web Archives. In: Proceedings of the 7th International Web Archiving Workshop. pp. 27–37 (2007)

[28] Vlassenroot, E., Chambers, S., Di Pretoro, E., Geeraert, F., Haesendonck, G., Michel, A., Mechant, P.: Web archives as a data resource for digital scholars. International Journal of Digital Humanities **1**(1), 85–111 (2019)

[29] Vlassenroot, E., Chambers, S., Lieber, S., Michel, A., Geeraert, F., Pranger, J., Birkholz, J.: Web-archiving and social media: an exploratory analysis [to be published]. International Journal of Digital Humanities (2021)

[30] Vsesviatska, O., Tietz, T., Hoppe, F., Sprau, M., Meyer, N., Dessi, D., Sack, H.: ArDO: An Ontology to Describe the Dynamics of Multimedia Archival Records [to be published]. In: ACM, Symposium On Applied Computing (2021)

Further with Knowledge Graphs. M. Alam et al. (Eds.)
AKA Verlag and IOS Press, 2021
© 2021 Akademische Verlagsgesellschaft AKA GmbH, Berlin
This article is published online with Open Access by IOS Press and distributed under the terms
of the Creative Commons Attribution License 4.0 (CC BY 4.0).
doi:10.3233/SSW210046

Embedding Taxonomical, Situational or Sequential Knowledge Graph Context for Recommendation Tasks

Simon WERNER [a,1], Achim RETTINGER [a], Lavdim HALILAJ [b] and
Jürgen LÜTTIN [b]

[a] *Trier University, Trier, Germany*
[b] *Bosch Research, Renningen, Germany*

Abstract. Learned latent vector representations are key to the success of many recommender systems in recent years. However, traditional approaches like matrix factorization produce vector representations that capture global distributions of a static recommendation scenario only. Such latent user or item representations do not capture background knowledge and are not customized to a concrete situational context and the sequential history of events leading up to it.

This is a fundamentally limiting restriction for many tasks and applications, since the latent state can depend on a) abstract background information, b) the current situational context and c) the history of related observations. An illustrating example is a restaurant recommendation scenario, where a user's assessment of the situation depends a) on taxonomical information regarding the type of cuisine, b) on situational factors like time of day, weather or location and c) on the subjective individual history and experience of this user in preceding situations. This situation-specific internal state of the user is not captured when using a traditional collaborative filtering approach, since background knowledge, the situational context and the sequential nature of an individual's history cannot easily be represented in the matrix.

In this paper, we investigate how well state-of-the-art approaches do exploit those different dimensions relevant to POI recommendation tasks. Naturally, we represent such a scenario as a temporal knowledge graph and compare plain knowledge graph, a taxonomy and a hypergraph embedding approach, as well as a recurrent neural network architecture to exploit the different context-dimensions of such rich information. Our empirical evidence indicates that the situational context is most crucial to the prediction performance, while the taxonomical and sequential information are harder to exploit. However, they still have their specific merits depending on the situation.

Keywords. knowledge graph embeddings, context-aware recommender systems, taxonomy embedding, hypergraph embedding

---

[1] Corresponding Author: Simon Werner, Universität Trier, FB II Computerlinguistik, 54286 Trier, Germany; E-mail: werners@uni-trier.de

1. Introduction

Recommender systems are a mature field in research and engineering. They have been applied in many diverse applications and the approaches and data sources used are equally diverse. Typically, specialized representation formalisms and methods are devised and optimized to exploit the specific information best. However, several applications of recommender systems in real world scenarios are faced with other challenges that should be considered in order to provide good recommendations. One factor is the consideration of context like location, time, etc. [1]. Another challenge is to deal with complex environments that are subject to greater variability and complexity of inputs to recommender systems rather than simple ratings or reviews. In some cases, the information structure that serves for recommendations is so complex that it is represented by a semantic model as a knowledge graph [2]. Similarly, some applications require more complex outputs than prioritized recommendation lists in the direction of composite or sequential recommendations.

We describe details of a concrete in-use application of a mobile location-based recommender system that makes use of semantic technologies for representing the complex information structure as well as for user information obtained from a social network. In this paper, we investigate three dimensions that provide additional information: a) symbolic background knowledge, b) situation-specific information and c) sequential information.

One illustrating example is a POI recommendation scenario, where a user's assessment of a situation depends on his preferences for a certain *type of cuisines*, situational factors like *time of day*, *weather* or *location* and on the subjective individual history and experience of this user in previous situations. For instance, a restaurant shouldn't be of interest to a user who just had something to eat.

An intuitive way of representing all this heterogeneous types of information are temporal knowledge hyper graphs that contain time-stamped hyper-edges to allow the extraction of the sequential history of previous interactions of a user in similar recommendation settings. Hereby, each concrete setting is accompanied by a list of contextual factors that are best modelled as an n-ary relation between the user and the recommendation target. Also, each entity is accompanied by symbolic background knowledge like taxonomical relations.

Knowledge Graph Embeddings (KGE) are a recent technique to transform such symbolic knowledge into predictive models, which operate on latent vector spaces. However, most current KGE methods produce exactly one embedding for each entity instance and relation type specified in a static Knowledge Graph (KG). Each embedding captures the global distributional semantic of the graph from the perspective of this entity or relation. This does not fit well to context-aware recommender systems.

In this paper, we test the hypothesis that a global KGE per entity and relation is not adequate for many recommendation tasks. Consequently, there is a need to customize static KGEs to situational and subjective contexts. More precisely we argue that most KGE models cannot generate embeddings that capture the current relational context and that contain the abstract conceptual background information as well as the subject's history of related observations.

Thus, we test different techniques to incorporate three dimensions of additional information: a) An ontology describing POIs for symbolic background knowledge, b) n-ary relations for capturing situation-specific information and c) sequential information about an individual's previous history.

Given such a formalization of contextualized observations over time, our goal is to learn embeddings that go beyond binary pre-trained KGEs by taking into account an ontology and the sequential history of contextualizing factors. We attempt that by a hypergraph- and a taxonomy embedding technique and recurrent neural networks. We make the following contributions:

- We propose a formal ontology for modeling abstract background knowledge in recommenation scenarios (addressing dimension a) and feed it into Knowledge Graph Embedding (KGE) methods.
- We apply a hypergraph embedding approach to include the situational context (addressing dimension b).
- We model the temporal context of an individual with a recurrent neural network
- We evaluate these methods on a context aware POI recommendation task to gain insights for the individual benefits of the dimensions to the recommendation performance.

2. Related Work

In this section we first survey previous work on the task of POI recommendation. Some more recent approaches rely on knowledge graph embeddings, which we also do in this work. Consequently, we discuss the fundamentals related to this area in more detail next.

2.1. Recommender Systems for Location Based Social Networks

Context information is particularly important for location based recommender systems where context like location, time, weather, or trip purpose has a large influence on the POI to recommend. Recommender systems based on location based social networks (LBSN) have been the subject of intensive recent research activities, see [3,4] for recent surveys. In-vehicle recommender systems provide even more context information such as vehicle sensor based information about occupants and driver, vehicle state, or surrounding traffic [5].

An early approach for POI recommendation based on models for human mobility and their dynamics in social networks is described in [6]. Another early approach for context-aware recommendation that considers social network information, personal preferences and POI popularity is presented in [7]. Nousal et al. [8] analysed simple measures such as popularity, category preference, temporal preference, social filtering, with supervised learning using linear regression model or decision trees for next place prediction. Baral et al. [9] propose a hierarchical contextual POI sequence recommender that formulates user preferences as hierarchical structure and exploits contextual trend to generate personalized POI sequences. Those works are method-wise not directly related to our approach, which is focused on knowledge graph embedding methods.

An approach presented by Baral et al. [10] describes a contextualized location sequence recommender that generates contextually coherent POI sequences relevant to user preferences exploiting recurrent neural networks (RNN) and extended Long-short term memory (LSTM) networks. A method based on matrix factorization to embed personalized Markov chains and localized regions for successive personalized POI recommendation is used in [11]. Feng et al. [12] propose a personalized ranking metric embedding method (PRME) which jointly models the sequential information and individual preferences. A fourth-order tensor factorization-based ranking methodology that captures long- and short term preferences simultaneously has been reported in [13]. We also investigate methods in this directions by using an LSTM-based approach in one of our experiments.

Even more closely related to methods investigated in this paper is a knowledge graph embedding method that learns semantic representations of both entities and paths between entities for characterizing user preferences described in [14]. Another knowledge graph embedding based approach [15] jointly captures the sequential effect, geographical influence, temporal effect and semantic effect by embedding four corresponding knowledge graphs (POI-POI, POI-Region, POI-Time and POI-Word) into a shared low-dimensional space. A state-of-the-art deep learning recommendation model has been reported in [16]. Categorical features are represented by an embedding vector, generalizing the concept of latent factors used in matrix factorization. A Spatial-Aware Hierarchical Collaborative Deep Learning model (SH-CDL) that jointly performs deep representation learning for POIs from heterogeneous features and hierarchically additive representation learning for spatial-aware personal preferences is presented in [17]. [18] propose LBSN2Vec, a hyper graph embedding approach designed specifically for LBSN data which we also use in our experiments.

2.2. Knowledge Graph Embedding

In recent years, Knowledge Graph Embedding (KGE) has been a very vibrant field in Machine Learning and Semantic Technologies, specifically in the area of Representation Learning (see [19] for a survey). Numerous methods for embedding knowledge graphs have been proposed and even more adaptations have been published. KGE methods can be roughly characterized by the representation space and the scoring function.

The vector representations of entities and relations are traditionally Euclidean $\mathbb{R}^d$, but many different spaces like Complex $\mathbb{C}^d$ (e.g., in [20]) or Hypercomplex $\mathbb{H}^d$ (cmp. [21]) have been used as well.

Standard KGE methods don't take into account temporal information or contextual factors that influence the plausibility of a fact. However, there have been attempts to address each limitation, as outlined next.

2.3. Contextual Knowledge Graph Embeddings

From the Knowledge Graph perspective, hypergraphs with n-ary relations and hyper-relational graphs with meta information encoded on the relations are exploited for modeling the context. Such approaches from Statistical Relational Learning are based on graphical models and tensor factorization [22]. A more recent approach extends the current KGE method SimplE [23] to hypergraphs [24] but does not take into account temporal or sequential information. This approach was used as the basis for our hypergraph embedding experiments. More details on our adaptions can be found in section 4.2.

Embedding temporal dynamics of a knowledge graph and thus tackling *(Lim2)* has received much attention recently. Knowledge graphs in which facts only hold within a specific period and where the evolution of facts follows a sequence have become increasingly available. This also increased the interest in learning embeddings that take the temporal information into account.

Basic approaches to temporal KGE model facts as temporal quadruples. They are optimized for scoring the plausibility of (unknown) facts at a given point in time [25], [26]. A more sophisticated approach is proposed in [27]. It even checks the temporal consistency given contextual relations of the subject and object. Besides the inability of those models to model *n*-ary sequential context, we are also taking a different focus by using the temporal dimension to model the history of experiences of a subject. A more entity-centric perspective is taken in [28], which attempts to model the temporal evolution of entities, where [29] take a relation-specific perspective instead. Similar to our approach, [30] proposes an LSTM-based approach, which exploits relation-specific embedding of entities.

3. Capturing Taxonomical, Contextual and Sequential Information for Recommendations

The goal of this paper is to investigate the potential of three different types of information, namely taxonomical, contextual and sequential, for their use in embedding-based recommender systems. We chose a knowledge graph as the underlying data structure, since it allows to include all those information types in one representation formalism. We first show how to model taxonomical information, before including situational context and the sequential history.

3.1. Modeling Taxonomical Information

This section describes the POI Categories (POICa) ontology used for representing information about POIs mainly by exploiting their hierarchical relationships.

3.1.1. Conceptualizing and Formalizing

The main objective of the POICa ontology is focused on representing: 1) *taxonomic knowledge*, encoding hierarchical information between different POIs, and 2) *auxiliary knowledge*, which comprises information for a specific check-in of a user in a particular POI including geo-spatial and temporal data, i.e. the location of the POI and the timestamp information about the check-in action. The underlying structure of the POICa ontology is built on top of Foursquare Categories[2] where the core concept is the *POI*. Several object and datatype properties describe a particular POI with respect to its attributes and relationships with other concepts.

As depicted in Figure 1, POICa ontology comprises a number of subcategories distributed in various levels, which for the sake of better readability are highlighted with different colors. The first level under the *POI* concept includes subcategories described in the following:

- *Art and Entertainment* - is the category for representing places related to art, culture, music, exhibitions, etc.

---

[2]https://developer.foursquare.com/docs/build-with-foursquare/categories

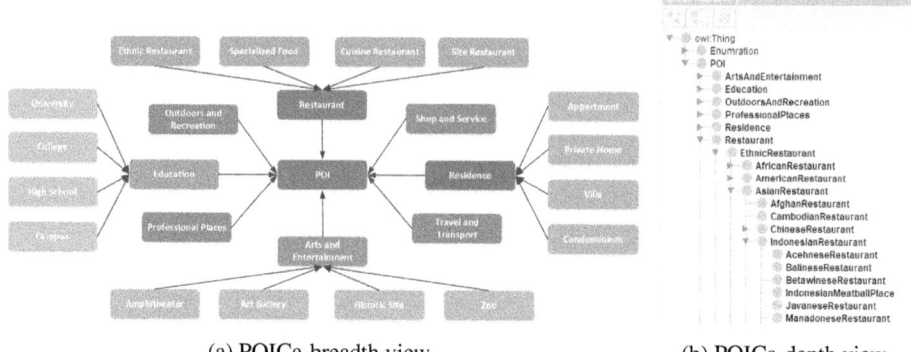

(a) POICa-breadth view.   (b) POICa-depth view.

Figure 1. POICa ontology. Main concepts representing different categories within the ontology: a) depicts all categories within the first level of the hierarchy including some important ones from the second level; b) depicts depth of a particular category i.e. *Restaurant*.

- *Education* - are entities which provide education-related services and learning environments.
- *Professional Places* - groups places which are involved or perform business activities.
- *Outdoors and Recreation* - are places where the recreation is commonly realized in natural settings.
- *Residence* - used to group POIs that mainly serves as living places.
- *Restaurant* - groups all types of restaurants split on various criteria, such as cuisine.
- *Shop and Service* - used to group POIs which are dedicated for selling goods or services.
- *Transportation* - containing POIs which enable carrying of people and goods from one place to another.

Each of these subcategories is further specialized utilizing *subClassOf* axiom in order to provide a detailed classification based on the shared characteristics, such as the type of the activity they perform combining with regional information. Several additional classes such *EthnicRestaurant, SiteBasedRestaurant, SpecializedFoodRestaurant* are introduced with the aim of grouping restaurants based on ethnicity or cuisine, style and flavour, respectively.

3.1.2. Alignment with and reuse of external ontologies

In order to ensure interoperability with other information from different sources, we reused a number of concepts from external ontologies such as *Schema.org*, *FOAF*, *DBpedia*, *DCTerms* and *Weather*[3]. For instance, in order to represent geo-spatial information for a given POI the following concepts from *DCTerms*, *Schema.org* and *DBpedia*: *dct:Location, schema:PostalAddress* and *dbo:City* are reused.

---

[3]https://schema.org/, http://xmlns.com/foaf/0.1/, http://dbpedia.org/ontology#, http://purl.org/dc/terms/, https://cutt.ly/QhQrFxv#

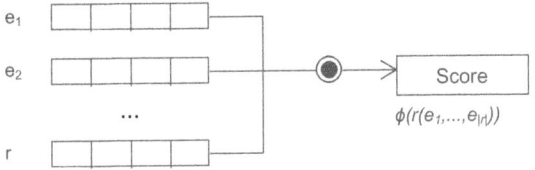

Figure 2. HypE architecture with scoring function

The current version of the POICa ontology contains 953 classes, 8 object properties, 12 datatype properties and 4 annotation properties. In this paper, our focus was to describe the core concepts that form the basis to understand the conducted work from the taxonomic point of view.

3.2. Context-aware Hypergraph-Embeddings

In traditional user-item-recommender systems, there is only one binary relation indicating which user interacted with which item. However, this cannot capture the multi-relational background knowledge described above and also cannot include situational context that describes the conditions when and how this interaction took place.

Thus, representing recommendation scenarios by only using binary relations can cause an information loss that might lead to poor performance on a recommendation task. To make full use of all the contextual information like day of the week and current time, that are contained in the dataset, the binary relations need to be extended to n-ary relations.

We therefore build on HypE [24], a recently introduced hypergraph embedding approach that showed promising results on other tasks and allows for easy adaption to our recommendation use-case. HypE uses a multilinear scoring function and additionally uses learnt convolutional filters to model the different importance of entities in different relations.

The recommendation itself is made through computation of a score, given n entities (depending on the arity of the relation) and the relation. As an example, given a context (i.e. the weather, day, time, proximity), all potential POIs can be ranked by computing the score for each and choosing the POI with the highest score as the recommendation. The scoring function of HypE is defined as $\phi(r(e_1,...e_{|r|}))$, and describes the sum of the element-wise product of the corresponding embedding vectors (cmp. Fig. 2).

3.3. Sequence-aware Recurrent Neural Nets

Having access to the full information and relying on a system that is constantly learning from new data is often an unrealistic assumption. Common issues are:

Cold start: In many situations the system encounters a new user or can't identify the current user and thus does not have access to the user's history and preferences.

Missing context: Often the full context of the recommendation situation is not available. The system still has to produce a recommendation without contextual factors.

Online Machine Learning: Most machine learning methods learn from (mini-) batches and can't be re-trained after each new data point arrives.

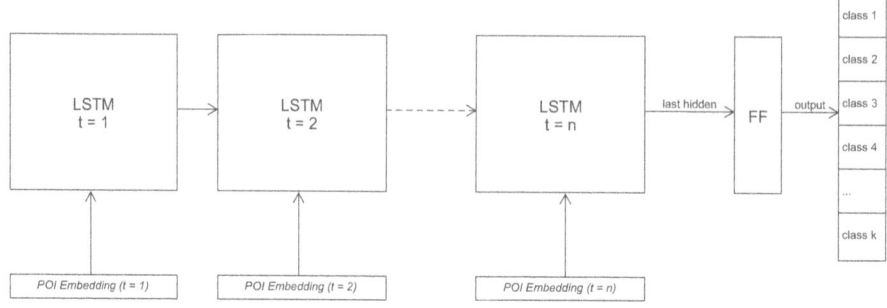

Figure 3. The architecture of the LSTM approach

A more realistic scenario is that a large data set of a LBSN is available for off-line training, but recommendations still have to be generated for new users without contextual information. Based on the assumption that a user chooses a POI not only based on contextual information, but also based on the last POI he visited, a personalized recommendation might even be possible for short individual histories.

For example, this captures that a user would typically not visit a restaurant right after returning from lunch and therefore should also not be recommended doing so.

To capture the sequential nature of such a scenario, we propose to use an LSTM network [31] that receives a sequence of check-ins without additional contextual information as input and predicts the next location in the sequence. We use the off-line trained HypE-Embeddings of the locations as our POI representations and minimize a Cross-Entropy-Loss to learn the next location in the sequence. As a proof-of-concept, we chose a simple network architecture, using an LSTM layer for modelling the sequential information followed by a fully connected layer for the prediction (see Fig. 3).

4. Experimental Setup and Results

The following section describes the experiments on POI recommendation based on the knowledge graphs described in the previous sections. We use two data sets that were introduced in a different knowledge graph embedding approach [18] for a POI recommendation scenario and use the reported hit@10 value from the same paper as a baseline to compare our results to. The experiments can be divided into three different sets of runs:

- Prediction based on binary KGE approaches [32]
- Prediction based on a hypergraph approach [24]
- Prediction based on sequential modelling

The first type of experiments were run on existing implementations[4] that were adapted for a more convenient usage without altering the core of the implementations. For the third set of experiments, we used a simple LSTM network that receives a sequence of visited POIs as input and outputs a prediction of the next POI in the sequence. The com-

---

[4]https://github.com/thunlp/OpenKE

bined approach was built using HypE[5]. Our implementation and experimental settings can be found in the repository[6] on GitHub.

The datasets in use consist of 104,997 and 376,077 data points, which represent the check-ins at locations in New York City and Jakarta over the course of two years. The larger Jakarta set contains 8,805 distinct POIs and 6,183 distinct users, while the NYC set contains 3,626 distinct POIs and 3,573 users. Since the original data represents a hypergraph, it had to be adjusted for usage with binary relations. The information loss in this procedure led to smaller datasets for the binary KGE approaches in comparison to the hypergraph approach. To make sure that the results are still comparable, splitting the data into test, validation and training set was the first step in data preparation, before the data was prepared for usage in the different settings.

As the results, we report the 'filtered' values for the binary and 'raw' values for the n-ary approaches. The filtered setting counts a "hit" as long as the the predicted value is an element of the ground truth, whereas the raw setting only considers the current sample value as a true result. In the third case (LSTM), we report the raw setting only, because we only want to model the sequential behaviour and therefore only consider a "hit" when the exact POI for this sequence is recommended.

4.1. Binary knowledge graph-embedding approaches

The first task was limited to represent the data as triples, consisting of subject, predicate and object. As there is no relation information that we can directly take from the original data, we introduced two different relations which we considered to be carrying most information. The first relation is checksIn(user, POI) and the second one is typeOf(POI, category). For the setting that incorporates the ontological data, we introduced an additional relation subclassOf(category, category) which is only present in the training data and is meant to provide further information for the recommendation task.

Based on the available implementations we conducted a series of experiments using a large variety of binary KGE approaches, including Complex[20], Distmult[33], Hole[34], Simple[23] and Transe[35]. As for the parameter settings, we tested across different embedding dimensions and left the other options to default values. We only report the best results for each method.

4.2. Knowledge hypergraph embedding

In preparation for the HypE approach, we defined one relation checksIn(user, hour of day, day of week, type, location) to represent the data. The hour of day and the day of week are derived from the timestamps in the original data. To achieve the results presented in table 2, we used a slightly different implementation of the HypE approach. The scoring function including the convolutions is still the same, but we made a few adaptions for faster runs on our dataset. We also slightly altered the training objective; instead of scoring against a fixed number of negative samples, we always scored against all possible locations. We only consider the 'raw' setting for evaluation.

For integration of background knowledge we implemented a model that combines the HypE approach for n-ary relations together with a binary approach (TransE) to em-

---

[5]https://github.com/ElementAI/HypE
[6]https://github.com/siwer/TaxonomicalKGE

bed the ontological information. The underlying idea is that the ontological information (in this case the POI categories) will be embedded in their own ontology space, while the other information (users, locations, etc.) will be embedded in a separate space. A translation layer (implemented as a feed-forward layer) learns to project from the ontology space to the general feature space. Algorithm 1 below shows the training procedure of our approach. We implemented a hyperparamer λ to control the influence of the ontological information during training. The training objectives are now to predict the location given (user, type, time, day) and to predict the superclass of a type given the provided ontology. For evaluation we still only consider the location prediction task. Across all experimental runs in different configurations, the results with $\lambda > 0$ outperformed the ones where $\lambda = 0$. Table 1 shows an example of the influence of λ on the training for both NYC and JAK data. The results shown there are averaged over runs with varying ontology space dimension (130,75,50,25). The general entity space dimension is fixed at 130 over those runs. As indicated by our empirical results, the most beneficial values for λ lie between 0.2 and 0.8. This behaviour is also consistent across the other observed metrics. In table 2, the '+ Ont' approaches denote $\lambda > 0$ for the HypE approach. As with the binary approaches, we also present the results from the best runs.

Lambda	0.0	0.2	0.4	0.6	0.8	1.0	Params
MR	23.66	**20.67**	21.76	20.95	21.06	20.90	NYC, lr = 0.01
MR	21.48	20.25	20.24	20.38	**19.98**	20.07	NYC, lr = 0.005
MR	21.73	20.52	19.60	20.18	**19.55**	20.21	JAK, lr = 0.01
MR	17.22	16.43	**15.76**	15.93	16.05	15.88	JAK, lr = 0.005

Table 1. Influence of Lambda on MR

Algorithm 1 Training of the combined approach

Input: batch, weightFactor = λ
typeVector = $ontologySpace_\Theta(type)$;
entityVectors = $entitySpace_\Theta(user, time, day)$;
relationVectors = $relationSpace_\Theta(checkinRelation, subClassRelation)$;
for all i in types **do**
    ontologyScores $\leftarrow \phi_{transE}(type, subClassOf, types_i)$;
end for
translatedType = $TranslationLayer_\Theta(type)$;
for all i in locations **do**
    locScores $\leftarrow \phi_{hypE}(checkin, user, translatedType, day, time, locations_i)$;
end for
lossOntology = $crossEntropy(ontologyScores, superType)$;
lossLocation = $crossEntropy(locScores, location)$;
combinedLoss = $lossLocation + (\lambda * lossOntology)$;
$\Theta \leftarrow update(\Theta, backProp(combinedLoss))$;

Approach	Jakarta	Jakarta + Ont	EmbDim	NYC	NYC + Ont	EmbDim
LBSN2Vec [18]	0.08	-	128	0.11	-	128
Complex	0.041	0.040	100	0.033	0.032	100
Distmult	0.045	0.045	150	0.035	0.039	100
HolE	0.031	0.030	100	0.024	0.023	100
SimplE	0.047	0.046	100	0.035	0.036	100
TransE	0.064	0.064	200	0.044	0.045	150
HypE	**0.742**	**0.771**	130/50	**0.722**	**0.738**	130/25
LSTM	0.085	-	100	0.080	-	100

Table 2. Best hits@10 results for different approaches with the corresponding embedding dimensions. For the KGE approaches, also results for adding information modeled in the POICa ontology (see Sec. 3.1) are reported.

4.3. LSTM-based Sequence-aware Recommendations

As the basis for experiments with the LSTM network, we use the location embeddings that were acquired in the experiments from the section above. Thus, some global contextual information is captured in the embeddings, however, the LSTM is not aware of any situational context, nor of the personalized history of the user, beyond a few previous check-ins. We chose the best performing HypE models for both datasets to provide the location representations.

Since sequential information is used, the original data had to be transformed to represent the check-in sequence(s) of a user. The extreme case would be assuming one sequence per user, i.e. taking all interactions of one user and transform it into a discrete sequence of check-ins. This, however, is not an assumption that would reflect real-word behaviour, because it is unlikely that a location which a user visited a month ago would influence a decision of today. To capture this, we assumed a new sequence after 6 hours passed between two check-ins. As a result, there are now 12,781 sequences in the NYC training set and 1,605 sequences in the NYC test set (For Jakarta: 56,670 and 5,319). Therefore, we consider at least two check-ins within a 6 hour window as a sequence. The choice of the duration after which a new sequence is assumed has a large influence on the final training data. A window of 24 hours would lead to fewer, but longer sequences, while a 4 hour window would yield more very short sequences. To ensure the relatedness of check-ins in the sequences, a shorter window is favorable, although at the cost of having shorter sequences. In the end, around 70% of the obtained sequences had a length of 2. Since we are interested in testing the performance also for cold start problems this is a suitable setup.

We modelled the neural network architecture as a classification problem, where the last hidden state of the LSTM is used as the input for the classification feed-forward layer. Due to the different dataset sizes, the NYC set has 3,626 classes (distinct locations) and the Jakarta set has 8,805 classes.

4.4. Discussion of results

Table 2 provides an overview of the best hits@10 results for each setup described above. First, the results reported in [18] are shown for comparison. Then, results of all binary KGE methods are reported and compared to when information from the POICa ontology is added. Throughout all experiments, the ontological information didn't make a significant difference. This is likely due to the naive way of introducing just the relational information from the ontology into the graph, without considering their semantics, like that of a taxonomical relation. Apparently, this adds more complexity than it provides valuable learning signals. We assume that a more sophisticated approach to exploit the ontology, as done in the HypE approach, can improve the results considerably.

All binary KGE approaches clearly show an inferior performance to LBSN2Vec. This is likely due to their inability to exploit contextual information. This observation becomes clear when looking at the HypE results. Like LBSN2Vec, HypE does exploit n-ary relation and thus the full situational context, however, their embedding techniques are fundamentally different. HypE's results are a quantum leap when compared to any other approach we tested. Since HypE is based on years of KGE research and optimized for use-cases with rich situational context an improvement was expected, but this extend was still surprising. As opposed to the naive approach of just adding the taxonomical information to the training data, the approach of jointly training embeddings for the prediction task and the ontology yielded a measurable increase in prediction performance.

Finally, the LSTM results based on sequential information show that its performance is below LBSN2Vec, specifically for the NYC data set. It is still noteworthy that such a result is obtained after only seeing one previous POI check-in without additional user-specific or contextual information. On the one hand, this seems reasonable since the POI embeddings from HypE are used as input and thus some global context of each POI is provided to the LSTM. On the other hand, there seems to be a valuable signal in the previously visited POI, that is not exploited by the other methods.

5. Conclusions and Future Work

In this paper, we obtained empirical evidence for how well state-of-the-art latent recommendation approaches can exploit ontological, situational and sequential information in a POI recommendation task. Our empirical evidence indicates that the situational context is most crucial to the prediction performance, while the taxonomical and sequential information are harder to exploit. As we have shown with the experiments based on HypE, a beneficial exploitation of ontological information requires a more sophisticated approach than just augmenting the knowledge graph with relations from the ontology. In our approach, we learn an additional dedicated ontology embedding space and train a translation layer to fuse both spaces. Besides of our approach, materializing implicit knowledge or deducing additional positive and negative training data might be another step in this direction. The LSTM approach seems to be an interesting option for cold start scenarios or whenever online learning is computationally not feasible. Also, this approach only initially requires KGE embeddings trained on the full information. Then it can be trained on sequence information only, without situational context, and applied to novel sequences of unknown users, again without situational context. Summing up, this work shows that the different dimensions each provide separate benefits, but exploiting all of them is non-trivial. Thus, promising future steps with great potential are methods for a tight integration of expressive formal ontologies with latent machine learning as well as deep learning architectures for a joined embedding of multi-ary knowledge graphs with sequential information.

References

[1] Gediminas Adomavicius and Alexander Tuzhilin. Context-aware recommender systems. In *Proceedings of the ACM Conference on Recommender Systems, RecSys*, pages 335–336, 2008.

[2] Hongwei Wang, M. Zhao, X. Xie, W. Li, and M. Guo. Knowledge graph convolutional networks for recommender systems. *The World Wide Web Conference*, 2019.

[3] Jie Bao, Yu Zheng, David Wilkie, and Mohamed F. Mokbel. Recommendations in location-based social networks: a survey. *GeoInformatica*, 19:525–565, 2015.

[4] Shenglin Zhao, Irwin King, and Michael R. Lyu. A survey of point-of-interest recommendation in location-based social networks. *CoRR*, abs/1607.00647, 2016.

[5] Juergen Luettin, Susanne Rothermel, and Mark Andrew. Future of in-vehicle recommendation systems @ bosch. *Proceedings of the 13th ACM Conf. on Recommender Sys.*, 2019.

[6] Eunjoon Cho, Seth A. Myers, and Jure Leskovec. Friendship and mobility: user movement in location-based social networks. In *KDD*, 2011.

[7] Josh Jia-Ching Ying, Eric Hsueh-Chan Lu, Wen-Ning Kuo, and Vincent S. Tseng. Urban point-of-interest recommendation by mining user check-in behaviors. In *UrbComp '12*, 2012.

[8] Anastasios Noulas, Salvatore Scellato, Neal Lathia, and Cecilia Mascolo. Mining user mobility features for next place prediction in location-based services. *2012 IEEE 12th International Conference on Data Mining*, pages 1038–1043, 2012.

[9] Ramesh Baral, S. S. Iyengar, Tao Li, and XiaoLong Zhu. Hicaps: Hierarchical contextual poi sequence recommender. In *Proceedings of the 26th ACM SIGSPATIAL International Conference on Advances in Geographic Information Systems*, SIGSPATIAL '18, page 436–439. Association for Computing Machinery, 2018.

[10] Ramesh Baral, S. S. Iyengar, Tao Li, and N. Balakrishnan. Close: Contextualized location sequence recommender. In *Proceedings of the 12th ACM Conf. on Recommender Systems*, RecSys '18, page 470–474. Association for Computing Machinery, 2018.

[11] Chen Cheng, Haiqin Yang, Michael R. Lyu, and Irwin King. Where you like to go next: Successive point-of-interest recommendation. In *IJCAI*, 2013.

[12] Shanshan Feng, Xutao Li, Yifeng Zeng, Gao Cong, Yeow Meng Chee, and Quan Yuan. Personalized ranking metric embedding for next new poi recommendation. In *IJCAI*, 2015.

[13] Xin Li, Mingming Jiang, Huiting Hong, and Lejian Liao. A time-aware personalized point-of-interest recommendation via high-order tensor factorization. *ACM Transactions on Information Systems (TOIS)*, 35:1 – 23, 2017.

[14] Zhu Sun, Jie Yang, Jie Zhang, Alessandro Bozzon, Long-Kai Huang, and Chi Xu. Recurrent knowledge graph embedding for effective recommendation. *Proceedings of the 12th ACM Conference on Recommender Systems*, 2018.

[15] Min Xie, Hongzhi Yin, Haifang Wang, Fanjiang Xu, Weitong Chen, and Sen Wang. Learning graph-based poi embedding for location-based recommendation. *Proceedings of the 25th ACM International on Conference on Information and Knowledge Management*, 2016.

[16] Maxim Naumov, Dheevatsa Mudigere, Hao-Jun Michael Shi, Jianyu Huang, Narayanan Sundaraman, Jongsoo Park, Xiaodong Wang, Udit Gupta, Carole-Jean Wu, Alisson G. Azzolini, Dmytro Dzhulgakov, Andrey Mallevich, Ilia Cherniavskii, Yinghai Lu, Raghuraman Krishnamoorthi, Ansha Yu, Volodymyr Kondratenko, Stephanie Pereira, Xianjie Chen, Wenlin Chen, Vijay Rao, Bill Jia, Liang Xiong, and Misha Smelyanskiy. Deep learning recommendation model for personalization and recommendation systems, 2019.

[17] Hongzhi Yin, Weiqing Wang, Hao Wang, Ling Chen, and Xiaofang Zhou. Spatial-aware hierarchical collaborative deep learning for poi recommendation. *IEEE Transactions on Knowledge and Data Engineering*, 29:2537–2551, 2017.

[18] Dingqi Yang, Bingqing Qu, Jie Yang, and Philippe Cudre-Mauroux. Revisiting user mobility and social relationships in lbsns: A hypergraph embedding approach. In *The World Wide Web Conference*, page 2147–2157. Association for Computing Machinery, 2019.

[19] Shaoxiong Ji, Shirui Pan, Erik Cambria, Pekka Marttinen, and Philip S Yu. A survey on knowledge graphs: Representation, acquisition and applications. *preprint arXiv:2002.00388*, 2020.

[20] Théo Trouillon, Johannes Welbl, Sebastian Riedel, Éric Gaussier, and Guillaume Bouchard. Complex embeddings for simple link prediction. In Maria-Florina Balcan and Kilian Q. Weinberger, editors, *Proceedings of the 33nd International Conference on Machine Learning, ICML 2016*, volume 48, pages 2071–2080. JMLR.org, 2016.

[21]   Shuai Zhang, Yi Tay, Lina Yao, and Qi Liu. Quaternion knowledge graph embeddings. In *Advances in Neural Information Processing Systems*, pages 2731–2741, 2019.

[22]   Achim Rettinger, Hendrik Wermser, Yi Huang, and Volker Tresp. Context-aware tensor decomposition for relation prediction in social networks. *Social Network Analysis and Mining*, 2(4):373–385, 2012.

[23]   Seyed Mehran Kazemi and David Poole. Simple embedding for link prediction in knowledge graphs. In Samy Bengio, Hanna M. Wallach, Hugo Larochelle, Kristen Grauman, Nicolò Cesa-Bianchi, and Roman Garnett, editors, *Advances in Neural Information Processing Systems 31: Annual Conference on Neural Information Processing Systems, NeurIPS 2018*, pages 4289–4300, 2018.

[24]   Bahare Fatemi, Perouz Taslakian, David Vázquez, and David Poole. Knowledge hypergraphs: Extending knowledge graphs beyond binary relations. *CoRR*, abs/1906.00137, 2019.

[25]   Julien Leblay and Melisachew Wudage Chekol. Deriving validity time in knowledge graph. In *Companion Proceedings of the The Web Conference 2018*, pages 1771–1776, 2018.

[26]   Shib Sankar Dasgupta, Swayambhu Nath Ray, and Partha Talukdar. Hyte: Hyperplane-based temporally aware knowledge graph embedding. In *Proceedings of the 2018 Conference on Empirical Methods in Natural Language Processing*, pages 2001–2011, 2018.

[27]   Yu Liu, Wen Hua, Kexuan Xin, and Xiaofang Zhou. Context-aware temporal knowledge graph embedding. In *International Conference on Web Information Systems Engineering*, pages 583–598. Springer, 2019.

[28]   Rakshit Trivedi, Hanjun Dai, Yichen Wang, and Le Song. Know-evolve: Deep temporal reasoning for dynamic knowledge graphs. In *Proceedings of the 34th International Conference on Machine Learning-Volume 70*, pages 3462–3471. JMLR. org, 2017.

[29]   Tingsong Jiang, Tianyu Liu, Tao Ge, Lei Sha, Baobao Chang, Sujian Li, and Zhifang Sui. Towards time-aware knowledge graph completion. In *Proceedings of COLING, the 26th International Conference on Computational Linguistics: Technical Papers*, pages 1715–1724, 2016.

[30]   Haoyu Wang, Vivek Kulkarni, and William Yang Wang. Dolores: deep contextualized knowledge graph embeddings. *arXiv preprint arXiv:1811.00147*, 2018.

[31]   Sepp Hochreiter and Jürgen Schmidhuber. Long short-term memory. *Neural computation*, 9(8):1735–1780, 1997.

[32]   Xu Han, Shulin Cao, Lv Xin, Yankai Lin, Zhiyuan Liu, Maosong Sun, and Juanzi Li. Openke: An open toolkit for knowledge embedding. In *Proceedings of EMNLP*, 2018.

[33]   Bishan Yang, Wen tau Yih, Xiaodong He, Jianfeng Gao, and Li Deng. Embedding entities and relations for learning and inference in knowledge bases, 2014.

[34]   Maximilian Nickel, Lorenzo Rosasco, and Tomaso A. Poggio. Holographic embeddings of knowledge graphs. In *Proceedings of the Thirtieth AAAI Conference on Artificial Intelligence*, pages 1955–1961. AAAI Press, 2016.

[35]   Antoine Bordes, Nicolas Usunier, Alberto Garcia-Durán, Jason Weston, and Oksana Yakhnenko. Translating embeddings for modeling multi-relational data. In *Proceedings of the 26th International Conference on Neural Information Processing Systems - Volume 2*, NIPS'13, page 2787–2795, Red Hook, NY, USA, 2013. Curran Associates Inc.

Further with Knowledge Graphs. M. Alam et al. (Eds.)
AKA Verlag and IOS Press, 2021
© *2021 Akademische Verlagsgesellschaft AKA GmbH, Berlin*
This article is published online with Open Access by IOS Press and distributed under the terms
of the Creative Commons Attribution License 4.0 (CC BY 4.0).
doi:10.3233/SSW210047

Adding Structure and Removing Duplicates in SPARQL Results with Nested Tables

Sébastien FERRÉ [a,1]

[a] *Univ Rennes, CNRS, IRISA,*
Campus de Beaulieu, 35042 Rennes, France
Email: ferre@irisa.fr

Abstract The results of a SPARQL query are generally presented as a table with one row per result, and one column per projected variable. This is an immediate consequence of the formal definition of SPARQL results as a sequence of mappings from variables to RDF terms. However, because of the flat structure of tables, some of the RDF graph structure is lost. This often leads to duplicates in the contents of the table, and difficulties to read and interpret results. We propose to use nested tables to improve the presentation of SPARQL results. A nested table is a table where cells may contain embedded tables instead of RDF terms, and so recursively. We introduce an automated procedure that lifts flat tables into nested tables, based on an analysis of the query. We have implemented the procedure on top of Sparklis, a guided query builder in natural language, in order to further improve the readability of its UI. It can as well be implemented on any SPARQL querying interface as it only depends on the query and its flat results. We illustrate our proposal in the domain of pharmacovigilance, and evaluate it on complex queries over Wikidata.

Keywords. Semantic Web, RDF Graph, SPARQL, Presentation of Results, Nested Table, Sparklis

1. Introduction

The SPARQL query language offers a powerful way to extract and compute information from RDF datasets. For the most common form of queries, SELECT queries, the results are structured and displayed as a table. Each column corresponds to a projected variable in the SELECT clause, and each row corresponds to a query answer, i.e. a mapping from those variables to RDF terms. Such tables have many advantages. They are universally understood. They can be read in two directions, by row or by column. They make a good use of the screen space, compared for instance to graph visualizations, and can therefore display a lot of information at once. They can be dynamically filtered and ordered according to each column. It is no surprise that they are found in all display and visualization frameworks, from HTML to D3js.

Despite all those advantages, tables in general and SPARQL results in particular have drawbacks due to the fact that they are in first normal form (1NF). 1NF is a notion from relational databases [1] that states that table cells only contain atomic values, RDF terms in the case of

---

[1]This research is supported by ANR project PEGASE (ANR-16-CE23-0011-08).

SPARQL results. It sounds like a reasonable constraint but it has negative consequences on the readability of query results. Imagine that a user wants to retrieve in a touristic dataset all hotels with rating 4 or more in Roma. She also wants to know for each hotel the available services and their cost, as well as reviews on that hotel. Because of the structure of SPARQL results, there will be a row for each combination of a hotel, an available service at that hotel, and a review on that hotel. If on average there are 10 services and 10 reviews per hotel, there will be on average 100 rows per hotel in the table of results, each repeating the same hotel name. Each service and review will also be repeated 10 times for each hotel. All those duplicates hinder the readability of the results. Moreover, the RDF graph structure where services and reviews are related to the hotel but not to each other is lost because of the flat structure of the table.

We propose an automated procedure to post-process SPARQL results into *nested tables* in order to address the previous drawbacks while retaining the advantages of tables. A nested table relaxes the 1NF constraint by allowing each table column to contain either RDF terms or nested tables, whose columns can in turn contain RDF terms or nested tables, and so on. In the above example about hotels, a nested table would have a single row per hotel, the service column would contain two-columns tables listing services with their cost, and the review column would contain one-column tables listing customer reviews.

The automated nesting procedure is decomposed into two algorithms. The first algorithm analyzes a SPARQL query to identify a *nested schema* describing the structure of the nested table to be produced. The second algorithm converts a standard table of results into a nested table, given the nested schema produced by the first algorithm. Together, those algorithms allow for the computation of nested tables with existing query engines, and without any additional requirement from users.

Automated nesting has been implemented in Sparklis[2] [2], a guided query builder that completely hides SPARQL queries behind a natural language interface. This improves further the usability of Sparklis by offering a more natural presentation of results. However, the nesting procedure can also be implemented on any SPARQL querying interface as it only depends on the query and its flat results.

The paper is organized as follows. Section 2 discusses related work. Section 3 defines nested schemas and nested tables in contrast to flat tables, and introduces two illustrative example queries and results. Section 4 presents the main contribution of this paper, the automated procedure from standard queries and flat tables to nested tables. Section 5 describes our implementation, and illustrates it with an application in pharmacovigilance. Section 6 presents a qualitative evaluation of our approach on a range of complex queries over Wikidata. Section 7 concludes and draws some perspectives.

2. Related Work

Nested tables were proposed and formalized in relational databases, where nesting is not only used for query results but also for data tables [3,4]. The motivation was to relax the first normal form (1NF) that states that only atomic values are allowed in table cells. The authors extend relational algebra with two operators: *nest* and *unnest*. To nest a table is to group a subset of columns into one higher-order column, whose values become nested tables. It is a form of aggregation, and it generally produces a table with fewer rows. To unnest a table is to explode a higher-order column into the set of columns it is made of. It is the inverse of the nest operation, and it generally produces a table with more rows. The authors also introduce a Partitioned Normal Form (PNF) that ensures that every nesting has an inverse unnesting by excluding some form of redundancy. Querying nested relational databases involves the application of the usual operations of relational algebra [1] on nested tables, plus nesting and unnesting operations.

---

[2]Available online at http://www.irisa.fr/LIS/ferre/sparklis/

Linked Data Query Wizard [5] is a tabular interface for the semantic web, where tables have a single row per subject, and possibly several values in cells. However, those tables are limited to the presentation of the direct neighborhood of entities (columns are entity properties, and column values are the objects of those properties) rather than results of arbitrary queries. Table cells can contain sets of values but not multi-column tables like in nested relational databases and what we propose in this paper. A lot of work have proposed various forms of visualization of SPARQL results in order to help their understanding [6,7,8,9]. Those visualizations generally include maps, charts, timelines, etc. They are definitely useful, especially for numerical data. However we think that they are a complement to a tabular view, and that they cannot fully replace it in the general case. A more general approach consists in supporting the transformation of SPARQL results into a broad set of data structures, e.g. using JSON as output [10], where nested tables are one possible output. However, this approach targets web developers, and does not fit end-users that can freely build their own queries, like with Sparklis [2].

Some features of SPARQL allow to structure query results to some degree. CONSTRUCT queries produce RDF graphs from query answers, hence offering a lot of flexibility in the produced structure but the concrete layout of the graph is left unspecified. A GROUP_CONCAT aggregate enables to pack a set of RDF terms into a single RDF term but this requires to convert all terms to strings, and the internal structure of aggregate values is lost, unlike with nested tables. Some extensions of SPARQL have also been proposed. For instance, a new CLUSTER BY clause was proposed to group the rows of the table of results into a hierarchical clustering [11]. In contrast, nested tables can be seen as a form of 2D hierarchical clustering because they involve grouping subsets of columns and subsets of rows at the same time. In a previous work [12], we have proposed to extend SPARQL 1.1 with a new kind of aggregation construct in order to have nested tables as a native SPARQL results. The work presented in this paper brings two new contributions. First, the structure of the nested table is automatically derived from a standard SPARQL query and its results. Second, it allows for the computation of nested results on top of standard SPARQL 1.1 endpoints, hence supporting a larger adoption of nested results, independently of the extension proposed earlier.

3. Motivating Nested Tables

The results of a SPARQL query are traditionally displayed as (flat) tables.

Definition 1 (flat table) *A flat table FT is a sequence of rows, where each row FT[i] is a partial mapping from column names to values. Notation FT[i].x refers to the contents of the cell (a value or nothing) that is at the crossing between the i-th row, and column x.*

In SPARQL results, rows are query answers, columns are SPARQL variables from the SELECT clause, and values are RDF terms. The ordering of columns is determined by the SELECT clause of the query, and the sequence of rows may be ordered or not depending on the existence of an ORDER BY clause in the query.

Table 1 shows an excerpt of the results of the following SPARQL query on DBpedia, which retrieves films directed by Danny Boyle, along with their music composers and actors, and also the birth year of actors[3].

```
SELECT ?f ?mc ?a ?y
WHERE { ?f a dbo:Film ;
            dbo:director dbr:Danny_Boyle ;
            dbo:musicComposer ?mc ;
```

---

[3]In table headers, variable names have been replaced by more explicit names for readability.

Table 1. Flat table of films by Danny Boyle with music composer, actor, and actor's birth year

film (f)	music composer (mc)	actor (a)	birth year (y)
Slumdog millionaire	A. R. Rahman	Dev Patel	1990
Slumdog millionaire	A. R. Rahman	Freida Pinto	1984
Slumdog millionaire	A. R. Rahman	Anil Kapoor	1959
Sunshine	John Murphy	Cilian Murphy	1976
Sunshine	John Murphy	Chris Evans	1981
Sunshine	John Murphy	Rose Byrne	1979
Sunshine	John Murphy	...	...
Sunshine	Underworld	Cilian Murphy	1976
Sunshine	Underworld	Chris Evans	1981
Sunshine	Underworld	Rose Byrne	1979
Sunshine	Underworld	...	...
...	...	...	...

Table 2. Flat table of countries with their capital, their most populated cities, and for each city, the population and the mathematicians who died in it.

country (c)	capital (cap)	city	population (pop)	mathematician (m)	death date (dd)
United States	Washington	New York	8 550 405	E. L. Post	1954-04-21
United States	Washington	New York	8 550 405	R. Schatten	1977-08-26
United States	Washington	New York	8 550 405	...	...
United States	Washington	Los Angeles	3 792 710	R. Montague	1971-03-07
United States	Washington	Los Angeles	3 792 710	R. E. Bellman	1984-03-19
United States	Washington	Los Angeles	3 792 710	...	...
United States	Washington	Chicago	2 707 120	E. Hellinger	1950-03-28
United States	Washington	Chicago	2 707 120	E. H. Moore	1932-12-30
...	...	...	...	...	...

```
        dbo:starring ?a .
     ?a dbo:birthYear ?y . }
```

It can be observed that the table contains a lot of redundancies. For instance, each actor and his birth year is repeated for each music composer. The number of rows for a film is equal to its number of music composers times its number of actors. When ordering by birth year, one needs to order first by film so as to keep rows grouped by film.

Table 2 shows an excerpt of the results of another SPARQL query that retrieves various information about countries: capital, most populated cities, and mathematicians who died in those cities.

```
SELECT ?c ?cap ?city ?pop ?m ?dd
WHERE { ?c a dbo:Country ;
           dbo:capital ?cap .
        ?city a dbo:City ;
            dbo:country ?c ;
            dbo:populationTotal ?pop .
        ?m a dbo:Scientist ;
           dbo:field dbr:Mathematics ;
           dbo:deathPlace ?city ;
           dbo:deathDate ?dd . }
```

Table 3. Nested table of films by Danny Boyle with music composers, and actors with birth year

film (f)	music composers	actors	
Slumdog millionaire	music composer (mc) A. R. Rahman	actor (a)	birth year (y)
		Anil Kapoor	1959
		Freida Pinto	1984
		Dev Patel	1990
		...	...
Sunshine	music composer (mc) John Murphy Underworld	actor (a)	birth year (y)
		Cilian Murphy	1976
		Rose Byrne	1979
		Chris Evans	1981
		...	...
...	...	...	

```
ORDER BY ?c DESC(?pop)
```

It can be observed again that the table contains redundancies, here about countries and capitals. More importantly, a lot of structure and dependencies are lost in the flat table. It is not clear, without reading the query, whether the population is about the city or the country, whether the listed mathematicians died in the city or more generally in the country.

The key idea of this paper is to present results in more structured tables, in order to make them more readable by removing redundancies and by exhibiting some of the underlying RDF graph structure.

Definition 2 (nested table and nested schema) *A nested table NT is a sequence of rows, where each row NT[i] is a partial mapping from column names to values or nested tables, according to a nested schema. A nested schema is an ordered forest, i.e. a sequence of ordered trees, such that there is a bijection between the forest nodes and the columns of the nested table. Nested table NT agrees with a nested schema $N = \alpha_1 \ldots \alpha_k$ if the following conditions are satisfied for every row i, and every tree α_j:*

1. *if $\alpha_j = x_j$ is a leaf, then $NT[i].x_j$ contains a value (or nothing);*
2. *if $\alpha_j = X_j[N_j]$ is an internal node N_j with children $N_j = \beta_1 \ldots \beta_l$, then $NT[i].X_j$ contains a nested table agreeing with nested schema N_j.*

A nested table agreeing with a nested schema follows a regular structure. For a given column, either all rows contain an RDF term or all rows contain a table following the same structure. Note that the definitions of nested tables and nested schemas are recursive, thus allowing arbitrary numbers of nesting levels.

In the following, we represent nested schemas using lowercase names for leaves, uppercase names for internal nodes, and square brackets to delimit the children of an internal node. For example, nested schema a b C[d E[e]] has three levels of tables: the outer table has two classical columns *a* and *b*, and a nested column *C*, which contains nested tables with a classical column *d*, and a nested column *E*, which in turn contains nested tables with a single column *e*.

Table 3 is the nested version of Table 1 for the nested schema

$$N_{film} = \text{f MC[mc] A[a y]}.$$

The outer table has a single row per film, and two of its columns, "music composers" (MC) and "actors" (A), contain nested tables. The former column contains one-column nested tables that

Table 4. Nested table of countries with their capital, and their most populated cities. Each city is described by its population, and a list of mathematicians who died there.

country (c)	capital (cap)	cities				
United States	Washington	*city*	population (pop)	*mathematicians*		
		New York	8 550 405	mathematician (m)	death date (dd)	
				E. L. Post	1954-04-21	
				R. Schatten	1977-08-26	
				...	...	
		Los Angeles	3 792 710	mathemtician (m)	death date (dd)	
				R. Montague	1971-03-07	
				R. E. Bellman	1984-03-19	
				...	...	
		Chicago	2 707 120	mathematician (m)	death date (dd)	
				E. H. Moore	1932-12-30	
				E. Hellinger	1950-03-28	
				...	...	
		...	...	...		
...	...	...				

contain the lists of music composers of each film. The latter column contains two-columns nested tables that contain the lists of actors of each film, along with their birth year. It can be observed that the nested table does not contain redundancies anymore, and that the dependencies between columns is made explicit: (a) music composers and actors are dependent on the film, but not on each other; (b) the birth year is dependent on the actor.

Table 4 is the nested version of Table 2 for the nested schema

$$N_{country} = \text{c cap CITIES[city pop M[m dd]]}.$$

The outer table has a single row per country, a column "capital" that contains RDF terms, and another column "cities" that contains nested tables, which themselves contain nested tables about the mathematicians who died in the city. The nested table structure clearly shows that countries have one capital but (possibly) several cities, that the population is about the city, and that the listed mathematicians are related to the city rather than to the country.

In the following section, we explain how a nested table can be automatically derived from the flat table, by analyzing the SPARQL query.

4. Automated Nesting of SPARQL Results

We here consider the computation of a nested table from the flat table resulting from the evaluation of a standard SPARQL query. Section 4.1 describes an algorithm *NestedSchema* that extracts a nested schema from the query. Section 4.2 describes an algorithm *NestedTable* that restructures the query results into a nested table agreeing with a given nested schema. By combining the two algorithms, it becomes possible to get nested tables as the result of a standard query evaluated on a standard SPARQL 1.1 engine. Given a query Q, this can be summarized by the definition

$$NestedEval(Q) = NestedTable(Eval(Q), NestedSchema(Q))$$

where *Eval* is standard SPARQL evaluation.

```
SELECT ?f ?mc ?a ?y
WHERE { ?f a dbo:Film ;
           dbo:director dbr:Danny_Boyle ;
           dbo:musicComposer ?mc ;
           dbo:starring ?a .
        ?a dbo:birthYear ?y . }
```

Figure 1. Example query on films.

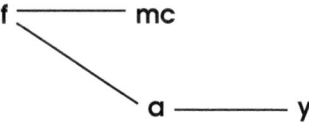

Figure 2. Dependency graph of the query in Figure 1 (ignoring non-connected vertices).

4.1. Nested Schema of a Query

Our procedure to compute the nested schema of a query relies on the dependencies between variables expressed by the SPARQL query, and on an ordering of those variables. We first explain the main principles of the automated procedure on the example about films, whose query we recall in Figure 1 for convenience. The expected nested schema is here $N_1 = $ f MC[mc] A[a y]. It has two nesting levels (tables in a table). Nesting $N_0 = $ f mc a y represents a flat table with no nesting (one level). Nesting $N_2 = $ f MC[mc A[a Y[y]]] represents a deep nesting with 4 levels. The reason why N_1 is better than N_0 and N_2 is that music composers and actors are related to films but not to each other. In other words, the set of music composers and the set of actors depend on the film but given a film, the set of actors does not depend on a particular music composer.

Dependencies between variables can be infered from the query abstract syntax. In short, two variables are dependent on each other if they occur in the same triple pattern, e.g. variables f and mc in the example. More generally, we formally define the dependency graph of an arbitrary SPARQL query.

Definition 3 (dependency graph) *The dependency graph of a SPARQL query Q is the undirected graph $G(Q) = (V,E)$, where the set of vertices V is the set of variables occuring in the query, and where the set of edges $E \subseteq V \times V$ is the set of dependencies $deps(g_0, Q)$, defined inductively on the syntax of the query according to the following equations, starting with the default graph g_0.*

$$deps(g, \text{SELECT } X \text{ WHERE } P) = deps_X(X) \cup deps_P(g,P)$$

$$deps_X(x_1 \ \dots \ x_n) = \emptyset$$
$$deps_X(x_1 \ \dots \ x_n \ (A_1(y_1) \text{ AS } z_1) \ \dots \ (A_k(y_k) \text{ AS } z_k)) = \{(x_i,z_j) \mid i \in [1,n], j \in [1,k]\}$$

$$deps_P(g,s \ p \ o) = \{(x,y) \mid x,y \in Vars(\{s,p,o,g\}), x \neq y\}$$
$$deps_P(g,P_1 \ . \ P_2) = deps_P(g,P_1) \cup deps_P(g,P_2)$$
$$deps_P(g,P_1 \text{ UNION } P_2) = deps_P(g,P_1) \cup deps_P(g,P_2)$$
$$deps_P(g,P_1 \text{ OPTIONAL } P_2) = deps_P(g,P_1) \cup deps_P(g,P_2)$$
$$deps_P(g,P_1 \text{ MINUS } P_2) = deps_P(g,P_1)$$
$$deps_P(g,P \text{ FILTER } E) = deps_P(g,P)$$
$$deps_P(g,\text{BIND } (E \text{ AS } x)) = \{(y,x) \mid y \text{ a variable occuring in } E\}$$
$$deps_P(g,\text{GRAPH } g' \ P) = deps_P(g',P)$$
$$deps_P(g,\text{SERVICE } s \ P) = deps_P(s.g_0,P)$$
$$deps_P(g,\text{VALUES } (x_1 \ \dots \ x_n) \ data) = \{(x_i,x_j) \mid 1 \leq i < j \leq n\}$$
$$deps_P(g,\{ \ Q \ \}) = deps(g,Q)$$

The inductive definition goes through queries ($deps(g,Q)$), projections ($deps_X(X)$), and graph patterns ($deps_P(g,P)$), given a current graph g: g_o is the default graph, and $s.g_0$ is the default graph of service s. Letter A denotes an aggregate operator (e.g. COUNT). Expressions in the SELECT and GROUP BY clauses are assumed to be rewritten as BIND clauses to simplify the definition. Solution modifiers (e.g., ORDER BY, LIMIT) do not produce dependencies.

Algorithm 1 $NestedSchema(G, X)$

Require: $G = (V, E)$ a connected dependency graph
Require: X a sequence ordering variables in V
Ensure: N a nested schema whose set of leaf columns is V
1: **if** $|X| = 1$ **then**
2:   $N \leftarrow X$
3: **else**
4:   $x, Y \leftarrow head(X), tail(X)$
5:   $G_x \leftarrow (V \setminus \{x\}, E \setminus (\{x\} \times V) \setminus (V \times \{x\}))$
6:   $G_1, \ldots, G_k \leftarrow ConnectedComponents(G_x)$
7:   $Y_1, \ldots, Y_k \leftarrow$ partition of Y according to $G_1, \ldots, G_k$
8:   $N_1, \ldots, N_k \leftarrow NestedSchema(Y_1, G_1), \ldots, NestedSchema(Y_k, G_k)$
9:   $N \leftarrow x\, X_1[N_1] \ldots X_k[N_k]$ {w}here each X_i is a fresh nested column name
10: **end if**

Figure 2 shows the dependency graph of the example query. Dependencies come mostly from the graph pattern in the WHERE clause, and also from aggregates. In triple patterns, each variable depends on other variables, including the current graph g if different from the default graph (quads). Then the dependencies from the different sub-patterns are collected, except for those at the right of MINUS as they do not produce any binding. Expressions in FILTER do not produce any dependency but in BIND, they produce a dependency from every used variable to the bound variable as the value of the latter depends on the value of each of the former. Similarly, every aggregate variable in the SELECT clause depends on each of the non-aggregate variables, i.e. on the grouping variables. In the GRAPH and SERVICE constructs, we produce the dependencies of the embedded graph pattern, only changing the current graph. In the VALUES clause, we have no information about the dependencies between the bound variables, and we have to consider that they are all mutually dependent. Indeed, the consequence of ignoring a dependency (a loss of information) is greater than considering a superfluous dependency (redundancy in results). However, such clauses are rare in practice. Finally, the dependencies of sub-queries are defined like for whole queries.

Algorithm 1 describes the recursive process of computing a nested schema given the connected dependency graph of query (see discussion below for non-connected dependency graphs), and given an ordering over the dependency graph vertices, i.e. the query variables. By default, we take the ordering of variables from their order of introduction in the graph pattern of the query. The SELECT clause can be used to alter this ordering. If a variable does not occur in the SELECT clasuse, it is pruned from the nested schema as a post-processing, which amounts to remove a leaf node from the forest sructure of the nested schema.

The base case of the algorithm is when there is a single variable. Otherwise, the first variable is used as a key (grouping), and other variables are organized into one or several nested tables. To determine the partitioning of the other variables into different nested schemas, we rely on the dependency graph. First, we remove the first variable x and its adjacent edges from the dependency graph. This may split the dependency graph into several connected components, which determine the partitioning of the remaining variables Y. The procedure is called recursively on each connected component G_i and its associated subsequence of variables Y_i.

In the unusual case where the dependency graph of a query is not connected, i.e. it has several connected components, we run the algorithm on each connected component, and get a set of nested schemas $N_1, \ldots, N_k$. From there, we generate the nested schema $N = X_1[N_1] \ldots X_k[N_k]$, which has no key variable, and hence specifies a main table with a single row. This implies that the query results are organized as a sequence of independent tables. Indeed, evaluating a disconnected query is equivalent to evaluating several queries, and hence to get several tables of results.

Applying   Algorithm   1   on   the   example   about   films   returns   nesting   schema

---

Algorithm 2 *NestedTable*(*FT*, *N*)

Require: *FT* a flat table with columns *X*

Require: *N* a nested schema over a subset of *X*

Ensure: *NT* a nested version of *FT*

1: **if** $N = x \{n\}$o nested table **then**
2:     $NT \leftarrow$ projection of *FT* on column *x*, and duplicate removal
3: **else**
4:     $N = x X_1[N_1] \dots X_k[N_k]$
5:     $\{FT_1, \dots, FT_n\} \leftarrow$ grouping the rows of *FT* by column *x* (*n* groups)
6:     $NT \leftarrow$ a table with $1+k$ columns $(x, X_1, \dots, X_k)$, and *n* rows
7:     **for** $i = 1$ **to** *n* **do**
8:         $NT[i].x \leftarrow FT_i[1].x$ {r}etrieving key value in first row of FT_i
9:         **for** $j = 1$ **to** k {f}or each nested column **do**
10:            $NT[i].X_j \leftarrow NestedTable(FT_i, N_j)$ {f}ill cells with nested tables
11:        **end for**
12:    **end for**
13:    **for** $j = 1$ **to** k {s}implification for empirical functional dependencies **do**
14:        **if** $NT[i].X_j$ has a single row for all $i \in [1, n]$ **then**
15:            replace the nested column $X_j[N_j]$ by the sequence of columns N_j
16:        **end if**
17:    **end for**
18: **end if**

$N_3 =$ f MC[mc] A[a Y[y]]. Note that N_3 is close to the expected nesting schema N_1 but not equivalent. The independency between music composers and actors has been identified but nested tables are introduced for actor's birth year inside the nested table of actors. The reason why this additional nested table is not relevant is that there is a functional dependency from actors to birth years as people are only born once. Unfortunately, the query does not provide this information. If there is access to the ontology or the data, it may be possible to get this information. In the following section, we show how the nested schema can be simplified during the nesting of flat tables by discovering such functional dependencies empirically. To give another example, the nested schema computed by our algorithm on the query about countries is c CAP[cap] CITIES[city POP[pop] M[m DD[dd]]], which is close to the expected nesting c cap CITIES[city pop M[m dd]] except for the additional nesting of functional properties (country's capital, city's population, and mathematician's death date).

The variable ordering has an important impact on the computed nested schema. Indeed, there is not a single good choice of nested schema given a dependency graph, and the variable ordering can be used to control which nested schema is produced. From the dependency graph in Figure 2, we obtain the different following nested schemas according to different variable orderings:

- a y f mc $\Longrightarrow$ a Y[y] F[f MC[mc]]: view by author,
- mc f a y $\Longrightarrow$ mc F[f A[a Y[y]]]: view by music composer,
- f a mc y $\Longrightarrow$ f A[a Y[y]] mc: another view by film, actors first.

4.2. Nesting a Flat Table into a Nested Table

The previous section explains how to automatically extract a nested schema *N* from a query *Q*. This provides all the necessary information to automatically lift the flat table $FT = Eval(Q)$ into a nested table agreeing with *N*.

Algorithm 2 computes such a nested table NT given the flat table FT and the nested schema N computed from the query (see Section 4.1). The base case (Lines 1-2) is when the nesting schema has no nested table, which implies it has the form $N = x$ for some variable x. The returned nested table is then column x of the flat table, in which duplicates are removed (like in a SELECT DISTINCT ?x). In the general case (Lines 3-18), the nesting has the form $N = x \ X_1[N_1] \ \dots \ X_k[N_k]$. Such a nesting involves a grouping of the rows of FT according to x (Line 5), like a clause GROUP BY ?x, and the computations of the k nested tables on each group (Lines 7-12). Each nested column $X_j[N_j]$ involves a recursive call on each group of rows FT_i with nesting N_j. A drawback of the nested schemas computed by Algorithm 1 is that it does not take into account functional dependencies. In the example about films, the computed nesting is f MC[mc] A[a Y[y]], which implies that in the nested tables about actors, the second column about actor's birth year is filled with one-column one-row tables. Lines 13-17 replaces those one-row nested tables by their single row contents, but only in the nested columns where all nested tables have a single row. This condition identifies *empirical functional dependencies*, i.e. functional dependencies that exist in the flat table but that may not be true in general. In the example, this results in the effective nested schema f MC[mc] A[a y].

5. Implementation and Application

The automated procedure to lift a flat table into a nested table has been implemented in the Sparklis[4][5] querying tool [2]. Sparklis is a SPARQL query builder that hides SPARQL behind a natural language interface, and guides the query construction so that the user does not need to know the schema of the RDF dataset. It works as follows. After each user interaction, the abstract representation of the query is updated, from which a new SPARQL query is derived. Then, the SPARQL query is sent to the SPARQL endpoint, which returns results as a set of mappings from variables to RDF terms. Originally, Sparklis displays those results as a flat table, only improving the display of RDF terms with labels and media contents. The new nesting procedure is applied to the generated SPARQL query and returned results, and feeds the final display process. Currently, Sparklis does not generate names for the nested columns, and their headers are left empty. In the future, those names could be generated in a way similar to classical columns whose names are derived from the labels of the classes and properties applying to the corresponding variable.

The display of results as nested tables was initially motivated by a use case in pharmacovigilance[6], where domain experts typically look for patient cases depending on the drugs they took, and the adverse reactions they suffered. In this use case, each patient case may have a number of different drugs and adverse reactions. In a flat table, the description of a patient case is therefore scattered over several rows, and a lot of duplicates occur when there are several drugs and several adverse reactions. In a previous user study [13], it was observed that this made it difficult for pharmacovigilance experts to read and interpret the results.

Figure 3 shows a screenshot of the first two rows of the nested table that describes patient cases who suffered adverse reactions to chloroquine. It can be observed that there is a single row per patient, and that this row is well organized. For each patient, the table shows its case id, its age, and two nested tables. The first nested table describes the drug event, giving the dose amount, and optionally the dose frequency. The second nested table gives the list of adverse reactions of the patient. The icons on the left of adverse reactions are taken from an iconic language for the graphical representation of medical concepts [14]. The anonymised patient data are a three-months sample from the FAERS database [15].

---

[4]Online application at http://www.irisa.fr/LIS/ferre/sparklis/
[5]Open source code at https://github.com/sebferre/sparklis
[6]This is part of ANR research project PEGASE. The dataset is not made available because of property rights on medical ontologies like SNOMED-CT and MedDRA.

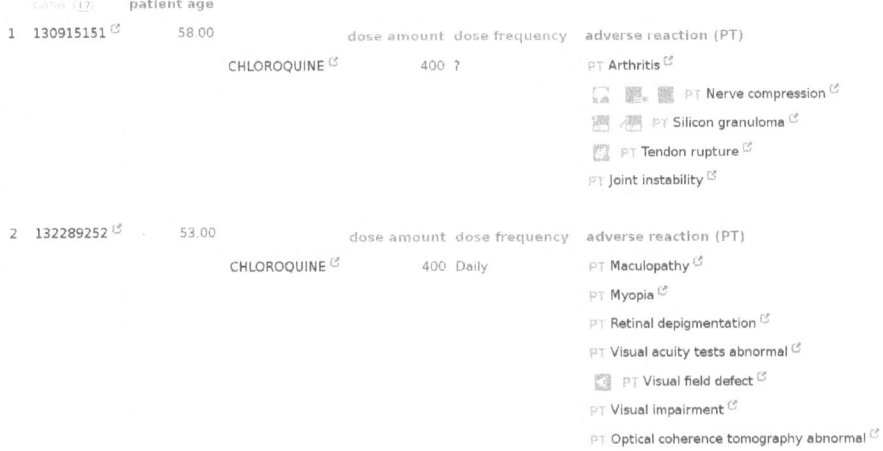

Figure 3. Screenshot of the nested table showing two patient cases (out of 17) with adverse reactions to chloroquine (in excerpt of FAERS data).

6. Evaluation

We evaluate our automated nesting procedure on a range of complex Wikidata queries, picked and adapted from an online list of Wikidata example queries[7]. We only pick queries with at least three different entities in the SELECT clause as otherwise, there is only one possible nested schema: $x\,Y(y)$, possibly unnested into $x\,y$ in case of functional dependency from x to y. Note that we do not count projected variables like ?xxxLabel as they only serve to capture the label of ?xxx. We also modify some queries by removing aggregates like SAMPLE and COUNT. Indeed, such aggregates replace sets of RDF terms by a single RDF term, and hence often remove the need for nested tables. For example, instead of retrieving one sample actor for each film, we retrieve a list of actors for each film.

For each of the nine queries below, we give:

(a) a title,
(b) a short URL[8] that opens the query in Sparklis and enables to visualize the results,
(c) an informal description of the information retrieved by the query,
(d) the obtained nested schema, in which we omit the nested column names, and replace the square brackets by round brackets in the case of unnesting due to a functional dependency in data,
(e) comments on the nested schema, and possibly alternative nested schemas based on a different column ordering.

The queries have been constructed interactively in Sparklis. Their verbalization in English is not always fully satisfying because it relies on the assumption that class and property labels are nouns, which is often but not always verified in Wikidata. However, we believe that those verbalizations are understandable in most cases. The ordering of variables used in the nesting procedure is defined by the order in which they appear (implicitly) in the verbalization.

---

[7]https://www.wikidata.org/wiki/Wikidata:SPARQL_query_service/queries/examples

[8]Real URLs and query previews are also available at http://www.irisa.fr/LIS/ferre/sparklis/examples.html, section "Nested results on Wikidata."

1. **Academy awards** (`http://rebrand.ly/xyw7nwf`): this query looks for people who received an Academy award for some work. It also retrieves work directors, if any, and the edition and time of the award

   N_1 = `person [work [director] [award (awardEdition (time))]]`

   Each person may have several awarded works. Each work may have several directors on one hand, and several awards (for the same person) on the other hand. According to results, each award belongs to a single Academy awards edition, which occurs on a single time. If the award column is put before the work column, one gets the less interesting nested schema `person [award (work [director] (awardEdition (time)))]`, where the grouping of awards by work is lost and a same work may be repeated across different awards.

2. **Ranking of film directors** (`http://rebrand.ly/qaelfdg`): this query retrieves film directors, counts their number of directed films, and number of cast roles, and rank them by decreasing sum of the two numbers.

   N_2 = `director (filmNb (roleNb (total)))`

   This query illustrates the fact that aggregates and expressions create functional dependencies, in which case there is not practical need for nesting.

3. **The Simpsons episodes** (`http://rebrand.ly/r2b4931`): this query retrieves all seasons and episodes of The Simpsons television series.

   N_3 = `seasonOrdinal (season [episodeOrdinal (episode)])`

   Each season ordinal number (1, 2...) determines a single season. Each season has a number of episodes, identified by their ordinal number in the season. By ordering by season ordinal and episode ordinal, we get a well-structured presentation of all episodes by season.

4. **Law & Order episodes** (`http://rebrand.ly/ib18whw`): this query retrieves all seasons and episodes of the Law & Order series, including publication dates for each episode.

   N_4 = `seasonOrd (season [episodeOrd (episode [pubDate])])`

   We get a similar nested schema compared to the previous query, except we get an additional nesting level for the episode publication dates. Indeed, many episodes have several publication dates.

5. **Dr Who performers** (`http://rebrand.ly/dpxfonc`): this query retrieves all regenerations of Dr Who with their ordinal and performers.

   N_5 = `doctor (ordinal) [performer]`

   The nested schema tells us that each regeneration of Dr Who has a single ordinal but several performers for the First Doctor. The ordinal enables to sort the results in chronological order.

6. **Movies about World War II** (`http://rebrand.ly/hv3hw1p`): this query retrieves narrative locations and countries of origins of films about WWII.

   N_6 = `film [narrativeLoc] [country]`

   The nested schema tells us narrative locations and countries of origin are independant, and that in general, there are several values of each for a given film. An alternative nested schema, `narrativeLoc [film [country]]`, provides WWII films grouped by narrative location.

7. **Longest rivers** (`http://rebrand.ly/xklfe8n`): this query retrieves rivers in decreasing length order, along with pictures of them.

$N_7 = $ `river [length] [picture]`

Surprisingly, it appears that some rivers have several lengths in their description. This typically happens when there are several sources of information. A nice consequence of having nested tables in Sparklis is that, when a river has several pictures, they are displayed as a kind of gallery in a table cell, rather than repeating the whole river row for each picture.

8. **Stations of Paris metro line 1** (`http://rebrand.ly/iolf4h3`): this query retrieves stations of Paris metro line 1, and for each station, it retrieves the connecting lines if any on one hand, and adjacent stations with directions on the other hand.

$N_8 = $ `station [line] [adjacent [adjacentLine [adjacentDir]]]`

The four-levels nested schema tells us that a station my have several connecting lines, what is not surprising. What is more surprising is that some adjacent stations can be reached through several lines, and sometimes for a given line, with several line directions. This happens because some metro lines have tree-shaped ends.

9. **Governments of countries** (`http://rebrand.ly/nlp8nex`): this query retrieves, for each country, the *current* forms of government (e.g., republic, parliamentary monarchy), and the heads of government since 2000 with their gender and start date. The current forms of government are selected by excluding those having an end date. We also retrieve the start date when available.

$N_9 = $ `country [form (formStart)] [head (gender) [headStart]]`

The nested schema shows that forms of government and heads of government are independent, as expected. Heads have a single gender but may have several start dates, corresponding to different mandates.

The above examples show a diverse range of nested schemas, which exhibit structures coming from the RDF graph and left implicit in flat tables. Those structures are often as one would expect but sometimes they reveal unexpected patterns or irregularities in the data: e.g., the fact that metro lines may have several directions through a same adjacent station, or the fact that some rivers have several competing lengths. The above examples also demonstrate the importance of empirical functional dependencies to simplify the structure of nested tables, in particular to reduce the number of nesting levels.

7. Conclusion

We have proposed an automated procedure to re-structure the flat results of a SPARQL query into a nested table. Nested tables improve the readability of results by avoiding redundancies in their contents, and by exhibiting the dependencies and independencies between their columns. The procedure is decomposed into two algorithms. Algorithm *NestedSchema* defines a nested schema given dependencies between variables and an ordering over those variables, both computed from the query. Algorithm *NestedTable* uses that nested schema to restructure the flat table of results into a nested table. One perspective is to generate nested schemas without giving a variable ordering, e.g. by finding a variable ordering that minimizes redundancies and maximizes readability.

References

[1] Codd EF. A Relational Model of Data for Large Shared Data Banks. Communications of the ACM. 1970;13(6):377-87.

[2]   Ferré S. Sparklis: An Expressive Query Builder for SPARQL Endpoints with Guidance in Natural Language. Semantic Web: Interoperability, Usability, Applicability. 2017;8(3):405-18. Available from: http://www.irisa.fr/LIS/ferre/sparklis/.

[3]   Scholl M, Abiteboul S, Bançilhon F, Bidoit N, Gamerman S, Plateau D, et al. VERSO: A database machine based on nested relations. In: Work. Theory and Applications of Nested Relations and Complex Objects. Springer; 1987. p. 27-49.

[4]   Roth MA, Korth HF, Silberschatz A. Extended algebra and calculus for nested relational databases. ACM Transactions on Database Systems (TODS). 1988;13(4):389-417.

[5]   Hoefler P, Granitzer M, Sabol V, Lindstaedt S. Linked Data Query Wizard: A Tabular Interface for the Semantic Web. In: The Semantic Web: ESWC 2013 Satellite Events. Springer; 2013. p. 173-7.

[6]   Bikakis N, Sellis T. Exploration and visualization in the web of big linked data: A survey of the state of the art. In: Int. Work. Linked Web Data Management (LWDM); 2016. .

[7]   Atemezing GA, Troncy R. Towards a Linked-Data based Visualization Wizard. In: Hartig O, Hogan A, Sequeda JF, editors. Int. Work. Consuming Linked Data (COLD), co-located Int. Semantic Web Conf. (ISWC). vol. 1264 of CEUR Workshop Proceedings. CEUR-WS.org; 2014. Available from: http://ceur-ws.org/Vol-1264/cold2014_AtemezingT.pdf.

[8]   Skjæveland MG. Sgvizler: A javascript wrapper for easy visualization of sparql result sets. In: Extended Semantic Web Conference. Springer; 2012. p. 361-5.

[9]   Martin M, Abicht K, Stadler C, Ngonga Ngomo AC, Soru T, Auer S. Cubeviz: Exploration and visualization of statistical linked data. In: Int. Conf. World Wide Web. ACM; 2015. p. 219-22.

[10] Lisena P, Meroño-Peñuela A, Kuhn T, Troncy R. Easy web API development with SPARQL transformer. In: Int. Semantic Web Conf. Springer; 2019. p. 454-70.

[11] Ławrynowicz A. Query results clustering by extending SPARQL with CLUSTER BY. In: OTM Confederated Int. Conf. on the Move to Meaningful Internet Systems. Springer; 2009. p. 826-35.

[12] Ferré S. A Proposal for Nested Results in SPARQL. In: Taylor K, Gonçalves R, Lecue F, Yan J, editors. ISWC 2020 Posters, Demos, and Industry Tracks. vol. 2721 of CEUR Workshop Proceedings; 2020. p. 114-9. Available from: http://ceur-ws.org/Vol-2721/paper527.pdf.

[13] Marcilly R, Douze L, Ferré S, Audeh B, Bobed C, Lillo-Le-Louët A, et al. How to interact with medical terminologies? Formative usability evaluations comparing three approaches for supporting the use of MedDRA by pharmacovigilance specialists. BMC Medical Informatics and Decision Making. 2020;20(261).

[14] Lamy JB, Duclos C, Bar-Hen A, Ouvrard P, Venot A. An iconic language for the graphical representation of medical concepts. BMC medical informatics and decision making. 2008;8(1):16.

[15] FDA Adverse Event Reporting System (FAERS);. Available from: https://open.fda.gov/data/faers/.

Further with Knowledge Graphs. M. Alam et al. (Eds.)
AKA Verlag and IOS Press, 2021
© *2021 Akademische Verlagsgesellschaft AKA GmbH, Berlin*
This article is published online with Open Access by IOS Press and distributed under the terms
of the Creative Commons Attribution License 4.0 (CC BY 4.0).
doi:10.3233/SSW210048

Object-Action Association Extraction from Knowledge Graphs

Alexandros Vassiliades [a,b,1], Theodore Patkos [b], Vasilis Efthymiou [b], Antonis Bikakis [c], Nick Bassiliades [a] and Dimitris Plexousakis [b]

[a] *Aristotle University of Thessaloniki, School of Informatics*
[b] *Institute of Computer Science, Foundation for Research and Technology Hellas*
[c] *University College London Department of Information Studies*

Abstract. Infusing autonomous artificial systems with knowledge about the physical world they inhabit is of utmost importance and a long-lasting goal in Artificial Intelligence (AI) research. Training systems with relevant data is a common approach; yet, it is not always feasible to find the data needed, especially since a big portion of this knowledge is commonsense. In this paper, we propose a novel method for extracting and evaluating relations between objects and actions from knowledge graphs, such as ConceptNet and WordNet. We present a complete methodology of locating, enriching, evaluating, cleaning and exposing knowledge from such resources, taking into consideration semantic similarity methods. One important aspect of our method is the flexibility in deciding how to deal with the noise that exists in the data. We compare our method with typical approaches found in the relevant literature, such as methods that exploit the topology or the semantic information in a knowledge graph, and embeddings. We test the performance of these methods on the Something-Something Dataset.

Keywords. Relation Pattern Method, Knowledge Graph, Semantics-Based Method

1. Introduction

Humans are able to understand relations between *real-world objects and actions* relying not only on observations, but also on their commonsense knowledge. Machines, on the other hand, need a large quantity of data, in order to learn and reason about object-action relations, as for instance to correlate the object *Knife* with the action *Cut*. Yet, recognizing such types of associations is crucial for a wide spectrum of applications involving autonomous entities. Commonsense Knowledge Graphs (KGs), such as ConceptNet [1] and WordNet [2], contain to some extent knowledge about object-action relations, and can help construct knowledge bases, which subsequently can be used by machines. However, inserting knowledge into a knowledge base from crowd-built KGs hides risks, as these may contain information that is noisy or false. Therefore, evaluation methods are crucial when exploiting knowledge from such KGs.

---

[1]This project has received funding from the Hellenic Foundation for Research and Innovation (HFRI) and the General Secretariat for Research and Technology (GSRT), under grant agreement No 188.

A method that correctly identifies positive and negative object-action associations in the presence of noise can increase the quality of data that a machine can utilize, which in turn can improve the performance of autonomous, artificial intelligence (AI) systems. Driven by this need, in this paper we compare a number of methods of different nature that are commonly used in practice to extract associations from KGs, organizing them into *topology-based*, *semantics-based* and *embeddings-based*. We also introduce a novel semantics-based approach to identify such object-action correlations that can achieve or improve state-of-the-art performance, while offering flexibility in ironing out noise. Its main characteristic is the exploitation of patterns of relations, which carry important information as to which associations to trust and which to dismiss.

Informally, the problem we aim to solve is the following: given a directed KG and a pair of nodes, one of which refers to a real-world object class and the other to a real-world action class, we try to infer whether these two nodes are associated or not, and to what degree, i.e., if the action can be performed by/on that object. This demand is amplified by the volume of current research in fields, such as robotic manipulation, where object affordances play a key role in enabling a robot to accomplish tasks (see for instance [3] for a recent survey of the relevant literature). Of course, the methods described in our study are not limited to the household domain, but can be applied for the detection of a broader class of associations; yet, framing our analysis on the given domain helps us compare more accurately the behaviour of diverse methods.

The main contributions of this paper are (a) a comparative analysis of popular methods for extracting associations from KGs focusing on a specific domain, that of household objects, (b) the proposal of a new, enhanced method that lays more emphasis on the semantic knowledge that exists in the KG, and (c) the generation of a dataset of positive and negative object-action relations, comprising labels that are commonly used for benchmarking both research and practical approaches. Our method and dataset are publicly available[2].

The rest of this paper is structured as follows. Section 2 discusses related work. Section 3 presents the existing and proposed methods for identifying object-action relations. Section 4 describes our experimental evaluation, and Section 5 concludes the paper.

2. Related Work

Extracting commonsense knowledge from problem-agnostic repositories has been applied to a diversity of AI-related domains to solve various problems. The authors of [4] rely upon ConceptNet to identify word similarities, which they then use in order to improve the performance of sentence-based image retrieval algorithms. A more elaborate use of KGs is presented in [5], where the authors approach the problem of zero-shot label learning in images by creating KGs based on labels detected visually and on correlations found in external sources. The authors rely on WordNet to populate the graph and use Wu Palmer similarity[3] to specify the properties. In [6], the authors assign labels to a visual scene using Bayesian logic networks and relying on commonsense knowledge extracted from WordNet, ConceptNet, and Wikipedia. WordNet is utilized in order to disambiguate seed words with the aid of their hypernym. ConceptNet properties, such as

---

[2]https://github.com/valexande/Semantics-2021
[3]https://www.nltk.org/howto/wordnet.html

LocatedAt or *UsedFor*, which may pinpoint the location of an object, are also retrieved. With this method, the system can generate a compact semantic knowledge base given only a small number of objects. Similar methods are used in [7,8,9,10].

The aforementioned studies attempt to integrate knowledge from general-purpose Web resources in a KG without, however, paying much attention to the validity of the information extracted from such resources. Moreover, they rely on the rather simplistic assumption that if two nodes are connected via any edge, then the two nodes are semantically related. We, on the other hand, try to iron out the noise or erroneous information that might exist in such Web resources before adding new knowledge to a KG.

The representation, as well as identification, of object-action relations has been the focus of interest of many studies in the field of cognitive robotics. In the projects KnowRob [11] and RoboSherlock [12], semantic correlation of physical entities is indeed captured, yet object-action relations are either learned exclusively through observed data, or captured in a problem-specific way. In [13], the authors integrate knowledge from ConceptNet in a KG. Given an object or action label, the authors construct subgraphs of ConceptNet with only two properties, in order to train a data-driven model, which can predict if an object is related with an action. Similar approaches are also used in RoboCSE [14], which uses embeddings to represent object and action labels and infer object-action relations based on the similarity of their vectors. Our proposed method exploits both semantically relevant and commonsense information captured in general-purpose repositories, which can complement and enrich the outcomes of the aforementioned studies.

The study of Zhou et al. [15] is more closely related to ours. The authors train a Long Short-Term Memory (LSTM) to predict the path between two nodes of the ConceptNet graph. They collect, for a set of node pairs, the most quality paths, defining quality as the most natural set of edges that connects two given nodes. For instance, the path *Lead* $\xrightarrow{\text{HasProperty}}$ *Toxic* $\xleftrightarrow{\text{RelatedTo}}$ *Lethal* $\xleftrightarrow{\text{RelatedTo}}$ *Poison* is considered the most natural among those connecting *Lead* and *Poison*. The quality of paths is annotated manually by a group of volunteers. Similarly, in [16,17] a data-driven model predicts a path between two nodes of ConceptNet; the quality of a path is hand-coded by the authors. Our method, on the other hand, aims to determine the importance of a path through training, rather than through manual annotation. This has two benefits: it takes into account, to a larger extent, the structural and semantic characteristics of the underlying KG and it is more adaptive to changes in the KG or the application domain.

3. Methodology

In this section, we formulate the problem and describe the different methods we evaluated. We classify the methods based on the information they utilize into *Topology-based*, *Semantics-based* and *Embeddings-based*. Topology-based methods exploit the structure of the graph, while semantics-based methods also take into account the types of relations connecting the two nodes. Embeddings-based methods use vector representations of graphs, potentially taking into account the structure of the graph, as well as the semantics of the node labels. Our novel **Relation Pattern Method** is part of the semantics-based methods.

3.1. Problem Formulation

The problem we aim to solve is the following. Given a directed knowledge graph $G = (E, R)$, where E is the set of nodes, corresponding to entities, and R is set of edges, corresponding to relations, and a pair of nodes (e_1, e_2) with $e_1, e_2 \in E$, where e_1 represents an action and e_2 an object (E may contain other types of nodes as well), find whether e_1 and e_2 are related. We consider the two nodes, e_1 and e_2, as related if the following question yields a positive answer: *"Can the action e_1 be performed by/on the object e_2?"*. For instance, the question *"Can the action Fold be performed by the object Knife?"* should yield a negative answer.

Before presenting the methods we evaluated to solve the aforementioned problem, we first describe how we can create the graph G from a given set of labels L that refer to real-world objects or actions. We extract the object and action labels from the Something-Something Dataset[4], a dataset that is commonly used by the Machine Vision community (see Section 4.1 for more details). Note, however, that any set of object and action labels can be used to create G. For every label $l_i \in L$, we generate a graph S_i, by appending information relevant to l_i from ConceptNet [1] and WordNet [2] in two steps. Then, we construct G by unifying all $|L|$ graphs $S_1, \ldots, S_{|L|}$, i.e., every graph S_i is a subgraph of G.

Step 1: For each object or action label, we search for a node with the same lemmatized label in the ConceptNet knowledge graph and extract a subgraph containing a subset of the properties found in ConceptNet that are considered relevant to the domain of interest. The subgraphs contain 2-hop paths from the object or action label. The edge types we consider are:

$$[RelatedTo, UsedFor, LocatedAt, FormOf, IsA, PartOf,$$
$$HasA, CapableOf, AtLocation, HasProperty, CreatedBy,$$
$$Synonym, LocatedNear, SimilarTo, MadeOf, ReceivesAction,$$
$$Causes, HasSubevent, HasFirstSubevent, HasLastSubevent,$$
$$HasPrerequisite, Antonym, DefinedAs, MannerOf, SimilarTo,$$
$$HasContext, EtymologicallyRelatedTo, EtymologicallyDerivedFrom,$$
$$DistinctFrom, DerivedFrom, SymbolOf]$$

We omit only 3 relations from ConceptNet[5]: *Causes* and *Desires*, which, although seemingly relevant, their use is human centric and they describe the sentiments that are caused to humans after an event, and *ExternalURL*, in order not to append information from other external resources, except WordNet.

Step 2: The next step is to insert context knowledge into the subgraph. We retrieve knowledge from WordNet by looking at the super-classes of each node in the subgraph created in **Step 1**, and if any super-class of a node falls into a domain-specific category of super-classes, then we keep the node in the graph, otherwise we delete it. The super-classes we consider are:

---

[4]https://20bn.com/datasets/something-something
[5]https://github.com/commonsense/conceptnet5/wiki/Relations

$$[abstraction, physical\_entity, thing, attribute, communication,$$

$$group, measure, otherworld, set, causal\_agent,$$

$$matter, object, process, substance, change]$$

We consider this specific set of classes following the findings of [18], which showed that almost all nodes in the WordNet graph that refer to a real-world object or action have at least one of these as a super-class. This pruning of nodes based on WordNet super-classes can give domain-specific concepts, e.g., when interested in household appliances. Figure 1 shows part of the subgraph for the label *Knife*. We highlight in red the node that is pruned in **Step 2**.

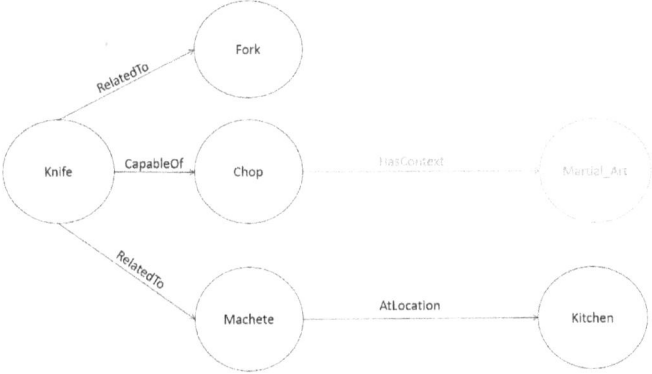

Figure 1. Part of the subgraph for the label *Knife*. The red node is pruned in **Step 2**.

After creating a graph for each object and action label, as described in **Steps 1** and **2**, we end up with a set of graphs $\{S_1, \ldots, S_n\}$, such that $S_i = (E_i, R_i)$ for $i = 1, \ldots, n$, where E_i is the set of nodes and R_i the set of edges in S_i. Thus, the final graph is defined as $G = (E, R)$, where $E = \bigcup_{i=1}^{n} E_i$, and $R = \bigcup_{i=1}^{n} R_i$.

3.2. Topology-based Methods

We apply the two most commonly used methods proposed in the relevant literature [10,9] that exploit the topology of a graph, in order to infer the extent to which two nodes are related.

The *Connecting Paths Method* takes into consideration each sequence of edges that begins from the object node and reaches the action node after a finite number of steps, or vice versa. The authors omit paths that contain loops, but do not take into account the type of edges a path contains. Given two subgraphs S_1 and S_2, as described in Section 3.1, corresponding to an object node and an action node respectively, the *connectPath* metric for S_1 and S_2 is defined as

$$connectPath(S_1, S_2) = \frac{|C_1 \cup C_2|}{|P_1 \cup P_2|} \tag{1}$$

where C_1 is the set of paths that start from the object node and reach the action node, C_2 is the set of paths that start from the action node and reach the object node, P_1 is the set of all paths that start from the object node, and P_2 the set of all paths that start from the action node. Since $(C_1 \cup C_2) \subseteq (P_1 \cup P_2)$, it follows that $0 \leq connectPath \leq 1$.

Example 1 *Let S_{knife} be the subgraph for the object node* knife *and S_{fold} be the subgraph for the action node* fold *and let S_{knife} have two paths that start from the node* knife, *namely* Knife $\xrightarrow{UsedFor}$ Butter *and* Knife $\xrightarrow{LocatedAt}$ Kitchen, *and S_{fold} have only one path,* Fold $\xrightarrow{HasContext}$ Cooking $\xleftarrow{UsedFor}$ Butter. *Then, the connectPath metric will return*

$$connectPath(S_{knife}, S_{fold}) = \frac{|C_{knife} \cup C_{fold}|}{|P_{knife} \cup P_{fold}|} = \frac{1+1}{2+1} = 0.666$$

Some recent studies that apply this method, as is or with small variations, are [16,4, 5,15]. In fact, they also focus on inferring object-action relations ([16,5]) and on object identification ([4,15]).

The *Common Nodes Method* divides the number of common nodes by the number of total nodes in two given graphs. Two nodes are considered common when they refer to the same entity in ConceptNet, i.e., the nodes have the same label. Duplicate nodes are cleared, allowing only one occurrence of each node. The commonNodes metric between two subgraphs S_1 and S_2 is defined as

$$commonNodes(S_1, S_2) = \frac{|E_1 \cap E_2|}{|E_1 \cup E_2|} \tag{2}$$

where E_i is the set of nodes in S_i. Essentially, the commonNodes metric between two graphs is the Jaccard similarity of the sets of nodes in these graphs. Example 2 shows how the commonNodes metric works.

Example 2 *Let S_{knife} and S_{fold} be the subgraphs from Example 1, for the nodes* knife *and* fold, *respectively. These two subgraphs have one common node,* Butter, *and 5 distinct nodes in total.*

$$commonNodes(S_{knife}, S_{fold}) = \frac{|E_{knife} \cap E_{fold}|}{|E_{knife} \cup E_{fold}|} =$$

$$\frac{|\{Knife, Butter, Kitchen\} \cap \{Fold, Cooking, Butter\}|}{|\{Knife, Butter, Kitchen\} \cup \{Fold, Cooking, Butter\}|} = \frac{1}{5} = 0.2$$

where E_{knife} is the set of nodes in the S_{knife} subgraph, and E_{fold} is the set of nodes in the S_{fold} subgraph. Recent studies that apply this method, as is or with small variations, are [4,19,20]. The focus is on object identification and on finding the similarity of two nodes in a knowledge graph.

3.3. Semantics-based Methods

As a semantics-based method, we consider the very popular WUP similarity, and we also present a novel **Related Pattern Method**, which exploits the pattern of connections in a KG to infer whether two nodes are semantically related.

The *Wu Palmer Similarity* (WUP) uses the acyclic graph of WordNet to calculate relatedness by considering the depth of two nodes in the WordNet taxonomies, along with the depth of their LCS (Least Common Subsumer). Given two nodes from the WordNet acyclic graph, the LCS of these nodes is their most specific common ancestor. The score can never be zero because the depth of the LCS is never zero (the depth of the root of the taxonomy is one). This metric calculates the similarity based on how close the nodes are to each other in the WordNet acyclic graph. The WUP similarity between an object node (n_o) and an action node (n_a) is defined as

$$WUP(n_o, n_a) = 2 * \frac{depth(LCS(n_o, n_a))}{depth(n_o) + depth(n_a)}, \tag{3}$$

where $depth(\cdot)$ is the depth of an entity in the WordNet graph.

Example 3 *The WUP similarity for the object* knife *and the action* fold *is*

$$WUP(knife, fold) = 2 * \frac{depth(LCS(knife, fold))}{depth(knife) + depth(fold)}$$

$$= 2 * \frac{depth(physical\_entity)}{depth(knife) + depth(fold)} = 2 * \frac{2}{12 + 6} = 0.222$$

Many studies use the WUP similarity in a wide spectrum of domains. Recent studies, such as [5,18], use WUP scores to infer object-action relations and object identification.

Our proposed method, the **Relation Pattern Method**, is based on the assumption that some of the paths connecting two nodes carry more semantically relevant information than others. For instance, the path *object node* $\xleftrightarrow{\text{Synonym}}$ *node0* $\xleftrightarrow{\text{ReceivesAction}}$ *action node* may appear more often in object-action pairs compared to paths composed of other relations. To verify this assumption, we selected a domain-specific subset

$$[RelatedTo, UsedFor, ReceivesAction, CapableOf, Synonym]$$

of the ConceptNet relations that we considered more relevant to the problem at hand; yet, this subset can change according to the context of the problem. An important aspect of our proposed method is the flexibility in deciding how to deal with the noise that exists in the data.

A *relation pattern* is any connecting path that is composed of at least one of the aforementioned relations, except from paths that only contain the relation *Synonym*. The latter are omitted, to avoid connecting an object and an action node having similar labels. In the end, 155 different relation patterns were produced; whenever a relation pattern is found between an object and an action node in the KG, we consider it as an indication that the two nodes are associated. If $\mathscr{P} = \{pattern_1, \ldots, pattern_{155}\}$ is the set of all relation patterns, then, for each $pattern_i \in \mathscr{P}$, the goal is to assign a weight of importance $W_{pattern_i}$, in order to specify how confident we are that the given pattern produces correct associations. For instance, in the next section, we assign the weights based on how well each pattern performs in our training data. Of course, other heuristics can be used instead.

Since it is reasonable to consider more than one patterns before reaching a conclusion about the relation between two labels, one can group together patterns, based on their performance, their domain-specific relevance, or other criteria. For quantifying the performance of a cluster W_C, one can consider, for instance, the weighted sum of the weights of each individual pattern, the max or min of these weights, or other heuristics-based metrics. In our evaluation, we adopt an even simpler approach as the baseline case, namely to treat all patterns with weight above a given threshold as equally relevant.

3.4. Embeddings-based Methods

Recently, there has been a surge of interest in the field of KG embeddings for the task of link prediction [21]. Studies following this methodology represent nodes of a KG as vectors in a latent space, which are generated by taking into account both the textual and structural features of those nodes. The textual features are considered by acquiring the word and sentence embeddings of node labels, from word embeddings that have been pre-trained on large document corpora, such as Wikipedia. The structural features consider, typically in an iterative way, the node embeddings of each node's neighbors in a KG.

For example, *AllenAI-CommonSense* [22], which constitutes the state of the art for link prediction in ConceptNet, employs a pre-trained BERT [23] model that is fine-tuned on ConceptNet, using Graph Convolutional Networks (GCN) [24] for embedding the ConceptNet graph. This model returns a list of possible relations between a given pair of ConceptNet nodes, ranked in descending order of likelihood (aka confidence score).

We can use the results of this system in two different ways for our purposes: a) we can either consider the confidence score returned by AllenAI-CommonSense for a specific relation (e.g., ReceivesAction), given two query nodes from our graph *G*, or b) we can consider that the answer to the problem formulated in Section 3.1 is positive for two query nodes, when the relation "ReceivesAction" is within the top answers for those query nodes.

4. Evaluation

In this section, we first describe how we created the ground truth from the Something-Something Dataset[6] and then we discuss the experimental setup and the results that each method achieved.

4.1. Data Collection

Rather than using a random set of action and object labels, aiming to achieve an adequate coverage of entities for the household domain, we decided to extract the set of labels for our evaluation from the Something-Something Dataset. Something-Something consists of a large collection of short video clips (more than 220k) containing actions performed on and with common household objects. The actions involve either one type of object (e.g., opening a bottle) or two distinct types of objects (e.g., putting coins inside a box). Due to its vast number of sample videos, the Something-Something Dataset has become a de-facto benchmark for the assessment of systems addressing the task of action recog-

---

[6]https://20bn.com/datasets/something-something

nition. The dataset provides for each clip a small description that contains action and object(s) labels.

Ground Truth Creation: From Something-Something we initially extracted 247 object labels and 35 action labels, which produced 8,645 object-action pairs. We replaced all object labels in plural form with their singular form, for example *notes* was replaced with *note*. Then, we removed certain object and action labels that we did not consider context related[7]. Next, for the remaining action and object labels, we issued a query to the ConceptNet KG using the ConceptNet Web API[8], in order to identify which labels are indeed part of the graph. We ended up with 148 object labels and 25 action labels. Since some actions have the same label with some objects (3 in total), we renamed these labels as follows: (a) pile → *pileO* and pile → *vpile*, (b) stack → *stackO* and stack → *vstack*, and (c) cover → *coverO* and cover → *vcover*, to refer to the object and action label, respectively.

Eventually, 3,700 object-action relations were kept in total. Those pairs that existed in the description of at least one video in the Something-Something Dataset were automatically characterized as positive pairs. The remaining were manually annotated, in order to determine if they are negative or if they are positive but it so happens that no clip in the dataset refered to them. At the end, 1,965 positive and 1,735 negative object-action relations were produced, forming our ground truth[9].

4.2. Experimental Setup

The evaluation of the methods described in Section 3 was performed using 10-fold cross validation over the 3,700 positive and negative relations described in Section 4.1. We used Sklearn[10] to split our data into 10 folds. Each fold contained 370 relations, 52% of which were positive and 48% negative, which reflects the distribution of the relations in the original dataset.

Each iteration of the 10-fold cross-validation process was used, in order to train the different models. Specifically, for the *Connecting Path Method*, the *WUP*, and the *Common Node Method*, the training folds helped specify the optimal threshold for each method that maximizes the F1 score. For the *Relation Pattern Method*, the training phase helped compute the weights of importance $W_{pattern_i}$ of each relation pattern $pattern_i \in \mathscr{P}$, as described in Section 3.3. During testing, we measured the performance of each method with the given thresholds and weights. Patterns that performed poorly during training were omitted completely.

We characterize the results as True Positive (TP), False Positive (FP), True Negative (TN), and False Negative (FN) according to the following definitions:

- TP is when a pair of object-action nodes (n_o, n_a) is related in the ground truth and also achieves a score above the threshold (for the threshold-based methods) or the pattern under consideration connects node n_o with n_a (for the pattern-based methods)

---

[7]The reader can find all the labels that were removed or replaced in our documentation: `https://github.com/valexande/Semantics-2021`

[8]`https://pypi.org/project/ConceptNet/`

[9]The dataset of positive and negative object action relations can be found in our documentation: `https://github.com/valexande/Semantics-2021`

[10]`https://scikit-learn.org/stable/modules/cross\_validation.html`

- FP is when a pair of object-action nodes (n_o, n_a) is not related in the ground truth, but achieves a score above the threshold (for the threshold-based methods) or the pattern under consideration connects node n_o with n_a (for the pattern-based methods)
- TN is when a pair of object-action nodes (n_o, n_a) is not related in the ground truth and also achieves a score below the threshold (for the threshold-based methods) or the pattern under consideration does not connect node n_o with n_a (for the pattern-based methods)
- FN is when a pair of object-action nodes (n_o, n_a) is related in the ground truth, but achieves a score below the threshold (for the threshold-based methods) or the pattern under consideration does not connect node n_o with n_a (for the pattern-based methods)

Finally, note that we define the weight of importance $W_{pattern_i}$ for *pattern$_i$* as the harmonic mean between precision P and recall R (Equation 4).

$$W_{pattern_i} = 2 * \frac{P * R}{P + R} \tag{4}$$

Example 4 *Consider the relation pattern* $\left(\xrightarrow{RelatedTo}, \xrightarrow{UsedFor} \right)$ *and the set of subgraphs* $\{S_{knife}, S_{cut}, S_{stab}, S_{fold}\}$, *which represent the nodes* knife, cut, stab, *and* fold, *respectively. For this example, let the knowledge graph G be composed only from the subgraphs* $\{S_{knife}, S_{cut}, S_{stab}, S_{fold}\}$. *The* knife *is related with* cut *and* stab, *but not with* fold, *according to the ground truth. For each such pair of object-action nodes, we search for a relation path* $\left(\xrightarrow{RelatedTo}, \xrightarrow{UsedFor} \right)$ *connecting the two nodes (see Section 3.2). Using this information, we get the following scores.*

$$P = \frac{TP}{TP + FP} = \frac{2}{2+1} = 0.666 \text{ and } R = \frac{TP}{TP + FN} = \frac{2}{2+0} = 1$$

$$W_{pattern \left(\xrightarrow{RelatedTo}, \xrightarrow{UsedFor} \right)} = \frac{4}{5} = 0.8$$

TP is 2 because the pairs knife-cut and knife-stab are related in the ground truth and the relation path $\left(\xrightarrow{RelatedTo}, \xrightarrow{UsedFor} \right)$ is a connecting path in both. FP is 1 because the pair knife-fold are not related in the ground truth and the relation path $\left(\xrightarrow{RelatedTo}, \xrightarrow{UsedFor} \right)$ is a connecting path. FN is 0 because we do not have a pair that is related in our ground truth and does not not have $\left(\xrightarrow{RelatedTo}, \xrightarrow{UsedFor} \right)$ as a connecting path. The final score of Example 4 shows that the weight of importance $W_{pattern \left(\xrightarrow{RelatedTo}, \xrightarrow{UsedFor} \right)}$ can predict 80% of the positive and negative object action relations. In other words, it shows the proportion of object-action pairs that can be classified correctly (i.e., related or not related), by this relation pattern.

Additionally, we evaluated the embeddings-based method AllenAI-Common Sense (top-k) over all ground truth object-action pairs, both positive and negative, by testing whether the relation "ReceivesAction" was within the top-k results for each pair, for $k \in \{1,3,5\}$. If "ReceivesAction" is within the top-k results, we consider this as a predicted positive pair, otherwise, a predicted negative, and follow the same conventions (TP, FP, TN, FN) as described above.

We note that another variation of this approach would have been to restrict the predicted results to those having a confidence score above a predefined threshold. However, our experiments showed that this method performs best when such minimum confidence threshold is 0 (confidence scores are extremely low in too many cases), so we do not report numbers for this variation.

4.3. Results

Table 1 summarizes the overall performance measures for each method. Although the differences among the first three popular approaches are small, the WUP similarity seems to achieve higher scores both in terms of accuracy (.555) and of F1 score (.696). We also see that there are patterns that achieve similar or better scores in the one or the other measure, but not in both (the weight of importance coincides with the F1 score). Due to the plurality of relation patterns, we display only the Top-20 relation patterns. The AllenAI-CommonSense (top-k) methods, despite their high accuracy, underperform in F1 scores, compared to the other methods. This is due to a considerable difference noticed in the accuracy for positive pairs (.19) with respect to that for negative pairs (.854).

An investigation of the figures for the Relation Pattern method reveals some interesting insights, not easily detectable with the other methods. First of all, we can see that at least one occurrence of the relation *RelatedTo* exists in almost all relation patterns. This is because, although not explicitly stated in the ConceptNet documentation[11], *RelatedTo* plays the role of a super-property, i.e., it subsumes the other relations. While one would expect that less abstract relations among nodes, such as *UsedFor*, would produce better results, this is not the case. This conclusion reflects, to some extent, the quality of data in ConceptNet and provides hints as to where there exists room for data cleaning.

We also observe that certain longer paths, such as $\left(\xleftarrow{\text{RelatedTo}}, \xleftarrow{\text{RelatedTo}}, \xleftarrow{\text{RelatedTo}}, \xleftarrow{\text{RelatedTo}} \right)$, achieve better performance than shorter paths involving the same type of relations, e.g., $\left(\xleftarrow{\text{RelatedTo}}, \xleftarrow{\text{RelatedTo}} \right)$. This might seem odd at first, as one would expect that the closer two nodes are in the graph, the more semantically tightly related they would be. This finding is probably owed to the nature of our problem. In contrast to entity resolution for instance, the nodes whose association we try to find are of different type, namely object and action.

Of course, such similar paths obtain practical meaning if considered as a group, rather than as individuals. For this reason, Table 1 also reports indicatively the performance of two clusters of patterns, one that is composed only of *RelatedTo* and *Synonym* relations, and one composed of *UsedFor* and *Synonym* relations. We adopt a simplistic approach in deciding what the answer of a cluster is: any pattern above a threshold is considered relevant. As such, even if a single pattern is found in the graph, the corresponding object-action pair is considered related. As we only wish to measure a baseline

---

[11]https://github.com/commonsense/conceptnet5/wiki/Relations

Table 1. Overall scores.

Method	Accuracy	Recall	Precision	F1 Score
Connecting Path	0.534	0.752	0.552	0.625
WUP	0.555	0.951	0.551	0.696
Common Node	0.551	0.956	0.548	0.695
AllenAI-Commonsense (top-1)	0.502	0.191	0.596	0.289
AllenAI-Commonsense (top-3)	0.582	0.599	0.608	0.603
AllenAI-Commonsense (top-5)	**0.596**	0.748	0.595	0.663

Relation Pattern	Accuracy	Recall	Precision	F1 Score ($W_{pattern}$)
→RelatedTo →RelatedTo →RelatedTo →RelatedTo	0.551	0.964	0.548	0.697
→RelatedTo →RelatedTo	0.539	0.985	0.536	0.695
→RelatedTo →Synonym	0.558	0.906	0.557	0.688
→RelatedTo →RelatedTo →RelatedTo	0.561	0.891	0.56	0.686
→RelatedTo →RelatedTo →RelatedTo →Synonym	0.561	0.835	0.564	0.67
→RelatedTo →Synonym →RelatedTo →RelatedTo	0.552	0.84	0.556	0.667
→Synonym →RelatedTo	0.528	0.611	0.556	0.579
→Synonym →RelatedTo →RelatedTo →RelatedTo	0.517	0.642	0.532	0.567
→RelatedTo →Synonym →RelatedTo →RelatedTo	0.525	0.543	0.561	0.549
→RelatedTo →Synonym →RelatedTo →Synonym	0.537	0.497	0.58	0.531
→UsedFor →UsedFor	0.528	0.484	0.569	0.521
→Synonym →Synonym →RelatedTo →RelatedTo	0.488	0.338	0.606	0.394
→RelatedTo →Synonym →RelatedTo	0.509	0.275	0.593	0.37
→Synonym →RelatedTo →RelatedTo	0.518	0.28	0.612	0.361
→RelatedTo →RelatedTo →Synonym	0.518	0.253	0.584	0.346
→Synonym →RelatedTo →UsedFor →RelatedTo	0.507	0.228	0.595	0.315
→Synonym →RelatedTo →RelatedTo →Synonym	0.509	0.213	0.588	0.301
→RelatedTo →Synonym →UsedFor →RelatedTo	0.488	0.192	0.575	0.283
→RelatedTo →RelatedTo →Synonym →Synonym	0.487	0.176	0.567	0.264
→Synonym →RelatedTo →Synonym →RelatedTo	0.494	0.162	**0.613**	0.248

Cluster Relation Pattern	Accuracy	Recall	Precision	F1 Score (W_C)
RelatedTo-Synonym	0.539	**0.985**	0.546	**0.702**
UsedFor-Synonym	0.582	0.636	0.569	0.597

case, we set a rather generous threshold for including patterns in the cluster, namely any pattern with weight above 0.1.

More elaborate methods can of course be implemented, e.g., by taking into consideration the weight of importance among the patterns of each cluster or by utilizing domain-specific criteria. Yet, even with this baseline, we notice that clustering paths can produce improved state-of-the-art F1 scores (.702). By ignoring the relative importance of each individual pattern though, we end up introducing noise, as shown in the precision scores if compared to the best performing patterns, an aspect that a more advanced method could eliminate.

Overall, probably the most important advantage of our proposed method, beyond its prominent performance, is the flexibility in deciding how to deal with noise in the data. By carefully choosing which patterns to trust, one can decide where to focus when importing new data. Such an adaptive behavior is not offered by the other methods, such as data-driven models, which are more vulnerable to noisy data, due to the domain-agnostic way of treating the KG.

5. Conclusion

In this paper, we present a novel method for extracting and evaluating relations between objects and actions from KGs, such as ConceptNet and WordNet. We compared our method with popular approaches proposed in relevant literature, such as methods that exploit the topology or the semantic information in a KG, and embeddings. Our method can improve state-of-the art performance in terms of F1 scores. But its most important advantage, beyond its very good performance, is the flexibility in finding and adapting to the noise in the data. In the future, we plan to integrate knowledge from other commonsense knowledge graphs, such as ATOMIC [25,26], and to evaluate our methods on other types of relations, such as those between an object and a state, and causal relations (i.e., in which states can the object be before and after we perform an action on it).

References

[1] Robyn Speer, Joshua Chin, and Catherine Havasi. Conceptnet 5.5: An open multilingual graph of general knowledge. In *AAAI*, pages 4444–4451, 2017.
[2] Christiane Fellbaum. Wordnet: An electronic lexical database and some of its applications, 1998.
[3] Paola Ardón, Èric Pairet, Katrin Lohan, Subramanian Ramamoorthy, and Ronald Petrick. Building affordance relations for robotic agents - a survey. In *30th International Joint Conference on Artificial Intelligence (IJCAI-21)*, 2021.
[4] Rodrigo Toro Icarte, Jorge A. Baier, Cristian Ruz, and Alvaro Soto. How a general-purpose common-sense ontology can improve performance of learning-based image retrieval. In *IJCAI*, pages 1283–1289, 2017.
[5] Chung-Wei Lee, Wei Fang, Chih-Kuan Yeh, and Yu-Chiang Frank Wang. Multi-label zero-shot learning with structured knowledge graphs. In *CVPR*, pages 1576–1585, 2018.
[6] Sonia Chernova, Vivian Chu, Angel Daruna, Haley Garrison, Meera Hahn, Priyanka Khante, Weiyu Liu, and Andrea Thomaz. Situated bayesian reasoning framework for robots operating in diverse everyday environments. In *ISRR*, 2017.
[7] Jay Young, Valerio Basile, Lars Kunze, Elena Cabrio, and Nick Hawes. Towards lifelong object learning by integrating situated robot perception and semantic web mining. In *ECAI*, pages 1458–1466, 2016.
[8] Jay Young, Valerio Basile, Markus Suchi, Lars Kunze, Nick Hawes, Markus Vincze, and Barbara Caputo. Making sense of indoor spaces using semantic web mining and situated robot perception. In *ESWC*, pages 299–313, 2017.
[9] Ganggao Zhu and Carlos Angel Iglesias. Computing semantic similarity of concepts in knowledge graphs. *IEEE Trans. Knowl. Data Eng.*, 29(1):72–85, 2017.
[10] Ganggao Zhu and Carlos A Iglesias. Exploiting semantic similarity for named entity disambiguation in knowledge graphs. *Expert Systems with Applications*, 101:8–24, 2018.
[11] Michael Beetz, Daniel Beßler, Andrei Haidu, Mihai Pomarlan, Asil Kaan Bozcuoglu, and Georg Bartels. Know rob 2.0 - A 2nd generation knowledge processing framework for cognition-enabled robotic agents. In *ICRA*, pages 512–519, 2018.
[12] Michael Beetz, Ferenc Bálint-Benczédi, Nico Blodow, Daniel Nyga, Thiemo Wiedemeyer, and Zoltán-Csaba Marton. Robosherlock: Unstructured information processing for robot perception. In *ICRA*, pages 1549–1556, 2015.

[13] Keerthiram Murugesan, Mattia Atzeni, Pushkar Shukla, Mrinmaya Sachan, Pavan Kapanipathi, and Kartik Talamadupula. Enhancing text-based reinforcement learning agents with commonsense knowledge. *CoRR*, abs/2005.00811, 2020.

[14] Angel Andres Daruna, Weiyu Liu, Zsolt Kira, and Sonia Chernova. Robocse: Robot common sense embedding. In *ICRA*, pages 9777–9783, 2019.

[15] Yilun Zhou, Steven Schockaert, and Julie Shah. Predicting conceptnet path quality using crowdsourced assessments of naturalness. In *WWW*, pages 2460–2471, 2019.

[16] Matt Gardner, Partha Pratim Talukdar, Jayant Krishnamurthy, and Tom M. Mitchell. Incorporating vector space similarity in random walk inference over knowledge bases. In *EMNLP*, pages 397–406, 2014.

[17] Yankai Lin, Zhiyuan Liu, Huan-Bo Luan, Maosong Sun, Siwei Rao, and Song Liu. Modeling relation paths for representation learning of knowledge bases. In *EMNLP*, pages 705–714, 2015.

[18] Alexandros Vassiliades, Nick Bassiliades, Filippos Gouidis, and Theodore Patkos. A knowledge retrieval framework for household objects and actions with external knowledge. In *SEMANTiCS*, volume 12378 of *Lecture Notes in Computer Science*, pages 36–52, 2020.

[19] Chuanming Yu, Xiaoli Zhao, Lu An, and Xia Lin. Similarity-based link prediction in social networks: A path and node combined approach. *Journal of Information Science*, 43(5):683–695, 2017.

[20] Palash Dey and Sourav Medya. Manipulating node similarity measures in networks. In *AAMAS*, pages 321–329, 2020.

[21] Andrea Rossi, Donatella Firmani, Antonio Matinata, Paolo Merialdo, and Denilson Barbosa. Knowledge graph embedding for link prediction: A comparative analysis. *CoRR*, abs/2002.00819, 2020.

[22] Chaitanya Malaviya, Chandra Bhagavatula, Antoine Bosselut, and Yejin Choi. Commonsense knowledge base completion with structural and semantic context. In *AAAI*, pages 2925–2933, 2020.

[23] Jacob Devlin, Ming-Wei Chang, Kenton Lee, and Kristina Toutanova. BERT: pre-training of deep bidirectional transformers for language understanding. In *NAACL-HLT*, pages 4171–4186, 2019.

[24] Thomas N. Kipf and Max Welling. Semi-supervised classification with graph convolutional networks. In *ICLR*, 2017.

[25] Maarten Sap, Ronan Le Bras, Emily Allaway, Chandra Bhagavatula, Nicholas Lourie, Hannah Rashkin, Brendan Roof, Noah A. Smith, and Yejin Choi. ATOMIC: an atlas of machine commonsense for if-then reasoning. In *AAAI*, pages 3027–3035, 2019.

[26] Antoine Bosselut, Hannah Rashkin, Maarten Sap, Chaitanya Malaviya, Asli Celikyilmaz, and Yejin Choi. COMET: commonsense transformers for automatic knowledge graph construction. In *ACL*, pages 4762–4779, 2019.

Further with Knowledge Graphs. M. Alam et al. (Eds.)
AKA Verlag and IOS Press, 2021
© *2021 Akademische Verlagsgesellschaft AKA GmbH, Berlin*
This article is published online with Open Access by IOS Press and distributed under the terms
of the Creative Commons Attribution License 4.0 (CC BY 4.0).
doi:10.3233/SSW210049

Members of Parliament in Finland Knowledge Graph and Its Linked Open Data Service

Petri Leskinen[1][0000−0003−2327−6942], Eero Hyvönen[1,2][0000−0003−1695−5840], and Jouni Tuominen[1,2][0000−0003−4789−5676]

[1] Semantic Computing Research Group (SeCo), Aalto University, Finland
[2] HELDIG – Helsinki Centre for Digital Humanities, University of Helsinki, Finland
http://seco.cs.aalto.fi, http://heldig.fi, firstname.lastname@aalto.fi

Abstract. This paper presents a prosopographical knowledge graph describing the Members of Parliament in Finland and related actors in politics, extracted from the databases and textual descriptions of the Parliament of Finland. The data has been interlinked internally and enriched with data linking to external data sources according to the 5-star Linked Data model. The data has been published together with its schema for better re-usability and is validated using ShEx. The knowledge graph presented is integrated with another knowledge graph about over 900 000 parliamentary plenary speeches in Finland (1907–) to form a larger parliamentary LOD publication *FinnParla* of the Parliament of Finland. The data is being used for Digital Humanities research on parliamentary networks, culture, and language.

Keywords: Parliamentary data · Biographies · Linked Data · Digital Humanities · Entity linking

1 Introduction

A key idea of Linked Data [1] is to enrich datasets by integrating complementary local information sources in an interoperable way into global knowledge graphs [2] to be used in applications. This involves harmonization of the local data models used, as well as aligning the concepts and entities (resources) used in populating the local data models.

This paper reports first results of the Semantic Parliament (SEMPARL)[3] project that produces a Linked Open Data (LOD) and research infrastructure for Finnish parliamentary data, and develops novel semantic computing technologies and applications to study parliamentary political culture and language. The project is related to various similar efforts in other countries [3,4,5] and in EU [6]; parliamentary open data is an important asset for rendering political decision making transparent, and such data is widely used for research on political language and culture.

SEMPARL aims at three major contributions:

---

[3] https://seco.cs.aalto.fi/projects/semparl/en/

1. The project responds to the demand for an easy to use and "intelligent" access to the newly digitized Finnish parliamentary data by providing the data as a national Linked Open Data (LOD) infrastructure and service for researchers, citizens, government, media, and application developers.
2. The project studies long-term changes in the Finnish parliamentary and political culture and language. These use cases are pioneering studies using the Finnish digital parliamentary data.
3. The new LOD service enriches semantically content in other related Finnish LOD services, such as LawSampo for Finnish legislation and case law [7] and BiographySampo [8] for prosopographical data.

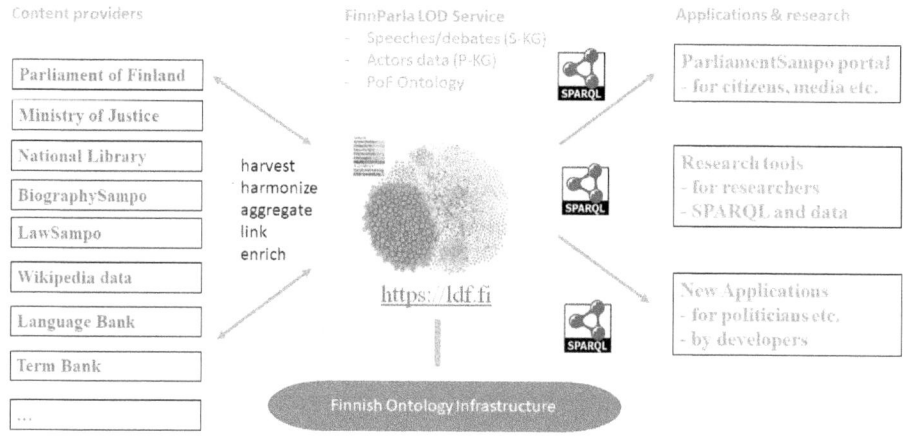

Fig. 1. Publishing model for Finnish parliamentary data in the SEMPARL project

The foundation of this work are two interlinked knowledge graphs (KG):

1. *S-KG* is a knowledge graph of all parliamentary debate speeches of Parliament of Finland (PoF) from 1907 to present time [9].
2. *P-KG* is a prosopographical knowledge graph of the Members of Parliament (MP), related other people, groups, and organizations, i.e., actors, pertaining to the parliamentary activities during the same period of time.

The two KGs are published as a LOD service called *FinnParla* about Parliament of Finland (PoF), based on an overarching ontology of PoF and the Finnish ontology infrastructure FinnONTO [10]. Fig. 1 illustrates the publishing model of SEMPARL. On the left, various content providing organizations and services are listed whose contents are transformed into, or linked with, the FinnParla LOD service in the middle. The data is used via SPARQL in research tasks and in developing applications on the right. These include the ParliamentSampo portal under development. The main data provider is PoF but also legislative data from related sources are planned to be linked to FinnParla, such as the LawSampo data [7] from the Ministry of Justice. From the National Library, ontologies served at the Finto.fi[4] service are re-used and well as bibliographical data[5]. The Language Bank of Finland[6] contains, e.g., lots of videos of the debates, and The Helsinki Term Bank for the Arts and Sciences[7] terminological definitions pertaining to legislation and politics. The BiographySampo system contains 763 biographies of MPs as linked data as part of over 13 100 national biographies of the Finnish Literature Society. Wikipedia/Wikidata is used in various ways for enriching the FinnParla data. Possibly also media content from the Finnish Broadcasting Company Yle will be used in the project later on.

This paper introduces the prosopographical knowledge graph P-KG and addresses the following more general research question:

> *How to represent and publish prosopographical data about parliamentary actors and their activities so that the data can be used easily for Digital Humanities research?*

As an answer, the modeling principles of P-KG are presented and its transformation and publication processes are explained. It is also shown as a proof-of-concept how the LOD service can be used for Digital Humanities [11,12] research.

In the following, we first describe the original open XML data of PoF to be transformed into Linked Data. After this the RDF data model for representing parliamentary actors and their activities, as well as the transformation process are described. The produced linked data has been published as a data service using the 7-star model [13] of the Linked Data Finland platform. As a demonstration of using the data service in research, data analyses are presented. In conclusion, contributions of the work are summarized, related works are discussed, and directions for further research are outlined.

2   Parliament of Finland Actor Data

The main data source used for the P-KG is the Members of Finnish Parliament data publication available at the Parliament Open Data portal[8]. This data is regularly updated, and contains at this moment information about 2605 Members of Parliament (MP) since 1907. The person data entries are in XML format which is available in Finnish and Swedish for all the members, and in English for 202 cases.

An extract from the XML data is shown in Fig. 2. All the tags are in Finnish, and in the English version only the content is in English. A person data entry

---

[4] http://finto.fi/en/
[5] http://data.nationallibrary.fi
[6] https://www.kielipankki.fi/language-bank/
[7] https://tieteentermipankki.fi/wiki/Termipankki:Etusivu/en
[8] https://avoindata.eduskunta.fi/#/fi/dbsearch

```
<?xml version="1.0" ?>
<Henkilo kieliKoodi="FI" tyyppiKoodi="Kansanedustaja">
   <HenkiloNro>126</HenkiloNro>
   <EtunimetNimi>Elsi Maria</EtunimetNimi>
   <SukuNimi>Hetemäki−Olander</SukuNimi>
   <LajitteluNimi>hetemäki−olander elsi</LajitteluNimi>
   <KutsumaNimi>Elsi</KutsumaNimi>
   <MatrikkeliNimi>Hetemäki−Olander(e. Rinne, e. Hetemäki), Elsi Maria</MatrikkeliNimi>
   <Ammatti>Master of Arts, Councellor of Parliament</Ammatti>
   <SyntymaPvm>1927</SyntymaPvm>
   <SyntymaPaikka>Oulainen</SyntymaPaikka>
   ...
   < Vaalipiirit >
      < EdellisetVaalipiirit >
         < VaaliPiiri >
            <Nimi>Electoral District of Uusimaa</Nimi>
            <AlkuPvm>23.03.1970</AlkuPvm>
            <LoppuPvm>21.03.1991</LoppuPvm>
            <Tunnus>uus01</Tunnus>
         </ VaaliPiiri >
      </ EdellisetVaalipiirit >
   </ Vaalipiirit >
   ...
   <Edustajatoimet>
      <Edustajatoimi>
         <AlkuPvm>23.03.1970</AlkuPvm>
         <LoppuPvm>21.03.1991</LoppuPvm>
      </Edustajatoimi>
   </Edustajatoimet>
   ...
   <EdustajanJulkaisut>
      <EdustajanJulkaisu>
         <Nimi>Suomen vaikuttajanaisia</Nimi>
         <Vuosi>1977</Vuosi>
         <Tekijat/>
      </EdustajanJulkaisu>
   </EdustajanJulkaisut>
   ...
</Henkilo>
```

Fig. 2. Partial extract from XML data for the politician *Elsi Hetemäki-Olander*

contains biographical basic information, e.g., family name (*SukuNimi*) and given names (*EtunimetNimi*), places (*SyntymaPaikka*) and times (*SyntymaPvm*) of birth and death (if applicable), and vocations (occupations). In addition, there are detailed descriptions of the person's political, professional, and educational career. The text sample has three examples of career events: being a candidate in an electoral district (*Vaalipiiri*), being a Member of the Parliament (*Edustajatoimi*), and being a member in a parliamentary group (*Eduskuntaryhma*). These descriptions contain the label (*Nimi*) and id (*Tunnus*) of the related group and the start (*AlkuPvm*) and end (*LoppuPvm*) timestamps pertaining to the data. The data may also contain information about the publications authored by the person or about him/her. Due to privacy issues the data does not contain family-related information about the spouses and children of the politicians in contrast to many other biographical dictionaries.

3   Data Model for Parliamentary Actors and Events

To represent the biographical information about MPs and other politicians the data model presented in Fig. 3 was developed. The key idea of the model is to represent an actor's life and activities as a sequence of events (*bioc:Event*) in places (*crm:E53_Place*) and in time (*:Timespan*) with the actors (*bioc:Person*) participating in different roles (*bioc:Actor_Role*), such as *:Member*, *:Representative*, etc. The data model follows the Bio CRM [14] ontology, an extension of CIDOC CRM[9] for representing biographical information based on role-centric modeling. Bio CRM makes a distinction among attributes, relations, and events, where entities participate in different roles in a qualified manner. The namespaces used in the model are described in the figure on the left. In this extended model, there are almost 200 different roles in use. The data model has been populated by using a set of domain ontologies, such as places based on YSO places[10], groups and organizations (harvested from the data), and vocations based on the AMMO ontology [15].

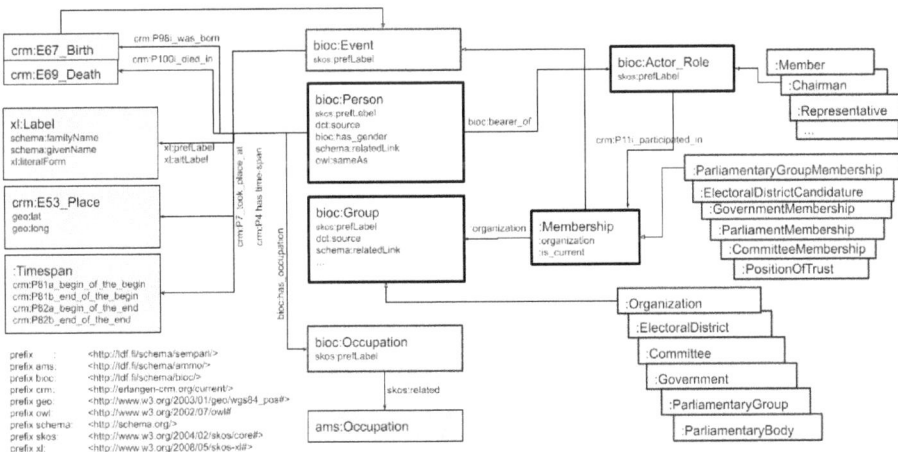

Fig. 3. Schema for the P-KG knowledge graph based on Bio CRM

For example, the XML data about the MP Elsi Hetemäki-Olander in Fig. 2 is translated into the RDF depicted in Fig. 4. Samples of extracted roles and events related to her life by the property *bioc:bearer_of* are listed in Fig. 5. As an example, *event:e2044* defines her the role of being a representative relating to *event:e2043*, being a MP during the time March 23 1970 to March 21 1991.

---

[9] https://cidoc-crm.org
[10] https://finto.fi/yso-paikat/en/

```
PREFIX bioc:        <http://ldf. fi /schema/bioc/>
PREFIX crm:         <http://erlangen—crm.org/current/>
PREFIX event:       <http://ldf. fi /semparl/event/>
PREFIX label:       <http://ldf. fi /semparl/ label />
PREFIX occupations: <http://ldf. fi /semparl/occupations/>
PREFIX people:      <http://ldf. fi /semparl/people/>
PREFIX rdf:         <http://www.w3.org/1999/02/22—rdf—syntax—ns#>
PREFIX rdfs:        <http://www.w3.org/2000/01/rdf—schema#>
PREFIX roles:       <http://ldf. fi /semparl/ roles />
PREFIX schema:      <http://schema.org/>
PREFIX semparl:     <http://ldf. fi /schema/semparl/>
PREFIX skos:        <http://www.w3.org/2004/02/skos/core#>
PREFIX times:       <http://ldf. fi /semparl/times/>
PREFIX xl:          <http://www.w3.org/2008/05/skos—xl#>

people:p126 a bioc:Person ;
    crm:P98i_was_born event:b126 ;
    bioc:bearer_of event:e2044,  ...,  event:e2050 ;
    bioc:has_gender schema:Female ;
    bioc:has_occupation occupations:o32,  occupations:o95 ;
    semparl:authored  publications:b114  ;
    semparl:id "126" ;
    schema:relatedLink <https://www.eduskunta.fi/FI/kansanedustajat/Sivut/126.aspx> ;
    skos:prefLabel  "Hetemäki—Olander, Elsi (1927—)"@fi ;
    xl:altLabel    label:l52 ,  label:l53 ,  label:l54  ;
    xl:prefLabel   label:l51  .

label:l51 a xl:Label  ;
    schema:familyName "Hetemäki—Olander" ;
    schema:givenName "Elsi" ;
    skos:prefLabel  "Hetemäki—Olander, Elsi"@fi .

label:l53 a xl:Label  ;
    schema:familyName "Rinne" ;
    schema:givenName "Elsi Maria" ;
    skos:prefLabel  "Rinne, Elsi  Maria"@fi .
```

Fig. 4. Partial extract from RDF data for the politician *Elsi Hetemäki-Olander*

4   Transformation of Parliamentary Actor Data into a KG

The data contains in total 2800 person entries, i.e., instances of the class *bioc:Person*. Out of this, 2605 are MPs from the main data source Parliament Open Data portal. This data was further enriched with data extracts from the web pages of the Finnish Government[11] and Wikidata in order to account for other people mentioned in the data and in the parliamentary speeches dataset S-KG [9] integrated with the P-KG. These ca. 200 additional resources are important people mentioned in the documents, such as Presidents of Finland, Ministers, or Parliamentary Ombudsmen[12] who have never been elected as MPs and therefore are not included in the MP database.

In addition to the people (*bioc:Person*), the groups and organizations (*bioc:Group*) mentioned in the XML data elements where extracted, disambiguated, and linked to the corresponding resources in the ontologies used. These groups contain the related parliamentary bodies and committees, governments,

---

[11] https://valtioneuvosto.fi

[12] https://www.oikeusasiamies.fi/en/web/guest

```
event:e2044  a  roles:r1  ;
    crm:P11i_participated_in event:e2043 ;
    skos:prefLabel "edustaja Hetemäki—Olander"@fi .

event:e2043 a semparl:ParliamentMembership ;
    crm:P4_has_time_span times:t814 ;
    skos:prefLabel "edustajuus 23.03.1970—21.03.1991"@fi .

event:e2050 a roles:r166 ;
    crm:P11i_participated_in event:e2049 ;
    skos:prefLabel "ehdokas Hetemäki—Olander"@fi .

event:e2049 a  semparl:ElectoralDistrictCandidature  ;
    crm:P4_has_time_span times:t814 ;
    semparl:is_current false ;
    semparl:organization  districts:uus01  ;
    skos:prefLabel "ehdokas: Uudenmaan läänin vaalipiiri "@fi.

districts:uus01  a  semparl:ElectoralDistrict  ;
    skos:prefLabel "Uusimaa constituency"@en,
        "Uudenmaan läänin vaalipiiri "@fi,
        "Nylands läns valkrets"@sv .

publications:b114 a  semparl:Publication  ;
    crm:P4_has_time_span times:t576 ;
    skos:prefLabel "Suomen vaikuttajanaisia " .
```

Fig. 5. Samples of resourses relating to the politician *Elsi Hetemäki-Olander*

electoral districts, and furthermore also groups out of political fields, such as companies, schools, and colleges. Also references to vocations (*bioc:Occupation*) were identified and linked to the resources of the AMMO ontology of historical occupations.

As a method for knowledge extraction, patterns of regular expressions were applied to the XML data fields, especially when extracting the person name variations and expressions of time. The source data contained all terms in Finnish. In addition, also the corresponding terms in English (1710) and Swedish (5420) were extracted. In the XML only recent data entries had translations in English. Since the main XML data came from a curated database, entities could be extracted with high precision and recall.

Table 1 summarizes the number of instances of the main classes of the data model of Fig. 3, and Table 2 lists the number of different event types extracted.

For validating the transformed P-KG data, the data model and its integrity constraints are presented in a machine-processable format using the ShEx Shape Expressions language[13]. We have made initial validation experiments with the PyShEx[14] validator. Based on the experiments, we have identified errors both in the schema and the data. We plan a full-scale ShEx validation phase integrated in the data conversion and publication process to spot and report errors in the dataset.

---

[13] https://shex.io
[14] https://github.com/hsolbrig/PyShEx

Table 1. Resources

Resource type	Count
Timespan	9168
Label	6061
Person	2801
Publication	1727
School, College	669
Place	607
Vocation	104
Parliamentary Group	89
Government	76
Committee	54
Organization	54
Electoral District	46
Parliamentary Body	38
Party	32
Ministry	12
Affiliation Group	10

Table 2. Events

Event type	Count
Career Event	14371
Position of Trust	12761
Committee Membership	6344
Municipal Position of Trust	4745
Event of Education	3712
Birth	2801
Electoral District Candidature	2205
Death	2025
Parliamentary Group Membership	1966
Government Membership	1622
Governmental Position of Trust	1621
Affiliation	1331
Parliament Membership	966
Honourable Mention	543
International Position of Trust	364
Membership Suspension	25

5   Prosopographical Data as a Linked Open Data Service

The prosopographical data P-KG presented above and the accompanying data model RDF schema have been published on the Linked Data Finland platform[15] [13] according to the Linked Data publishing principles and other best practices of W3C [1], including, e.g., content negotiation and provision of a SPARQL[16] endpoint.

In our work, the "FAIR guiding principles for scientific data management and stewardship" of publishing Findable, Accessible, Interoperable, and Re-usable data are used[17]. The data can be used via the SPARQL endpoint in two ways. Firstly, the underlying SPARQL endpoint can and is being applied to custom data analyses in Digital Humanities research using tools, such as YASGUI, Google Colab, and Jupyter notebooks. Secondly, a portal called *ParliamentSampo – Finnish Parliament on the Semantic Web* is under development, a new member in the "Sampo series" of semantic portals and LOD services[18]. The portal is targeted to both researchers and the public for studying parliamentary debates, the language used, networks of Finnish politicians, and political culture. ParliamentSampo is based on the Sampo model [16] for sharing collaboratively enriched linked open data, using a shared ontology infrastructure.

---

[15] https://ldf.fi
[16] https://www.w3.org/TR/sparql11-query/
[17] https://www.go-fair.org/fair-principles/
[18] https://seco.cs.aalto.fi/applications/sampo/

The SPARQL endpoint is hosted on an Apache Jena Fuseki[19] SPARQL server. The LDF platform provides dereferencing of URIs for both human users and machines, and a generic RDF browser for technical users, which opens when a URI is visited directly with a web browser. The URI routing, content negotiation, and caching is implemented using the Varnish Cache web application accelerator[20]. The LDF data service is based on a microservice architecture, using Docker containers[21]. Each individual component (Fuseki with the KG data and Varnish) is run in its own dedicated container, making the deployment of the services easy due to installation of software dependencies in isolated environments, enhancing the portability of the services. The data and the service are currently used internally in the SEMPARL project but will be opened by the CC BY 4.0 license to external users later on.

6   Using the SPARQL Endpoint for Data Analysis

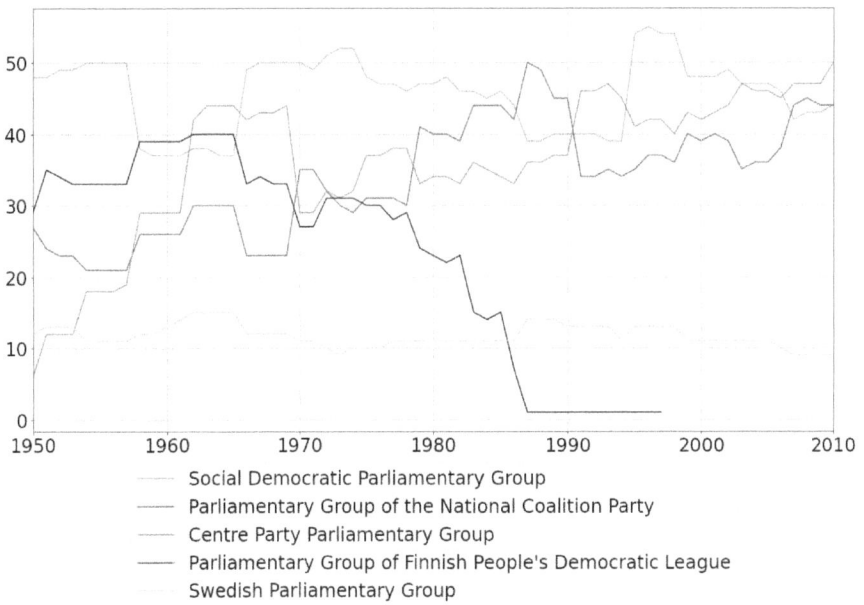

Fig. 6. Number of MPs of five most common Parliamentary Groups on a timeline

This section illustrates how the P-KG data can be used in researching the parliamentary culture in Finland, as suggested in Fig. 1.

---

[19] https://jena.apache.org/documentation/fuseki2/
[20] https://varnish-cache.org
[21] https://www.docker.com

A typical question in politics is to find out or forecast popularity of parties among the voters. Such data is available for recent times but not for historical times. By using P-KG such questions can be answered starting from 1907. For example, Fig. 6 depicts the number of MPs of the five most common Finnish parties during the years 1950–2010. The curves show how the *Social Democratic, National Coalition,* and *Centre Party* constantly share the top three positions. However, the *Finnish People's Democratic League* had a significant number of representatives from 1950's to the end of 1980's; the party was later replaced by the *Left Allience.* Furthermore, during the entire period of time, the *Swedish Parliamentary Group* has had an almost constant number of MPs.

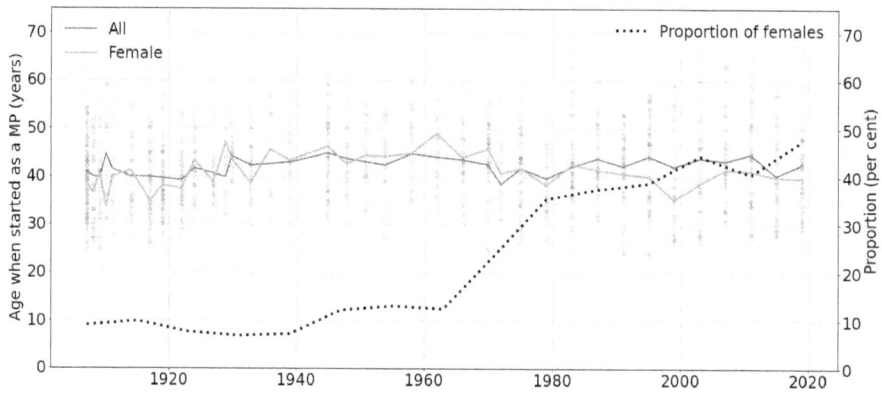

Fig. 7. Timeline with average ages of new MPs

Fig. 7 depicts on a timeline the ages of people when they were selected as MPs for the first time. The blue curve shows the average age for all MPs, and the red curve for female MPs. The values are calculated in time windows of four years. The black dotted line shows the relative proportion of female MPs in percents. It can been observed that between the years 1960 and 1980 this proportion constantly grows approximately from 10% to 40%. Generally, the average age of entering the Parliament is 42.1 which remains relatively constant during the entire timeline. However, after the 1980's the new female representatives are a few years younger than the men.

An interesting part of the P-KG is information about the vocations of the people, based on the AMMO ontology that has been aligned with the international HISCO classification[22] [17]. It provides an international comparative classification system of history of work, particularly for occupational titles in the 19th and early 20th centuries. HISCO encodes not only occupations, but also information about prestige, property, and family relations can be included. As an example of a data analysis based on vocations, Fig. 8 depicts a correlation matrix between

---

[22] https://iisg.amsterdam/en/data/data-websites/history-of-work

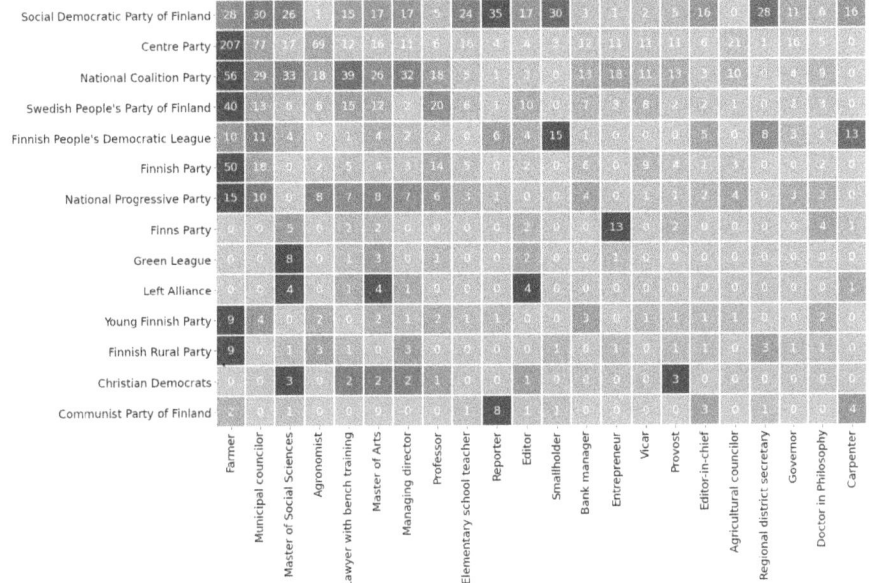

Fig. 8. Correlations between parties and vocations

the parties and vocations of the MPs. In the figure, the rows correspond to the ten parties with most MPs and columns to their vocations. The figure shows the vocations during the entire time period from 1907 to 2021. Finland was a before the Second World War a rural country, which explains why the vocation Farmer is on the first rank. From the results it can be noticed that, e.g., *Smallholder* and *Carpenter* have been common vocations for MPs of *the Finnish People's Democratic League* or *Provost* and *Master of Social Sciences* are common among the MPs of *the Christian Democrats*.

As a final example of data analysis, Fig. 9 depicts a correlation matrix between the parties and committees of PoF. In this figure, each row corresponds to a party and each column to a committee. The darker the cell background color is, the more members of that party haves been in the corresponding committee. Generally, the largest committee *the Grand Committee* has had a large amount of members from most of the parties. It can be noticed that, e.g., *the Finns Party* has had more members in *the Legal Affairs Committee* and *the Swedish People's Party of Finland* in *the Finance Committee*. The data model facilitates to easily analyze similar correlations between, e.g., parties, vocations, or genders.

These data analyses and visualizations were created easily by using a SPARQL query and then analysing its result with Python scripting and libraries on Google Colab Jupyter documents. According to our experiences in these and several other examples, the underlying data model and the populated data seems useful, semantically rich, and complete enough for studying political culture in versatile

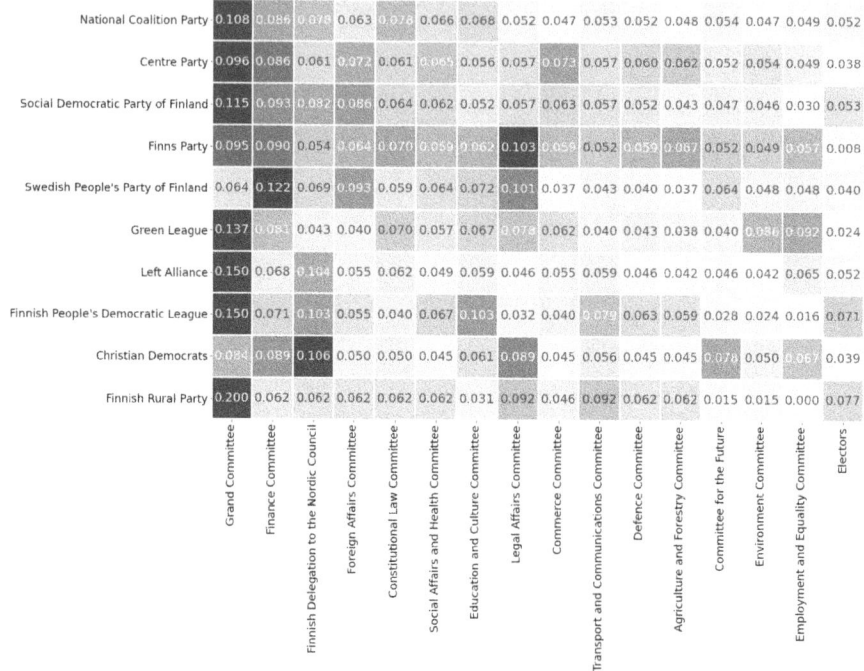

	Grand Committee	Finance Committee	Finnish Delegation to the Nordic Council	Foreign Affairs Committee	Constitutional Law Committee	Social Affairs and Health Committee	Education and Culture Committee	Legal Affairs Committee	Commerce Committee	Transport and Communications Committee	Defence Committee	Agriculture and Forestry Committee	Committee for the Future	Environment Committee	Employment and Equality Committee	Electors
National Coalition Party	0.108	0.086	0.078	0.063	0.078	0.066	0.068	0.052	0.047	0.053	0.052	0.048	0.054	0.047	0.049	0.052
Centre Party	0.096	0.086	0.061	0.072	0.061	0.065	0.056	0.057	0.073	0.057	0.060	0.062	0.052	0.054	0.049	0.038
Social Democratic Party of Finland	0.115	0.093	0.082	0.086	0.064	0.062	0.052	0.057	0.063	0.057	0.052	0.043	0.047	0.046	0.030	0.053
Finns Party	0.095	0.090	0.054	0.064	0.070	0.059	0.062	0.103	0.059	0.052	0.059	0.087	0.052	0.049	0.057	0.008
Swedish People's Party of Finland	0.064	0.122	0.069	0.093	0.059	0.064	0.072	0.101	0.037	0.043	0.040	0.037	0.064	0.048	0.048	0.040
Green League	0.137	0.081	0.043	0.040	0.070	0.057	0.067	0.073	0.062	0.040	0.043	0.038	0.040	0.086	0.092	0.024
Left Alliance	0.150	0.068	0.104	0.055	0.062	0.049	0.059	0.046	0.055	0.059	0.046	0.042	0.046	0.042	0.065	0.052
Finnish People's Democratic League	0.150	0.071	0.103	0.055	0.040	0.067	0.103	0.032	0.040	0.079	0.063	0.059	0.028	0.024	0.016	0.071
Christian Democrats	0.084	0.089	0.106	0.050	0.050	0.045	0.061	0.089	0.045	0.056	0.045	0.045	0.078	0.050	0.067	0.039
Finnish Rural Party	0.200	0.062	0.062	0.062	0.062	0.062	0.031	0.092	0.046	0.092	0.062	0.062	0.015	0.015	0.000	0.077

Fig. 9. Correlations between parties and committees of PoF

ways. In order to get feedback from external users, too, the data was used in the Helsinki Digital Humanities Hackathon in May 2021 for research purposes.

Of course, the data is limited to what is openly available from PoF and to additional data and links aggregated into the P-KG from related data sources during the data transformation into RDF. When using a dataset such as P-KG, where much of the content has been created or transformed automatically, new kind of data literacy [18] is needed when interpreting the results. Tools based on distant reading [19] are good for finding and exploring efficiently interesting patters of information in the data but for the final interpretation and error analysis close reading is needed, too.

7   Discussion

Related Work Many national projects have transformed parliamentary data[23], such as plenary session debates [9], into structured formats and enriched the data with biographical metadata, including, e.g., the Canadian Lipad project [3] and the Norwegian Talk of Norway [4]. Linked data has also been used in some

---

[23] See the CLARIN page www.clarin.eu/resource-families/parliamentary-corpora for a list of various national parliamentary corpora projects.

works, such as the LinkedEP about the European Parliament linked data 1999–2017 [6], the Latvian LinkedSAEIMA project [5], and the Italian Parliament[24]. Speech data can be used for analysing the language and topics of speeches (cf. e.g. [20,21,22]) and also the activities of the parliament and networks of its members. For example, speeches of male and female MPs or other groups, such as political parties, can be analyzed and compared [23].

The P-KG is in nature a biographical dictionary even if focused on parliamentary data and events. The idea of analysing such proposographical data quantitatively, as was illustrated in section 6, have been already made for some national dictionaries of biography, such as for the British ODNB [24] and the Irish Ainm [25]. As is [26], our goal is to combine quantitative approach and distant reading methods with the qualitative approach, often based on close reading, typical to biographical research.

Contributions This paper introduced the first Linked Data model and publication of the Finnish parliament actor data, covering the whole history of PoF since 1907. In comparison to related works, the underlying data model is arguably unique in employing the semantically rich event-based ontology model presented for harmonizing data about the politicians and their lives, extending CIDOC CRM to representing prosopographical data. Our experience on developing biographical Sampo systems [8] suggests that an event-based approach is needed for integrating biographical data of different kinds instead of using only traditional document-centric models, such as Dublin Core. Furthermore, the actor data is enriched and interlinked with several additional external data sources, and is based on a national level ontology infrastructure [10] for even more extensive interlinking. The first experiments presented in using the data service for Digital Humanities research suggest that the model is fit for its purpose and can be used effectively in SPARQL queries for visualizations and parliamentary data analyses, and for creating the large Finnish parliamentary debate dataset [9] and the larger *FinnParla* LOD cloud.

Future Research Digital humanities studies are underway in the Semantic Parliament project project using the P-KG interlinked with its sister dataset S-KG about the Finnish parliamentary debates. The P-KG will also be used as part of the semantic portal *ParliamentSampo – Finnish Parliament on the Semantic Web* that is being developed based on the Sampo model [16] and the Sampo-UI framework [27].

Acknowledgements Thanks to Ari Apilo, Sari Wilenius, and Päivikki Karhula at the Parliament of Finland for co-operation, and the Semantic Parliament project team for discussions. Our work was funded by the Academy of Finland as part of the Semantic Parliament project, the EU project InTaVia: In/Tangible European Heritage[25], and is related to the COST action NexusLinguarum[26] on linguistic data science. CSC – IT Center for Science, Finland, provided computational resources for the work.

---

[24] http://data.camera.it/data/en/datasets/
[25] https://intavia.eu
[26] https://nexuslinguarum.eu

References

1. Heath T, Bizer C. Linked Data: Evolving the Web into a Global Data Space (1st edition). Synthesis Lectures on the Semantic Web: Theory and Technology. Morgan & Claypool; 2011. Available from: http://linkeddatabook.com/editions/1.0/.
2. Gutierrez C, Sequeda JF. Knowledge Graphs. Commun ACM. 2021 Feb;64(3):96—104. Available from: https://doi.org/10.1145/3418294.
3. Beelen K, Thijm TA, Cochrane C, Halvemaan K, Hirst G, Kimmins M, et al. Digitization of the Canadian Parliamentary Debates. Canadian Journal of Political Science. 2017;50(3):849-64.
4. Lapponi E, Søyland MG, Velldal E, Oepen S. The Talk of Norway: a richly annotated corpus of the Norwegian parliament, 1998–2016. Language Resources and Evaluation. 2018 Sep;52(3):873-93.
5. Bojārs U, Darģis R, Lavrinovičs U, Paikens P. LinkedSaeima: A Linked Open Dataset of Latvia's Parliamentary Debates. In: Acosta M, Cudré-Mauroux P, Maleshkova M, Pellegrini T, Sack H, Sure-Vetter Y, editors. Semantic Systems. The Power of AI and Knowledge Graphs. Cham: Springer; 2019. p. 50-6.
6. van Aggelen A, Hollink L, Kemman M, Kleppe M, Beunders H. The debates of the European Parliament as Linked Open Data. Semantic Web. 2017;8(2):271-81.
7. Hyvönen E, Tamper M, Oksanen A, Ikkala E, Sarsa S, Tuominen J, et al. LawSampo: A Semantic Portal on a Linked Open Data Service for Finnish Legislation and Case Law. In: The Semantic Web: ESWC 2020 Satellite Events. Revised Selected Papers. Springer; 2019. p. 110-4.
8. Hyvönen E, Leskinen P, Tamper M, Rantala H, Ikkala E, Tuominen J, et al. BiographySampo - Publishing and Enriching Biographies on the Semantic Web for Digital Humanities Research. In: The Semantic Web. ESWC 2019. Springer; 2019. p. 574-89.
9. Sinikallio L, Drobac S, Tamper M, Leal R, Koho M, Tuominen J, et al. Plenary Debates of the Parliament of Finland as Linked Open Data and in Parla-CLARIN Markup. In: Proceedings, Language, Data and Knowledge (LDK 2021); 2021. Forth-coming.
10. Hyvönen E, Viljanen K, Tuominen J, Seppälä K. Building a National Semantic Web Ontology and Ontology Service Infrastructure—The FinnONTO Approach. In: Proceedings of the 5th European Semantic Web Conference (ESWC 2008). Springer; 2008. p. 95-109.
11. McCarty W. Humanities Computing. Palgrave, London; 2005.
12. Gardiner E, Musto RG. The Digital Humanities: A Primer for Students and Scholars. New York, NY, USA: Cambridge University Press; 2015. https://doi.org/10.1017/CBO9781139003865.
13. Hyvönen E, Tuominen J, Alonen M, Mäkelä E. Linked Data Finland: A 7-star Model and Platform for Publishing and Re-using Linked Datasets. In: Presutti V, Blomqvist E, Troncy R, Sack H, Papadakis I, Tordai A, editors. The Semantic Web: ESWC 2014 Satellite Events. ESWC 2014. Springer-Verlag; 2014. p. 226-30. Available from: https://doi.org/10.1007/978-3-319-11955-7_24.
14. Tuominen J, Hyvönen E, Leskinen P. Bio CRM: A Data Model for Representing Biographical Data for Prosopographical Research. In: Proceedings of the Second Conference on Biographical Data in a Digital World 2017 (BD2017). vol. 2119. CEUR Workshop Proceedings; 2018. p. 59-66. Available from: http://ceur-ws.org/Vol-2119/paper10.pdf.

15. Koho M, Gasbarra L, Tuominen J, Rantala H, Jokipii I, Hyvönen E. AMMO Ontology of Finnish Historical Occupations. In: Proceedings of the First International Workshop on Open Data and Ontologies for Cultural Heritage (ODOCH'19). vol. 2375. CEUR Workshop Proceedings; 2019. p. 91-6. Available from: http://ceur-ws.org/Vol-2375/.

16. Hyvönen E. "Sampo" Model and Semantic Portals for Digital Humanities on the Semantic Web. In: DHN 2020 Digital Humanities in the Nordic Countries. Proc. of the Digital Humanities in the Nordic Countries 5th Conference. CEUR Workshop Proceedings, vol. 2612; 2020. p. 373-8. Available from: http://ceur-ws.org/Vol-2612/poster1.pdf.

17. Van Leeuwen MHD, Maas I, Miles A. HISCO: Historical international standard classification of occupations. Leuven University Press; 2002.

18. Koltay T. Data literacy for researchers and data librarians. Journal of Librarianship and Information Science. 2011;49(1):1-14.

19. Moretti F. Distant reading. Verso Books; 2013.

20. Greene D, Cross JP. Exploring the Political Agenda of the European Parliament Using a Dynamic Topic Modeling Approach. Political Analysis. 2017;25(1):77-94.

21. Won M, Martins B, Raimundo F. Automatic extraction of relevant keyphrases for the study of issue competition. EasyChair; 2019. EasyChair Preprint no. 875.

22. Kettunen K, La Mela M. Digging Deeper into the Finnish Parliamentary Protocols – Using a Lexical Semantic Tagger for Studying Meaning Change of Everyman's Rights (allemansrätten). In: DHN 2020 Digital Humanities in the Nordic Countries. Proc. of the Digital Humanities in the Nordic Countries 5th Conference. CEUR Workshop Proceedings, vol. 2612; 2020. p. 63-80. Available from: http://ceur-ws.org/Vol-2612/paper5.pdf.

23. Blaxill L, Beelen K. A Feminized Language of Democracy? The Representation of Women at Westminster since 1945. Twentieth Century British History. 2016;27(3):412-49.

24. Warren C. Historiography's Two Voices: Data Infrastructure and History at Scale in the Oxford Dictionary of National Biography (ODNB). Journal of Cultural Analytics. 2018.

25. Bhreathnach Ú, Burke C, Mag Fhinn J, Ó Cleircín G, Ó Raghallaigh B. A quantitative analysis of biographical data from Ainm, the Irish-language Biographical Database. In: Proceedings of the Third Conference on Biographical Data in a Digital World (BD 2019). CEUR-WS; 2019. Forth-coming.

26. Jänicke S, Franzini G, Cheema MF, Scheuermann G. Visual text analysis in digital humanities. Computer Graphics Forum. 2017;36(6):226-50.

27. Ikkala E, Hyvönen E, Rantala H, Koho M. Sampo-UI: A Full Stack JavaScript Framework for Developing Semantic Portal User Interfaces. Semantic Web – Interoperability, Usability, Applicability. 2021. Accepted.

Further with Knowledge Graphs. M. Alam et al. (Eds.)
AKA Verlag and IOS Press, 2021
© *2021 Akademische Verlagsgesellschaft AKA GmbH, Berlin*
This article is published online with Open Access by IOS Press and distributed under the terms
of the Creative Commons Attribution License 4.0 (CC BY 4.0).

Subject Index

Further with Knowledge Graphs. M. Alam et al. (Eds.)
AKA Verlag and IOS Press, 2021
© 2021 Akademische Verlagsgesellschaft AKA GmbH, Berlin
This article is published online with Open Access by IOS Press and distributed under the terms
of the Creative Commons Attribution License 4.0 (CC BY 4.0).

Author Index